JAZZ
America's Gift

FROM ITS BIRTH TO GEORGE GERSHWIN'S RHAPSODY IN BLUE & BEYOND

RICHIE GERBER

Illustrations by Miguel Covarrubias

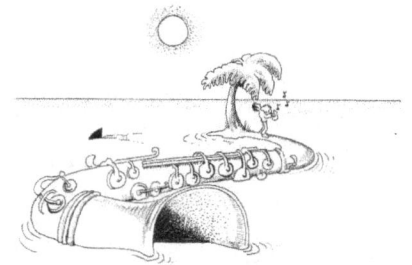

GERBER'S MIRACLE PUBLISHERS LLC
Fort Lauderdale, Florida

Gerber's Miracle Publishers LLC
Fort Lauderdale, Florida

Copyright © 2015 Richie Gerber

ISBN: 978-0-69244-553-2

LCCN: 2015907863

All rights reserved. No part of this book may be reproduced, stored in a retrieval system, or transmitted by any means, electronic, mechanical, photocopying, recording, or otherwise, without written permission from the author.

Copyeditor: Carol Killman Rosenberg • www.carolkillmanrosenberg.com

Cover and interior design: Gary A. Rosenberg • www.thebookcouple.com

Gerber's Miracle Publishers LLC Logo: Tim Sample • www.timsample.com

Photos by Angelo Orlando—Angelo's Gallery

Miguel Covarrubias images used by permission of María Elena Rico Covarrubias

Miguel Covarrubias Images Courtesy of Private Collector

Prints and Photographs Division, Library of Congress

National Portrait Gallery, Washington, D.C.

Smithsonian Institution, Washington, D.C.

Carnegie Hall Programs used by permission of The Carnegie Hall Trust: Special thanks to Gino Francesconi, Director of Archives and Rose Museum at Carnegie Hall for researching and providing the program images

Cover Illustration "Whiteman at Carnegie Hall" by Miguel Covarrubias: a concert for the benefit of The American Academy in Rome, Carnegie Hall, Monday evening, April 21, 1924.
Bottom, far left in audience: Miguel Covarrubias chatting with George Gershwin.
Bottom, far right in audience: Tallulah Bankhead.

Printed in the United States of America

For Julie and Isaac—the miracles of my life

In memory of my brother Stacy

Contents

Acknowledgments, ix

INTRODUCTION

Prelude #1, 2

Welcome Song, 3

You Can't Unscramble Scrambled Eggs, 4

THE ROOTS OF JAZZ

The Yankee Doodle Blues, 9

Hooray for the U.S.A.!, 11

Dead Men Tell No Tales, 13

O Land of Mine, America, 16

Follow the Minstrel Band, 19

Black and White, 22

We Go to Church on Sunday, 29

Dixie Rose, 31

Pay Some Attention to Me, 37

The Real American Folk Song (Is a Rag), 39

Trumpeter, Blow Your Horn, 43

Show Me the Town, 47

I'd Rather Charleston, 49

New York Rhapsody, 51

Harlem River Chanty, 53

Changing My Tune, 55

I Love to Rhyme, 59

Harlem Serenade, 61

Blue, Blue, Blue, 65

Midnight Blues, 71

Blah, Blah, Blah, 74

For You, For Me, For Evermore, 78

Little Jazz Bird, 81

You Started It, 91

THE LIFE & TIMES OF GEORGE GERSHWIN

Who's the Greatest?, 100

I'm Somethin' on Avenue, 102

Official Resume, 105

I'm On My Way, 109

Any Little Tune, 112

Wake Up, Brother, and Dance, 116

Cinderelatives, 120

Swanee, 122

Blue Monday Blues, 125

Soon, 129

Oh, Lady Be Good!, 131

What's the Big Idea?, 135

Tonight's the Night, 143

Somebody Loves Me, 153

Stiff Upper Lip, 158

Could You Use Me?, 163

Concerto in F, 165

A Typical Self-Made American, 171

The He-Man, 179

When You Live in a Furnished Flat, 182

Climb Up the Social Ladder, 184

Quite a Party, 187

A Wonderful Party, 190

My Cousin in Milwaukee, 193

Lovers of Art, 197

The Matrimonial Handicap, 199

Drifting Along With the Tide, 203

The Man I Love, 205

Nice Work if You Can Get It, 209

If I Became the President, 211

An American in Paris, 213

An American in Paris—
The Movie, 217

The Dybbuk, 220

Strike Up the Band!, 223

Cuban Overture, 225

Money, Money, Money, 229

Delishious, 231

Second Rhapsody, 233

Of Thee I Sing, 235

I Got Rhythm, 237

Variations on "I Got Rhythm", 241

George Gershwin's Song Book, 242

Tune In (to Station J.O.Y.), 245

I Loves You, Porgy, 247

The Senatorial Roll Call, 257

(I've Got) Beginner's Luck, 259

What Causes That?, 261

AND BEYOND

I'll Build a Stairway to Paradise, 268

I Found a Four Leaf Clover, 271

They Can't Take That Away From Me, 273

Overflow, 275

Boy Wanted, 277

The Illegitimate Daughter, 279

Do It Again!, 281

Love Is Here to Stay, 285

Notes, 288

Bibliography, 307

Index, 310

About the Author, 323

Acknowledgments

I would like to thank the following people for their contributions to this work and to my musical life:

Jim Oppenheimer, my best friend and former business partner, for all of his support over the decades, and of course his lovely wife, Sue.

Rudy Shur, publisher extraordinaire at Square One Publishers, for his friendship, help, and advice (www.squareonepublishers.com).

Carol Killman Rosenberg and Gary A. Rosenberg, The Book Couple (the dynamic duo), for taking my manuscript and transforming it into a book (www.thebookcouple.com).

Linda Kleinschmidt, the Write Watchman, copyeditor and content reviewer, for offering continual words of encouragement as I worked to deliver these remarkable stories.

María Elena Rico Covarrubias, for granting me permission to use Miguel Covarrubias's images.

Adriana Williams, who literally wrote the book on Miguel Covarrubias.

Ric Emmett, who introduced me to Miguel Covarrubias back in the early 1980s, when I first saw the poster hanging on the wall of his Modernism Gallery, and the rest is history (www.modernismgallery.com).

The late Eddie Higgins, who was the greatest piano player I have ever known.

Dr. Don Wilner, for helping me create a world-class jazz venue and for booking some of the greatest jazz players at the Bread of Life.

Tim Sample, who hired me to play sax in the Dubious Brothers band and created the "Alone on the Saxophone" logo seen in this book.

Elliot Zimmerman, for his friendship and guidance into the world of MIDI music.

The late Larry Sanborn, who shared his musical knowledge so generously with me.

My cousin Pamela Dunn for helping me get started.

Angelo Orlando, for his generous help with the photos in this book.

Williams College, Paul Whiteman Collection.

Sylvia Kennick Brown, Williams College, Archivist, Special Collections Librarian.

Mar Hollingsworth, Visual Arts Curator and Program Manager, California African American Museum.

Peter Mears, Curator of Art, Harry Ransom Center, The University of Texas at Austin.

Gino Francesconi, Director of Archives and Rose Museum at Carnegie Hall.

Chelsea Weathers, Ph.D., Research Associate, Art, Performing Arts Collections, Harry Ransom Center, The University of Texas at Austin.

My cousin Howard Stern for using his far-reaching microphone to support my projects over the years.

My son, Isaac Pablo, for sharing his vast knowledge of technology and book publishing with me, for keeping me connected with current trends and for filling my heart with love.

My wife, Julie, for patient and loving help reading, rereading and critiquing innumerable drafts and redrafts and listening to countless stories about jazz and George Gershwin. For always giving me excellent advice. Words cannot express my gratitude.

The following is a list of alumni musicians who performed at the Bread of Life and some others with whom I played over the years, including musicians from the South Florida music scene and beyond, and others that I admire (in no particular order):

The late great Eddie Higgins, the late great Pete "Fingers" Minger, Ira Sullivan, the late Larry Sanborn, Dr. Donald Wilner, Elliot Zimmerman, Ken Katz (MAE Music), Othello, Grady Tate, Duffy Jackson, Mike Renzi, Pamela Stanley, David Shelley, the late David Wertman, Lynne Meryl, Phil Flanigan, Roger Wilder, Dolph and Tony Castellano, the late Lou Colombo, Hank Ballard, Ed Bell (Jazz DJ), Larry Brown (The Blue Notes), Dennis Marks, Mike Gerber (no relation to me), Billy Ross, Joe Donato, Eddie Crocetti, Bruce Brown (recorded my tune "Radiation" in Waterville, Maine back in the late 70s), Don Miller, Turk Mauro, John Doughten, Richie Cole, Jon Frangipane, Gary Mayone, Tim Schiavone (The World Famous Parrot Lounge), Paul Lorenzo (The Candy Store), Danny Burger, Al Shikaly, Randy Emerick, Dave Wilkinson, the late China Valles, Lenny Steinberg, Sheri Brooks Garlock, Michael Levine, Jeff T. Watkins, Iris van Eck, Karen Shane, Meredith d'Ambrosio, John Eatmon, Irving Weiner, Dick Cully, Tim Sample, James Martin, John Belt, Randi Fishenfeld, Kitty Ryan (O'Hara's), Dr. Lonnie Smith, Jesse Jones Jr., Melton Mustafa, Jerry Mascaro and the late Don Cohen (The Musicians Exchange), Stu Grant (Jazz DJ), Sam Chiodo, Rich Franks, Randy Bernsen, Lawrence Dermer, Stan Street, Harry Allen, Nicole Yarling, Captain Reese Singleton, Motel Mel, Big Mama Blu, Ken Peplowski, Chuck Redd, Jaco Pastorius, Ramon Justicia, Frank Tiberi, Roswell Rudd, Eddie Shaw & the Wolfgang, Hubert Sumlin, Larry Rivers, Bill Stevens, and Eric Allison

INTRODUCTION

Prelude #1*

*(1926)

Although this book is about the history of jazz, a majority of the work centers on the life and works of the jazz genius George Gershwin, who has been a hero of mine since childhood. Gershwin spent the first three years of his life in the East New York section of Brooklyn, just blocks from where I grew up. Since my boyhood, I have always felt a special bond with this virtuoso musician.

Gershwin composed hundreds of songs during his brief twenty-year career. I use his song titles as section headings in this book, tipping you off to that choice with an asterisk (*) following the song title. Underneath the emboldened Gershwin song title is another asterisk. It indicates the name of the show or movie for which the song was written and then the date of its publication or first performance. For example, "You Can't Unscramble Scrambled Eggs*" is the title of a Gershwin tune. Underneath that is *Girl Crazy (Unused) (1930), meaning Gershwin wrote the song for the show *Girl Crazy*, but it was not used. It was published in 1930.

There is one other convention you will find in your reading: To get a better understanding of the value of the money from days past, I thought it wise to convert those old values into today's dollars. To do so, I used the United States Department of Labor, Bureau of Labor Statistics online CPI Inflation Calculator.[1] So, for example, I plugged in $1,000 and chose the year 1913 (the first year this gizmo offers). The calculator spit out the fact that in 2014 (one hundred and one years later) the value of that one grand would be $24,000! You will see throughout this book that I first give you the dollar amount in the historical context and then convert that value into today's dollars. It really puts the money thing into today's context and makes it more understandable.

---

1. http://www.bls.gov/data/inflation_calculator.htm

Welcome Song*

*The Shocking Miss Pilgrim (Unused) (1947)

America has always been a melting pot, a combination of the world's peoples, cultures, religions, and soul. America is a nation of immigrants. Even the Native American Indians are believed to have traveled to North America in the very distant past. Our "melting pot" past has blessed us with a unique history and culture. It has also professed the idea of rugged individualism.

My wife, Julie, fled from Cuba several years after the Communist Castro brothers took control of that island. She arrived in Brooklyn where we met several years later. To escape city living, we fled to Maine from Brooklyn in the early 1970s to build our own house and start an organic farm. We both left well-paying teaching jobs to become modern-day pioneers. All we had in Maine was 29 acres (more or less) and a barn, which we moved from the center of a small rural town, three miles to our remote property in the summer of 1973. With no jobs lined up, we were committed to making our way no matter what. America was built by people just like us, risking it all and depending on their wits to survive. We were just a small microcosm of the brave founders of America.

Jazz is also based on rugged individualism. Those who perform jazz stand naked (both emotionally and musically) in front of an audience and improvise before complete strangers "to play what no man has played before." To express your feelings, your soul, to total strangers can be both frightening and exhilarating. Talk about modern-day pioneers. Every song, every note becomes a journey into new, uncharted waters. To me, this is why jazz is so unique to America because, out of all the countries that have ever existed, this is the one nation that is based on the value of the individual. Our constitution protects our God-given, individual rights. That is not to say that people can do whatever they want, as there are limits. However, in jazz, there are no limits at all.

In a standard jazz tune, the band, whether it is a trio, quartet, or other format, states the melody. So just like in America, everyone in the band works together as a group with a common goal. Then, after stating the melody, all the individual musicians take their improvised solos. This is where the idea of American rugged individualism comes in and shines. The soloist is backed up by the rhythm section, but that person is out there telling his or her personal story through the magic of improvisation.

After the musicians have a chance to express themselves individually as soloists, they meet back again at the original melody to close out the song. My point here is that in jazz, like in America, the group works together toward a common cause with lots of room left for each individual to shine.

You Can't Unscramble Scrambled Eggs*

Girl Crazy (Unused) (1930)

Jazz came to America three hundred years ago in chains.
—PAUL WHITEMAN, JAZZ (1926)[1]

At this point, I should make a personal disclaimer regarding the use of some offensive words and terms you will encounter while reading this book. After lengthy contemplation on how or even if I should use certain offensive and racist words and terms in the following sections, I decided to include them because I wanted to document the historical facts accurately and as they were. Yes, I wanted to show the good, the bad, and the ugly with all the warts.

Please note that in no way, shape, or form do I want to perpetuate their use today, but rather, I do find it important to relay the history as accurately as possible. Therefore, for the sake of presenting the facts without succumbing to so-called political correctness or rewriting history to whitewash the truth, I present the story as faithfully as I can in its historical context.

Over time, things change and that can certainly be said about the racial issues in this wonderful country of ours. America had a sordid past as far as racial issues are concerned. What was permitted and popular years ago is now seen through our new, clearer eyes. Only a short fifty years ago, our country passed the Civil Rights Act of 1964, making it illegal to discriminate against any person based on race, ethnicity, religion, gender, and national origin. It also granted equal voter registration rights and outlawed segregation. The Jim Crow laws of the South were no longer permitted. It is truly unbelievable that a law like this needed to be passed in the "Land of the Free, and Home of the Brave." And to think that this monumental achievement happened in *my* lifetime no less, one hundred years after the Civil War and the emancipation of slaves from their bondage, I guess actions do speak louder than words. In the following pages, I felt compelled to share with you some of these words that we consider unspeakable today to demonstrate how much things have changed.

Some readers may think that I included too much stuff on this topic, and others may think too little. Damned if I do . . . Prejudice and racism are a part of our history, and we are still dealing with the wounds. Of course our country has traveled far from those bad days. We have even elected and then reelected our first black president, which would make some folks from those times roll over in their graves.

Here is one example of this *mishegas* (craziness) from a November 1906 article. It appeared in the periodical *The Musician* and was entitled "Lafcadio Hearn and Congo Music" by the then American music critic and musicologist Henry E. Krehbiel:

> I would also try to show a relation between Negro physiology and Negro music. You know the blood of the African black has the highest human temperature known—equal to that of the swallow—although it loses that fire in America. I would like you to find out for me whether the Negro vocal chords are not differently formed and capable of longer vibration than ours. Some expert professor in physiology might tell you; but I regret to say the latest London works do not touch upon the Negro vocal chords, although they do show other remarkable anatomical distinctions.[2]

This is an amazingly racist comment by a highly respected elite musicologist and written just over one hundred years ago. Can you imagine him writing this same copy today?

Over time, words, terms, and mores always change. What was once considered unfit for polite company is now generally accepted. The word "jazz" was actually born in the brothels and was considered taboo because it referred to the act of sex. So our words and morays change and hopefully evolve in positive ways over time. During the "Roaring Twenties" the word "gay" had a completely different meaning than today as well. Terms such as "Gay Paree" and "The Gay Nineties" used the word "gay" to indicate happiness and cheerfulness, a kind of party atmosphere. Today the word "gay" is commonly associated with homosexuality.

How is it possible that just a few decades after Japan bombed Pearl Harbor and the United States bombed Japan with atomic bombs, killing over 200,000 Japanese citizens, our two countries are now the best of friends? How do we explain the Jewish State of Israel being trading partners and on good diplomatic terms with Germany after the atrocities committed by the Nazi regime on so many European Jews? These are very complicated issues that are far removed from the scope of this book. But maybe time can help us heal some of the wounds inflicted on and by our ancestors if we learn more history.

I was born in Brooklyn to European Jewish parents who left everything behind and immigrated to the United States in the early 20th century in order to save their lives. They instilled in me a strong sense of my Jewish heritage as well as my love for America. Yiddish was their first language, but they did learn to speak English. This background gives me my own unique perspective of America and New York City, the Melting Pot of America.

As you read on, you will see quite clearly what I am talking about. I hope I strike the right balance and you appreciate the historical significance of my decision of inclusion. I like the way Merle Armitage put it in the book he edited in a tribute to George Gershwin shortly after Gershwin's untimely demise. Armitage said, "The fact that George Gershwin was a Jew, and that many of his musical sources were Negroid confirms his basic Americanism. For this is not a country of race, it is a country of races."[3]

Let the music begin!

Many thanks,
Richie

THE ROOTS OF JAZZ

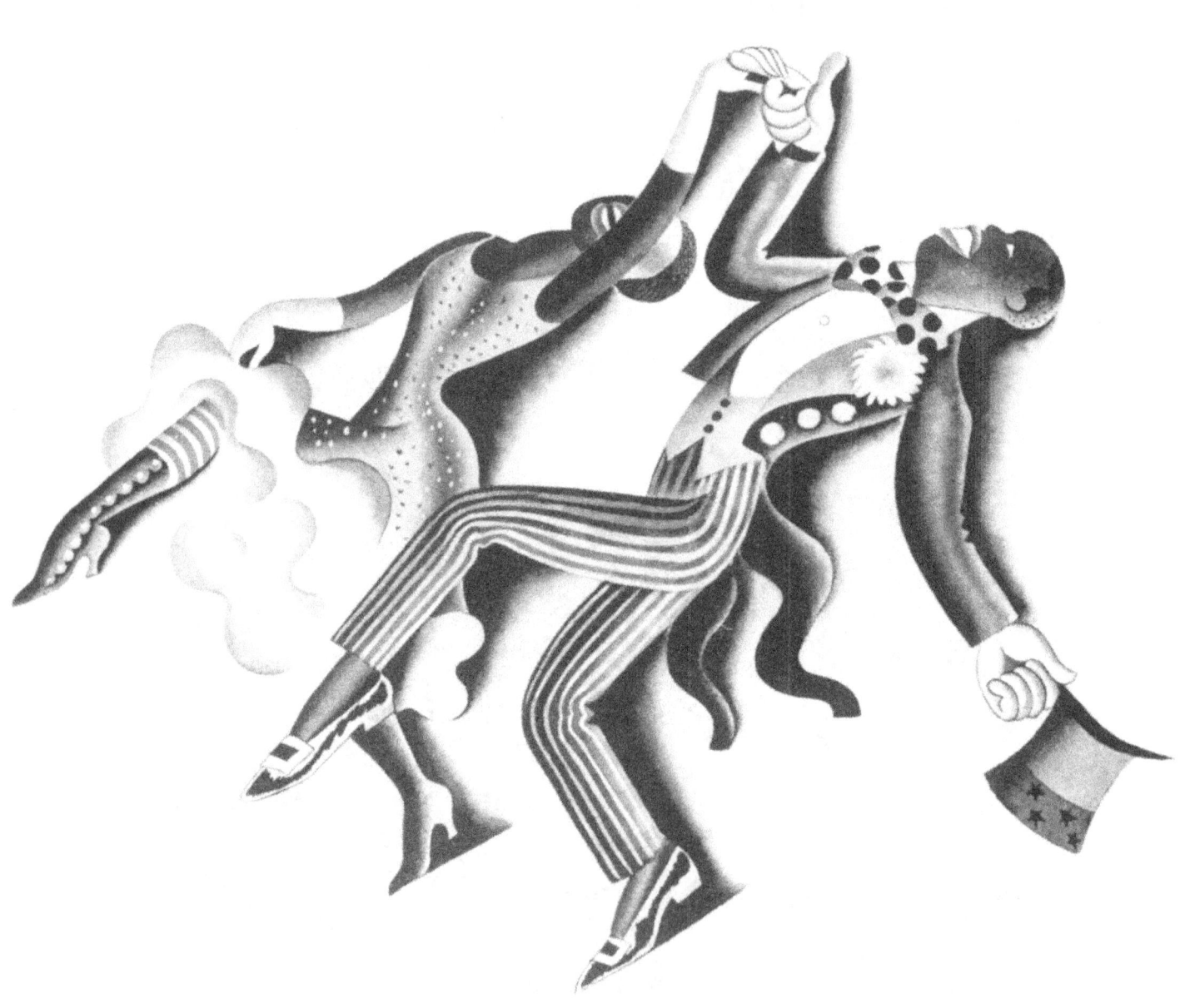

The Yankee Doodle Blues*

*Spice of 1922 (1922)

In the earliest years of our country, American songs were born out of religion, politics, or war—and sometimes a mix of all three. So, of course, we must begin our journey through American music with a look at the first popular composer of North America, William Billings. Born in Boston in 1746, he was a composer of psalms. His first of several books of music was titled *The New England Psalm Singer*, published in 1770.

This book included a song called "Chester," and in light of the fact that Billings was a close friend of Paul Revere and Samuel Adams, it should come as no surprise that this composition became the theme song of the American Revolutionary Army. He inspired colonial soldiers to fight against the tyranny of Great Britain with such rousing lyrics as:

Let tyrants shake their iron rod,
And Slav'ry clank her galling chains,
We fear them not, we trust in God,
New England's God forever reigns.

It's interesting to note that the lyrics "We trust in God" were inverted to form the phrase that Americans now hold as our nation's motto: "In God we trust." The phrase was adopted as the official motto of the United States in 1956. According to many historians, the first use of "In God we trust" was as a lyric in "The Star-Spangled Banner," written during the War of 1812. Now we can see where the inspiration for Frances Scott Key's words perhaps came from.

The Colonists took great pride in changing the words of British songs as an act of defiance. Songs like "God Save the King" were changed by the Colonists to proclaim, "God Save the Thirteen States." This new iteration praised, ". . . our famed Washington, Brave Stark at Bennington, Glory is due."

Our first American hit song, "The Liberty Song" (1768) was also a song of defiance, a modification of the old English tune "Hearts of Oak," to reflect the growing American desire for liberty. Ironically, "Hearts of Oak" was the anthem of the British Royal Navy!

. . . Come, join hand in hand, brave Americans all,
And rouse your bold hearts at fair Liberty's call;
No tyrannous acts shall suppress your just claim,
Or stain with dishonor America's name . . .

In the fourth verse is the first appearance of the famous words: "By uniting we stand, by dividing we fall."

*Then join hand in hand, brave Americans all,
By uniting we stand, by dividing we fall;
In so righteous a cause let us hope to succeed,
For heaven approves of each generous deed.*

It seems this song inspired the famous line that Patrick Henry ("Give me liberty or give me death") used in his last public speech.

After the Revolutionary War, independence and freedom proved to be a potent, even intoxicating source of musical inspiration. Many new songs rang out across the nation.

The first presidential campaign anthem, "Adams and Liberty," was heard in 1800, promoting the Federalist John Adams in his battle against Democratic-Republican Thomas Jefferson. Jefferson won the election, proving that you need more than a good song to become president. Robert Treat Paine (a signer of the Declaration of Independence) wrote the song based on the British song "Anacreon in Heaven." Although Adams lost the election, the song "Adams and Liberty" lives on. The lyrics have been changed, but the music became the melody of our national anthem, "The Star Spangled Banner."

The lyrics of "The Star Spangled Banner" were composed as a poem by 35-year-old Francis Scott Key, a lawyer and poet who witnessed the bombing of Baltimore's Fort McHenry from a British ship two years into the War of 1812. The poem became very popular and, in the days and weeks that followed, was printed repeatedly in broadsides and newspapers. (Broadsides were large oversized documents printed on only one side so that they could be posted on a public wall.)

Hooray for the U.S.A.*

*Sweet Little Devil (1924)

During this time, the United States was struggling with a deeply split personality—identifying itself as the Land of the Free, a land of liberty, yet operating as a hotbed of slavery. The American Revolution was a fight for freedom, and yet many patriots owned other human beings who had been forcibly relocated from their homes in West Africa. Patriots glorified their battle against an oppressor from another continent and yet functioned as oppressors in their own homes. It reeks of irony.

Irony indeed! The thirteen colonies were in fact colonies of the colonialist/imperialist British nation, where slavery was permitted by law. So the colonies had no way to discard slavery legally. During the writing of the U.S. Constitution, some of our Founding Fathers (including George Washington) tried to include a passage to get rid of slavery. They were not successful because the Southern colonies refused to sign on the dotted line for economic reasons. This threat from the Southern colonies forced the hand of the antislavery delegation into a compromise that permitted slavery (a slave was counted as three-fifths of a "real person"). Thus, the United States of America might not have ever existed without the compromise of the legalization of slavery. The antislavery crew did say that they would continue to push for abolition in future years, which is what eventually happened. Sadly, it took nearly another eighty years and thousands of deaths in the Civil War and a brave president to finally get the job done.

Another interesting, yet less known, fact regarding slavery is the system of indentured servants. This was a system in which a person can voluntarily commit to servitude of a master, or owner, for a defined number of years before being set free. Both parties agreed to a legally binding commitment and were required by law to live up to the contract. North America had tens of thousands of indentured servants. Many did it in order to pay back the master for the cost of travel from Europe to America.

Just as slavery was not unique to North America, neither was indentured servitude. Similarly, both are mentioned in the Bible. We are all familiar with the story of Moses freeing the enslaved Hebrews from the Pharaoh, but a less known story is one of indentured servitude. Jacob, one of the Jewish patriarchs, voluntarily became an indentured servant for seven years in order to get the hand of marriage to Rachael from her father, Laban. The deal was made between the two men, and Jacob worked as a servant of Laban for seven years. Laban then tricked Jacob at the wedding and switched Rachael with her older sister, Leah. Jacob's love for Rachael was so strong that he actually signed on for an additional seven years of indentured servitude to get her hand in marriage. The point being here is the U.S. was neither the first nor the last country to condone such behavior. These acts go back thousands of years to Biblical days. Even Thomas Jefferson—one of the Founding Fathers of the United States, a Declaration of Independence signatory (which contained his words, "all men are created equal"), and third president of our nation—owned hundreds of slaves during his lifetime. At Monticello, Jefferson's Virginia plantation, slaves were treated very well. Yet a well-treated slave is a slave nonetheless.

Thomas Jefferson was probably the first white man to make note of the musical culture of his slaves. An exceptionally gifted and intelligent man, he listened to the music of his slaves and recognized how special it was. In his *Notes on the State of Virginia* (1784), Jefferson wrote, "In music they are more generally gifted than the whites, with accurate ears for tune and time, and they have been found capable of imagining a small catch."[1]

Although he didn't know it at the time, Jefferson was bearing witness to the beginning of a new musical era of a later time—one that began in the melting pot of America, where European music blended with a distinctive American spirit, and simmered in the spicy undertones imported by African slaves. Indeed, even in America's early days during a time of deep division, music began to unify us all.

A contemporary of Jefferson who was untimely born into slavery eventually gained his freedom and became a preacher. His powerful voice quickly lifted him from obscurity to renown as he crossed over from all black audiences to whites as well. His name was Harry Hosier, but as a former slave, he was still always referred to as "Black Harry."

"Black Harry" Hosier (1750–1806) gained his freedom after the Revolutionary War and became a traveling Methodist preacher. Although illiterate, he was a supremely gifted orator. His singing voice was even more compelling. He stirred worshipers into a frenzy with his vocal prowess, blending African and American musical techniques into his own very unique signature style. He turned stuffy psalms into extravagant, rhythmic, bent-note creations by using a slave field-worker technique called "lining out." He would sing a few lines and then wait for the congregation to repeat the lines, in the way the slaves often used "call and response" in the fields. Since most of his parishioners were also illiterate, this style became a popular and effective way to unify the people in song and spirit. Many preachers copied Black Harry's style, both during and after his time, collectively weaving African culture still deeper into the evolving fabric of American music.

Dead Men Tell No Tales*

*Treasure Girl (Unused) (1928)

Washington Square Park, once known as "The Land of the Blacks," is located at the southern tip of 5th Avenue in New York City. A quadrangle of land, just shy of ten acres, it sits in the heart of Greenwich Village. In my younger days, I often hung out in the park, playing street music with other local cats. Jazz, blues, rock 'n' roll, salsa, and folk music could be heard coming from all directions. Especially powerful were the drummers, beating out their rhythms. Congas, bongos, timbales, guiros, claves, and steel drums competed for the park's airwaves and its listeners. Described as such, it may seem like a cacophony to many, but in person, it seemed perfectly natural . . . perhaps because this space has always been competed for by artists of all sorts.

Today, "The Land of the Blacks" is practically surrounded by New York University, and the area remains a magnet to artists and bohemians. So how did such a famous park and diverse bit of land, named after our first president and home of the iconic Washington Arch, become known as "The Land of the Blacks"? Like so much of American history, the answer lies deep in the dark, murky times of slavery.

In the mid-17th century, Dutch settlers drove the Native Americans from this slice of their ancestral land. Although history credits Dutchman Peter Minuit for purchasing Manhattan Island from the Native Americans, a deal is not necessarily a *real* deal. The Native Americans were completely unfamiliar with the concept of land ownership. They were nomadic, and so various tribes were in the area at the time. Making a deal with one tribe did not mean the other tribes in the vicinity were included. Again, they did not understand how someone could own land; therefore, that famous $24 deal was virtually meaningless. The Dutch walked away thinking they got the deal of a lifetime (Donald Trump agrees), and the Native Americans thought they were "given" valuable trinkets as some sort of gift. Thus, they in turn thought they got the deal of a lifetime. Win-win!

The Dutch intended to farm the area, but the displaced Native Americans from other tribes who were not part of the original transaction wouldn't give up the land without a fight. Maybe my use of the word "displaced" is not perfectly accurate, but close enough. So, to resolve this security (or, more accurately, insecurity) problem, the Dutch freed a number of slaves to live on and farm the land. In effect, they created a human buffer zone, with freed slaves standing between Dutch colonists and the angry, displaced Native Americans. In return for their freedom, the blacks had to give a portion of their crops to the Dutch East India Company. Further, any children born to the "freed" slaves had to be turned over to their former owner.

A *Fact Sheet* by the New York Historical Society describes the "Land of the Blacks" this way:

The Dutch West India Company began to grant partial freedom, referred to by historians as half-freedom, in the 1640s. These former slaves owed a tax to the Company; white colonists did not. They also had to work for the colony whenever they were needed, and their children were automatically slaves. However, these blacks no longer lived the life of the enslaved. They were able to farm their own lands, sell their produce, and keep the profits beyond what they owed in tax. They also created the first black community in Manhattan, on farms granted them in the Land of the Blacks, located where Washington Square is now.[1]

Around 1800, the land became a potter's field, and later a burial ground for indigent people. In the early 1800s, an epidemic of yellow fever struck the region. "The Land of the Blacks," being somewhat removed from the population center in lower Manhattan, was deemed a suitable site for mass graves. The cemetery was closed in 1825, with over 20,000 bodies resting at the site.

The Washington Square scene in its Post Revolutionary potter's field days was said to have blacks:

. . . dancing the whole afternoon in the present Washington Square, then a general burying ground—the blacks (danced) joyfully above, while the sleeping dead reposed below! In that field could be seen at once more than one thousand of both sexes, divided into numerous little squads, dancing and singing, 'each in their own tongue,' after the customs of their several nations in Africa.[2]

It is hard to believe that so much suffering and death still lies just below the surface of this world-famous park, especially with so much music filling the air above it. However, this history lends the insight required to recognize the truly iconic nature of Washington Square Park, both as a historically significant location and as an enduring point of historical reference in the culture of American music.

One of my favorite songs is a jazz classic by Rahsaan Roland Kirk entitled "Serenade to a Cuckoo." The song was later made famous when the rock group Jethro Tull recorded it. A little-known fact is that Kirk created "Serenade to a Cuckoo" based on an old instrumental folk song named "Washington Square." It's common practice for jazz cats to use the chord structure of a song to create a completely different song. In jazz, this is called a contrafact (discussed in more detail in the "I Got Rhythm" section). From folk song to jazz classic to rock hit, "Washington Square" has indeed made its mark across many genres.

I will always remember seeing Rahsaan Roland Kirk at the Newport Jazz Festival in Rhode Island on July 4, 1969, just weeks before Woodstock. Kirk was angry and bitter, for good reason, in my humble opinion. The festival had changed from a gathering of jazz aficionados to a rock 'n' roll event, featuring bands like Blood Sweat and Tears and Jethro Tull. Kirk ripped into the crowd, telling us just how he felt, namely, that white rockers were ripping off black artists. His case in point was "Serenade to a Cuckoo," a song he wrote and made very little money on—yet when Jethro Tull covered it, suddenly it was a chart topper, showering the band with money and fame. He was disgusted by the injustice of it all—and to punctuate his point, he proceeded to regale the crowd with a phenomenal display of his own formidable talent.

With his great percussionist, Joe Texidor, Kirk held that rock crowd and me in awe. As a blind, multi-woodwind-instrumentalist who could play three saxophones at one time, he owned that stage like no one else—and he refused to leave it. As a form of protest against the white music establishment's exploitation of black musicians, Kirk continued playing and playing. Eventually, the producers shut off the stage lights, but Kirk kept on blowing. They turned off the microphones, but Kirk kept on blowing. Finally, Kirk was escorted off the stage by security, all the while still blowing his horns. As I heard those final sweet strains of "Serenade to a Cuckoo," I instinctively knew I had witnessed a defining moment in jazz.

O Land of Mine, America*

*Winner of a 1919 song contest conducted by the *New York American*

By the mid-1800s, there were over 4 million slaves in North America. Many white Americans thought that blacks were an inferior race, lacking in reason and intellect, and thus needing a paternal figure to watch over them. They were considered childlike in their spontaneous behaviors, including singing.

This view was well documented in a November 22, 1856, article in the *Charleston Mercury* entitled "The Lilliputian Musicians." The journalist described five black boys. One was characterized as an "uncivilized African." Of another, it was noted, "No human being can control him but his master . . ." And of a third, the journalist wrote, "a mild and gentle disposition, very submissive to his master, but never succumbs to one of his own race."[1]

Slave owners believed that blacks needed to be "cleansed" of their African traditions, beliefs, and culture. Still, despite their best efforts, slave traders and owners could not erase the indomitable spirit and culture of the Africans or the ubiquitous influence of their music. In time, their musical style began to take strong root in popular American music.

The music of the slaves differed from Euro-American music because, unlike their masters' music, drumming and rhythm dominated it, and the melody was secondary. In time, these rhythms melted into American music. Then, as European music and instruments mixed with Afro-American styles, something new and unique began to emerge.

This new blend of music was carried across the land by roving minstrels, and it wove itself into a wide variety of musical institutions: plantation hollers, slave songs, voodoo ceremonies, funeral music, spirituals, work songs, cotton and tobacco field slave songs, even marching bands. Because slave owners thought that music, dancing, and singing made slaves feel better about their hopeless plight, they encouraged their captives to sing and dance as a way to blow off steam, kind of like the pressure-release valve on a pressure cooker. The slave owners wanted to keep their "property" healthy and happy for various reasons. Slaves were very expensive, so keeping them happy and healthy made sense from an investment perspective. Another factor was that a happy slave was generally more docile, which reduced the chances of an uprising (a hungry man is an angry man). It also meant that their slaves would be more productive at their particular job. Therefore, slave treatment really boiled down to economics (take care of your investment and your investment will take care of you).

As more and more blacks converted to Christianity, African music blended into church music and spirituals. It also began their connection to the Jewish people. Blacks and Jews shared a special bond through the horrors of slavery, as evidenced by the black spiritual "Go Down Moses," which ends in a refrain to "let my people go." For several thousand years, the Jewish people have relived their experience of slavery under the Egyptians and their ultimate flight to freedom. Each and every year, Jews relive their personal slavery and flight from bondage during the Passover Seder. Black slaves related to this story of bondage and quest for freedom and hoped someday they too would live in freedom. And yet, to sing of this hope overtly would have been viewed as subversive by their owners and earn them extremely harsh reprisals. So, slaves veiled their longing for freedom in songs about Moses and the Children of Israel. Clearly, the plight of the African slaves and their musical influence was a cross-cultural symbol of spirit and resilience.

The slave trade was a worldwide phenomenon, reaching deep into Central and South America, the Caribbean, Cuba, Jamaica, Haiti, Trinidad, and Brazil. Slave traders plundered African tribes, often aided by African tribes themselves, who sold as slaves prisoners they captured in wars or kidnapped from other tribes. They intentionally separated tribes and families to weaken their cultural identity and familial bonds. But it was not an exact science. In Cuba, for example, there was a strong concentration of people from the Yoruba tribe, and their close proximity helped them preserve much of their music and religious practices.

Religion and music were deeply connected in the African society and then the Afro-Cuban one. For example, Santeria, a religious practice characterized by drumming and animal sacrifices, was imported from Africa to Cuba and is still practiced secretly in Cuba and the United States today. The Shango cult was also imported to Cuba. A Bantu-derived Afro-Brazilian religion moved into Haiti and then into Louisiana. Voudun or voodoo, which originated in Africa, is still practiced as well. Drums, rhythm, and dance are paramount in these African religious practices.[2]

Virtuoso trumpeter, Dizzy Gillespie, became deeply connected to Afro-Cuban music through his friendship with the jazz trumpeter Mario Bauzá and the conga drummer Chano Pozo. Although he is most widely known for the creation of Bebop with Charlie Parker, Dizzy was also instrumental in the creation of a form of jazz called CuBop (as in Cuban Bebop). Dizzy understood the deep roots of jazz, as he expounded in his 1979 memoir, *To Be, or Not . . . to Bop*:

A student of music, if he goes back far enough, will find out that the main source of our music is Africa. The music of the Western Hemisphere (not just our music)—the music of Cuba, the music of Brazil, the music of the West Indies, although they haven't made such a big impact on humanity as a whole, as jazz, spirituals and blues which were created by the blacks in the United States—is primarily of African origin.[3]

In this memoir, he goes on to talk about his own personal attraction to Latin rhythms.

I've always been a Latin freak. Very early in my career, I realized that our music and that of our brothers in Latin America had a common source. The Latin musician was fortunate in one sense. They didn't take the drum away from him, so he was more polyrhythmic.[4]

Dizzy was a great innovator, weaving together many threads of musical culture from around the globe. And, by all accounts, he was also a wonderful man. My old pal, the late great piano legend Eddie Higgins, played with Dizzy on the Jazz Cruises out of the Port of Miami, and he always spoke very highly of Dizzy. Their shared stories, illustrating his talent, character, and influence, were chronicled by the *Associated Press* on the morning Dizzy passed out of this world and into jazz history.

Follow the Minstrel Band*

*Show Girl (1929)

From the mid-to-late 19th century, traveling minstrel shows were a popular form of American entertainment. White performers presented comical musical acts in blackface, mimicking black people and portraying them as dim-witted, lazy, superstitious buffoons. They roved from town to town, speaking and singing in a manner that was very degrading to blacks.

In 1828, Thomas D. Rice wrote "Jump Jim Crow," a derogatory song and dance routine that mimicked a disabled, deformed slave. Rice wrote the song's chorus after hearing a disabled slave mutter, "Wheel about an' turn about and do jis so, an' eb'ry time I wheel about I jump Jim Crow." Rice's routine, performed in blackface, became a big hit, as he traveled far and wide. It earned him both fame and fortune. During the 1828–1829 season at Cincinnati's Columbia Street Theatre, it brought down the house. In a December 1832 performance by Rice in New York's Bowery district, the audience insisted that Rice repeat his Jim Crow song and dance act an extraordinary twenty times.[1] This racist blackface song and performance, like so many others like it, became entrenched in the popular vernacular, eventually providing widespread support for the Jim Crow laws of segregation, which became popular in the aftermath of the Civil War.

I was shocked to discover while researching this book that a song I had learned as a young saxophone student was derived from a racist blackface song of this era. "Turkey in the Straw," which shares its history and its melody line with the 1830s song "Zip Coon" ("coon" being a derogatory term for blacks), was in fact performed in blackface at the Bowery Theatre in New York City in 1834. One of the lyrics to "Zip Coon" mentions hootchy-kootchy, a black term for sex, "Did you ever go fishin' on a warm summer day When all the fish were swimmin' in de bay With their hands in their pockets and their pockets in their pants Did you ever see a fishie do the Hootchy-Kootchy dance?"[2]

One of the first recipes for blackface make-up included ham fat, so that became part of the racist vernacular of the era. In fact, a popular hit song at the time was "The Ham-fat Man." In the chorus, we hear the phrase "A hootchy, cootchy, cootchy, the ham-fat man." Yes, folks were doing the "hootchy-cootchy" back in the early-19th century, decades before it became popular at the 1893 World's Columbian Exposition in Chicago. (As for me, blues giant Muddy Waters holds the title as "The Hoochie Coochie Man.")

In 1843, a cat named Edwin Pearce Christy formed a blackface minstrel group dubbed

Christy's Minstrels. They became quite popular, innovating and organizing the minstrel show into a form that would be copied by many acts over the years. (This group is not to be confused with the 1960s folk music group called the New Christy Minstrels, which did not perform in blackface.) Despite its shameful legacy, minstrelsy still produced something quite notable—America's first blockbuster composer, Stephen Foster (1826–1864).

Known as the "Father of American Music," Foster penned over 200 songs, including classic American tunes like "Camptown Races" and "Oh! Susanna." While living in Cincinnati, Foster wrote "Oh! Susanna," which became the theme song of the Gold Rush forty-niners, miners who flocked to California's Sutter's Mill with "a banjo on their knee." The banjo was a favorite of the traveling minstrels, and Foster's songs were soon featured in many minstrel shows. Christy's Minstrels played Foster's songs just as soon as he could compose them, which fueled Foster's popularity and pushed him to grind out hit after hit. In 1853 he wrote a controversial song titled "Old Black Joe," which was both denounced and praised for its depiction of blacks. Yet, despite his meteoric rise to notoriety, Foster struggled to generate financial success. He died completely destitute, with just a few pennies in his pocket, on Manhattan's Lower East Side at the young age of thirty-seven.

Even P. T. Barnum, the legendary leader of "The Greatest Show on Earth," engaged in the blackface minstrel business. Beyond his role as a circus operator, he was also a producer and promoter of minstrel shows, featuring white performers in blackface. Even Barnum himself performed in blackface. Few people know that Barnum got his start in show business by buying an elderly, blind slave woman who claimed to be over 160 years old. The character was a big draw in New York. Never one to shy away from a scam, Barnum also promoted and sold an herb that supposedly turned black skin white.

Believe it or not (oops . . . that's Ripley) in time, Barnum became ardently opposed to slavery, eventually switching from Democrat to Republican and entering the political fray in support of the abolition of slavery and then the right of blacks to vote. In a speech he gave on May 26, 1865 Barnum said:

> Let the educated free negro feel that he is a man; let him be trained . . . let him support himself, pay his taxes, and cast his vote, like other men . . . A human soul that G-d has created and Christ died for, is not to be trifled with . . . It is still an immortal spirit . . . without regard to color or condition, all men are equally children of the common Father.[3]

It was indeed a radical transformation, from slave-owning blackface performer to staunch antislavery activist. Only in America!

Celebrated author Mark Twain was another notable fan of minstrelsy. He was quoted as saying, "The genuine nigger show, the extravagant nigger show, was the show which to me had no peer . . . a thoroughly delightful thing." At one point, he publicly declared that minstrel shows were preferable to opera, and he never hesitated to mention them in his books. In *The Adventures of Tom Sawyer* (1876), Twain wrote, "The first of all negro minstrel shows came to town, and made a sensation." He also mentioned minstrels in *The Adventures of Huckleberry Finn* (1884). Of course, at the time, they were a dominant feature of the American entertainment industry. Although this whole chapter in American history seems abhorrent to us today, we should be careful and recognize that this was well over one hundred years ago, and the times then were vastly different from what they are in the 21st century.

It's important to recognize the context surrounding these minstrel shows. For generations, American blacks had lived under the power of their slave owner. They were fed, housed, clothed, doctored, and bred with virtually no say so on their part. Another human being controlled a slave's very existence, from cradle to grave. And then, practically overnight, the slaves became former slaves, 100 percent responsible for their own lives.

Being "free" meant that emancipated slaves had to fend for themselves. Post-Civil War blacks had to find shelter, food, clothing, and security—and the stakes were life or death. They were completely unprepared. As they fled the plantations, many blacks became sharecroppers or tenant farmers. Some traveled to the cities to work in the ports, industry, or railroads. Others became musicians, snapping up the brass instruments shed by the Civil War bands, and some joined the minstrel shows to eke out a living.

It's ironic that the minstrel show industry was based on a mockery of black music and culture, and that so many blacks sought refuge in this genre of entertainment. After the Civil War, black minstrel "darkies" made a living by imitating the white minstrels, who had been imitating the blacks. They wore huge, oversized shoes and applied burnt cork on their faces to enhance the ridiculing "darkie" effect. But hey, whatever pays the bills, right?

One of the most successful men of this new black minstrel industry was "The World's Greatest Minstrel Man," James A. Bland (1854–1911). Born in Flushing, New York, he was a black man who composed over 700 songs for black minstrel shows. Some of his tunes, such as "Carry Me Back to Old Virginny" (1878) and "Oh, Dem Golden Slippers" (1879), eventually became American folk classics. He toured the world, playing for queens and princes in Europe. Sadly, he died in obscurity from tuberculosis.

By the turn of the century, there were many traveling minstrel shows featuring black musicians, singers, dancers, and entertainers. It is rumored that Jelly Roll Morton and Ma Rainey traveled the circuit, infusing the blues into the musical lexicon of America. White audiences were beginning to hear directly from black musicians a new sound that was the called the blues, with its flattened thirds, fifths, and sevenths. Unfortunately, blackface continued on well into the 1930s. Legendary white entertainers like Al Jolson, Eddie Cantor, Bing Crosby, and Judy Garland performed in blackface at various points in their careers.

As America moved beyond minstrel shows, two other kinds of shows became popular—vaudeville and burlesque. Both were variety shows and helped move the evolution of America's taste in entertainment. Vaudeville was a series of separate, unrelated acts that included musicians, dancers, singers, comedians, impersonators, acrobats, trained animals, jugglers, and one-act plays. Burlesque shows were much more risqué, relying heavily on exposed female skin, but they also included a heavy dose of slapstick comedy. Many new songs were written to support these shows, bringing new rhythms, sounds, and other musical concepts from the black community to the American public.

Despite its many faults, the era of minstrelsy and the years that followed introduced black music to millions of white Americans, and provided a career to countless black musicians who were struggling to find their way along the jagged edge of post-Civil War America.

Black and White*

*Show Girl (1929)

At this time, let me address the 800-pound matzo ball in the room. It's the complicated relationship between the Jewish and the black communities.

Let's jump right in with blackface and how it relates to George Gershwin and his first blockbuster hit, "Swanee," which was written in 1919. At first, the song did not go anywhere. But when the Jewish performer Al Jolson, nicknamed "The World's Greatest Entertainer," heard twenty-year-old Tin Pan Alley hack George Gershwin playing "Swanee" at a party at Bessie Blood's House of Fame (in truth, a whorehouse), he fell in love with it. Jolson worked it into his Broadway show *Sinbad,* which was running at the Winter Garden. (Sadly, Jolson performed the tune in blackface, but to raving white audiences.)

In 1920, Columbia Records recorded Jolson covering the song, and it soared to the top of the national charts, holding the number-one hit position for nine weeks running. It lingered on the charts for eighteen weeks total, selling well over 2 million records, plus a million copies of sheet music! George Gershwin hit the big time with a song performed in blackface by "The World's Greatest Entertainer" of the time, Al Jolson.

Several years later in 1927, a motion picture was made—the first movie featuring sound, talking, and singing. The movie was *The Jazz Singer,* and it featured none other than Al Jolson performing the Gershwin song that boosted his fame and fortune: "Swanee." Now all of America, as well as the whole world, saw the blackface Jewish singer/dancer Al Jolson performing his big hit, written by a Tin Pan Alley hack, who was also of Jewish heritage. It was certainly a Two Jews Blues phenomenon. It's absolutely amazing that folks from diverse religious, cultural, and racial backgrounds can borrow from each other to produce such a song and performance. I contend that the reason for this rests squarely in the uniqueness of America.

Viewing the "Swanee" story through our 21st-century Google glasses stirs up some negative feelings, and rightfully so, but we should temper that negativity in the backdrop of an evolving American culture. It was a complex interplay of racial factors. So let's take a closer look at this complicated chapter of our nation's history. Before I delve too deep into the relationship between the blacks and Jews, I would like to add a bit of context to the blackface narrative.

Many of us are aware of the stereotypical indignities of blackface in America's history, but few are aware of a similar phenomenon targeting Jews that is called "Jewface." In 2006, a CD released on Reboot Stereophonic and curated by Jody Rosen introduces us to a term that Rosen calls "Jewface," which is the title of this CD as well. A very informative booklet written by Rosen accompanies the CD. First, he describes the Jewish comedian as having a distinctive "shtick and look" with "bulging eyes that darted above the ubiquitous beard and enormous hook nose." The Jewfaces' stereotypical wardrobe consisted of "oversized shoes, a tattered black overcoat, and a derby cap pulled tightly across his head so that his ears jutted out." Rosen continues his description of the Jewface: "A hodgepodge of Jewish stereotypes old and new, both a crafty grasper and a bumbling immigrant greenhorn: Shylock lifted out of Venice and deposited in the bewildering polyglot scrum of the Lower East Side ... And was obsessed above all with money-making schemes. He was a buffoon, forever losing his shirt in pinochle games and his best girl to an Irishman who would beat him up for good measure. Occasionally he'd leave New York and head west determined to become a cowboy or Indian chief, an adventure that would invariably end with a pratfall into a cactus."

Jewface portrayed Jews both onstage as well as in the print media. Onstage the entertainer in Jewface spoke and sung in a thick Yiddish dialect. Here are a couple of song titles on this CD; see if you can guess which stereotypical Jewish trait is being mocked: "Cohen Owes Me 97 Dollars"; "When Mose With His Nose Leads the Band." If you answered cheap money grubbing for the first song and the huge hooknose for the second, then give yourself an A+. Mazel Tov! As with blackface, Jewface was, in many cases, written and portrayed onstage by many of its own, Jews, as well as non-Jews.

Some folks in the black community had then and some still have today a very negative view of Jews, saying the Jews ripped off the black culture for fame and fortune in the same way that slave owners derived wealth from the black man's toil. Others in the black community still have a common bond with the people of the Old Testament, since they too had to break the chains of oppression. As W. E. B. Du Bois once said, "The Negro race looks to the Jews for sympathy and understanding." Many blacks recognized that Jews have been terribly oppressed, just as they had been. So, within these large and diverse two groups of people, we do have many different perspectives. The feelings and actions of a few should never represent the sentiments of an entire community; however, it is interesting and informative to explore these resentments in our quest for knowledge.

Perhaps because of their shared roots in slavery and persecution, Jews had a special affinity for jazz and its bluesy expression of suffering. Some have compared the singing of synagogue cantors to the blues, suggesting that the Jewish ear was already attuned to the sound of the blues because of their use of minor keys. Samson Raphaelson was inspired to write *The Jazz Singer* after seeing Jolson perform in blackface. He said, "My G-d, this isn't a jazz singer. This is a cantor." Jolson was the son of a cantor so perhaps he was born for the part. Further still, the blues are some of the building blocks of jazz, and cantorial music shares these same blue notes.

Harlem's leading newspaper, *The Amsterdam News*, wrote of the movie *The Jazz Singer*, "One of the greatest pictures ever produced," and of Jolson they said, "Every colored performer is proud of him."[1] Time and music have a way of healing the wounds of the past. Aretha Franklin, the "Queen of Soul," showed us how her wounds had healed by recording "Swanee," Gershwin's hit song made famous by Jolson singing it in blackface. Why she chose this extremely controversial song is anybody's guess, but she took that song and transformed it into something completely different and deeply compelling, and she recorded it for posterity. Her rendition can be heard on the album entitled *Black Sabbath: The Secret Musical History of Black-Jewish Relations* (produced by the Idelsohn Society for Musical Preservation). The compilation is chock full of surprises. The first track is Lady Day (Billy Holliday), singing a home recording of "My Yiddishe Momme" with enormous passion and soul and a spirit that highlights the universality of motherhood from a black/Jewish perspective. She sweetly implores us to remember that all humans are the same.

Blues great Alberta Hunter is also featured on this album, singing "Ich Hob Dich Tzufil Lieba" ("I Love You Much Too Much") in Yiddish. I remember seeing Ms. Hunter in person, at The Cookery in Greenwich Village. Alberta sang this same Yiddish song there and autographed an album that I still have to this day. My wife, Julie, and I were in total shock, hearing her sing in Yiddish. Having grown up in a home where my parents spoke Yiddish, I knew Alberta's pronunciation and inflection were spot on.

Other black musicians on this album sing and play the soul of the Jewish people, including Eartha Kitt, singing "Sholem"; jazz alto-sax legend Cannonball Adderley, playing "Sabbath Prayer"; the Slim Gaillard Quartet covering "Dunkin' Bagel"; and Nina Simone singing the Israeli folksong "Eretz Zavat Chalav" ("A Land Flowing with Milk and Honey"). Even the fabulous Motown sensations The Temptations joined in the Jewish spirit with a medley of songs from *Fiddler on the Roof*.

If you are not *kvelling* or "bursting with pride" by now, then hearing Johnny Mathis belting out "Kol Nidre" (the holy song/prayer that begins the Yom Kippur service) as if he studied in a cantorial yeshiva for decades will surely make you a believer that the music of the Jews was loved, respected, and integral to many black entertainers and the black community in general. In his arpeggios, Mathis hits more blue notes (I call them Jew notes) per second than anyone can imagine. What a *mensch!*

Before moving on, I must pay homage to one last tune from this album, the Yiddish song "Utt Da Zay" ("That's the Way"), about the motions of a tailor. Sung by jazz great Cab Calloway ("the hi-dee hi-dee hi-dee ho man" from the song "Minnie the Moocher,"), the song was written by Callaway's Jewish agent, Irving Mills, with Cab and Clarence Gaskill. It was the first number-one U.S. hit by a black artist. The song became such a hit that Cab followed it up with another Yiddish ditty, "Abi Gezunt" ("If You Got Your Heath, You Can Be Happy"), and then added several other Yiddish songs to his repertoire as the years progressed. Some say Callaway became quite fluent in Yiddish. Many of his songs echoed the arpeggios of the Jewish cantors with Cab's jive "hepster" twist, as only he could pull off. To sum up, on the album *Black Sabbath: The Secret Musical History of Black-Jewish Relations*, some songs will make you laugh, some will make you cry, some will tear at your heartstrings, and some will make you dance. The album made me proud to be an American—not a Jewish-American or a black-American . . . a melting-pot American! It's what makes this country unique.

In his autobiography, *James Brown: The Godfather of Soul,* Brown expressed a deep love for and connection to the Jewish culture. In fact, he attributed his success to a couple of Jewish businessmen. Brown insisted that the white people he liked must have had "some Jewish in them." He related his affinity to Jewish people to the fact that they, like him, were cultural outsiders, and he admired the way they achieved success a few decades before him and thus cleared the path for him.[2] Many of his contemporaries also recognized this unique connection.

Rhythm and blues, gospel, soul and jazz great, Ray Charles (the "Georgia on My Mind" cat) was honored as "Man of the Year" by the Beverly Hills lodge of B'nai B'rith in 1976, and in his acceptance speech, Brother Ray drew some very poignant parallels between blacks and Jews:

> Blacks and Jews are hooked up and bound together by a common history of persecution. . . . If someone besides a black ever sings the real gut bucket blues, it'll be a Jew. We both know what it's like to be someone else's footstool.[3]

At Brown University in November 1969, the American literary critic Leslie Fiedler said in front of the esteemed annual Wetmore Lecture series on black author Ralph Ellison (*Invisible Man*), "He's a black Jew." Ellison then replied, "Leslie's been trying to make me a Jew for years. But someone should have said that *all* us old-fashion Negroes are Jews."[4]

Ellison also stated:

> Thus I feel uncomfortable whenever I discover Jewish intellectuals writing as though they were guilty of enslaving my grandparents, or as though the Jews were responsible for the system of segregation. Not only do they have enough troubles of their own, as the saying goes, but Negroes know this only too well. . . . I consider the United States freer politically and richer culturally because there are Jewish Americans to bring it the benefit of their special forms of dissent, their humor and their gift for ideas which are based upon the uniqueness of their experience.[5]

Another black author, James Baldwin (*Notes of a Native Son*), also felt a kinship between Jews and blacks, saying, "The hymns, the texts, and the most favored legends of the devout Negro are all Old Testament and therefore Jewish in origin: the flight from Egypt, the Hebrew children in the fiery furnace, the terrible jubilee songs of deliverance."[6]

Baldwin also acknowledged that Jews, like blacks, are in a vulnerable position, so both groups have to lean toward and even favor the white side to avoid the wrath of the mob. He relates the two as scapegoats, saying, "Georgia has the Negro and Harlem has the Jew."

Harlem's poet laureate, Langston Hughes, wrote a poem that later shared its title with his 1927 poetry collection, *Fine Clothes to the Jew*. Later in life, Hughes bravely joined forces to help rescue European Jews during the Holocaust and also supported the formation of the State of Israel. He joined other prominent black celebrities, like Paul Robeson and W. E. B. Du Bois, to rescue Jewish refugees from Europe and relocate them to Palestine.

But not every black celebrity has felt so closely aligned with the Jewish community. Jazz cat Miles Davis had a rocky road with his record label, Columbia, and he wasn't shy in expressing his feelings about the company. He felt very strongly that Columbia failed to promote black artists as vigorously as they did whites and Jews. In *Miles: The Autobiography*, he wrote, "I had said in an interview that Columbia Records was a racist place to be, and it was. Now they seemed to be interested in pushing only white music. . . . I wanted them to push black music like they were pushing white rock and that sad-assed hillbilly shit they were doing. . . ."[7] In another quip about Columbia Records, Davis complained, "They don't do anything for you unless you're white or Jewish." Miles was one heck of a complicated cat to say the least, so perhaps we should take his comments with a grain of NaCl (salt to you non-chemistry majors).

It seems human nature always drives folks to take out their own personal frustrations on someone else. Comedian Lenny Bruce hit the nail on the head when he said, "Let's get together, Jews, Catholics, Protestants, Blacks, Whites, everybody. Let's get together and beat up on the Puerto Ricans." It appears that some folks want to kick others who are more vulnerable than they are.

Jazz trumpeter, composer, and Lincoln Center's director of jazz, Wynton Marsalis, also made a shocking anti-Semitic statement on national television, saying blacks have been held back for many, many years because the music business is controlled by "people who read the Torah and stuff."[8] This is quite a surprising statement from such a virtuoso musician.

Auto magnate, Henry Ford, would have readily agreed. He believed that Jews were the invisible hand of jazz. In 1921, in his very own newspaper, *The Dearborn Independent,* Ford wrote an article entitled, "Jewish Jazz—Moron Music—Becomes Our National Anthem." Ford was on an anti-Semitic rampage, noting:

> Jazz is a Jewish creation . . . The invisible Jewish baton, which is waved above them for financial and propaganda purposes. Just as the American stage and motion picture have fallen under the control of Jews and their art-destroying commercialism, so the business of handling "popular songs" has become a Yiddish industry . . . The Jews do not create; they take what others have done, give it a cleaver twist and exploit it.

Ford was a *putz* racist *meshugganah* whose company, years later, ironically hired many Jews and blacks. Have you driven a Ford lately? The history of relations between blacks and Jews can be both depressing and inspiring, which is understandable, given the complicated relationship between these two minorities that both experienced the wrath of prejudice and racism, sometimes from whites and sometimes from each other.

In the book *A Right to Sing the Blues: African Americans, Jews, and American Popular Song,* written by Harvard University Ph.D. Jeffrey Melnick in 2001, the author opines about Jews being guilty of "the rip-off of African-American culture." He asserts, "Jews (were) responsible for perverting 'authentic' African-American music." He then declares that Jews did a "takeover of popular music." In another section he writes, "Jews had come to function as modern-day slaveholders."[9] In my opinion, this "professor" is totally off the wall. Are kids really taking out college loans to be taught by this pedagogue?

Race was always an integral component of the music scene. Paul Whiteman hired gifted black musician/arranger Don Redman in the mid-1920s, but only as a behind-the-curtain arraigner, because a black man was not permitted to perform onstage with a white band like Whiteman's Orchestra. Jim Crow laws were in effect at the time, and the American Federation of Musicians (a musicians' union) had separate locales for black and white musicians.[10]

The racial barrier began to break down in the 1930s with band leaders like Benny Goodman, who hired pianist Teddy Wilson, and the clarinetist, composer, and bandleader Artie Shaw, who featured the great vocalist Billie Holiday in 1935. Interesting that Goodman and Shaw were both Jewish, which kind of refutes Dr. Melnick's thesis. I guess the esteemed Harvard professor might need a bit more schoolin'!

Although the Jim Crow barrier was finally shattered in the 1930s by some very brave jazz cats, it took more than a decade to slap down the reverse racial discrimination practiced by the black bands of the time. The practice of not including white musicians in black bands was called "Crow Jim." In 1949 Count Basie ended the "Crow Jim" policy practiced by the black bands. The count hired two excellent white sax cats—Serge Chaloff (a Jew) and George Auld—to play on the bandstand with his band. It took an additional two years for Duke Ellington to bust the "Crow Jim" policy in his outfit by hiring white drum sensation Louis Bellson. Jazz was finally becoming color blind as well as accepting Jews on the bandstand.

We Go to Church on Sunday*

*Our Nell (1922)

The first slaves in America, about nineteen, arrived at Jamestown, Virginia, in 1619. A Dutch ship had seized them from a Spanish slave ship. As soon as they arrived, slave owners began the process of separating slaves from their roots by forbidding rituals and customs they had practiced in Africa. Their owners superimposed a new culture on their "property," requiring the slaves to adopt Christianity. Fortunately, this new religion gave many slaves a measure of hope and comfort.

Because music and dance had been such an integral part of the rituals and traditions of their homeland, slaves quickly took to singing the praises of Jesus, which was legal and highly encouraged. Since it was illegal to teach a slave to read or write, knowledge of Christianity was passed on verbally through preaching. The only book that preachers were allowed to read to slaves was the Bible. So spirituals, such as "Go Down, Moses" and "Turn Back the Pharaoh's Army" (both reflections of the blacks' connection with the Hebrews' bondage in Egypt) were memorized and sung and re-sung.

In 1866, shortly after the end of the Civil War, Fisk University opened its doors in Nashville, Tennessee. Fisk billed itself as a liberal arts university, and it was open to students of all colors. This was a radical groundbreaking event in a segregated America and an amazing opportunity for newly emancipated slaves. But then, just a few short years later, the university ran into financial problems. So, music professor, George White, a white Northern missionary and music director for the school, recruited students to form a choral ensemble, which then went on tour in support of the financially strapped institution. Calling themselves the Fisk Jubilee Singers, these black men and women performed spirituals to predominately white audiences.

A bit of insight into why the Fisk University Singers added the word "jubilee" to their name: the word "jubilee" comes from a passage in the Old Testament (*Leviticus* 25:10) that references the final year of "seven cycles of seven years plus one"—in other words, it is a 49-year cycle with the jubilee being the 50th year. The Bible states that:

> The 50th year is sacred—it is a time of freedom and of celebration, when everyone will receive back their original property, and slaves will return home to their families.[1]

For a singing group of former slaves, singing the songs of the slaves, the word "jubilee" had a deep personal meaning.

As a side note, in Hebrew, the word "jubilee" is related to the word "shofar" (meaning ram's horn), and at the beginning of the jubilee year, the *shofar* is sounded on Yom Kippur. I have been the shofar sounder in my *shul* for decades, and yet I have never sounded the shofar for the jubilee. I asked the rabbi if, on the jubilee year, I would perform special sounds. He told me no one knows which year is the jubilee year because we don't know when to start the count. He did say, however, that when the temple is rebuilt in Jerusalem, we will be able to start the tradition again, so my sounding the shofar on the jubilee year will have to wait until the coming of the Messiah. (I hope it is soon because I have been practicing very diligently for that gig!) Let's get back to the Fisk Jubilee Singers.

As you might well imagine, the singers traveled a rocky road at first. It wasn't a minstrel show, which the public had grown so accustomed to seeing. The Fisk Jubilee Singers were forging an entirely new paradigm, and eventually, their brave tour began to pay off. The group turned a profit, enabling them to pay for the tour and still send money back to the school.

A profitable group of emancipated slaves was quite a sensation at that time, so their fame and fortune skyrocketed. In fact, at the end of 1872, President Ulysses S. Grant invited them to the White House to perform.

The group continued to tour the country and then went to Europe, performing for the King and Queen of England and other nobility as well as commoners. It is said that Queen Victoria wept when she heard the singers. The Fisk Jubilee Singers introduced a new formerly obscure type of black American music and culture to other parts of Europe as well. They traveled to France and Germany and other European nations, and were very well received.

Dixie Rose*

*Same music as *Swanee Rose* (1921)

I heard a story once. As a matter of fact, I've heard a lot of stories in my time. They went along with the sound of a tinny piano, playing in the parlor downstairs. "Mister, I met a man once when I was a kid," they'd always begin. Well, I guess neither one of our stories is very funny.

—HUMPHREY BOGART IN *CASABLANCA* (1942)

New Orleans has always been a gumbo pot of diversity and activity. In its youth, it was an action-packed port city, teeming with barges' hauling goods up and down the Mississippi River. Ships from other countries also used the port for commerce. So, of course it follows that during the era of slavery, New Orleans was a major center for slave traders. Yet, for Africans, it was more. It was also a hub of cultural expression.

On Sunday afternoons, slaves were allowed to gather in Congo Square (now located inside of Louis Armstrong Park) to dance the African Bamboula and blow off steam. This practice dated from before the Louisiana Purchase and continued long after the United States took over the territory. The event was so popular that up to 3,000 slaves would gather every Sunday afternoon to sing and dance. Many African tribes were represented, including the Zulus, Mandingas, and Gangas. It was in Congo Square that the slaves also first elected a big black man as "King of the Zulus" to spearhead the Mardi Gras celebrations.

Music has always been a core component of New Orleans' culture and identity. Further, with rich folks living in close proximity to poor folks, music also served to bridge the socioeconomic and racial sectors of the city.

Before the Civil War, the city boasted three opera companies and two symphony orchestras that catered only to the upper class. Then after the Civil War, when soldiers' brass marching band instruments flooded the market, trumpets, trombones, and many other instruments were easy to find and also very reasonably priced. Soon, brass marching bands, both white and black, appeared in every sector of society—in funeral processions, at weddings, at parties, and even at the occasional bar mitzvah. During the eight-week Carnival season that culminated in Mardi Gras, marching bands filled the streets.

In time, an entire sector of the city assumed the task of merging cultures and classes through the amazing spirit of music, pleasure, and self-expression.

STORYVILLE: THE BIRTHPLACE OF JAZZ

Storyville, also known as "The District," was a section of New Orleans where the black community was cooking up a spicy musical mix. Blending together Afro, Afro-Cuban, ragtime, slave songs, work songs, gospel, marching brass bands, spasm bands, Mardi Gras music, and Creole tunes, many types of music and culture now simmered together and eventually served up the iconic music we now call jazz.

Yet in Storyville, people rubbed elbows with more than musicians. From the late 1800s until 1917, Storyville served as the red-light district of New Orleans, home to the honky-tonks, barrelhouses, gambling venues, and whorehouses. It was home to pimps, gamblers, whores, porters, criminals, whores, folks looking for a good time . . . and even more whores! It became very popular with white men who were looking to partake of the pleasures of the quadroons and octoroons, fair-skinned women of mixed ethnicity. The city government didn't legalize prostitution; it just ignored it in Storyville, effectively containing the culture of sin and vice within a 38-block section of the French Quarter.

The infamous Basin Street (celebrated in "Basin Street Blues") was an integral part of "The

District" and home to many "palaces" (whorehouses), as well as honky-tonks, sporting houses, and barrelhouses, such as The 25 Club, Madame White's Mahogany Hall, Aunt Lucy's, The Red Onion, The Keystone, and Spanola's. Can't you just imagine Spencer Williams's "Mahogany Hall Stomp" playing in the background at Madame White's Mahogany Hall? He must have been a prince on the street, as he also wrote the blues classic "Basin Street Blues." Stories about Storyville of course added to its notorious reputation, such as the renaming of a dive called the 601 Ranch to the 602 Ranch after its owner was killed.[1]

Storyville had its own royal court. There was Buddy "King" Bolden (unfortunately he went mad and was committed to an insane asylum), Freddie "King" Keppard, and Joseph "King" Oliver—all trumpet greats. In fact, a number of the earliest jazz legends played in New Orleans, including Kid Ory (trombone), Johnny Dodds (clarinet and alto sax), Jimmy Noone (guitar and clarinet), and the one and only Louis Armstrong (trumpet, coronet, and vocalist extraordinaire). It was also home to many famous Creole players, including Sidney Bechet (soprano sax) and Jelly Roll Morton (piano).

Some say New Orleans got its nickname, "The Big Easy," from the musicians who found it easy to find a gig there. Riverboats, such as the S.S. President of the Streckfus Line, ferried countless jazz bands along the Mississippi River and its tributaries and also back and forth to New Orleans.

Unfortunately, as Geoffrey Chaucer once said, "All good things must come to an end." In 1917, within a period of a few weeks, four Navy sailors were killed in "The District." Shortly thereafter, the U.S. Army prohibited its soldiers from visiting Storyville to partake in its most popular retail product, prostitution, proclaiming whores to be a public health hazard. Eventually, on November 12, 1917, Mayor Martin Behrman closed down Storyville "under protest." He had no choice, as both the U.S. Army and the U.S. Navy insisted. He reluctantly relented, saying:

> Preterpermitting the pros and cons of legislative recognition of prostitution as a necessary evil in a seaport the size of New Orleans, our city government has believed that the situation could be administered more easily and satisfactorily by confining it within a prescribed area. Our experience has taught us that the reasons for this are unanswerable, but the Navy Department of the Federal Government has decided otherwise.[2]

The closure of Storyville produced a mass exodus, and hundreds of black musicians became jobless. They scattered north, east, and west, many heading for Texas and California. Some went upriver, playing music on the riverboats to Kansas City and St. Louis, and points further north like New York and especially Chicago. The Windy City was a bustling town with stockyards and decent paying jobs, and in 1920, when Congress passed the 18th Amendment, Prohibition became the law of the land, catapulting Chicago into a major hotspot of speakeasies and bootleggers. Wherever you found a speakeasy, you also found a thriving subterranean jazz scene.[3]

Despite the fact that its key players had scattered to the winds, the legacy of Storyville lived on. A movie (now on DVD) entitled *New Orleans—The All-Musical Tribute to the Birth of Jazz 1947*—starred Louis Armstrong, Billie Holiday, Woody Herman, and more. It is a rich compilation of musicians who carried the roots of jazz into the rest of America. Chock full of classic Louis Armstrong and Billie Holiday music, it includes other jazz legends, such as Kid Ory on the trombone, Zutty Singleton on drums, Bud Scott on guitar, Red Callender on bass and tuba, Barney

Bigard on clarinet, and the legendary Meade "Lux" Lewis on piano. But one song stands out from them all—Lady Day singing a haunting blues rendition of "Farewell to Storyville." She was leading what resembled a funeral procession out of that infamous section of town, right after the U.S. government shut it down. What an eerie scene it was. Holiday's voice resonated with the despair and helplessness of the Storyville people, as only Lady Day could do.

New Orleans—The All-Musical Tribute to the Birth of Jazz 1947 also includes two memorable shorts: a 1932 film featuring Louis Armstrong, appropriately titled *A Rhapsody in Black and Blue* (1932), and *Symphony in Black: A Rhapsody of Negro Life* (1935) that featured Duke Ellington and Lady Day. Just as memorable is an essay written by Orson Welles called *The Story of Jazz.* Campy as all these flicks may be, these snapshots of history are worth every cent you pay for them.

Storyville was an abundant source of timeless stories. One told of Creole trumpet great Freddie Keppard (1889–1933), leader of the Original Creole Orchestra that toured the United States on the Vaudeville circuit. Keppard was an exceptional musician, but also a paranoid guy who feared that other trumpeters wanted to steal his "stuff." Because of his paranoia, he played the horn with a handkerchief draped over his hand, so no one could see his fingering. In fact, he was so frightened of musicians stealing his "stuff" that in 1915 he turned down a Victor Records offer to record his orchestra. If he had accepted this recording gig, he would have gone down in history as the one who produced the first jazz record. Because Keppard did refuse, the title of "the first jazz record in history" ironically went to a white jazz band.

Two years later, Victor Records signed a deal with a white band, The Original Dixieland Jass Band, to record "Livery Stable Blues," with "Dixie Jass Band One-Step" on the flip side. This 78-RPM became the biggest-selling record of its time, selling over 250,000 records at 75 cents each ($187,500 then, which translates to $3.5 million in today's dollars). Yet, musical snobs looked down their noses at it, calling this new jazz hit "barnyard noise" because of the farm-animal sounds featured in the song.

"Livery Stable Blues" gave most Americans their very first opportunity to hear this new type of music called jazz, and boy, did they LOVE it! In fact, even five years after its release, at the historic Aeolian Hall concert (which I will discuss later), the still popular "Livery Stable Blues" opened the show to thunderous applause.

The year 1919 was an interesting one for New Orleans jazz. After Storyville closed and a great majority of its gigs had vanished, most musicians had moved north to find work. Jazz had settled into a paternal sort of relationship with Joseph K. Gorham, which the *New Orleans Item* dubbed the "Daddy of the Jazz." Gorham was a theatrical impresario who booked jazz bands in his shows, as well as scheduling some far-off gigs in Chicago.

Another jazz cat who prevailed through these troubled times went by the street name "Stale Bread." "Stale Bread" was a blind newsboy who taught himself to play the violin that he picked up as a leftover from a traveling minstrel band. Around 1901, he learned to play some swinging tunes and performed them on street corners while selling his newspapers. His style was fresh and unique, and when his popularity increased, he formed a band known as Stale Bread's Spasm Band. Despite their moniker, their tunes were fresh baked and lively. (An interesting article on this unique group can be found in the April 26, 1919, issue of *Literary Digest*. It's titled "Stale Bread's Sadness Gave 'Jazz' to the World.")

Long after the closure of Storyville, its legacy

was living on. Piano legend, Dave Brubeck was quoted as saying:

> In New Orleans, of course, is where it all started. Kind of a combination of cultures, the fusion of which produced a uniquely American art form. There was the African influence, you know, the drive, the beat. Then, via French New Orleans, from Western Europe, came the harmonic sense, the tonal structure, the instruments employed.[4]

In 1950, jazz impresario and Newport Jazz Festival producer, George Wein, opened a jazz club in Boston's Copley Square Hotel; appropriately, he named it Storyville. Many jazz greats of the day played at that club, including Charlie Parker, Louis Armstrong, Duke Ellington, Billie Holiday, and Dave Brubeck, all paying homage to their roots, which reached deeply into the heart of New Orleans.

Pay Some Attention to Me*

*A Damsel in Distress (Unused) (1937)

Jelly Roll Morton, born Ferdinand Joseph LaMothe (1890–1941), was a man who wore many hats—that of a part-time pimp, a vaudevillian who played in minstrel shows, a self-proclaimed "Inventor of Jazz and Stomps," "The Originator of Jazz, Stomps and Swing," and "The World's Greatest Hot Tune Writer." A practicing Catholic raised by his godmother, a voodoo witch named Laura Hunter, this light-skinned Creole pianist is best known as a legendary pianist, composer, and bandleader.[1]

Morton's Creole heritage and light skin helped him land a gig at LuLu White's, the largest and most highfalutin' whorehouse in Storyville. Lulu was widely known as a purveyor of light-skinned ladies for her white clientele, so she did not want a dark-skinned piano man. Morton, being both light skinned and an excellent piano player, was perfect for the job.

But even Jelly Roll could not escape the degrading racism of the Jim Crow days. As Louis Armstrong put it:

> Jelly Roll, with lighter skin than the average piano player, got the job because they did not want a black piano player for the job. He claimed he was from an Indian or Spanish race. Not culled at all. He was a big Bragadossa. Lots of big talk. They had lots of players in the District that could play lots better than Jelly, but their dark color kept them from getting the job. Jelly Roll made so much money in tips that he had a diamond inserted in one of his *teeth*. No matter how much his diamond sparkled, he still had to eat in the *kitchen*, the same as we blacks.[2]

By the age of seventeen, Jelly Roll hit the road, playing in Memphis, Kansas City, Chicago, and New York. And he took his roots with him. As a native of the New Orleans melting pot, he incorporated rhythms from the Caribbean and the Habanera into his repertoire. (The Habanera, as in Havana, was imported from Africa to Cuba.)

Jelly Roll was a very outspoken cat, and one of Storyville's most famous, controversial, and flamboyant personalities. Some said he was an exaggerator; others verified his stories. Yet his controversial nature caused many people and musicians as well to dislike him. As Duke Ellington once said, "Sure, Jelly Roll Morton has talent . . . talent for talking about Jelly Roll Morton."

Some jazz historians consider Jelly Roll to be the first jazz composer, and no one disputes the fact that his hit song, "Jelly Roll Blues" (1915), was the first jazz song ever published. As the jazz musician/expert/conductor/composer and author, Gunther Schuller, put it, "The legendary Ferdinand Joseph ('Jelly Roll') Morton, pianist, gambler, pimp, self-proclaimed 'inventor of jazz,' but above all the first of that precious jazz elite: composer."[3]

Later in life, Mr. Jelly Lord, Morton's nickname, (he chose Lord since Duke, as in Ellington and Count, as in Basie were already taken, so Lord it was) got into a public spiff with none other than blues innovator, W. C. Handy. On March 26, 1938, while listening to a Ripley's *Believe It Or Not* radio broadcast, Morton heard Handy introduced as the originator of jazz and blues. Jelly Roll went berserk! (Little did he know, the radio script had been written by one of Ripley's staff; Handy had nothing to do with that verbiage.)

He wrote a 4,000-word letter to Ripley and sent a copy to *Downbeat* magazine as well. The letter opens with: "W. C. Handy is a liar!" And it closes with the signature, "JELLY ROLL MORTON, Originator of Jazz and Stomps, Victor Artist, World's Greatest Hot Tune Writer."[4] Let me tell you, this letter is packed with put-down after put-down of Handy and other musicians. One critic then wrote an article in *Downbeat*, defending Handy and calling Morton "a loud-mouth whorehouse piano player." Others acknowledged that there was some truth in what Jelly Roll said. Despite this public feud, Morton remained widely respected in the jazz community. Mister Jelly Lord died in 1941 at the young age of fifty-one.

The Real American Folk Song (Is a Rag)*

*Ladies First (1918)

Although the younger generation today may know the word "ragtime" as the code name of a top-secret intelligence program of the National Security Agency (as discussed in the book *Deep State: Inside the Government Secrecy Industry*) (John Wiley & Sons),[1] jazz cats and their loyal fans have a very different understanding of the word and its relationship to American history.

Ragtime, a distinctive segment of American jazz music, burst into public awareness in 1899 with the sheet music publishing of "Maple Leaf Rag" by Scott Joplin. The song sold hundreds of thousands of copies, unprecedented at the time, and catapulted Joplin into national prominence, earning him the title "The King of Ragtime."

This style of music, characterized by syncopation, is named for its complex, "ragged" rhythms that accent the second and fourth beats (offbeats) of a measure instead of the first and third. It first emerged in 1896 as dance music in the New Orleans' brothels, honky-tonks, and Creole community, with further connections to voodoo, prostitutes, gambling houses, riverboats, and drunks. It was an early piano solo format, and people loved to dance the cakewalk to it. It was happy, infectious dance music, fully challenging the Victorian mores of the day.

New York City piano man Ernest Hogan is widely credited as its innovator and key pioneer and also with coining the term "ragtime." In 1896, he introduced New York to ragtime with "All Coons Look Alike to Me," a million-dollar sheet-music seller with lyrics like:

All coons look alike to me,
I've got another beau, you see,
And he's just as good to me
As yon nig ever tried to be.
He spends his money free;
I know we can't agree;
So, I don't like you nohow,
All coons look alike to me.

Strangely enough, Hogan was a black man, and he later regretted the racist nature of this song. Yet, to him, the song was a bad/good thing because it helped open up new opportunities for black musicians. Also strange is the fact that "All Coons Look Alike to Me" was not a true ragtime tune, despite its role in popularizing this new genre of music.

In addition to Hogan, Scott Joplin was notorious for championing the ragtime style, writing and promoting many celebrated rag tunes, including "The Entertainer," later made famous in the Paul Newman/Robert Redford movie, *The Sting*.

If we wander back in time to the ancient Greek philosopher and mathematician Plato (ca. 428–348 B.C.), we find that the rhythms of music also carried tremendous significance. In *The Republic*, Plato wrote:

> Beauty of style and harmony and grace and good rhythm depend on simplicity—I mean the true simplicity of a rightly and nobly ordered mind and character, not that other simplicity which is only an euphemism for folly?
>
> . . . Musical innovation is full of danger to the State, for when modes of music change, the laws of the State always change with them. . . . Musical training is a more potent instrument than any other, because rhythm and harmony find their way into the inward places of the soul on which they may fasten.

It seems likely that Plato would have found ragtime, with its sophisticated rhythms, to be an "enemy of the state" and a "corrupter of orderly minds"! Perhaps he would have agreed with (some early) 20th-century Christians in calling jazz, "The Devil's Music." Truly, ragtime and jazz were contentious phenomena.

A September 13, 1899, editorial in the *Musical Courier* cited a scathing review of ragtime:

> A wave of vulgar, of filthy and suggestive music has inundated the land. Nothing but ragtime prevails . . . The pabulum of theatre and summer-hotel music is "coon music." No seaside resort this summer has been without its ragtime orchestra, its weekly cakewalk. Worse yet, the fashionable idle folk of Newport have been the chief offenders. Society has decreed that ragtime and cakewalk are the thing, and one reads with amazement and disgust of historical and aristocratic joining in this sex dance, for the cakewalk is nothing but an African danse du ventre (i.e. belly dance), a milder edition of African orgies, and the music is degenerative music. Ragtime rhythm's present usage and marriage to words of veiled lasciviousness should banish it from polite society . . . it is artistically and morally depressing, and should be suppressed by press and pulpit.[2]

Wow! So ragtime was vulgar, filthy, degenerative music, a sex dance derived from African orgies. Little did this pious man know that such words were bound to increase its popularity. Bring on the ragtime many said!

In 1901, the American Federation of Musicians (the musicians union) condemned ragtime and issued a ruling that its members were not allowed to play ragtime. The resolution pledged that members should "make every effort to suppress and discourage the playing and publishing of such musical trash."[3] The president of the union even said:

> That does not mean . . . that we are to play nothing but Beethoven's symphonies to park Sunday crowds, but it does mean that we will substitute music of some real merit for ragtime trash, and show the people the difference. We don't have to play classics to play good music. We intend to play popular airs instead of a senseless jumble of words and notes. The musicians know what is good, and if the people don't, we will have to teach them. . . . The ragtime craze has lowered the standard of American music as compared with other countries. We have duty as well as business to look after, and we will not give way to a popular demand that is degrading.[4]

Yet, all these efforts were futile; ragtime was taking America by storm. In 1903, Axel Christensen opened the first ever school of ragtime in New Orleans, promising, "ragtime taught in ten lessons." By 1908, his business expanded to four schools in Chicago with widespread sales of ragtime lessons in sheet music form. His system became so popular that Christensen later opened locations in hubs like San Francisco and Cincinnati, and other locations as well. He also wrote many ragtime songs, and by 1910, he was dubbed "The Czar of Ragtime." By 1918, the Christensen School of Popular Music was operating in twenty-five locations around the United States.

As ragtime surged, many sectors of society continued to protest. In 1913, *The New York Times* warned of the imminent danger of ragtime music, due to the "primitive and low moral nature" of ragtime, its practitioners, and its fans. Others tried to calm these fears. W. C. Handy, "The Father of the Blues," insisted, "ragtime, essentially, is nothing more than a pepped-up secular version of the Negro spirituals."[5] And Dr. Isaac Goldberg, musical historian and George Gershwin biographer, aptly stated, "The spirituals translate the Bible; ragtime translates the other six days of the week."[6]

With the passage of time, ragtime was eventually viewed as an integral part of the jazz legacy. As composer, conductor, author and musician, Gunther Schuller explained,

> The development of the minstrel show provided the Negro with an outlet in the area of popular entertainment, absorbing in the process various popular musical forms from Europe—jigs, marches, polkas, quadrilles, etc.—and finally spawning a pianistic descendant: ragtime. All these forms contributed vitally to the development of jazz in its full-fledged form in the first decades of this century.[7]

Gilbert Seldes wrote in his book, *The 7 Lively Arts* (1924):

> What makes the first rag period important was its intense gaiety, it naïveté, its tireless curiosity about itself, it unconscious destruction of the old ballad form and the patter song. The music drove ahead; the half-understood juggling with tempo which was to become the characteristic of our music led to fresh accents, a dislocation of the beat, and to a greater freedom in the text. For half a century syncopation had existed in America, anticipating the moment when the national spirit should find in it its perfect expression; for that half century serious musicians had neglected it; they were to study it a decade later when ragtime had revealed it to them.[8]

However, ragtime's place in the evolution of jazz remained hotly contested. Many members of the musical intelligentsia argued that ragtime was just syncopation and nothing new or unique. They compared it to the syncopation of Bach, Mozart, Mendelssohn, Handel, Schubert, Haydn, and even Beethoven.

In the March 1900 issue of *The Musician*, an article titled "Ragtime" argued:

> The song from Carmen, "Love is a Wild Bird," is one of the best examples of ragtime in modern music. In the overture to Don Juan, by Mozart, and in some compositions of Bach we have good examples of syncopation.. . . . Ragtime is simply having its day. It will be forgotten as a craze in a few years.[9]

In 1927, Jewish-American composer Aaron Copland declared that "Ragtime is much inferior to jazz, and musically uninteresting; it consists of old formulas familiar in the classics which were rediscovered one day and overworked."

In his book, *American Popular Song: The Great Innovators, 1900–1950*, American composer, Alec Wilder opined:

Post-slavery Negro music into the white community occurred in whore houses, which provided an early home for ragtime, and jazz. . . . The origins of ragtime cannot be dated. It assumed the form of complex piano composition by the 1890s. A classic cause-and-effect can be found in the rise of ragtime (the same cause-and-effect evolution that was probably present in country fiddling): a new dance evolved and it required new music. The cakewalk, a walking, strutting dance, could not be performed to European instrumental music (gallops, polkas, waltzes). It required something new; ragtime filled the bill. Probably both evolved together.[10]

Stunningly, some of the music elite waxed fondly about "the good old days of slavery" and "True Negro Music," as journalist Jeannette Robinson Murphy stated in her July 23, 1903, *Independent* article titled, "The True Negro Music and Its Decline."

They should be taught that slavery, with its occasional abuses, was simply a valuable training in their evolution from savagery and not look upon their bondage and their slave music with shame. For during that period these songs could develop because the Negro was kept in such perfect segregation, and its instincts and talents had full ply. He received then those things which he needed most—viz., work for his hands and God's revealed word for his heart and mind.[11]

Ragtime composer and piano legend Eubie Blake (1887–1983) said:

People ask me where did ragtime come from and I say I didn't know, I heard it all my life . . . when my mother would go out and wash white folks' clothes, I'd play music lessons the way I liked and when she came home and heard me, she'd say, "You take that ragtime out of my house, don't you be playing no ragtime."[12]

Despite its many detractors, ragtime gradually found its way into the hearts of many Americans and jazz aficionados and earned a respectable place in the ever-evolving field of American music. Among the most notable ragtime composers and the songs ragtime was best known for were:

Eubie Blake: "Charleston Rag" (1917)

Zez Confrey: "Kitten on the Keys" (1921) (performed at the Aeolian Hall concert where Gershwin premièred *Rhapsody in Blue*)

Scott Joplin: "Maple Leaf Rag" (1899) and "The Entertainer" (1902)

Jelly Roll Morton: "Frog-I-More Rag" (1918)

Luckey Roberts: "Junk Man Rag" (1913)

Igor Stravinsky: "Piano-Rag-Music" (1919)—yes, Stravinsky. This is not a typo!

Clearly, many high-profile and widely revered musicians aligned themselves with this then widely disparaged style of music. But then again, that fit with the trend then; so much of the jazz we celebrate today indeed did emerge from the shadowy corners of society.

Trumpeter, Blow Your Horn*

*Of Thee I Sing (1931)

Who was the greatest trumpet player in jazz? Louis Armstrong—there's no question there! Louis played from his heart and soul. . . .
—NEW ORLEANS TRUMPETER, MUTT CAREY[1]

Just after midnight on January 1, 1913, the world of jazz hit a pivotal moment. Deep in the heart of New Orleans, a twelve-year-old boy was arrested for firing his stepfather's 38-caliber revolver into the air to celebrate the New Year. The judge sentenced the boy to serve time at the New Orleans Colored Waifs Home—a decision that would change that boy's life and the course of jazz forevermore.

The name of this young juvenile delinquent was Louis Armstrong. In time, he would become known as Satchmo, Pops, Satchel Mouth, Dippermouth, Boat Nose, Hammock Face, and Rhythm Jaws—and also as a legendary singer, entertainer, actor, and jazz's most incomparable trumpeter.

As legend tells it, Armstrong was born in New Orleans on the 4th of July in 1900. His father abandoned the family early on, so Louis, his mother, and sister shared a one-room apartment with an outhouse in the backyard. His mother worked as a domestic servant for white folks; she later became a prostitute, leaving the young boy and his sister with their former-slave grandmother.

Around 1907, the then seven-year-old Louis began working for the Karnofskys, a Jewish family in New Orleans. The Karnofskys had two sons, Alex and his older brother, Morris. The family ran a couple of horse-drawn wagons, collecting and selling junk, and selling coal by the bucketful.

Riding on the junk wagon with Alex, Louis would blow a little tinhorn at the top of his lungs for all to hear. This little noisemaker would always draw a crowd, which was good for business—more customers would come outside to buy or sell their own stuff.

Day after day on the wagon route with Alex, Louis often admired a beat-up old cornet in a pawnshop window. One day, Alex stopped at the shop, went inside, and put down a $2 deposit on the horn. The price of the cornet was $5, and Louis paid 50 cents a week out of his salary until he could call it his own. This sale might have been the single most important act ever to affect jazz history!

In the first chapter of a book of his writings titled, "Louis Armstrong + the Jewish Family in New Orleans, La., the Year of 1907," Armstrong related in a very open and honest manner how his life was elevated and transformed by the Russian-Jewish Karnofsky family. They gave him meaningful employment and mentored him in matters of family, work ethics, and many other aspects of life—lessons that supported Armstrong throughout his life.

Night after night, eating Russian Jewish food for supper after a hard day of work, Louis grew to love Jewish food and culture. Louis also always joined in when the family sang a Russian lullaby to put the family's baby to sleep. The kindness of this poor, but entrepreneurial, Jewish family transformed Satchmo, and he became an unwavering supporter of Jews for the rest of his life.

Louis noticed that the Jewish family experienced prejudice, and although it wasn't as bad as what the blacks endured, Louis recognized their shared discrimination.

Late at night, after the wagon had completed its junk route, Louis and Alex Karnofsky delivered coal to the white whorehouses of Storyville for five cents a water-bucket full to help the ladies keep their one-room "cribs" warm and toasty for their customers.

In honor of the Karnofsky family, and his love and appreciation of the Jewish people, Armstrong wore a Jewish star around his neck at all times. He said of the Jews:

> I had a long admiration for the Jewish people. Especially with their long time of courage, taking so much abuse for so long. I was only seven years old but I could easily see the ungodly treatment that the white folks were handing the poor Jewish family whom I worked for.[2]
>
> ... If it wasn't for the nice Jewish people, we would have starved many a time. I will love the Jewish people, all of my life.[3]
>
> They were always warm and kind to me, which was very noticeable to me—just a kid who could use a little word of kindness, something that a kid could use at seven, and just starting out in the world ... I liked their Jewish food very much. Every time we would come in late on the little wagon from buying old rags and bones, when they would be having "supper," they would fix a plate of food for me, saying, "You've worked, might as well eat here with us. It is too late, and by the time you get home, it will be way too late for your supper." I was glad because I fell in love with their food from those days until now. I still eat their foods (matzos). My wife Lucille keeps them in her bread box so I can nibble on them any time that I want to eat late at night.[4]
>
> ... It was the Jewish family who instilled in me singing from the heart. They encouraged me to carry on. ... I shall always love them. I learned a lot from them as to how to live—real life and determination. God bless them. Whatever they accomplished they certainly deserve it.[5]
>
> Helping on the coal and junk wagons every day with those fine Jewish boys was a great schooling for me. If I would say a word such as dat—they the whole family would say "no Louis, that, and not dat."[6]

Armstrong also made a distinctive statement on racial issues. Of his own people, he wrote:

> The Negroes always hated the Jewish people who never harmed anybody, but they stuck together. And by doing that, they had to have success. Negroes never did stick together and they never will. They hold too much malice—Jealousy deep down in their heart for the few Negroes who tries. But the odds were (are) against them. ...

> I think that I have always done great things about uplifting my race (the Negroes, of course) but wasn't appreciated.[7]

These are explosive words, and many will find them hard to hear. But they are the thoughts of arguably the greatest jazz figure of all time. They also go to show that Louis Armstrong was a fervent He-Bro!

Joe Glaser, a Jew with mob connections and the owner of the Sunset Cabaret in Chicago, was Armstrong's decades-long manager and friend. The two men were very devoted to each other. In fact, Louis dedicated his book to him and called Joe his best friend.

However, when, in 1913, young Louis found himself in the Crescent City's Colored Waifs' Home for Boys (the orphanage), serving a one-year sentence for firing a gun into the air on New Year's Eve, he had reached a turning point. It was there that one of the staff, Peter Davis, noticed Louis's gifts and bought him a trumpet. Mr. Davis went on to teach Louis music and eventually became the leader of the Colored Waifs' Home for Boys Band.

Upon his release, fourteen-year-old Louis had gained a certain degree of musical training and experience as a band member and as a bandleader. At the time, most musicians in New Orleans did not have any formal training, so his year in the orphanage put Louis way ahead of the game. He formed a band that played in Storyville for several years.

After bouncing around Storyville for nearly three years, Louis hooked up with Joe "King" Oliver, the trumpet master in Kid Ory's Jazz Band. The elder horn man took an interest in the kid and tucked him under his wing, teaching him the various tricks of the trade. This relationship reaped huge rewards for young Louis because King Oliver relocated to Chicago, but recommended that Kid Ory hire Armstrong to replace him in the band. Ory did. Now seventeen-year-old Armstrong was sitting in the first trumpet chair of Kid Ory's Band—and folks were starting to notice his virtuoso talents.

When Louis was twenty-two, his musical mentor, "King" Oliver, who was living in Chicago, called Armstrong to come join his band in Chicago. Musically and physically, Louis was ready to spread his wings, so in 1922, he left New Orleans to play second trumpet behind the great "King" Oliver in Chicago.

In taking on the gig, Armstrong became part of what became known as "The Great Migration." Blacks were leaving the South and relocating to northern cities like Chicago in search of jobs and freedom from the oppressive Jim Crow laws. Chicago was bursting at the seams with economic activity, and it soon translated into jobs in the stockyards, steel mills, the railroad, and other industries.

After Armstrong arrived in Chicago, he soon built a reputation for himself in the Windy City, and word of his extraordinary talents spread throughout the country.

As Louis matured into manhood, so did his musical chops. He grew stronger and better—much better! If the truth be told, he was developing into a force to be reckoned with.

Louis Armstrong was a great innovator of the jazz form. As well-known jazz critic Martin Williams said:

> Louis Armstrong's genius as an intuitive improviser affected the work of every jazz musician. Certainly as a soloist, Armstrong inevitably had his limitations. But more important, he had his legitimate followers who worked out some of the implications of his style for themselves without doing imitations.

That Louis Armstrong was a powerful and compelling player should go without saying. He also had a more sophisticated sense of harmony and melody than any who had gone before him, and he gave the music a new stylistic language. Further, he had a rhythmic sense that was not only surer than what had gone before him but different, and, as Andre Hodeir pointed out in *Jazz: Its Evolution and Essence* (Grove Press), his rhythmic message was the essence of his contribution to jazz.

It is no coincidence that the word swing came into use among musicians while the music was under Armstrong's tutelage, for it is their word to describe his idea of jazz rhythm. He could play a phrase that had been around long before his time, but he would inflect it, accent it, pronounce it in such a way that it had a very different impetus and momentum, and this basic rhythmic impetus opened up the music to twenty years of development in melody and harmony as well.

In short, his influence was profound, and from 1923 to 1943 most jazz, big band or small, is significantly "Louis Armstrong Style."[8]

And then there was Gunther Schuller's take on Satchmo:

When, on June 28, 1928, Louis Armstrong unleashed the spectacular cascading phrases of the introduction to *West End Blues*, he established the general stylistic direction of jazz for several decades to come.... This was music for music's sake, not for the first time in jazz, to be sure, but never before in such a brilliant and unequivocal form. The beauties of the music were those of any great, compelling musical experience: expressive fervor, intense artistic commitment, and an intuitive sense for structural logic, combined with superior instrumental skill. By whatever definition of art—be it abstract, sophisticated, virtuosic, emotionally expressive, structurally perfect—Armstrong's music qualified.[9]

As Schuller noted, although Armstrong had already been playing and recording for years, with the highest quality and ability, his particular recording of *West End Blues* elevated both him and jazz to a new dimension. Schuller suggested that Armstrong's playing started at a very high level and was now evolving rapidly from there. (Indeed, Satchmo was playing at a very high level in more ways than one. He was known to have a fondness for "muggles"—and not the Harry Potter type. In the 1930s, "muggles" was slang for marijuana, and Pops was a big fan! Go figure!)

Show Me the Town*

*Rosalie (1928)

Chicago became the next hotspot for jazz, inheriting many of its musicians from New Orleans. Hundreds of Storyville musicians traveled up the Mississippi, and most of them ended up in Chicago. Lots of gigs and good pay was a huge magnet for the cats, and jazz was all the rage.

World War I, "The War to End All Wars," concluded at the end of 1918, producing a sense of jubilation and a "live for today" mentality. This view carried well into the 1920s, widely known now as the Roaring Twenties, and Chicago became the new capital of both corruption and vice. With both, the Jazz Age was born. Great jazz musicians, both black and white, were now playing this new music in the Windy City.

A 1916 issue of *Variety* declared, "Chicago has added another innovation to its list of discoveries in the so-called 'jazz bands.'"[1] So, apparently the word "jazz" was not only associated with New Orleans, but now also with Chicago. That's not surprising, since many New Orleans ragtime musicians had migrated north. In fact, some even considered jazz to be just a renaming of ragtime.

When Armstrong arrived in Chicago in 1922 the 18th Amendment was already two years old. When one speaks of Prohibition, a specific vernacular comes to mind: Chicago, mobs, racketeers, speakeasies, bootleggers, loose women, gambling, booze, and crime. One might say that 1922 Chicago was Storyville North. Although the best and brightest players were definitely there, none could compare with the brilliant Louis Armstrong.

Yet, the times they were a-changin'. By 1929, the Windy City had relinquished its title as Jazz Capital to the shiny new Big Apple. Armstrong had traveled east to New York City, where his star as a trumpeter, singer, performer, radio, and movie star rose even higher.

Over the following decade, Armstrong crisscrossed the United States, performing for a wide range of audiences. He even went across the Pond to perform for royalty throughout Europe. What a radical time it was becoming then.

I'd Rather Charleston*

*Lady, Be Good! (1926)

*It was an age of miracles, an age of art,
an age of excess, an age of satire. . . .*
—F. SCOTT FITZGERALD[1]

As America recovered from the ravages of World War I, the nation was in a state of upheaval. It was the era of Prohibition, women winning the right to vote, and deep racial tensions. Politically and socially, the concept of freedom was being thoroughly tested and contested, and it seemed everyone had a stake in redefining our national identity.

At the time, Americans were feeling a new sense of power, independence, and *carpe diem* (live for today). America emerged as the new global superpower, a land of unbridled innovation, rich with technology, culture, and new ideas. We were riding a heady wave of radio broadcasts, musical records, flappers, x-rays, automobiles, and airplanes. Groundbreaking products and ideas were suddenly within reach of the masses, and visionaries like Freud, Einstein, and Picasso were ushering America into the Modern Age.

It was an era when the men were dapper and the women wore flappers. The decade could perhaps be best characterized by the lyrics of the hit song "Ain't We Got Fun," which was featured in the movie *The Great Gatsby*.

F. Scott Fitzgerald dubbed the 1920s era "The Jazz Age," and as much as the music made its mark, the dances also helped define the times. "The Charleston," "The Varsity Drag," and "The Black Bottom" were all the rage. And of course "The Cakewalk," a leftover from the days of minstrelsy, was there too and mimicked and mocked the highfalutin' white man.

New York City became the new epicenter of American culture, but when it came to music, New York had multiple personalities. There was the Midtown Tin Pan Alley scene, the Uptown Sugar Hill Harlem scene, and the densely packed tenements in the San Juan Hill neighborhood around Columbus Circle where Lincoln Center sits today.

Uptown Harlem gave birth to the Harlem Renaissance, and its black-elite Talented Tenth became a new voice in American culture. The Apollo emerged and also The Cotton Club and small cabarets like Small's Paradise and Minton's Playhouse. From Sugar Hill to the seedier stretch of 5th Avenue, known as "The Jungle," the city was oozing music.[2]

The Roaring Twenties also featured parlor socials, then known as rent parties, which gave black musicians countless opportunities to conduct jam sessions and their fabled cutting sessions. From house to house and club to club, the city swelled with a newfound appreciation of jazz. As jazz slowly began to take over New York, one thing was clear—a new day and a new sound had arrived in the Big Apple.

New York Rhapsody*

*Delicious (1931)

Let's backtrack a couple of decades to the turn of the century to examine the seeds of change that led to the Roaring Twenties and the Modern Age. The year 1898 was a transformational year for the United States, New York City, and American music.

The United States flexed its military muscle that year to quickly defeat Spain in the Spanish-American War. That victory was, in essence, America's first real show of military strength to the world, and it gave the United States a higher standing in the global hierarchy of nations. National pride further increased with Teddy Roosevelt's Rough Riders. The war ended with the signing of the Treaty of Paris of 1898. Spain was humiliated, surrendering control of Cuba to the United States and ceding Puerto Rico, the Philippines, and other areas to the United States. This event was both an ending and a beginning—the end of Spain as a colonial power and the beginning of the United States as a global power. Hawaii was also annexed that year, and Pierre and Marie Curie discovered radium.

That same year, New York City was in a transformational stage as well. On January 1, 1898, the five boroughs (Brooklyn, Queens, Staten Island, Manhattan, and the Bronx) were consolidated into what is now New York City. It was a fast-growing city with a huge port, financial district, and a large population.

It was in this transformational year that George Gershwin was born in the East New York section of Brooklyn (as I was, but fifty years later). George spent most of his youth in Manhattan's Lower East Side and Harlem, where many European Jews had settled, and as he grew up, so did the city around him. Over the next two decades, New York added the infrastructure that let it evolve into a world-class metropolitan area. Massive construction projects like the subway system, roads and bridges, made it easier to commute from one borough to another, and the advent of the skyscraper increased population density, especially in Manhattan.

New York was truly a melting pot with a tremendous diversity of people. They had come from many countries bringing many different religions and traditions. There was also a huge influx of Southern blacks into the city. They were fleeing the humiliation of the Jim Crow laws and searching for jobs and a bit of dignity.

Jazz first appeared in the Big Apple on the evening of January 16, 1917. The bandleader and trumpeter Nick LaRocca and The Original Dixieland Jass Band appeared at Reisenweber's, a restaurant in Columbus Circle. Ironically, it was an all-white band, and they were playing songs like "Livery Stable Blues" and "Tiger Rag."

At first, this new music confused the audience that night, and they all remained in their seats.

No one got up to dance . . . until the manager politely explained, " 'Ladies and gentlemen, this is *jazz*. It is meant for dancing!' There was some good-humored laughter, and the ice was broken. A few venturesome partners started dancing; others (sic) followed. The music went to town, and so did the dancers. Jazz had come to New York. For better or for worse, it had come to stay."[1]

Just a few weeks after this momentous remarkable night, Victor Records recorded LaRocca's Original Dixieland Jass Band's songs—"Livery Stable Blues" and "Dixie Jass Band One-Step." They released the record quickly and it was an instant hit. Not only was it the first jazz recording, but it was also the first record to sell a million copies! (This success reflects a serious quirk of history. How is it that a white band holds the honor of producing the first-ever jazz recording?!)

Although jazz took New York by storm, Chicago was still the center of the jazz universe. But that was rapidly changing. New York bands, led by Fletcher Henderson and Duke Ellington, snapped up some of the most gifted and talented jazz musicians of the time, and the epicenter of jazz gradually shifted from the Windy City to the Big Apple.

New York was the perfect spot for jazz to mature. Thanks to the Volstead Act, Prohibition was still in full force. The era of speakeasies, bootlegging racketeers, and (ironically) alcoholism flourished. Jazz fit right in.

The city became a magnet for America's musicians. New York City had over 5,000 speakeasies, which produced plenty of jazz gigs for black and white musicians. Broadway musicals and nightclubs also provided plenty of musical gigs. Tin Pan Alley, capitol of the sheet music and song publishing industries, came into its own, and the new recording industry was growing and sinking its roots deep into the heart of New York City.

The hotbed of jazz was uptown in Harlem where The Cotton Club, Shim Sham, Club Ebony, Connie's Inn, The Savoy Ballroom, Green Cat, The Jungle, and The Nest were serving up round after round of hot, savory jazz. Rent parties, nightclubs, and other nightspots drew flocks of white folks uptown, eager to party, dance, drink, and have fun. Black performers played to white audiences, and the white folks couldn't get enough of them. It was a vibrant, colorful, fun-loving time.

W. E. B. Du Bois popularized the phrase "The Talented Tenth," which declared that one in ten blacks could get a formal education. With this education, "The Talented Tenth" would become leaders of the black community and thereby the new agents of change. They were the writers and intellectuals who could begin preaching the gospel of the new, self-reliant black. They wanted to shatter all vestiges of the weak/dependent slave mentality that relied on the white master to solve problems. "The Talented Tenth" spawned the Harlem Renaissance, also known as the New Negro Movement, with their black music, poetry, art, and literature. In 1925, Langston Hughes published his first book of poems, *The Weary Blues*. In the same year, an anthology of essays from Harlem authors was published as *The New Negro: An Interpretation*, emphasizing a cultural shift from the pre-World War I "Old Negro" sense of subservience to a newfound sense of personal and cultural self-reliance and pride.

However, not everyone was celebrating the black community's new emerging spirit of self-reliance and freedom. In some parts of town and also the country at large, these changes further stoked the fires of resentment, prejudice, and hatred.

Harlem River Chanty*

Tip-Toes (Unused) (1925)

Many folks of a certain age are familiar with Jesse Jackson's famous early 1980s line about "Hymietown," which was referring to New York Jews in a derogatory way. To Jews, Hymie is the "H word" (comparable to the "N word" for blacks), despite the fact it is a common Jewish name (I had an uncle named Hymie). Jackson's words reflected the fact that from the early 1900s onward, certain quarters of the black community harbored a negative sentiment toward Jews and the Jewish community.

In the early 1900s, the black nationalist Marcus Garvey defamed the Jews after he lost a mail fraud case presided over by a Jewish judge, a Jewish prosecutor, and several Jewish jurors. He loudly and bitterly blamed them for his legal defeat and incarceration.

Perhaps the most vocal and flagrant example of the anti-Semitic black sentiment was a cat up in Harlem called the "Black Hitler of Harlem." Eugene Brown, born in Massachusetts in 1903, was a firebrand labor leader who spouted tremendous hatred toward the Jews. Brown changed his name to Sufi Abdul Hamid after converting to Islam. In the 1930s, using a stepladder as his pulpit, he perched in front of businesses owned by Jews in Harlem and repeatedly preached hatred and intimidation of Jewish business owners, as well as any black folks who supported them. He shouted for a boycott of all Jewish-owned businesses, insisting that Jews spread filth and disease. He even encouraged his followers to tear out the tongues of Jews. His rhetoric earned him the name "Black Hitler of Harlem."

On the other hand, W. E. B. Du Bois renounced anti-Semitism as "poison," referring to Jews as "our best friends." These comments reflected a significant evolution in his personal perspective, as earlier in his career, he had made many negative comments about Jews and indeed accused them of becoming the new slave barons.

Lest we forget, Jews were very involved in the creation of the NAACP (the National Association for the Advancement of Colored People). In fact, Jews provided major financial support as well as organizational and leadership expertise in the early years. In 1909, one of the founders, Henry Moskowitz, was a Jew. Decades later, the Jews also served as vigorous supporters of blacks during the Civil Rights Movement of the 1960s, Rabbi Abraham Joshua Heschel marched shoulder to shoulder with Dr. Martin Luther King in Selma.

Changing My Tune*

*The Shocking Miss Pilgrim (1947)

> *Tin Pan Alley, in a word, is a unique phenomenon, and there is nothing in any other country of the world to compare with it. New York, being the musical and theatrical center of the nation, where most songs and stage acts are made, naturally gave rise to the Alley of the Tin Pans.*
>
> —GEORGE GERSHWIN[1]

Starting in the 1890s, Union Square in New York City was the center of music publishing, theater, and entertainment businesses. Music publishers started churning out songs in a factory mode.

Later in the early 20th century, the publishers moved north to 28th Street, between 5th and 6th Avenues, when Irving Berlin worked there. The Alley was just a few blocks north of the Flatiron Building, at the intersection of 5th Avenue, Broadway, and East 22nd Street. As America ascended, so did its buildings. The sky was the limit.

The Flatiron Building was built in 1902. It was one of the first of many skyscrapers to come. The building declared the new confidence of America, and especially New York City, as America was emerging as a new world power with its quick and definitive military victory against the old world colonizer, Spain.

Tin Pan Alley became America's song factory. The publishing houses hired song pluggers to go near and far to promote the newest songs to the public. The music publishing companies moved north to the West 40s, but the Tin Pan Alley name still followed them uptown.

Where did the strange name Tin Pan Alley come from?

It started around 1885, down on 28th Street between Broadway and Sixth Avenue. One could hear many pianos playing all at once, streaming from the various cubicles of different publishing houses. Back then, sheet music was their major moneymaker.

It was said that Monroe H. Rosenfeld, a writer for the *Herald*, said the sound of all those tinny pianos playing at one time made him think of a bunch of folks beating on tin pans. The image stuck, and the name of the industry became Tin Pan Alley.

Tin Pan Alley was the epicenter of the sheet music industry, a music factory grinding out formulaic tunes. Creativity was frowned upon. Let's say that in Tin Pan Alley popular music was manufactured, not created. Most of the tunesmiths could not read or write a lick of music, so they had to dictate their tunes to someone who could write the notes.

It is said too that the young Irving Berlin's "Alexander's Ragtime Band" breached this old-school, formulaic, factory-music assembly-line and created a new paradigm in the Alley—it opened up to new ideas, and both inspiration and creativity rushed into Tin Pan Alley.

In the early part of the 20th century, the majority of middle-class homes had a piano. It gave rise to the sheet music industry to satisfy the public's desire for fresh, new music they could play. In 1910, sheet music sales totaled over $2 billion! Adjusting for inflation, that would equal about $50 billion today![2] The Alley published millions of sheet music scores, and the dollars came flowing in.

Tin Pan Alley gave rise to fad dances as well. Think of songs like "Mashed Potato Time," "The Stroll," and of course "The Twist" (made famous by Chubby Checker but written by my old pal, Hank Ballard, leader of The Midnighters—a man and a band I had the honor of touring with in the early 1980s as lead saxophonist). However, back in the early Tin Pan Alley days, there was the "Texas Tommy," "The Bunny Hug," "The Turkey Trot," and the still popular "Fox-trot." (Apparently they liked animal dances!) Back then, they had the "Shim Sham Shimmy," and we later had the "Boogaloo." They had the "Grizzly Bear" and we then had the "Monkey." We sure have come a long way, baby!

Music publishing was (is!) a huge industry, with many fortunes to be made and also lost. In retrospect, it looks like those tin pans were truly cast in solid gold. The industry provided work for accountants, lawyers, song composers, lyricists, arrangers, song pluggers, office staff, cleaning crews, printers, orchestrators, and many others.

They also paid the rent to landlords and paid many checks at restaurants and bars. Are you starting to see how huge the economic impact of this industry actually was, and still is?

In 1917, a Supreme Court decision exploded Tin Pan Alley's profitability and power. That story begins in 1915 when the famous composer Victor Herbert, the founding member of the American Society of Composers, Authors and Publishers (ASCAP), walked into Shanley's Restaurant in Times Square and heard his music being played for the diners there. Herbert felt he should be compensated for this "free" performance of his intellectual property (and rightly so!). His music had been created for paid performances in concert halls, and he felt that if the restaurant wanted the live house band to play his songs, it owed him royalties.

Herbert and his publisher filed a lawsuit that took two years to wind its way to the Supreme Court. In 1917, Chief Justice Oliver Wendell Holmes sided with Herbert, saying that if the music did not pay for itself, then the restaurant owner would not feature it. Holmes wrote, "It is true that the music is not the sole object, but neither is the food." This landmark decision opened the floodgates; waves of revenue started flowing to the licensing agencies like ASCAP and its artists. This was a boon for the entire industry, effectively monetizing their creations and securing their financial position for the future.

> *(Tin Pan Alley) isn't a place . . .*
> *(it's) a state of mind.*
>
> —GEORGE GERSHWIN ON A 1934
> RADIO BROADCAST[3]

Of course, in such racially charged times, certain vocal people took tremendous issue with this change of fortune—and they simply deemed it a Jewish conspiracy.

Automaker Henry Ford despised the Jews. In *The Dearborn Independent*, a newspaper he owned, Ford wrote a series of Jew-bashing articles, which he later combined into a 1920s book titled *The International Jew: The World's Foremost Problem*. Ford said the Jews had a grand conspiracy to control the world's financial markets and banks, the U.S. press and radio stations, and world politics. He argued that Jews were the fomenters of World War I, eager to make huge profits selling munitions and war supplies to both sides. Essentially, Ford believed that Jews controlled most of America and the world. He even accused the Jews of fixing the World Series.

Ford also wrote that Jews controlled the entertainment industry. In one article, titled "Jewish Jazz—Moron Music—Becomes Our National Music—the Story of Popular Song Control in the United States," published on August 6, 1921, in Ford's very own newspaper, *The Dearborn Independent*, Ford wrote about Tin Pan Alley and the Jews as follows:

> The song-pluggers of theatre, vaudeville and radio, are paid agents of the Yiddish song agencies. Money, and not merit, dominates the spread of the moron music which is styled Jewish jazz and swing. Non-Jewish music is stigmatized as "highbrow." The people are fed from day to day on the moron suggestiveness that flows in a slimy flood out of "Tin-Pan Alley," the head factory of filth in New York which is populated by the "Abies," the "Izzies," and the "Moes," who make up the composing staffs of the various institutions. "Tin-Pan Alley" is the name given to the region. . . . where the first Yiddish song manufacturers began business. . . . Needless to say, scandal became rampant, as it always does when so-called "Gentile" girls are reduced to the necessity of seeking favors from the Jew. . . . All of America is now one great Tin-Pan Alley, its entertainment, its youth, its politics, a blare of moronic Judaism. . . . There is something Satanic about it, something calculated with demonic shrewdness. And the stream flows on and on, growing worse and worse, to the degradation of the non-Jewish public and the increase of Jewish fortunes. . . . Common sense dictates a cleaning out, and a clearing out, of the sources of the disease. The source is in the Yiddish group of song manufacturers who control the whole output and who are responsible for the whole matter from poetry to profits.[4]

Oy, vey! What a *putz*.

Ford's tirade accused Tin Pan Alley of being controlled by the "Abies, Izzies and Moes." He did miss one name, however, that rung out from all the rest on the Alley. It was a Russian-Jewish kid named Irving—Irving Berlin! (Actually, Izzy was a nickname for Irving Berlin.)

I Love to Rhyme*

*The Goldwyn Follies (1938)

I want to say at once that I frankly believe that Irving Berlin is the greatest songwriter that has ever lived . . .
—GEORGE GERSHWIN[1]

Irving Berlin was born Israel Baline in Siberia on May 11, 1888. His only memory of Russia was the sight of his house burning down during one of the anti-Semitic pogroms. "Pogrom" is the Russian word for the vicious, brutal, barbaric murders, rapes, and destruction of property inflicted on Jews by the Russians. These savage acts were repeatedly committed on Jews and Jewish communities over hundreds of years. Like many other Russian Jews of the late 19th century, Berlin's family immigrated to New York's Lower East Side. They arrived in 1892 and lived in abject poverty. His father died shortly thereafter, but he left his son one enormous inheritance—a paternal lineage of cantors. Through this rich musical heritage, Izzy was gifted with a nuanced voice and a brilliant sense of music.

In 1904, Berlin landed his first job as a singing waiter in a club owned by the Jewish businessman and mobster Mike Saulter. Located in Chinatown, at 12 Pell Street, it was just south of Canal Street, near the entrance to the Manhattan Bridge. (Unfortunately, the name of this fashionable Chinese joint was "Nigger Mike's.") This is where Berlin wrote the lyrics to his first hit, "Marie from Sunny Italy," which earned the young man a whopping 37 cents. More important, it landed his name on sheet music for the first time. Unbeknownst to him, this modest start was the beginning of many much bigger things to come.

Ragtime exploded in 1911 when this twenty-three-year-old Tin Pan Alley American-Russian-Jewish composer (Berlin) swept the nation with his hit song, "Alexander's Ragtime Band." The tune sold over a million copies of sheet music! Although it wasn't true New Orleans ragtime, its captivating freshness and syncopation took the country by storm and held it in its grip for years to come. In the March 1925 issue of *Vanity Fair* magazine, over a decade after the song's release, the noted American writer and photographer Carl Van Vechten wrote: "*Alexander's Ragtime Band* was real American music . . . while it completely routed the so-called art music of the professors."[2]

In just two short years, Berlin had escalated from complete oblivion to national fame and without any formal musical training! In the process, he revolutionized Tin Pan Alley and its prolific song factory system and reshaped the entire music distribution industry.

Because Irving Berlin could neither read nor write music, he searched for someone to write down the musical notation of his songs. As fate would have it, he interviewed a very young fellow named George Gershwin for that job.

Berlin and Gershwin had a lot in common. They were both descendants of Russian Jews and had spent parts of their childhoods on Manhattan's Lower East Side. Both dropped out of school to pursue careers in music. At first glance, they seemed a great fit. But after hearing Gershwin play piano like a master, Berlin famously told him, "What the hell do you want to work for anybody else for? Work for yourself!"[3]

Yet, Berlin continued the job interview and told George:

The job is yours, if you want it. But I hope you don't take it. You are too talented to be an arranger and secretary. If you worked for me you might start writing the way I do, and your own style might become cramped. You are meant for big things.[4]

You're more than a skilled arranger that I am looking for. You're a natural-born creator.[5]

An incredible degree of mutual respect was instantly established between these two virtuosos, and it endured for all the years to come. Gershwin always spoke of Irving Berlin and his songs with the highest regard. As revealed by musician, songwriter, and Gershwin lover Kay Swift, in a biography on Gershwin:

She once told Gershwin she felt his songs had far greater musical variety and interest than Irving Berlin's. Gershwin immediately went to the piano and for over an hour played Berlin to prove to Kay Swift how much versatility and greatness there was to Berlin's writing. "He's a master," Gershwin kept on saying, "and let's make no mistake about that."

"And he proved his point," she commented. "Many of the songs he played I knew, but I didn't realize that they were Berlin's."[6]

Speaking of Berlin, Gershwin wrote:

Irving Berlin was the first to free the American song from the nauseating sentimentality which had previously characterized it, and by introducing and perfecting ragtime he had actually given us the first germ of an American musical idiom.[7]

Gershwin also said:

Irving Berlin is the greatest American songwriter that has ever lived. He has that vitality—both rhythmic and melodic—which never seems to lose any of its exuberant freshness; he has that, rich, colorful melodic flow which is ever the wonder of those of us who, too, compose songs; his ideas are endless. His songs are exquisite cameos of perfection and each one of them is as beautiful as its neighbor. Irving Berlin remains, I think, America's Schubert.[8]

In 1917, Berlin wrote a tune that never took off, so he threw it in the junk bin where it was forgotten over time. Then in 1938, he revived the tune for Kate Smith, who made it her theme song. This song was "God Bless America." It became an overwhelming hit. Some considered it our second national anthem, and yet, he never accepted one thin dime for this great American song. He donated all the royalties, valued at over $100,000, to the Boy and Girl Scouts of America. What a patriot!

There's a funny thing about two of Berlin's most beloved and popular tunes: "Easter Parade" ("In Your Easter Bonnet") and "White Christmas"—both of which became Christian American classics—they were composed by a Jew named Irving Berlin! Only in America . . .

Harlem Serenade*

*Show Girl (1929)

Stride piano, a sophisticated urban style of piano playing, first emerged in Harlem, just after World War I. The earliest stride player, James P. Johnson, wrote the music for the "Charleston" (it launched that Roaring Twenties dance craze), and it was featured in the 1923 black musical comedy *Runnin' Wild*. Other great practitioners (or ticklers after the old phrase "ticklin' the piano keys" as they were called) included Eubie Blake, Fats Waller, Luckey Roberts, Willie "The Lion" Smith, and Art Tatum.

Stride piano is often viewed as a bridge between ragtime and jazz, and it was widely accepted as a modernized style of ragtime. Stride was part of an evolutionary process. Those who mastered it were great ragtime players as well, but stride players felt they were playing a more "city sophisticated" form of ragtime than their country brothers. It's not that they turned their backs on ragtime; rather, they just "jazzed it up" a bit. They took ragtime in stride, so to speak!

Stride piano players carried a strong left-hand bass line that at times could stride long distances across the keys, hence the name "stride." It was a more sophisticated bass line that added a feeling of intensity through both dramatic hand motion and speed. Stride players also relied on improvisation, as opposed to simply playing the ragtime songs of the day as written.

Let's take a moment to honor my favorite stride piano cat, a black Jew who went by the name of Willie "The Lion" Smith. "The Lion" was a brilliant stride piano innovator who also had a remarkable personal story.

William Henry Joseph Berthol Bonaparte Bertholoff was born in Goshen, New York, in 1897. The son of a black mother and a Jewish father (who died in 1901), Willie eventually shed his Jewish surname, Bertholoff, and took the last name of his stepfather, John Smith.

> I wanted to become a rabbi. I got as far as becoming a cantor. Because of my devotion to Judaism, I was called "The Lion of Judea," later abbreviated to "The Lion."[1]

A World War I hero, he proved his strength and fortitude long before he proved his musical abilities.

> I was one of the few volunteers to go to the front and fire a French seventy-five—and of those who did, few returned. I stayed at the front for 51 days without relief. I was known from that time on as Sergeant William H. Smith, "The Lion."[2]

"The Lion" was known for his straight talk, his signature derby hat, and the ever-present cigar that dangled from his mouth. A mentor to many jazz cats, including Duke Ellington (who honored "The Lion" with his musical composition "Portrait of the Lion"), he became good friends with George Gershwin and even attended the world premiere of *Rhapsody in Blue* at Aeolian Hall.

Gershwin was acquainted with many stride piano players. Living on the Upper West Side, his proximity to the Harlem club scene and the great music created there also helped form his own musical personality.

There's another interesting point regarding the connection between black musicians and Jews. Harry T. Burleigh (1866–1949), a little-known black American composer, arranger, and singer, was a long-time member of the choir in the huge Temple Emanu-El, where the funeral services for George Gershwin were held in 1937. In life and in death, Gershwin's ties to the community of black musicians remained constant and strong.

Boogie-woogie was another style of piano-based blues that emerged in the early 1920s. It burst into American pop culture when Pine Top Smith recorded "Pine Top's Boogie Woogie" in 1928.

Distinct from ragtime and stride piano, Boogie-woogie was defined by a rapid and rolling eight-beats-to-the-bar bass line. Relying heavily on the twelve-bar blues, repeated with infinite (often improvised) variations, this style highlighted the percussive, polyrhythmic nature of the piano as an instrument.

Its fast-paced, driving, left-hand bass line made the music very danceable, which helped lift this lively piano style into national prominence. From poor Southern barrelhouses to uptown Harlem rent parties, it eventually rose all the way to Carnegie Hall, where Albert Ammons and Meade "Lux" Lewis performed it (with Pete

Johnson) in 1938. That was quite an accomplishment for a couple of former taxicab drivers who both drove for the Silver Taxicab Company in Chicago!

The name Boogie-woogie reeks of racial overtones. Yet the term was, and still is, widely accepted by folks of all races. Although the style started with black piano players, it was eventually adopted by white musicians and celebrated by white audiences and featured in small ensembles and even big bands. The style also made its mark in the movies. I bet you can still hear that rollicking Boogie-woogie piano as the Andrews Sisters sing "The Boogie Woogie Bugle Boy from Company B" (in the 1941 Abbott and Costello film *Buck Privates*)?

Blue, Blue, Blue*

*Let 'Em Eat Cake (1933)

*The blues came from the man farthest down. The blues
came from nothingness, from want, from desire.
And when a man sang or played the blues, a small
part of the want was satisfied from the music.*
—W. C. HANDY, "THE FATHER OF THE BLUES"[1]

Why did the word "blues" come to signify a universal melancholy feeling? Why not purple or cyan? "I got the cyans?" Of course, nothing really fits the depth of such an emotion as perfectly as "the blues." But where did this terminology get its start?

Most of us take for granted the idea that black slaves attached the word "blues" to this feeling of melancholy, but in truth, it preceded them.

The term "blue devils" first shows up in Great Britain print around 1600 in a poem and is described as, "the horrors, or remorse, that usually follows an ill course of life."[2]

In the 1700s, the English continued using the expression "the blue devils" to indicate a melancholy or dark spirit. "He has a case of the blue devils," they would say, indicating that someone was depressed or sad. In time, the word "devil" fell off and just "the blues" remained. This phrase migrated with the English to America and once here rooted itself in our vocabulary. (An interesting fact is the term "blue funk" being shortened to "funk" has a similar evolutionary history dating back to the same time period in English history. "Blue Funk" and "Funk" indicated a state of fear or panic.)[3]

In 1807, American author Washington Irving (author of *The Legend of Sleepy Hollow* and *Rip Van Winkle*), included "the blues" in his writings, marking the first time this phrase was used in American literature. In Irving's satirical periodical, which he published called *Salmagundi*, he wrote:

> I saw he was still under the influence of a whole legion of the blues, and just on the point of sinking into one of his whimsical and unreasonable fits of melancholy abstraction, I proposed a walk.

Earlier in *Salmagundi,* Irving wrote:

> He is worried to death with inquiries, which answer no other end but to demonstrate the good will of the inquirer, and put him in a

passion; for everybody knows how provoking it is to be cut short in a fit of the blues, by an impertinent question about "what is the matter?" when a man can't tell himself.[4]

We cannot know when slaves started using this term, but we do know their music reflected a strong sense of "the blues." And for good reason!

In a July 1901 article in the *American Musician* titled "Suppression of Ragtime," the author used the word "blues" in relation to the connection between music and melancholy.

> To most people music is not a serious matter. It is amusement and relaxation. It drives away the blues, and makes happy thrills run all over our system. It is refining and has a natural tendency to elevate mankind.[5]

What exactly are "the blues" musically speaking? So much can be said on that topic . . . the answer could fill books! But here are a few succinct comments "about" the blues.

The blues chord progression is the most widely used structure in American music, and possibly all around the whole world. From France to Germany to Japan, it is common to hear the blues. They can be heard in theater, rock 'n' roll, country and western, gospel, and even classical music. Even looking through the lens of jazz, it should be noted that Duke Ellington scholar Maestro Maurice Peress once estimated that half of all the music that the Duke wrote was based on the blues.[6]

The flattened third, fifth, and seventh notes of the musical scale are called "blue notes," because they deliver that unique, melancholy sound.

Let's consider the very familiar solfège scale—Do, Re, Mi, Fa, So, La, Ti, and then back to the beginning Do in the next octave range. The third note of the scale is Mi, the fifth is So, and the seventh is Ti. The "blue" notes are a flattened Mi, So, and Ti. (Flattening these notes means you lower their pitch by half a tone. A flattened third note is the pitch that rests halfway between Mi and its lower neighbor, Re. The flattened seventh is halfway between Ti and its lower neighbor, La.) These notes have a unique and distinctive sound, which we call the "blue" sound. Although the notes impart a melancholy feeling, they can also express great happiness and exhilaration. The amazing diverse feelings imparted by the blues are what make notes and thus the music so very unique and universal.

In addition to the blue notes, we also have the "twelve-bar blues." Not to get overly technical, this is simply a twelve-measure chord progression. To musicians, it is the I-IV-V chord progression, where the (I) chord is tonic, the (IV) chord is sub-dominant, and the (V) chord is dominant.

However, to dissect the blues down to some technical chord progressions or only a few "blue notes" would be doing it a great disservice. There are many other factors that make up the blues and give the music its unique sound and feel.

The blues is a very personal form of expression and thus an art. For example, when Ray Charles sang "America the Beautiful," he masterfully transformed a traditional non-blues song into one of the bluest tunes you will ever hear. By incorporating a deep sense of emotion with his vast knowledge, experience, and ability to express the blues, Charles created a true blues classic.

Brother Ray tended to *blue up* every song he sang. Take a listen to his rendition of Hoagy Carmichael's song "Georgia on My Mind," and you will surely agree that Charles was the King of the Blues.

It's important to note that neither of these songs features the typical twelve-bar blues chord progression (I-IV-V) or blue notes. And yet, they are undeniably "bluesy"! How can that be?

The "blues" are not just derived from certain techniques or notes or patterns. It is mostly a vehicle for expressing feeling, and in order to do so, it employs a wide variety of techniques. We've already covered the twelve-bar blues; blue notes; flattened thirds, fifths, and sevenths; and the I-IV-V chord progression. But there is so much more! Think wailing, honking, screaming, moaning . . . licks, riffs, extensions, elaborations . . . spirituals, Jive, Rhythm & Blues . . . harmonic progressions, bending notes, chord patterns, blues scales . . . Walkin' Blues, head arrangements, alterations . . . and so many other features of the blues! It's truly an art, not a science.

Let's take a closer look at some of the more technical aspects of this iconic musical style as viewed through the lens of history.

When slaves brought their music here from Africa, it was different from European music in some very significant ways, especially in the scales. The European musical scale is comprised of twelve notes: C, C#, D, Eb, E, F, F#, G, G#, A, Bb, B, and then it ends on the C in the next register. The African (microtonal) music scale includes notes between the twelve European ones—something like C## or Ebb. So, African music features smaller intervals between notes. Instead of just a C#, the African system includes notes between C# and D, or a pitch between D and Eb, which might look something like Ebb. It is just a smidgen flat of Eb, somewhere between Eb and D or better yet, halfway between Eb and D# . . . like an Ebb.

Because there are so many more notes on the African music scale, it provides players with a broader range of sound with which to express their feelings.

Over the years, the African microtonal scale was superimposed on and then combined with the European musical scale, producing something that was neither African nor European. This new creation became the seed of a unique American sound—THE BLUES!

Many musicologists have opined that the use of blue notes is an attempt to adapt the African microtonal scale to the European diatonic scale. As poet/author/critic Hayden Carruth stated:

> But, this meant a loss of purity; the African pitch would have been neither flattened nor natural, but, something in between. Purity was lost, and before long it was forgotten—at least on the level of conscious musicality—and in its place came a bending, slurring, and wavering of pitch that is the primary melodic quality of the blues. And this, I believe, is what accounts, musically, for the expressiveness of the blues.[7]

The combining of the African microtonal scale with the European scale started with the first slaves when they were brought to America. They were encouraged by their owners and overseers to sing, both to release tension and to pace their fieldwork. As mentioned earlier, some of these work songs were the "call and response" type, where one slave would sing out a phrase, and the rest of the field crew would sing out a response. The slaves would place private hidden jokes in the songs to secretly poke fun and mock their bosses and masters. Although it was frowned upon to teach a slave to read, some house slaves were encouraged to learn to read music and play instruments for entertainment purposes. It increased a slave's value if he or she could play music. But to be clear, the overwhelming number of slaves did not play a musical instrument.[8]

So, in the plantation fields and parlors, the European and African scales began to merge, and thus, the "blue" notes first rang out in America in the culture that was slavery.

The blues provided an outlet for the sorrows, fears, and conflicts of black folks, expressing love and hate, joy and anger, hopeless and resentment toward their harsh and inhumane treatment in the "land of the free and home of the brave," where "all men are created equal and endowed by their creator with certain inalienable rights" or were supposed to be. The blues was a most suitable soundtrack for this very troubling and conflicted time.

When emancipation from slavery presented the need for blacks to provide for themselves, the blues served the black community in an entirely new way—as a source of income. Street performers started singing and dancing for tips, improvising both blues tunes and musical instruments. Their songs reflected the events and feelings of the time—just as the blues continue to do today. (Think about "Sequestration Blues" or even "Bluetooth Blues," entertaining and current songs that illustrate the ever-changing and vibrant nature of this enduring musical style.)

Many ethnomusicologists believe that the human voice was the first musical instrument. It was followed by objects one could pound on (the human body and drums), then devices one could pluck (stringed instruments), and then appliances one could blow (wind instruments, horns).

My friend, jazz expert, teacher, and Bebop saxophonist, Larry Sanborn described this playing the "instrument" of the human body—or, as it came to be known, the "hambone"—with the "pat." As the performer slapped various parts of his body—the knees, hips, butt, thighs, cheeks, and other areas—each part produced a unique sound. "Hambone" performers added grunts, growls, clucks, and lyrics, creating a dynamic, malleable and very affordable(!) instrument. The "hambone" is still played in prisons and rural areas today.

Sanborn reminds us that Bobby McFerrin made it to the top of the charts in 1988 and even earned a Grammy with his hit song, "Don't Worry, Be Happy"—a song that McFerrin wrote, sang, and used his body for the musical accompaniment.[9]

Due to the lack and affordability of "real" instruments, makeshift instruments became popular in black and rural areas. These included washboards, pieces of wood, combs, earthen jugs, and the tub bass, to name a few. Sanborn called these instruments "musical devices" and shared stories of playing with "tubmen" in some Chicago gigs when the union restricted regular bass players. Sanborn said the pay was so far below union scale that he had to find a "tubman" instead. These "tubmen" proved to be very accomplished, and the audiences loved the novelty. Just think of a Bebop cat playing the washtub . . . now that's jazz! Although these performers never studied "wash tub bass" at the Juilliard School of Music, they certainly held their own in a band and also had a washtub to use to clean their clothes when times got really bad.

Clarinetist and bandleader Johnny Dodds' Washboard Band made several recordings featuring Jimmy Bertrand on the washboard, including "Blue Washboard Stomp." Many musicians felt the washboard was an "illegitimate" instrument, but upon hearing Bertrand play some of these rare tunes, people did appreciate the musical talent that shone through. Check out The Washboard Rhythm Kings of 1933 or Spike Jones for that matter. It's impressive!

Before 1900, blues tunes were not as formalized as they are today. At the beginning of the 20th century, the blues were played by whorehouse piano players, laborers, field workers, and solo street-corner guitar players. With the advent of the record industry in the 1920s, black blues musicians started to become popular nationally, recording on "race records." In the early 1900s, W. C. Handy formalized the blues idiom as we know it today by writing the blues on paper.

The blues spread quickly, from its epicenter in New Orleans up the Mississippi via riverboats, and then throughout the Gulf Coast along the railroad lines. As the blues became harder and harder to ignore, white bands started imitating the black blues bands. Still, that doesn't mean it was widely accepted.

Like ragtime, the blues was originally considered by many to be a corrupting influence. A 1916 music journal article read:

> For the last several years the most popular type of Negro song has been that peculiar, barbaric sort of melody called "blues," with its irregular rhythm, its lagging briskness, its mournful liveliness of tone. It has a jerky tempo, as of a cripple dancing because of some irresistible impulse.[10]

Clearly, some circles of society judged it quite harshly. And yet, during the 1920s, the blues moved from the fringes of American society to its center. It became a national craze and a permanent fixture in the American musical lexicon.

Many unconventional sounds are also incorporated in the blues, such wails, glisses, yelps, slap tongue, the laugh, flutter tongue, growls, moans, honks, screams, bends, trills, grunts, slides, fall offs, and slurs, to name a few. Blues tenor sax players, like me, employ many of these sounds and techniques. How I love honking and screaming on my sax!

In the words of the avant-garde tenor sax man Ornette Coleman, as quoted from the liner notes of the 1979 album *Honkers and Screamers* (Arista Records):

> The tenor is a rhythm instrument, and the best statements Negroes have made, of what their soul is, have been on the tenor saxophone. Now you think about it, and you'll see I'm right. The tenor's got that thing, that honk, you can get into people with it. Sometimes you can be playing that tenor and I'm telling you, the people want to jump across the rail.[11]

The blues is an integral part of all jazz; it's the common denominator. You can also hear the blues in ragtime, bebop, swing, and post-bop. Because of its simple and universal nature, most jazz performers will play the blues at one point or another. For example, jazz legend Charlie "Bird" Parker, the co-founding creator of Bebop jazz, was also a master blues man, and recording the blues served as the fitting bookends to his career. His first recording session was as the soloist on *Hootie's Blues* and *Dexter Blues* with the Jay McShann Orchestra in 1941, and in his last recording session, he played his own blues tune, "Now's the Time."[12] Some cats found a way to insert the blues into any song they played. Think of Ray Charles singing "Georgia," or Charlie Parker playing "White Christmas"—just two examples of how a musical master could turn any song into a blues tune by using blue notes and other blues techniques. Even though these songs were not harmonically, melodically, structurally, or rhythmically considered blues tunes, these highly versatile performers transformed them into blues songs with their brilliance.

In Abbe Niles's 1949 foreword to the title *Blues: An Anthology*, he wrote about the first blues songs ever published:

> (There had been 19th-Century tunes with such titles as *The Richmond Blues*, but these were actually marches, named for the local military organizations, and "blue" was merely the color of a uniform—cf., in New York, the *"Knickerbocker Greys."*) The first so-called "blues" was *Baby Seals Blues*, which appeared in St. Louis, on August 3, 1912; *Dallas* was published in Oklahoma City, on September 6,

1912. The third was *Handy's Memphis Blues*, in Memphis, on September 28, 1912, but this had already been played for three years before its publication.[13]

An interesting side note to Handy's "Memphis Blues" story is that Handy was fooled into selling the rights to "Memphis Blues" to an unscrupulous white guy, who then made a small fortune selling the sheet music. The owners of the rights even refused to give Handy permission to include "Memphis Blues" in his 1926 book, *Blues: An Anthology!* But Handy did get some satisfaction years later; the rights were returned to him after the first copyright term ran out.

Musician, composer, and radio host Ben Bernie, who in 1925 wrote the famous jazz standard "Sweet Georgia Brown" (the theme song of the Harlem Globetrotters), said:

The blues . . . seem to me the complaint of a fellow who's in trouble just now, but who all the time has a feeling way down inside of him that it's all going to come out right in the end.[14]

I agree with "The Old Maestro" (Ben Bernie's nickname) that although the blues at times felt bitter and hopeless, they also reflected a ray of sunshine. Instead of bitter, we could choose to hear them as deeply bittersweet. Tomorrow is a new day and better times are just around the corner.

The blues can express an enormous range of human experience—sorrow, lost love, poverty, happiness, joy, dreams, yearnings, sex (or lack thereof), success, failure, wit, depression, poetry, suffering, melancholy, and many, many more aspects of what is called humanity. Although blue notes quite easily reflect a sense of melancholy, the blues can also express great happiness and exhilaration. That's quite a range! An amazing one!

The blues was born and then reared in the American black community, but over time, it has evolved to become an integral part of the full jazz art form—and an integral part of those who play it. As blues great, singer Alberta Hunter said:

The blues? Why the blues are a part of me. To me, the blues are—well, almost religious. They're like a chant. The blues are like spirituals, almost sacred. When we sing the blues, we're singin' out our hearts, we're singin' out our feelings. Maybe we're hurt and just can't answer back, then we sing or maybe even hum the blues. Yes, to us, the blues are sacred.[15]

And further, the blues are uniquely American. As Isaac Goldberg's biography of George Gershwin explained:

Perhaps our native theorists have over-philosophized the blue note of the Negro, for the most popular scale of the Khassid has a blue note that is quite as cerulean or indigo, as the black man's blues may be. The Negro blue note, of course, has its peculiarities of origin and of use . . . although George does not minimize the contribution of the Negro to the psychology, the rhythms and the words of our popular song, he maintains that jazz is essentially an American product.[16]

Midnight Blues*

The Rainbow (1923)

So the blues helped fill the longing in the hearts of all kinds of people. They took it to their hearts and felt the same thing we felt. Now when you hear a white person sing the blues, he can put as much into it as a Negro. The blues and jazz have become a part of all American music and will be developed farther and farther on into infinity.

—W. C. HANDY[1]

W. C. Handy (1873–1958), well known as the "Father of the Blues," was born in Florence, Alabama, the son and grandson of Methodist ministers who considered music to be the devil's pastime. Handy's father once said he would rather follow his son's hearse than see him become a professional musician.[2]

If only he knew what was to come. . . .

Gershwin biographer Isaac Goldberg asked and answered the question *Where the "Blues" Came From*, writing:

> William Christopher Handy, "the father of the blues," is not the inventor of the genre; he is its Moses, not its Jehovah. It was he who, first of musicians, codified the new spirit in African music and sent it forth upon its conquest of the North. The "rag" had sung and danced the joyous aspects of Negro life; the "blues," new only in their emergence, sang the sorrows of secular existence.[3]

In 1896, at the age of twenty-three, Handy became the leader of Mahara's Colored Minstrels in Chicago; he played lead cornet. Later, he authored the "Memphis Blues" and "St. Louis Blues," which served to formalize the blues for the American public with the three-line, four-bar stanza. Each song was composed of four bars, repeated three times, epitomizing the then very popular twelve-bar blues.

Craft a tune following the I-IV-V chord progression and throw in a few "blue notes" (a flattened third, fifth, and seventh) and you end up with a real, down-home blues song. Add some sort of suffering to the lyrics, and you really make it blue.

Here is a quick and dirty template to blues lyrics:

STATE THE ISSUE OR CONFLICT IN THE
 FIRST FOUR BARS:
My baby left me . . . and moved uptown. . . .

THEN REPEAT THE ISSUE IN THE SECOND
 FOUR BARS:
I said, my baby left me . . . and moved uptown.

THEN RESOLVE THE ISSUE IN THE FINAL
 FOUR BARS:
She left a note sayin'—You're a lying lowdown clown!

Simple enough! Keep repeating this conflict/release pattern, and add in a few more personal issues to ramp up the drama. Finish up with a resolution, and you have yourself a full-blown, down and dirty, gutbucket blues tune.

Of course, blues can be much more complicated, but this form is its most basic—tension and conflict followed by release. This simple and repetitious pattern made it perfect for a gig.

Handy's first blues tune was a political one about the 1909 mayoral campaign of Edward "Boss" Crump. Appropriately titled, "Mr. Crump," the tune was very popular and helped "Boss" Crump win the election. The song was a classic twelve-bar blues tune that was chock full of blue notes from start to finish. In 1912, Handy changed the lyrics and renamed the tune, "Memphis Blues." Handy then struck a deal to have the song published, but in doing so, he made the rookie mistake of selling the rights to the song for only $50. It then went on to become a national hit. Handy had to sit on the sidelines with his head in his hands, suddenly realizing just how easily a creative artist could lose a fortune to industry predators.

He certainly wasn't alone. Many black artists throughout the twenties, thirties, forties, fifties, sixties, and even today have shared this same fate. It's so common it's practically a cliché: the artist struggles to get by while his work climbs to astronomical success, raining down riches on capitalizing businessmen. I heard many of these tragic stories in person, while touring with music-industry victims.

In retrospect, Handy later said:

> The melody of Mr. Crump was mine throughout. On the other hand, the twelve-bar, three-line form of the first and last strains, with its three-chord basic harmonic structure (tonic, subdominant, dominant seventh) was that already used by Negro roustabouts, honky-tonk piano players, wanderers, and others of their underprivileged but undaunted class from Missouri to the Gulf, and had become a common medium through which any such individual might express his personal feelings in a sort of musical soliloquy. My part in their history was to introduce this, the "blues" form to the general public, as the medium for my own feelings and my own musical ideas. And the transitional flat thirds and sevenths in my melody, by which I was attempting to suggest the typical slurs of the Negro voice, were what has since become known as "blue notes."[4]

Handy was under tremendous financial pressure to write another hit, so he sequestered himself in a room in St. Louis. He was hungry, drunk, broke, and on the verge of becoming a "one hit wonder." Deep in despair, he remembered an encounter he'd had with a woman who was even more depressed than him. He had heard her say, "Ma man's got a heart like a rock cast in de sea." Handy dredged up these blue words and put them into his new tune, and a masterpiece was born—"St. Louis Blues."

Yet, as his luck would have it, he couldn't sell the song. Every single publisher he approached passed on it. So in an act of great courage, Handy decided to publish it himself. This decision was unheard of at the time—especially for a black man! In partnership with Harry Pace, Handy formed his own publishing company, Pace & Handy, and in 1914, they released and promoted "St. Louis Blues." It became a national hit, unleashing a flood of cash, but also a ton of confidence for Handy personally. After all, a financially independent black man was nearly unheard of at that time! Pace & Handy later morphed into Handy Bros. with a new partner, Handy's brother, Charles.

"St. Louis Blues" has earned a rightful place in the fabric of American culture. Today, it is an integral part of our musical heritage. Jazz cats played it for years and years, and even today people still call out requests for this classic in clubs.

Handy also introduced the *habanera* rhythm to the popular culture of the time. Think of it as a syncopated tango rhythm. "The Charleston," one of the most popular hits of the Roaring Twenties, was loosely based on this particular rhythm.

In 1920, the blues singer Mamie Smith became the first black singer to make a blues recording: "Crazy Blues" (Okeh Records). Due to contractual issues, the record label had not been able to work with their first choice, Jewish "red hot momma" Sophie Tucker, so they gambled with a black blues singer, and in doing so, they crossed over into the jazz community. The record was a giant hit, selling over 100,000 copies, and made Ms. Smith a very wealthy woman. It should also be noted that Willie "The Lion" Smith was the featured pianist on this record.

In 1921, the stride piano legend James P. Johnson recorded the first jazz piano solo record. It was called "Carolina Shout," also on the Okeh label.

Blah Blah Blah*

*Delicious (1931)

Like ragtime and blues, jazz got off to a very controversial start. Many religious men and women spoke out against jazz music, loudly declaring it responsible for the moral decay of men, women, and children in America. (Pretty reminiscent of the things later said about rock 'n' roll, rap, and hip-hop. Right?) Even the word "jazz" (or "jass") was considered crass and profane because of its sexual connection, reflecting its early connection to the brothels of New Orleans.

To put this phase of American music in a better context, in 1918, we had just emerged from World War I, "The War to End All Wars," and the United States was celebrating its new position as a global power. Our nation was ecstatic, bursting at the seams with a powerful sense of nationalism and modernity. Then, late in 1919, the Volstead Act was passed and the 18th Amendment ratified—laws we now refer to as Prohibition. The Anti-Saloon League, a progressive movement representing many Protestant congregations, led the charge in caricaturizing jazz as a "corruptor of morals," just as bad as alcohol. Other churches, the government, and the media chimed in and all campaigned to wipe out jazz. It was now "the devil's music."

Leading the pack was Wilbur Glen Voliva, head (or should we say dictator?) of the Zion Community, based just outside of Chicago. A strict vegetarian, Mr. Voliva was a controversial man who adamantly declared that the Earth was flat and predicted he would live to the ripe old age of 120. (He died at seventy-two, missing his target by a mere forty-eight years.) He also predicted that the world would end in 1923. When this prediction did not come to pass, he pushed the date back to 1927 . . . then 1930 . . . then 1935 . . . and again to 1943. (Because he died in 1942, that was the last of his prognostications.) Anyway, in January 1921, the highly influential Voliva issued an edict to his religious community, banning all jazz records. Any jazz record found in the community would be "summarily confiscated and destroyed as unholy and disagreeably noisy."

Later, in August 1921, the *Ladies' Home Journal* featured an article written by Anne Shaw Faulkner, the National Music Chairman of the General Federation of Women's Clubs. In a piece titled, "Does Jazz Put the Sin in Syncopation?" she asked, "Can music ever be an influence for evil?" She then went on to declare that "Government studies show jazz and its evil influence is destroying the morality of young people. . . . Jazz is an influence of evil." She backed up this assertion with news that some high-class country clubs were providing "corset check rooms" where young women could remove their binding garments before heading to the dance floor to shimmy and shake. "Dancing to Mozart minuets, Strauss waltzes, and Sousa two-steps certainly never led to the 'corset check room,'" she wrote.[1] I guess Anne never heard of SPANX!

She further wrote that jazz had been banned in some industries because it distracted the workers and caused "inferior workmanship." Ms. Faulkner went on to say:

> Jazz originally was the accompaniment of the voodoo dancer, stimulating the half-crazed barbarian to the vilest deed. The weird chant, accompanied by the syncopated rhythm of the voodoo invokers, has also been employed by other barbaric people to stimulate brutality and sensuality. That it has a demoralizing effect upon the human brain has been demonstrated by many scientists.[2]

(No wonder I act like a demoralized barbarian! Did you hear that, Julie? No more jazz for me!)

In another remarkable quote, Faulkner wrote:

> A number of scientific men who have been working on experiments in music-therapy with the insane, declare that while regular rhythms and simple tones produce a quieting effect on the brain of even a violent patient, the effect of jazz on the normal brain produces an atrophied condition on the brain cells of conception, until very frequently those under the demoralizing influence of the persistent use of syncopation, combined with enharmonic partial tones, are actually incapable of distinguishing between good and evil, between right and wrong.[3]

She then predicted America would sink into degeneracy because of jazz.

Around the same time, *The New York Times* featured an article titled, "Both Jazz Music and Jazz Dancing Barred from All Louisville Episcopal Churches," explaining that the reason jazz was banned was to prevent "jazz manners and jazz morals."[4]

Louis Armstrong opined on the Jim Crow restrictions that separated black from white musicians back in the day, saying:

> Those people who make the restrictions, they don't know nothing about music, it's no crime for cats of any color to get together and blow. Race-conscious jazz musicians? Nobody could be who really knew their horns and loved music.[5]

In December 1921, the *Ladies' Home Journal* was at it again, publishing an article titled, "Unspeakable Jazz Must Go!" Written by John R. McMahon, it stated that the American National Association Masters of Dancers "director of reform," Fenton T. Bott, had declared that jazz was degrading to young people, lowered moral standards, and led to undesirable things. "The jazz is too often followed by the joyride. The lower nature is stirred up as a prelude to unchaperoned adventure."[6] (And what could be worse than an unchaperoned adventure?! Banning them?!)

The American National Association of Dance Masters also published a booklet, which they provided to the United States Public Health Services and Surgeon General. It draws a connection between jazz dancing and "social diseases." Because they felt that, "The road to hell is too often paved with jazz steps," the association issued a BOLO (**Be On the Look Out**), ordering its Masters of Dance in high schools and civic centers to be on the alert for "animal names for dances, such as cat step, camel walk, bunny hug, turkey trot, and so on."[7] These were certainly indicative of:

> . . . a degrading tendency. Rapid and jerky music is condemned . . . They call for more

police censors.... The police class in censorship is told not to permit cheek-to-cheek dancing, abdominal contact, shimmy, toddle or the Washington Johnny, in which the legs are kept spread apart.[8]

The article also indicated the Association was offended by a newspaper cartoon depicting a dance teacher as "... a wasp-waisted, effeminate young man. He has a tiny mustache and a violet-edged perfumed handkerchief."[9] They would likely arrest a gay man doing the Macarena at a bar mitzvah. Mazel Tov!

Just a few months later, on March 3, 1922, *The New York Times* published an article entitled "Primitive Savage Animalism, Preacher's Analysis of Jazz" by Reverend A. W. Beaven. It declared:

It has gotten beyond the dance and the music and is now an attitude toward life in general. We are afflicted with a moral and spiritual anemia for which the Church has the only transfusion that will cure.[10]

The New York Times jumped into the fray once again in April 1922 with an article headlined, "Musician Is Driven to Suicide by Jazz: Wouldn't Play It, Couldn't Get Employment."[11] It described a cello player who would not "insult his instrument" by playing jazz on it, which meant bandleaders would not hire him for a gig.

Are we having fun yet? G-d Save the Queen, but the Hell with Jazz! *The Chicago Tribune* even pulled the English royal family into the fray with an article titled, "Queen Mary Bars Jazz: She Dances a Fox Trot at Goodwood—The King Only a Spectator." It described how Queen Mary "requested the orchestra not to play jazz music" at an informal dance at the Goodwood racetrack.[12]

In an August 1922 sermon, Harvard-educated American Protestant-Episcopalian clergyman, Reverend Percy Stickney Grant, asked, and then answered his own question:

What is jazz, then? ... A music of animal noises which makes you want to chatter and twist your tail around a tree. It is going back to the tom-tom and beating upon a hollow log of savage times for music. It is a gesture of the devil—jazz goes back to the jungle.[13]

Anti-jazz proponents even tried to get the law involved. According to a December 10, 1922, article in *The New York Times* ("Shady Dance Steps Barred by Police"), Deputy Police Commissioner, Mrs. George W. Loft, called dancehall proprietors to a meeting at the West 37th Street police station, asking for their help in eliminating certain "impure" dance steps like the "Chicago" (a slow step that sounds like grinding in my day), "balconading" (described as "rough"), slow dancing, and "parking" (when a couple stops dancing and just "park" themselves, which also sounds like grinding to me) from public dancehalls.

She told the group that police departments were flooded with complaints from mothers who regarded these "impure" dancehall practices, and asked them to introduce "noticeable distance and a brisker motion into public dancing." Mrs. Loft also said that if the new moral dancing standards were not adopted "voluntarily," police would be dispatched to secure law and order in the offending establishments. Police Commissioner Enright suggested he might even revoke licenses or arrest those who did not control these dancers.[14]

Why was the public getting whipped up into such a frenzy over jazz? Beyond the perceived moral and cultural risks of this music, many believed it also posed a threat to mental health! In a February 1923 article, "Detrimental Effects of Jazz on Our Younger Generation," author A. E. Guilliams wrote:

I can say from my knowledge that about 50 percent of our young boys and girls from the age of 16 to 25 that land in the insane asylums these days are jazz crazy, dope fiends and public dance hall patrons. Jazz combinations, dope fiends and public dance halls are all the same, "one." Where you find one you will find the other. This "jazz" life is great while it lasts but it is short-lived with many, as I have seen from three to five young boys and girls land in our asylums one after another from the effect of too much jazz, dope, and public dance halls.[15]

In a May 31, 1923, edition of the *Musical Courier*, an article screamed the headline, "Representatives of 2,000,000 Women, Meeting in Atlanta, Vote to Annihilate Jazz." It declared that the General Federation of Women's Clubs, representing 40,000 clubs and 2 million members, had passed a resolution saying:

> Jazz is having a bad effect on our girls and boys and on society in general. It must go and concerted action by the women's clubs of America will wipe it out of existence. Let us furnish real music to our young folks—but no jazz.[16]

Of course, as one layer of American society rallied against jazz, another layer championed it, fully recognizing its cultural value, musical ingenuity, and American roots. As American composer and conductor John Philip Sousa (the "Stars and Stripes Forever" guy) explained:

> When jazz is buried, and the funeral is not far distant, it will be buried so deep that God himself can't find it then—and the flat-footed man and the unmusical souls will be the mourners at the grave.

Fortunately, the anti-jazz campaigns faded by the end of the decade. In a book titled *George Gershwin*, edited by Merle Armitage and published in 1938 as a tribute to the great artist, we can read the following:

> We have already forgotten the tumult and the shouting which existed in the early 1920s in regard to the decadence of the jazz age. Reactionaries of both continents found jazz a most satisfactory target for their invective. Case in point: In London, on October 8, 1927, Sir Henry Coward, one of England's leading musicians and a world authority on choral technique, said: '. . . a lowering of our moral standards and a consequent loss of the prestige to the white race in the world would be among the dire results of the vogue of jazz. We had not recognized that anything vital, anything convincing, anything important in American art must have its roots in our own soil and our own environment.'"[17]

For You, For Me, For Evermore*

*The Shocking Miss Pilgrim (1947)

THE RECORD INDUSTRY

In 1877, Thomas Edison invented the phonograph, otherwise known as the record player. While other inventions could record sound, his was the first that could play it back.

At the turn of the century, Emile Berliner advanced the technology from cylinders to two-sided flat discs, the record format we are familiar with today. Much easier and cheaper to mass-produce, records revolutionized the music industry. After patenting his invention in 1887, Berliner launched the Gramophone Company to mass-produce both records and players.

Its trademark image of the dog staring into a gramophone, titled "His Master's Voice," became one of the best-known trademarks in the world—but not until Berliner's company was nearly out of business. The rights to the image were passed on to Eldridge R. Johnson, whom Berliner had worked with to improve the playback machine. Johnson launched the Victor Talking Machines Company in 1901, and a few short years later, they started selling their most popular record player, the Victrola. Johnson continued to use that wildly popular image of the dog, printing it on his Victor record catalogs and the paper labels of the discs. Although the Gramophone brand of products faded into obscurity, its name is today immortalized by the Grammy Awards.

As the popularity of the phonograph record exploded, our language changed to reflect its growing commonality. The term "phonograph record" was shortened to "record" and the brand name "Victrola" came to signify any record player. Growing up in Brooklyn in the 1950s, we had a generic record player that we all referred to as the Victrola, just like today we ask for a Kleenex instead of a tissue or speak of "Xeroxing" when we copy something on a copy machine made by HP or Brother.

In 1948, the record industry took another technological leap forward when Columbia Records introduced the LP (long play) record. Turning at $33 1/3$ revolutions per minute, as opposed to its predecessor, which turned at 78 revolutions per minute, this new format extended recording time from four minutes per side to over twenty-two minutes. It was quickly adopted as the new standard in the record industry.

This new format breathed new life into the jazz world. With over twenty-two minutes of music available per side, it gave musicians plenty of room to express their talents fully with improvisation. Under the time constraints of a 78, they had only one minute to play the melody, two minutes to improvise, and one last minute to repeat the melody. It was very hard to "jazz up!" But on a 33$^1/_3$ LP, they could improvise for over twenty minutes and fully explore a tune, as they often did in live performances. Cats like John Coltrane took full advantage of this newfound freedom.

Not every jazz song on a 33$^1/_3$ was a long one, however. Artists sometimes recorded multiple songs on each side, thereby delivering much greater value to the consumer. Instead of just two songs, they might get ten or more songs on a single record. This ability also greatly benefited composers, artists, and publishers, who earned more royalties with each record sale. So from manufacturers to producers, to composers, publishers, and artists to consumers, the 33$^1/_3$ LP indeed revolutionized, monetized, and economized the record industry. It was a technological revolution that affected the artistic one.

Little Jazz Bird*

*Lady, Be Good! (1924)

If you ask 99 different musicians for a definition of jazz, you get 99 different answers.
—ANONYMOUS

Trying to define jazz is a fool's trap. Even the jazz greats have struggled with the question *What is jazz?* In 1926, "King of Jazz" Paul Whiteman finally admitted, "I have been dodging this question for years, because I haven't been able to figure out an adequate answer."[1]

Jazz trumpeter Louis Armstrong dodged it as well. When he was asked, "What is jazz?" Armstrong replied, "If you have to ask what it is, you'll never know it." Good answer, Pops.

Although the definition of jazz has always remained elusive and is also often contested, most would agree on two defining traits of the art form: improvisation and spontaneity. Of course, that begs the question, how can we have "real jazz" records, when spontaneous improvisation is frozen in time? In a sense, jazz records are a contradiction in terms. Although at the time the musicians were performing spontaneously, once that spontaneous performance is recorded and frozen on the record, replaying it is in fact not spontaneous. One can keep playing over and over again the greatest jazz solo by Bebop legend Charlie Parker, but it will be the exact same way each and every time for eternity. Playing a recorded solo of a spontaneous event by definition makes listening to that recording not spontaneous because the event is now being repeated. Does that leave us without any definition then? Not exactly. As jazz educator, Bebop musician and my friend/teacher/mentor, Larry Sanborn, so eloquently stated:

> Jazz improvisation embodies many artistic elements, including ingenuity, risk, astonishment, excitement, technical brilliance, and delayed response or anticipation, that are employed in various combinations by the performer to produce a well-crafted solo. Jazz performance is an art; and art, like love, is easier to experience than to define.[2]

Like love, the word "jazz" is both a verb and a noun. The noun, of course, refers to jazz as a form of music. As a verb, people often say *jazz it up*, meaning to speed it up and/or add a sense of spice, sexiness, excitement, and appeal to something, often to music, but of course, to any part of life. In fact, the word "jazz" has become so ubiquitous that it can be found in the names of a professional basketball team, certain styles of exercise and dance, a line of cosmetics, a Puerto Rican food company, a line of jewelry, a Honda car, and a Microsoft motherboard. In 2002, the Argonne National Laboratory funded a teraflop-class computing cluster named Jazz!—a 350-node computing cluster for high-end scientific research. Clearly, this word and its inferences and implications are all around us—not just in music. Jazz is everywhere!

As far as music is concerned, jazz embraces many styles. Avant-garde, bebop, Chicago style, cool jazz, Dixieland, East Coast, free jazz, fusion, mainstream, modal, new jazz, New Orleans, progressive, ragtime, swing, and West Coast all reside under the broad canopy of jazz.[3]

Yet, none really answers the original question: *What is jazz?*

Perhaps another way to approach this question is to absorb internally the comments of a number of jazz experts. Let's start with George Gershwin. He appreciated jazz as a uniquely American phenomenon.

> Jazz is the result of the energy stored in America. It is a very energetic kind of music, noisy, boisterous and even vulgar. One thing is certain. Jazz has contributed an enduring value to America in the sense that it has expressed ourselves.
>
> It is an original American achievement that will endure, not as jazz perhaps, but which will leave its mark on future music in one way or another.[4]

Gershwin always acknowledged the fact that the roots of jazz were firmly planted in the American black experience. He was widely quoted as saying:

> Jazz—certainly the most efficacious means, to date, for the recreation of American music—has its roots deeply embedded in the Negro spiritual.[5]

In his book, *Tin Pan Alley*, Gershwin biographer Dr. Isaac Goldberg wrote:

> Before the various types of jazz was the modern coon song; before the coon song was the minstrel show; before the minstrel show was the plantation melody and the spiritual. It is safe to say that without the Negro we should have no Tin Pan Alley; or, if this sounds like exaggeration, certainly Tin Pan Alley would have been a far less picturesque Melody Lane than it is today.[6]

Most agree that the roots of jazz do belong to the African-American community, and that the genre then radiated out through white America into the rest of the world. As Goldberg explained:

> [Jazz] traces its origins back to the African jungle; it becomes transformed in the hearts and on the lips of the American Negro; it travels North and is taken up by the white, by Gentile and Jew. At the hands of such Jews as Irving Berlin, George Gershwin, Jerome Kern and—in the symphonic realm—Gershwin, Gruenberg and Aaron Copland, it acquires international recognition. The African Negro has dwelt in other countries, without producing a characteristic music; only in America did jazz arise and could jazz have arisen. We must accept it, then, as a phenomenon peculiarly American.[7]

As George Gershwin was known to say:

> Jazz is not Negro, but American. It is the spontaneous expression of the nervous energy of modern American life.[8]

These remarks are widely accepted as accurate. However, many aspects of jazz's heritage have been hotly contested. Jazz pianist, composer and author, Leonard Feather, addressed these conflicts, writing that,

> There are many common misconceptions about jazz, most of them the result of special pleading on the part of experts in whom romanticism has displaced realism. The most widespread is the concept that New Orleans was the exclusive American nursery of jazz. A second is that jazz originally was African music. Another is the racial theory of jazz nurtured since the 1930s by critics in France.[9]

Feather went on to disprove these misconceptions. First, he quoted several jazz legends from the early days, revealing that an abundance of jazz was played in the North and numerous places other than just New Orleans. Regarding the second misconception, that jazz was originally African music, Feather stated:

> The second misconception—that jazz grew wholly out of "African music"—is based on what is at best a half-truth. The music we recognize today as jazz is a synthesis of six main sources; rhythms from West Africa; harmonic structure from European classical music; melodic and harmonic qualities from 19th Century American folk music; religious music; work songs, and minstrel show music, with of course, a substantial overlapping of many of these areas.[10]

Gershwin's comments also reflected the overlapping heritage of jazz. In 1926, he said:

> The "voice of America" is jazz cooked up in our "great melting pot" . . . And what is the voice of the American soul? It is jazz developed out of ragtime, jazz that is plantation song improved and transformed into finer, bigger harmonies. . . . I do not assert that the American soul is negroid. But it is a combination that includes the wail, the whine, and the exultant note of the old "mammy" songs of the South. It is black and white. It is all colors and all souls unified in the great melting pot of the world. Its dominant note is vibrant syncopation. . . . the voice of America, the expression of its soul, is jazz. . . . Jazz is young. It is no more than ten years old. Ragtime is dead.[11]

Defining the music further, Gershwin said:

> [Jazz] is really a conglomeration of many things. It has a little bit of ragtime, the blues, classicism and spirituals. Basically, it is a matter of rhythm. After rhythm in . . . importance come internals, music intervals which are peculiar to the rhythm.[12]

Gershwin saw jazz as a type of American folk music that would eventually transform into long-lasting works.

> Jazz, ragtime, Negro spirituals and blues, Southern mountain songs, country fiddling, and cowboy songs can all be employed in the creation of American art music. . . . I regard jazz as an American folk music . . . a very powerful one which is probably in the blood and feeling of the American people more than any other style of folk music. I believe that it can be made the basis of serious symphonic works of lasting value.[13]

History proved him right. Gershwin's symphonic jazz works are still performed by orchestras around the world many decades after his demise.

In addition to Gershwin, Goldberg, and Feather, other musicians and experts have offered valuable insight on the infinitely challenging question: *What is jazz?* From truly informative to condescending to humorous, their comments lend a unique perspective to the discussion and help us get a grip on this very slippery topic.

Whitney Balliett, jazz critic for *The New Yorker,* called jazz "the sound of surprise."[14] American critic and composer Virgil Thomson took it one step further, declaring that "Jazz is the most astounding spontaneous musical event to take place anywhere since the Reformation."[15]

In his 1926 book, *So This Is Jazz,* Henry O. Osgood referred that "Jazz, a state of mind!"[16] Developing his definition further, Osgood wrote:

> Let us prepare a stately definition which may be used without credit or acknowledgment by any future dictionary or encyclopedia that so desires:
> Jazz; (*orig.* Africa) v. to enliven; pop. To pep up; adj. jazzy, applied to manners, morals, and especially music; n. jazz, pepped-up music—or pepped-up most anything else.[17]

Of course, his definition clashed totally with the 1925 etymological *Dictionary of Modern English,* which defined jazz as:

> A number of Niggers surrounded by noise— a kind of ragtime dance introduced from the United States . . . a word taken from Negro jargon.

Phonograph inventor Thomas Edison considered jazz to be noise. In fact, he said he usually played jazz records backward because they sounded better that way.

In 1921, English art critic Clive Bell shared his disdain, noting in a racist rant that jazz was:

> . . . headed by a band and troupe of niggers, dancing. . . . We shall beat our swords into plowshares and our jazz bands into unconsciousness.

Echoing this rhetoric, former Princeton professor Henry van Dyke said at the 1925 meeting of the National Education Association (NEA) that jazz was, "a species of music invented by demons for the torture of imbeciles." Indeed, he might have enjoyed the company of Don Alfonso Zelaya, son of a former Nicaraguan president and student of "musical vibrations," who proclaimed in 1926, "Jazz will turn America's future generations into a 'bunch of jumping jackals' unless it is curbed soon."

The "King of Jazz" Paul Whiteman said that people unfairly blamed "the devil's music" for all sorts of unrelated problems, from drunkenness and insanity to sin and crime. He framed these unfair allegations by telling a little story:

> "I don't believe in vaccination," said the farmer, "my neighbor's little boy was vaccinated in school and within a week he was dead. None of my children will ever be vaccinated—not if I know it."
> "Did the little boy die of the vaccination or of the smallpox?" somebody asked.
> "Neither. He fell out of a tree and broke his neck."[18]

In a clear nod to its association with the shadowy depths of American culture, author Orson Welles said, "Let's face it. Jazz has made some dangerous friends."[19]

Many people did see jazz in that same light, including some of its best-known personalities. One notable example was Duke Ellington, who said:

> Jazz always has been like the kind of man you wouldn't want your daughter to associate with. The word "jazz" has been part of the

problem. The word never lost its association with those New Orleans bordellos.[20]

His comments reflect on the fact that jazz was first spelled "jass" (as in The Original Dixieland Jass Band)—a throwback to Storyville, where jasmine was the prostitutes' perfume of choice. Jasmine was shortened to "jass," and then the term took on a life of its own. Later, "jass" evolved into "jazz," and it became the recognized term for the music that the bordello bands were playing.

The 1925 anthology *The New Negro* also addressed the origins of the word, although it took a different tack:

> [Jazz] . . . seems to have come into being this way, however; W.C. Handy, a Negro, having digested the airs of the itinerant musicians referred to, evolved the first classic, *Memphis Blues*. Then came Jasbo Brown, a reckless musician of a Negro cabaret in Chicago, who played this and other blues, blowing his own extravagant moods and risqué interpretations into them, while hilarious with gin. To give further meanings to his veiled allusions he would make the trombone "talk" by putting a derby hat and later a tin can at its mouth. The delighted patrons would shout, "More, Jasbo. More, Jas, more." And so the name originated.[21]

But Jazz was an encapsulation of the spirit of America:

> Some say jazz is this, and some say jazz is that . . . But I say fiddle-de-dee for all these learned definitions. Jazz is American, and that's that. Now let's hear you define America. Difficult, isn't it? . . . nervous energy, joy, humor, youth, lack of repression, freedom of expression. It is because the spirit of jazz so admirably paints this musical picture of America that the coming of George Gershwin at this time was so propitious.[22]

Gershwin served as a crucial bridge between the rigid and refined culture of classical music and the hot, uninhibited spirit of jazz. With his classical training and his soul-level affinity for jazz, his work connected people that were otherwise worlds apart.

Let's take a closer look at some of the other fundamental differences between the buttoned-up classical musicians and the freewheeling jazz artists:

> "Classical" musicians strive to produce purity of tone. In contrast, jazz uses a broader range of timbre, and there are conscious attempts to produce a dirty tone, raucous and husky qualities on all instruments, as well as with the voice. Musicians in the classical field are usually trained to develop perfect accuracy of pitch, although violinists, and trumpeters and other wind musicians consciously play sharp to achieve greater brilliance, just as the highest 10th of the piano range is tuned sharper than the true pitch. Jazz musicians, however, at times consciously play and sing slightly flat, and with a wavering tone, smears, and glissandi to produce hot intonation.[23]

Some musical purists have asserted that these unconventional techniques placed jazz beyond the realm of music. American journalists toyed with this idea and challenged jazz musicians to counter it. Of course, the musicians had no time for such games. They were busy playing it. "When I was first asked, 'Is jazz music?'" avant-garde composer, pianist George Antheil said, "I was tempted to reply, 'What is music?'"[24] When Tin Pan Alley legend Irving Berlin faced the same question, he replied inquisitively, "What is jazz?"

Poet and professor, Hayden Carruth, resolved this conflict by saying:

Some people can hear jazz, and others, by far the greater number, cannot.[25]

The past 60 years of jazz have produced an eruption of both individual and correlative genius that is truly astounding, and because of the nature of jazz this has placed the emphasis in creative intuition precisely where it should be, on the fusion of "tradition and the individual talent," on the concurrence of discipline and freedom, and on the mutuality of creative transcendence.[26]

"Creative transcendence"—what a concise way to describe the art of improvisation, which is so very central to jazz and understanding its essence!

This comment speaks to another primary difference between jazz and classical music. Classical musicians strive to re-create the composer's vision as closely as possible, carefully following the written score. Classical composers specify details, such as the tempo at which a section should be played, or the volume, from very low to very loud, and so forth. This places the performer secondary to the composer, as he/she is only delivering the composer's ideas to the audience as precisely as possible and like the composer wrote it.

In jazz, the performer uses the composer's tune as a launching pad to improvise, thereby decomposing and recomposing the tune spontaneously, thus crafting a new song on the spot. In doing so, the performer becomes a spontaneous composer, using the spotlight as a creative force, while the composer holds a secondary position, supplying the basis for the musician's improvisation.

Typically, a jazz band presents the basic melody and then gives each performer a chance to improvise on that melody. Finally, the band restates the melody at the end. As jazz saxophonist, professor and author Jerry Coker explains it:

The most important characteristic of jazz, however, is improvisation. Virtually every jazz selection will focus on improvisation, even when many other characteristics remain optional. Jazz continues to develop, absorb new styles and techniques, and change with great rapidity, but improvisation, the blues, and the vigorous pulse remain reasonably constant throughout its history of development from folk music to art music.[27]

To put it quite succinctly and as Gunther Schuller said, "Improvisation is the heart and soul of jazz."[28]

Jazz piano legend, Dave Brubeck echoed this same sentiment, declaring:

If I didn't improvise every night, I'd quit. I've got to keep improvising.[29]

What is jazz? When there is not complete freedom of the soloist, it ceases to be jazz. Jazz is about the only form of art existing today in which there is this freedom of the individual without the loss of group contact.[30]

Hayden Carruth explained the idea further when he wrote:

Jazz musicians work out their improvisations in jam sessions, but not only there; they do it too on the stand, in rehearsal halls, in studios, at home by themselves, and sometimes—many have testified to this—while walking, driving a car, performing actions distantly related, if at all, to jazz; sometimes even in dreams, which are, no matter what anyone thinks, work. In these ways improvisations grow.[31]

Bebop innovator Charlie Parker further added:

> Music is your own experience, your thoughts, your wisdom. If you don't live it, it won't come out of your horn. They teach you there's a boundary line to music, but, man, there's no boundary line to art.[32]

Parker's pal and fellow Bebop innovator, Dizzy Gillespie, also embraced the artistic aspect of jazz, describing it this way:

> In improvisation, the first thing you must have is the sight of a gifted painter. You've got to see colors and lines in music, and then you've got to be able to mix the colors and draw the lines. The better you mix colors and draw lines the better the painting is going to be.[33]

When Gillespie was asked whether jazz should be considered "serious" music or not, Dizzy remarked, "Men have died for this music. You can't get more serious than that."[34]

Billie Holiday, widely and affectionately known as Lady Day, celebrated jazz with a sincere and distinctive passion.

> I don't think I'm singing. I feel like I am playing a horn. I try to improvise like Les Young, like Louis Armstrong, or someone else I admire. What comes out is what I feel. I hate straight singing. I have to change a tune to my own way of doing it. That's all I know.[35]

Record producers and writers Orrin Keepnews and Bill Grauer wrote:

> Jazz . . . is music and the truest way to know it is to hear it. . . . Jazz has always served as an expression of people and of their environment—of a great many different people who have created it and reacted to it, in a great many different settings. Perhaps the truest measure of the validity of jazz is that it can be all things to all men: a mild form of amusement; an emotional or an intellectual stimulant; an art form; a social commentary; a cult; something to like, love, or even hate for a wide variety of esthetic, emotional or social reasons. Thus jazz is both simple (no more than the combinations of notes you hear) and incredibly complex (as complex as human beings and as the world we inhabit). . . . Jazz, then, is many things (simple, complex, young, old; changing, constant).[36]

Gilbert Seldes further stated in his 1924 book, *The 7 Lively Arts*, "Jazz is good—at least good jazz is good"[37]

Pianist and avant-garde composer George Antheil shared Lady Day's feelings, writing:

> Jazz is not a craze. It has existed in America for the last hundred years and continues to exist each year more potently than the last. As for its artistic significance, the organization of its line, and color, its new dimensions, its new dynamics and mechanics—its significance is that it is one of the greatest landmarks of modern art.[38]

There is an interesting aside to know about George Antheil: In addition to being a notable pianist and composer, Antheil was also an inventor and jack-of-all-trades genius. In fact, he patented a secret code-breaking system using unique radio communication concepts developed by his partner, none other than the Jewish actress, mathematical prodigy, and gifted scientist Hedy Lamarr.

Movie magnate Sam Meyer (of the Metro Golden Meyer empire) called Lamarr "the most beautiful woman in the world" after watching her run naked through the Austrian countryside in a

European movie titled *Ecstasy*. The movie caused quite a stir back then.

Lamarr fled Austria shortly before Hitler annexed it. Being a Jewess, her timing could not have been better. She ended up in the United States and went on to become a huge Hollywood movie star. But fame, riches, and accolades proved unfulfilling to her. She fiercely despised Hitler and his Nazis, and so she committed her huge intellect and resources to bringing the evil Nazi empire down.

Using her mathematical and scientific brilliance, she invented and patented novel ideas that were secretly used by the United States Navy in the war. Her patented intellectual concepts proved invaluable in guiding torpedoes and other military weapons. Some of her concepts, such as frequency hopping and spread spectrum, are still widely used in wireless communication and secure military communications. Today's Wi-Fi networks, BlackBerrys, and fourth-generation "LTE" wireless technology all capitalize on Lamarr's genius.

Yet, when this noted genius applied for membership in the National Inventors Council, Lamarr was told that the best way for her to help the war effort was to use her celebrity status to sell U.S. war bonds. Clearly, gender discrimination was one tyrant that her brilliance couldn't conquer. So here we have a brilliant mathematician/scientist/actress teaming up with a famous jazz pianist and avant-garde composer, George Antheil, also a bona-fide genius, to help beat the Nazis. Jazz has made some strange bedfellows. But I digress a bit here.

So what exactly does the "J" in jazz stand for? Apparently, to some people, it stands for Jew. Wilfrid Sheed, in his book, *The House That George Built*, wrote, "The standards have actually been referred to as a Jewish response to black music."[39] Gershwin biographer Isaac Goldberg agreed by writing, "A goodly part, then, of what we know as jazz is Jewish."[40]

In his article, "Aaron Copland and His Jazz," which appeared in the *American Mercury* in September 1927, Goldberg wrote:

> In the course of its filtration from the South to a small but noisy point called Manhattan Island it has undergone something decidedly more than a sea change. It reaches from the black South to the black North, but in between it has been touched by the commercial wand of the Jew.[41]

His comments are tempered by Wilfred Sheed, who very wisely reminded us:

> Music is not produced by whole groups, but by one genius at a time, and it may be significant that the two families that gave us Irving Berlin and George Gershwin both fled Russia on the same great wave of czarist pogroms, only to find American black people not only singing about a similar experience, but using the Hebrew Bible as their text.[42]

(Here's my take on it: if the "J" in jazz stands for Jew, then the "B" in blues must stand for bagels! Pass the lox!)

In 1920, the music magazine, *Melody*, essentially published an 'official' obituary for jazz, declaring, "'Jazz' is now dying that natural death . . . 'Jazz' has had its day."[43] I guess the author must have meant that jazz was going to die a very *slow* death since this article was published almost 100 years ago.

Jazz pianist and composer giant Thelonious Monk gave his thoughts when questioned in an interview, "Where's jazz going?" His Thelonious assault answer was "I don't know where it's going. Maybe it's going to hell. You can't make anything go anywhere. It just happens."[44]

Miles Davis then stripped jazz of all intellectualizing when he stated, "No critic can put it into any words. It speaks in the music. It speaks for itself."[45]

Jazz tenor sax great John Coltrane agreed with Davis, saying that words couldn't capture the essence of jazz when he said, "If the music doesn't say it, how can words say it *for* the music?"[46] He continued on with his point by saying, "The music has to speak for itself."[47]

Defining jazz seems to be an impossible task, and perhaps that is a good thing. For some, it is the music of the devil, but to others it is the epitome of freedom. Exemplified as a spontaneous art form based on improvisation, just because a musician is improvising a song does not automatically transform that song into a jazz performance. Something very important needs to be added to the mix for a tune to be transformed from a bunch of improvised notes into a first-rate jazz performance. I think the title of the classic jazz tune by the great Duke Ellington with lyrics by his Jewish partner, Irving Mills, does capture the true spirit of jazz: "It Don't Mean a Thing (If It Ain't Got That Swing)"

You Started It*

*Delicious (1931)

*What jazz represents is the indefinable thing....
That essence, if I may be forgiven for taking the
liberty of attempting to describe anything so elusive,
is energetic, wistful, enterprising and self-confident.*

—PAUL WHITEMAN (1926)[1]

Paul Whiteman (1890–1967) was born Paul Wightman in Denver, Colorado. Both parents were classical musicians; his father was the director of music for the Denver school district and his mother sang in the Denver choir.

As a young boy, Whiteman aspired to be a mechanical engineer, but once he learned to play the violin, his dreams and ambitions turned to music. By 1907, at the tender age of seventeen, he held the first chair viola seat in the Denver Symphony Orchestra. He then moved west to play in the San Francisco Symphony Orchestra. There, he played viola at the 1915 World's Fair. To make ends meet, he occasionally moonlighted as a taxicab driver, as so many "perspiring" musicians have done (me included).

Whiteman's introduction to jazz happened on "one of the worst days" of his life. That fateful day had started off with him in a grumpy mood and only got worse from there. He broke a mirror shaving, then drank some cold coffee, and ate overcooked eggs. He described the rest of the day in a tongue-in-cheek manner. That evening, one of his musician buddies visited him at home and coaxed him to go slumming. The moment he agreed, he knew that his fortune had taken a dramatic turn. Here's how he described it:

We first met—jazz and I—at a dance dive on the Barbary Coast. It screeched and bellowed at me from a trick platform in the middle of a smoke-hazed, beer-fumed room. And it hit me hard. I had been blue all day. . . . We ambled at length into a mad house. Men and women were whirling and twirling feverishly there. Sometimes they snapped their fingers and yelled loud enough to drown the music—if music it was.

My whole body began to sit up and take notice. It was like coming out of blackness into bright light. My blues faded when treated to the Georgia blues that some trombonist was wailing about. My head was dizzy, but my feet seemed to understand that tune. They began to pat wildly. I wanted to whoop. I wanted to dance. I wanted to sing. I did them all. Raucous? Yes. Crude—undoubtedly. Unmusical—sure as you live. But rhythmic, catching as the smallpox, and spirit-lifting. That was jazz then. I liked it, though it puzzled me. Even then it seemed to me to have vitality, sincerity and truth in it. In spite of its uncouthness, it was trying to say something peculiarly American. . . . The fantastic beat drummed in my ears long after the strident echoes had died, and sleep for nights became a saxophonic mockery.[2]

Shortly after that life-altering night, Whiteman resigned from the San Francisco Symphony Orchestra and went in search of a gig with a jazz band. Little did he know, however, that he was once again a novice and just beginning a new phase of his musical education.

He was hired by a jazz band that was playing at Tait's in San Francisco—and then promptly fired after only two nights. A classical square, he was trained to play notes precisely as written. Whiteman had no idea how to "jazz up" a song.

At the time, most jazz cats could not read a single note of music—or even a word on a page. Their musical competence was judged entirely by their improvisational skills—their ability to compose on the spot—extemporaneously. Whiteman hadn't honed that skill as yet; he was an expert at playing someone else's music exactly as written but not playing spontaneous music of his own creation.

Without a steady gig, Whiteman lived for a while as a struggling musician, taking all sorts of odd jobs to pay the rent. After many hours behind the wheel of a taxicab and even more hours of trial and error as a jazz musician, he finally figured out "how to fake it," meaning he learned how to improvise. This skill was the ticket into the vibrant world of jazz musicians. The only ticket.

I was thirteen when I got my first "fake book"—368 pages of music, with a cover promising 1,000 tunes. (Most pages noted the melody line for three different tunes.) I had to buy it "under the counter" because the publisher hadn't received permission from the music's copyright owners. Although the sale and the book were illegal, this one tool gave me the ability to play countless jazz gigs over the years. (After all these years, it's still one of my most prized possessions!)

"Fake books" weren't just for youngsters and novices. For decades, most professional jazz cats brought a fake book with them to all their gigs, including weddings and bar mitzvahs. When the bandleader called out, "Rhythm 210," they knew he meant "I Got Rhythm" on page 210 of the fake book. Band members would first play the melody, and then the improvisation would begin. This improvisation was the actual "faking it," and that skill is what separated the jazz cat from other musicians.

Paul Whiteman was one of those "other musicians"; at first, he did not have a clue about how to "fake it." Yet he was a persistent artist and a stubborn man, and so he committed himself to learning the vernacular of this new music called jazz, "I'd learn if it took a year."[3]

Whiteman proceeded to "wood shedding." This term, used by jazz cats, means intense study and practice. He visited clubs that were hosting jazz bands to learn their techniques, but since he was flat broke and couldn't buy any food or beverages in the clubs, he ran into trouble with the headwaiters. So he started to wear his old symphony suit. By looking the part of a well-to-do patron, he learned that management didn't bother him.

In his "disguise," Whiteman was able to study the improvised snippets being played onstage; he then returned to his apartment to work out what he had just heard. For a highly trained and accomplished musician, this technique proved to be a very successful way for him to explore the emerging art of jazz. He was literally taking notes from the seasoned jazz cats!

In those days, the song repertoire of most bands and musicians was based on memory and laced with loads of improvisation (again, because most musicians could not actually read music). Eager to merge his classical composing skills with his newfound passion for jazz, Whiteman created a new and unique concept. He began writing out jazz-infused orchestral scores for bands to play, blending various elements of black music (like blues and polyrhythms) into western style (white) symphonic music. In the process, he gave birth to what he named "symphonic jazz."

In his autobiography, Whiteman declared that as far as jazz was concerned, he was the right man at the right time:

> My notion is that the chief contribution of the white American to jazz so far has been his recognition of it as legitimate music.[4]
>
> It is a relief to be able to prove at last that I did not invent jazz. . . . All I did was to orchestrate jazz. If I had not done it, somebody else would have. The time was ripe for that. Conditions produce the men, not men the conditions. It merely happened that I was the fortunate person who combined the ideas, the place and the time. At least, I think I was fortunate. Others are not so sanguine.[5]

Many agree that this man was far too modest. As Duke Ellington said, "Paul Whiteman was known as the King of Jazz, and no one as yet has come near carrying that title with more certainty and dignity."[6]

Unlike any musician who came before him, Whiteman converted the raw and unharnessed music of the black community into a style that was much more palatable to the mainstream American audience. Escorting this new music from uncivilized whorehouses to refined concert halls, he poured ice water on "hot" jazz and then sweetened it with honey, eventually creating a "sweet, syrupy" jazz.

This shift from hot to sweet was done through strategic orchestration by easing up on the horns and playing up the strings (remember that Whiteman was a string player). Since horns are hot and strings are sweet, more of an emphasis on soft, sweet strings and less focus on loud, hot horns simplified and minimized the (hot) rhythms and emphasized the sweet melody instead.

He then shaped a song with the same musical restraints of an orchestra, replacing improvisation with meticulously scored pieces. Despite the fact improvisation was one of jazz's foundational elements, it was not allowed in any Whiteman symphonic jazz performances. Musicians had to stick to the written score, note by note, or they would be fired.

Of course, this directive meant a new type of musician was needed—one who could read music. Most black musicians were not equipped to play this new style. A "help wanted" ad for Whiteman's orchestra thus might have read something like this:

> **Wanted:** Experienced musicians for a steady gig. Chart reading a must. Whites only. Blacks and improvisers need not apply.
> Call Pennsylvania 6–5000

When World War I broke out, Whiteman was still struggling to form a jazz band. Even though he was called a "starving musician," he weighed over 300 pounds. Being so portly, he was unfit for combat duty, so he enlisted in the Navy as a bandleader. This decision turned out to be an invaluable experience, schooling him in the operations and intricacies of leading a band.

After the war, Whiteman bopped around California until he met and then hired genius orchestrator/arranger Ferde Grofé. Then Whiteman met John Hernan, a benefactor who believed in him enough to book an orchestral gig at the Alexandria Hotel in Los Angeles. The gig lasted for over a year, giving the Whiteman Orchestra a platform to develop and deliver unique music that fused the soul of jazz with the western symphonic model.

Fame and fortune quickly followed. In just one month, cover receipts rose from $300 to $1,200 a night. (In today's dollars, that's an increase from about $4,500 to about $18,000 a night.) The band caused so much buzz that the Hollywood elite, including Charlie Chaplin, Harold Lloyd, and Cecil B. DeMille, flocked to the Alexandria Hotel. It was the Club 54 of its day.

Before long, S. W. Straus gambled $2,600 (about $40,000 in today's scratch) to take the band east to Atlantic City's newly opened Ambassador Hotel. On a chance encounter at this new venue, Victor Phonograph Company representative, Calvin Child, went wild for the band and signed them to a two-year contract. Things were really starting to "jazz up" for Whiteman!

As his career continued to escalate, Whiteman starred in musical performances, recordings, radio shows, and more. His writing and composing duties got to be too much for one man alone. Whiteman knew he needed an arranger who could bridge the gap between black and white cultures, someone who could lift the lowly black jazz music into a high form of music acceptable to the white American public. (Forgive me for saying this, but Whiteman wanted to whitewash black music.) Then, one evening in a dance hall, Whiteman saw and heard a man who was able to make the right connection between the two cultures—piano player, arranger, and dance hall bandleader Ferde Grofé.

In 1920, Whiteman and Grofé hit it big in the record industry with the blockbuster hit "Whispering." How big a hit was it? In his 1972 book, *American Popular Song: The Great Innovators, 1900–1950*, Alec Wilder concluded that the then sales of "Whispering" would equate to over 20 million copies in 1972.[7] What would that number equate to today, given all the iPods, MP3 players, and other devices in circulation? It's impossible to say, but we can certainly appreciate the fact that "Whispering" was an enormous commercial success.

Whiteman and his orchestra were now the toast of the town. New York town that is. He signed a contract for his band to be the house orchestra at New York City's largest café, the Palais Royal at West 48th Street and Broadway. This was just a few blocks south of the Roseland Ballroom, where jazz innovator Fletcher Henderson's band was featuring a trumpet phenomenon, Louis Armstrong. Duke Ellington's band was also playing nearby. Clearly, midtown New York was the hotspot of world-class jazz.

Amidst so much competition, Whiteman decided to rename his outfit "Paul Whiteman and His Palais Royal Orchestra." It was a wise strategic move, because the clientele of the Palais Royal read like a who's who of New York City's high society, hoity-toity, artsy-fartsy, hoi polloi intelligentsia highfalutin' one percent. Whiteman's orchestra was now playing for royalty, the Vanderbilts, and other movers and shakers of the day.

(Incidentally, Whiteman held rehearsals for the *Rhapsody in Blue* concert at the Palais Royal club in the days leading up to that Aeolian Hall concert. The orchestra also played a season with the *Ziegfeld Follies*.)

It was a well-known fact then that Whiteman featured the most talented musicians of the time. He attracted the best and the brightest, in part because he paid his men extremely well. In an interview in 1924, Whiteman asked:

> Have you ever wondered why each man in my orchestra makes from $65 to $300 a week all the year round while the best men in a big symphony orchestra are lucky if they earn $200 a week for six months of the year?

To put this statistic more into perspective, his musicians earned between $48,000 and $230,000 a year in today's dollars. At the time, this pay was unprecedented. Still, Whiteman's orchestra was in great demand, and we all know how the principle of supply and demand works.

In addition to paying his men exceptionally well, Whiteman (also known as Pops) was known to give amazing bonuses. Henry Busse, Whiteman's top trumpeter and fluegelist, was given an ultra-expensive Pierce Arrow luxury automobile. When you pay your musicians that extravagantly, you get the best of the best and in both regards: Whiteman did just that.

In March 1923, his group sailed across the Atlantic to play for European royalty, including the Prince of Wales. Five months later, returning to the outstretched arms of New York City, Whiteman was officially crowned "The King of Jazz." Local and national papers trumpeted the news, celebrating and broadcasting Whiteman's new title as "The King of Jazz."

This title stayed with him for the rest of his life—but not everyone felt he deserved such a comprehensive jazz title. As some folks put it:

> Paul Whiteman, who once had a band which could really swing, concerns himself now with "what the public wants." He specializes in what strikes me as empty, pompous performances—nicknamed "symphonic jazz."[8]

A word as to Paul Whiteman. From the number of pages indexed to his name in almost any book on hot jazz one may know in advance how often he has been insulted in the text. I, too, do not particularly care for "sweet jazz," yet I should like to risk the scorn of partisans by testifying that Whiteman has quite a band, that it took courage and ability first to perform the Gershwin *Rhapsody In Blue* and *Concerto in F* (as it did for Damrosch to introduce *An American in Paris*), and that Whiteman tided things over from the first shock of "Dixieland" until the public was tough enough to take its hot jazz neat.[9]

Whiteman's billing as "King of Jazz" should not be taken too seriously in a musical sense; no more so than the overall designation of all the goings-on of the Roaring Twenties as "The Jazz Age." But he was a friend and steady employer of bona fide jazz musicians.[10]

Indeed, Paul Whiteman did employ many musicians over the years, both black and white, including some of jazz's greatest players, like Bix Beiderbecke and Joe Venuti. Of course, during the 1920 Jim Crow days, Whiteman kept his black arrangers behind the scenes, since it was forbidden to have mixed-race musicians on stage together at that time.

By 1926, Paul Whiteman's Orchestra was incredibly popular—and lucrative. His outfit was pulling in $12,000 to $15,000 a week (which equates to about $160,000–$200,000 today)—and he received a percentage of all the receipts exceeding that guarantee. But the gross receipts tell only part of the story. Whiteman was supporting a huge orchestra of thirty musicians, as well as arranger Ferde Grofé and a manager. Those professionals were the cream of the crop, and they cost money—lots of money.[11] Still, when you're the best of the best, you can command top dollar and top talent.

FERDE GROFÉ

Ferdinand Rudolph von Grofé was born in New York City in 1892 to a family of classically trained professional musicians that stretched back four generations. Both of his parents worked as professional musicians.

As a young boy, Grofé showed tremendous ability in playing and composing classical music. Later in life, he became a teacher at the Julliard School of Music, teaching orchestration.

At the young age of fourteen, Grofé left home and bounced around, doing various jobs, finally ending up as a piano player in a "sporting house" (bordello). When his family got wind of what he was doing, they brought him home to Los Angeles in 1909. There he landed a job playing the viola in the Los Angeles Symphony Orchestra where both his grandfather and uncle worked. He stayed with this gig for ten years, learning a tremendous amount about the music industry.

A talented multi-instrumentalist who played strings (including banjo), piano, and horns, Grofé also moonlighted in ragtime and pop bands. Ragtime really captured his interest, and so he began writing down ideas for a band.

On that fateful evening when Whiteman "discovered" Grofé, Grofé was leading his band through an original arrangement. Whiteman was blown away and made him an offer he could not refuse. Grofé became Whiteman's top arranger and the relationship soon propelled them both into national prominence. Their first national blockbuster was "Whispering," arranged by Grofé and performed by Paul Whiteman and his Ambassador Orchestra. It stayed on the charts for twenty weeks, eleven of them at number one, and sold over 2 million records!

Over the years, Ferde Grofé composed many other compositions for both orchestras and films. In 1931, Grofé composed his most famous work, "Grand Canyon Suite," which received widespread critical acclaim. For his work in elevating the art of jazz, he was dubbed "The Prime Minister of Jazz," a tongue-in-cheek poke at his longtime boss, Whiteman, "The King of Jazz."

KING OF JAZZ THE MOVIE

In 1930, Universal produced a movie featuring Paul Whiteman titled *King of Jazz*. As the first Technicolor film, it had a huge budget—over $1.5 million (just under $21 million in today's dollars). This budget paid for elaborate staging, rich royalties (including a whopping $50,000 [about $700,000 today] to Gershwin and his publisher Harms, for the rights to use *Rhapsody in Blue* in the flick), and top-notch talent. It even featured the debut performance of Bing Crosby in his trio "The Rhythm Boys."

The movie premiered at New York's Roxy Theatre on May 2, 1930. As a marketing ploy, Whiteman's Orchestra, featuring George Gershwin, performed an abridged version of *Rhapsody in Blue* for live movie theater audiences, joined by the Roxy Orchestra and Chorus. This combination live show and movie was offered five times a day for a week.

Gershwin performed *Rhapsody* over thirty times that week. Unaccustomed to such a grueling work schedule, he *kvetched* about his aching back, but he also said it was great fun. He even signed on for an additional week of performances.

The movie turned out to be a box-office dud. Universal lost hundreds of thousands of dollars on it (although it recouped its losses several years later).[12] But it was quite a windfall for Gershwin. The Roxy Theatre paid him the astounding sum of $10,000 for that two-week gig! (That would be about $140,000 today.)

Why was the movie such a flop? Mainly because it lacked a cohesive plot. It was a series of musical performances, comedy sketches, and vaudeville gags simply strung together.

The film was introduced as a Paul Whiteman scrapbook. The movie started with a short cartoon by Walter Lantz (the Woody Woodpecker guy) showing Whiteman in "darkest Africa," being crowned "The King of Jazz" while the reigning "King of the Jungle" chased him.

Much of the film's music was excellent, showcasing some of Whiteman's virtuoso musicians' strutting their stuff, as well as vaudeville acts that did amazing things on their instruments. Several scenes reminded me of the Radio City Rockettes or a Busby Berkeley film with beautiful leggy women in scanty outfits, strutting their stuff (which always gets my attention!). The videography in some scenes was exceptional, especially since it was produced so early in the evolution of film technology.

The high point of the flick by far is the Paul Whiteman Orchestra performing Gershwin's *Rhapsody in Blue*. It was a huge production number with amazing visual and audio effects and elaborate sets. With something for everyone, *King of Jazz* was a worthwhile and entertaining hour and a half.

The film sent Broadway gossipers into orbit spreading the rumor that Paul Whiteman and George Gershwin had a friendly feud going. Supposedly, Whiteman claimed that he made Gershwin famous by commissioning him to compose *Rhapsody in Blue*, whereas Gershwin declared he made Whiteman famous by his writing such a great and historically significant piece.

It's the age-old question: Which came first, the chicken or the egg . . . kugel? But let's not cry fowl too soon!

THE LIFE & TIMES OF GEORGE GERSHWIN

Who's the Greatest?*

*Let 'Em Eat Cake (1933)

Music must reflect the thoughts and aspirations of the people and the time. My people are Americans. My time is today.
—GEORGE GERSHWIN[1]

In 1895, Russian-born Jews Rose Bruskin and Morris Gershovitz were married in New York. In the years that followed, they had four children: Ira (Israel), George (Jacob Morris), Arthur, and Frances. Over time, the family name morphed from Gershovitz to Gershwine, then to Gershvin, and finally to Gershwin. (Some also say George changed it to Gershwin in honor of his hero, comedian Ed Wynn.)

George was born in Brooklyn on September 26, 1898, two years after his brother and future lyricist/partner, Ira. Young George was a rough-and-tumble streetwise kid with a strong athletic streak. He prided himself on being the champion roller skater on Seventh Street, and he loved to play stickball, a popular pastime for kids then on New York City's streets. George also had a streak of delinquency and at times was busted for stealing and street fighting. In fact, one picture of George clearly shows a scar over young George's right eye. His friends called him "Cheesecake," a nickname given him because his father owned a bakery at one time or another.[2]

At some point during his childhood, George found himself on the wrong end of a horse and got kicked in the nose, an injury that caused a lifetime of nasal and sinus issues. (Then again, to my knowledge, all Jewish males have some nasal and/or sinus issues. I have never met a Jewish guy without a deviated septum and sinus problems, myself included. Please pass the Kleenex!)

Unlike Paul Whiteman, the Gershwin kids were not born into a lineage of musical talent. There were no musical geniuses or famous cantors in their family tree. In fact, in his younger years, George was most definitely *not* interested in music. As Gershwin's biographer Isaac Goldberg wrote:

> In the days of the roller skate and the hockey stick, it was George's firm conviction that there was something radically wrong with youngsters who went in for music. To scrape away at the fiddle, to wear out one's fingers on piano keys, was to be a "little Maggie," a sissy. Music was effeminate; it was taught by women to women and little girls, and if little boys submitted to instruction, they at once classified themselves.[3]

In author/critic Henry O. Osgood's 1926 book titled *So The Is Jazz,* the author tells us of an interview with Gershwin in which he asks the question, "Didn't you play anything when you were a youngster." Gershwin prankishly replied, "Nothing but hookey."[4]

When George was born on September 26, 1898, his family was living in the East New York section of Brooklyn at 242 Snediker Avenue, between Sutter Avenue and Belmont Avenue. (My father's grocery store was on Sutter Avenue, just 1.2 miles away. Thus, only twenty-five short blocks separated Gershwin's first digs from my own childhood home, and just like my parents, George's parents spoke Russian, Yiddish, and English in the home.)

A quick search on Google Maps reveals that the Gershwin house was next door to a synagogue that is still standing, but like the rest of the *shuls* in this area of Brooklyn, it has been converted to a church. This synagogue is today a Pentecostal Church. So George Gershwin and I were really neighbors living in a different time and different dimensions.

The Snediker Avenue house had:

A front room, a dining room, a kitchen, and a maid's room on the ground floor; upstairs there were three or four bedrooms, one of which was rented to a Mr. Taffelstein for $3 a week. The Gershwins paid $14 a month rent for the house. George's father was earning $35 a week as a skilled designer of uppers for women's shoes, an income that enabled Mrs. Gershwin to employ a maid.[5]

I'm Somethin' on Avenue A*

*Tell Me More (1925)

The Gershwin family moved from Brooklyn to Grand Street, just off the Bowery north of Chinatown on the Lower East Side of Manhattan. A hotspot of pushcarts and peddlers, the Lower East Side was the finish line for many European Jewish immigrants. They flocked to this overcrowded neighborhood, living in small apartments in rundown, crowded tenement buildings. (Even though my family lived in the East New York section of Brooklyn, living quarters were similar to those on the Lower East Side. My family of six lived in a tiny two-bedroom, one bathroom apartment behind my father's grocery store [more accurately, an appetizing store]. There was no living room. Trust me, I had to learn early on to carefully schedule my bathroom time or else I was s**t out of luck, so to speak. Lucky for me we had a *pish-glassel* (jar) just in case. If the bathroom was in use, I would be handed the *pish-glassel* and learned to be a straight shooter.)

When George's parents got married in 1895, there were 300,000 Jews in all of New York City. By 1910, just fifteen years later, the Lower East Side alone had over 500,000 Jews! It was like a European Jewish *shtetl* in downtown New York City. Everything was smooshed together—tenements, grocery stores, bakeries, and *shuls*. I suspect the Lower East Side had the highest concentration of deviated septums in the world!

George went to P.S. 20 and then P.S. 25 at 5th Avenue and 2nd Street—and he was a very poor student, which made him the opposite of his older brother, Ira, who was a diligent student and often got George out of jams. Studious Ira would do homework assignments for his hooky-playing kid brother.

Yiddish music and theater were part and parcel of the Lower East Side, so George was exposed to many Yiddish composers and performers. Older brother, Ira, remembered the famous Yiddish Theatre composer Joseph Rumshinsky, playing cards with his father Morris while the Gershwin family lived on 2nd Avenue.

The Yiddish musical was king during the early 20th century; composers, musicians, and singers of Yiddish songs were popular celebrities of the day, especially on the Lower East Side. George did odd jobs for some of them and became friendly with many of these players, singers as well as the rest of the milieu. These early experiences proved to be formative in terms of George's musical development. Like the blues, Yiddish music expresses a wide range of emotions—melancholy, sadness, exuberance, and joy, sometimes all at once. Both genres utilized many of the same musical techniques; let's just say the "blue notes" and the "Jew notes" had much in common.

When the Gershwins moved to 91 2nd Avenue, between 5th and 6th Streets, they were smack dab in the middle of the Yiddish Theatre District. The area was so vibrant with the arts that it rivaled the Broadway Theatre District in sales, number of shows, and quality of performers.

The building occupied by the Gershwins was just a few doors down from the old Fillmore East Auditorium (105 2nd Avenue), which was built in the mid-1920s as the showcase theater of the Yiddish Theatre District. It fell into disrepair after World War II and stayed that way throughout the mid-1960s. In 1968, however, rock impresario Bill Graham took over the derelict theater, transforming it into the hippy rock capital of the East Coast. I have many fond memories of the Fillmore East, being the winning bidder of King Curtis' (sax soloist on rock classic "Yakety Yak") saxophone mouthpiece at a benefit auction and being kicked out of the legendary theater by none other than Bill Graham himself! That second memory is a story well worth telling.

My friend—and band mate in "The Feather Factory"—Irving (aka Irk) worked at the Fillmore East and often would sneak our band members into the shows. We would spread out and hunt for empty seats, and when one of us found them, we would yell our code word "Chino!" to signal the others to join us. One night, I found a few empties in the front row. The announcer's mic was directly in front of me. Unfortunately, the announcer was Bill Graham himself. While Mr. Graham was going through his preshow announcements, I was yelling, "CHINO! CHINO!" at the top of my lungs. I was so excited to have scored such amazing seats. (And, I must admit, my judgment may have been impaired at the time.) Bill Graham stopped his announcements and walked off the stage, down the steps, and directly to my seat. To my sheer horror, he asked to see my ticket. Of course I could not produce one, so he personally escorted me to the back of the house and passed me off to an usher, instructing him to show me the door.

My pal Irk intercepted the usher and pulled me to the side, educating me on the advantages of laying low. (I'm pretty sure the word *"schmuck"* was used—probably more than once.) Then he let me blend back into the crowd. This experience earned me a legendary reputation within our band. "Sax great Richie Gerber stopped the show at the Fillmore East!"

But, I digress . . . let's get back to George Gershwin.

The wandering Jewish Gershwin family moved often. In George's earliest years, they moved up to Harlem and then returned to Brooklyn for a short stint. Upon returning to Brooklyn, they lived at 1310 8th Avenue, just one block from Prospect Park. On page 3 of *The Gershwins* by Robert Kimball and Alfred Simon, there is a full-page photo from 1901, when George was just three years old.[1] He is sitting in front of a tree with his mother, older brother Ira, younger sister Frances, and their maid.

That very same tree is where my wife, Julie, and I met and fell in love. When I saw this picture, I called her into my office and, pointing to the page, asked her if anything looked familiar. Without the slightest hesitation, she gasped and exclaimed lovingly, "PROSPECT PARK!" We hugged and laughed, reminiscing about meeting in the park while walking our dogs some forty-four years earlier. To think that sixty-nine years before that fateful day, three-year-old George Gershwin sat with his family in that exact spot, under that same tree. Amazing!

Ira Gershwin said the family moved twenty-eight times, living mostly in Manhattan and three times in Brooklyn. Their father, Morris, always wanted to live within walking distance of his work, which is why he relocated the family so many times. "Papa" Morris had an incredibly restless and entrepreneurial nature. He was a serial businessman. On this topic, biographer David Ewen stated:

> He opened a small stationery store in Brooklyn. Before long, he abandoned it for a restaurant on the East Side, in partnership with his brother-in-law, Harry Wolpin. After that he passed from one business venture to another, always in partnership with his brother-in-law. At different periods he owned several restaurants: one on Forsyth Street, another on downtown Broadway, a third on upper Broadway near 145th Street, a forth near the Hotel McAlpin on 34th Street and Broadway. There was one period when he ran four restaurants simultaneously. Also at different times he owned and operated several Turkish and Russian baths, including the St. Nicholas Baths on Lenox Avenue and 111th Street, and the Lafayette Baths downtown. He was also at one time or another the proprietor of several bakeries, and of two rooming houses at or near 42nd Street; the owner of a cigar store which included a pool parlor on what is now the Grand Central Station; and a bookmaking establishment at the Belmont Race Track. One summer, in 1904, he operated a summer hotel in Spring Valley, New York, which accommodated 200 guests.[2]

Gershwin tells of his first real memory of music. He discovered music as a barefoot six-year-old boy in overalls, standing outside a Harlem penny arcade on 125th Street, mesmerized by a player piano belting out Rubinstein's "Melody in F."[3]

When Gershwin was about ten years old, a neighborhood friend invited George to his house. There was a player piano in the parlor, and George was spellbound by it. From that day forward, he spent countless hours at his pal's house, perched on the piano stool, his small fingers shadowing the automated depressions of the keys. Young George was teaching himself to play the most popular music of the day.

Two years later, when George was twelve, Mother Rose purchased a secondhand upright piano on an installment plan. (Her sister had recently bought a piano, so she had to have one too. A little sibling rivalry, perhaps?) The idea was for Ira to learn to play it.

The piano movers hoisted the piano through a front parlor window, and as soon as it was set in place, George spun the piano stool to his height, sat down, and started to play a series of popular tunes. Everyone gasped. The kid was a natural! George was so enamored with the piano that he completely took it over. Fortunately, Ira did not mind one bit.

George was eager to study and learn as much as he could. Amazingly, he even requested a piano teacher. Remember, in his day, the word on the street was that women gave piano lessons to other women and girls. If a boy took lessons, he faced a great deal of name calling on the street. However, George knew he was strong enough to defend his tough-guy reputation.

Official Resume*

*Strike Up the Band (1930)

*Studying the piano made a good boy out of a bad one.
It took the piano to tone me down . . . I was
a changed person after I took it up.*

—GEORGE GERSHWIN IN A 1924 INTERVIEW[1]

The piano had a transformative effect on George. This streetwise kid exhibited amazing virtuosity, and his teachers could not keep up with his brilliance. After studying with several run-of-the-mill teachers, George finally met the one who would nurture and inspire him to new musical heights. In 1912, the fourteen-year-old boy hooked up with his first "real" teacher. That's when things started to change for this young teenager.

Charles Hambitzer had a prestigious musical pedigree. His great grandfather was court violinist for the Czar of Russia, and his father owned a music store in Milwaukee, Wisconsin. Charles was a gifted classical pianist who also played a number of other instruments. After arriving in New York in 1905, he taught piano, violin, and cello and then assumed a position with the Waldorf-Astoria Orchestra. In addition to playing concert piano, he did some of their orchestrations.

Hambitzer immediately recognized Gershwin's musical genius. In a letter to his sister, he crowed:

I have a new pupil who will make his mark in music if anybody will. The boy is a genius, without a doubt; he's just crazy about music and can't wait until it's time to take his lesson. No watching the clock for this boy! He wants to go in for this modern stuff, jazz and what not. But I'm not going to let him for a while. I'll see that he gets a firm foundation in the standard music first.[2]

Hambitzer was so taken by the young genius that he taught him free of charge. They went to concerts together, and in doing so, George acquired what he called:

My habit of intensive listening. I had gone to concerts and listened not only with my ears but with my nerves, my mind, my heart. I had listened so earnestly that I became saturated with the music.

Then I went home and listened in memory. I sat at the piano and repeated the motifs.[3]

Speaking of Hambitzer, George said to his biographer:

> I revere the man. . . . Under Hambitzer, I first became familiar with Chopin, Liszt and Debussy. He made me harmony-conscious. . . . I was crazy about the man. I went out, in fact, and drummed up 10 pupils for him.[4]

In 1915, Hambitzer decided it was time for Gershwin to receive formal training in music theory and harmony. He sent the boy to Edward Kilenyi, Sr., a Hungarian émigré, who then taught George counterpoint, harmony, form, and orchestration. Gershwin was still just a teenager, but he was being taught and trained by some of the best in the music industry.

As Kilenyi stated:

> Our lessons consisted of analyzing and discussing classical masterpieces. George understood that he was not to learn "rules" according to which he himself would have to write music, but instead he would be shown what great composers had written, what devices, styles, traditions—later wrongly called rules—they used.[5]

Kilenyi also imparted a sense of freedom to his young, impressionable student, guiding him to express his own thoughts, ideas, and feelings without concern for formal technique. Instead, Kilenyi relied on the great musical masters as examples of expressionism, thus showing Gershwin how the masters expressed their ideas musically.

To gain a richer and more nuanced understanding of each of the orchestra instruments, Gershwin asked Kilenyi to arrange a lesson for him on each one. As biographer Merle Armitage wrote:

> Kilenyi engaged orchestral players to come and explain, and play, each instrument in the orchestra. This invaluable experience enabled George to grasp the meaning as well as the possibilities of each instrument. When George began his larger works, he had an excellent knowledge of how far he could push his ideas within the compass of the conventional orchestra. In later years he showed many players latent or unsuspected powers of instruments they had played for years. Only a few conductors and not many composers have been so informed and armed.[6]

One of my favorite songs is a little-known ditty titled "Lullaby for String Quartet," which Gershwin composed during the Kilenyi period. Brother Ira dated its creation to 1919 or 1920.[7] It was George's first serious piece of concert music, composed by a twenty (or twenty-one-year-old) just starting to spread his creative wings, and it is truly spectacular. (I listen to this song all the time; indeed the Julliard Quartet performs it beautifully.)

George studied with Kilenyi for about five years, continuing sporadic lessons with him until the early 1920s. Unfortunately, his original teacher, Hambitzer died unexpectedly in 1918 of tuberculosis while working with Gershwin on the Chopin *Preludes*. After Hambitzer's death, George always spoke reverently of him as, "the first great musical influence in my life" and "the greatest musical influence in my life."[8]

Gershwin continued to study with a number of musical masters over the next few years. *The New Yorker's* January 1, 1927, issue indicated that Gershwin "was studying piano with Ernest Hutcheson and harmony with Rubin Goldmark."[9] It went on to note:

> After the manner of Beethoven, Gershwin sets down in a sketch-book every musical idea that occurs to him, with the date of its birth

and its subsequent development. Sometimes there is no subsequent development, for he is his own severest critic, and the volume is dotted with forlorn little ideas that never grew up.[10]

In the course of his early musical studies, somewhere between Hambitzer and Kilenyi, George decided to devote himself entirely to music, since he was a horrible student and constantly in and out of trouble when he wasn't playing hooky. He officially dropped out of the High School of Commerce, a vocational school, at the age of fifteen. Yes, George Gershwin was a high school dropout—much to the dismay of his mother, Rose. Like all Jewish mothers (including mine), Rose felt music was nice . . . but you still needed a profession to pay the bills. She wanted her son to become an accountant. However, his passion for music was all consuming and undeniable, and in time, she had no choice but to let her son pursue his musical ambition and his genius.

I'm On My Way*

*Porgy and Bess (1935)

After dropping out of high school, George took a job as a song plugger, piano pounder, and staff pianist with the music publisher Jerome H. Remick & Company, for $15 a week ($350 today). The job earned George the title of Tin Pan Alley's youngest song plugger ever.

Jerome Remick had moved his publishing company from Detroit to New York City in 1902. The office was located on West 28th Street off of Broadway, and although it started out as a small business, Remick eventually became a music-publishing heavyweight thanks to blockbuster hits that included "Bye Bye Blackbird"; "Oh, You Beautiful Doll"; "I'm Looking Over a Four Leaf Clover"; and "Shine On, Harvest Moon." By the time George was hired, Remick's was a big force in the music publishing biz.

As a song plugger there, Gershwin was ideally positioned to develop his musical chops. He played the piano for hours on end, selling songs to a wide variety of customers who included singers, dancers, vaudeville types, Broadway producers, and more. His sight-reading skills grew by leaps and bounds. Singers needed him to transpose songs on the spot to suit their vocal ranges. It was an intense on-the-job training immersion that would help young George for many years to come.

Playing for hours on end, day after day, can easily blow out a piano player's hands and fingers. Fortunately, Charles Hambitzer had taught Gershwin to play with a "loose wrist." This technique prevented the permanent damage that the long, arduous hours of playing would surely have inflicted on his hands and fingers otherwise.

While working at Remick's as a teenager, Gershwin was able to rub elbows with the show biz elite—and the not so elite, for that matter. He met Broadway stars, up and comers, unknowns, losers, winners, composers, lyrists, shysters, and gangsters, all part of the vast array of chaos known as Tin Pan Alley. As the lyricist and composer Irving Caesar remembers:

> I met him for the first time at Remick's when it was on 46th Street. Remick's was an amazing place. There was always something happening. Performers would be there to hear new songs for their acts, and it was a real beehive of rehearsal activity. George was a much-sought-after accompanist there. They all loved to have George play the new songs for them. He was like a salesman exposing the inventory, and the songs were inventory. He was a great salesman because the way he played the piano was unique.[1]

A notable friendship formed between Gershwin and two other talented teens, the fabulous dance team of Fred and Adele Astaire. In Fred Astaire's autobiography, *Steps in Time*, he described his first encounter with Gershwin:

> I would go to the various music publishers looking for material, and George was a piano player demonstrating songs at Jerome H. Remick's. We struck up a friendship at once. He was amused by my piano playing and often made me play for him. I had a sort of knocked-out slap left-hand technique and the beat pleased him. He'd often stop me and say, "Wait a minute, Freddie, do that one again."
>
> I told George how my sister and I longed to get into musical comedy. He in turn wanted to write one. He said, "Wouldn't it be great if I could write a musical show and you could be in it?" That thought materialized only a few years later when Adele and I were in *Lady, Be Good!* at the Liberty Theatre, New York, music by George Gershwin, lyrics by Ira Gershwin. I was fortunate later on to do several pictures with scores by George and his brother, Ira.[2]

What an interesting retrospect and look into the formative days of these talented teens with big dreams—and the fortitude to make them come true!

George was building a reputation at Remick's as the go-to guy to play the piano. In fact, after a visit to Remick's, the theater critic Max Abramson began calling Gershwin "the genius." The black cats were taking notice of George as well. All the heavyweight black piano players of the day knew his name, and when ragtime piano great Eubie Blake (who wrote the hit song "I'm Just Wild About Harry") arrived in New York in 1916, he said of Gershwin:

> James P. Johnson and Luckey Roberts told me of this very talented ofay (white guy) piano player at Remick's. They said he was good enough to learn some of those terribly difficult tricks that only a few of us could master.[3]

Stride piano innovator Luckey Roberts (composer of the hit tune "Moonlight Cocktail") also encountered the young Gershwin at Remick's. As he remembers that meeting:

> Bert Williams and Will Vodery (Ziegfeld's conductor) were the ones that got me to teach George Gershwin. At that time he couldn't play. He didn't have a tune in his head. He was selling orchestrations at Remick and stood behind the counter, and Will Vodery said, "Son, help him along. He's very ambitious." He couldn't play jazz, but he had two good hands for the classics.[4]

In 1916, when his song "When You Want 'Em, You Can't Get 'Em, When You've Got 'Em You Don't Want 'Em" was accepted by a Remick publishing competitor, Harry Von Tilzer, George officially stepped up from plugger to composer. He now also gained new insight into the business of music publishing.

Believe it or not, the lyrist Murray Roth earned $15 from the deal, and Gershwin got only $5. Why did the lyricist get $15 and the composer only $5? Were the words more important than the music? Not really. It was George's first business deal, and he decided to take a risk. Murray Roth and George were both offered a $15 advance for the song. Roth took the offer, but George opted for nothing up front and a lump sum *with* royalties on the back end. After some time, Gershwin approached Tilzer and asked him for some cash for the song. Tilzer reached into his pocket and handed Gershwin a $5 bill. Those five bucks were all Gershwin ever received for his first tune. As far as Tilzer was concerned, however, the deal was paid in full. Books closed.[5] Young George learned an important lesson that day . . . something about a bird in the hand . . . ?

George stayed at Remick's for three years, playing day in and day out. He then decided to move on to greener pastures. One reason for his leaving was that Remick's management showed absolutely no interest in publishing any of his songs. To management, Gershwin was a song plugger, and that was all. They already had songwriters on staff, so George's skills were not needed in that department, and they made that point crystal clear to him.

Gershwin quit his $15-a-week Remick job in March 1917 without any job prospects in sight. As Gershwin told interviewer George Newell, "I just walked out. It wasn't what I wanted. No, I did not have any other job in view. That $15 was all I was making."[6]

For George, enough was enough. This decision was before he had any income from royalties, so times were tough, money was tight, and Gershwin had to begin "paying his dues." To make ends meet, he cut piano rolls and worked some club dates and small gigs, including a several week stint with a small combo in a Brooklyn nightclub.

His friend, black conductor/arranger Will Vodery, helped him find some gigs. One was at Fox's City Theatre on 14th Street, where George replaced none other than—get this—Groucho Marx's older piano playing brother, Chico! George was asked to play piano while the orchestra took their supper break. It was an incredible opportunity that paid $25 a week (just shy of $500/week today)—but for George, it was a disastrous one-night stand. He screwed it up royally. Being unfamiliar with show tunes, he started playing different songs than the chorus was singing. Smelling blood in the water, the show's comedian ripped the young kid apart. Everyone, from the singers to the audience, laughed at him. It was just too much for George to bear. He stopped playing mid-song. As the old saying goes, "the show must go on," so the singers continued even without their piano accompaniment. Humiliated, George left the theater without even stopping for his check. Later on in life, he admitted, "The whole experience left a scar on my memory."[7]

If even a virtuoso can have an off day, perhaps we mere mortals shouldn't be so hard on ourselves. At least, when we screw up, it isn't in front of a large audience with a professional comedian roasting us!

George refused to let this one miscue slow his momentum. His youth, vitality, and exceptional piano skills quickly landed him other pianist jobs around town, and he soon became a local darling, so to speak.

He caught the attention of the major music publisher Max Dreyfus, head honcho of T.B. Harms Publishing, and in February 1918, Dreyfus made George an offer he could not refuse, that of staff composer for $35 per week ($550 today). All he had to do was compose songs—no more grueling song plugging for him. In addition, if Harms published any of George's songs, he would earn another $50 ($800 today) per tune plus three cents (fifty cents today) per each copy of sheet music sold. This was a great deal for the young upstart, and it marked the beginning of a long and mutually beneficial relationship between George and Harms. In fact, Gershwin remained with Harms and its sister companies for the rest of his life.

During that first year at Harms, George didn't exactly set the world on fire. Only one composition was published: "Some Wonderful Sort of Something." But with $35 a week in steady income, plus side gigs moonlighting as a rehearsal pianist for Broadway shows and cutting piano rolls to boot, the kid was working hard and finally making some real loot.

Any Little Tune*

*The Rainbow (1923)

I stood outside a penny arcade listening to an automatic piano leaping through Rubinstein's Melody in F. The peculiar jumps in the music held me rooted. To this very day I can't hear the tune without picturing myself outside the arcade on 125th Street, standing there barefoot and in overalls, drinking it all in avidly.

—GEORGE GERSHWIN[1]

Let's turn the clock back a few years to late 1915, when George first started to cut piano rolls. He was still a full-time song plugger at Remick, making $15 a week. The piano roll business was where he always turned to pick up some additional scratch.

Although just a teenager, Gershwin was hired by piano roll manufacturers to perform the music that would ring out of player pianos on piano rolls across the nation. On Saturday afternoons, he traveled out to Standard Music Company's Perfection Studios in East Orange, New Jersey, to cut piano rolls. He earned $5 per roll and $35 for six rolls ($100–$800 today ... the average American weekly salary at the time was $15). This extra income was crucial to George, and so he continued to cut piano rolls for eleven years, achieving a total of about 130 rolls. In 1916 alone, he cut a total of 40 rolls for the two competing piano roll industry giants, the Standard Company as well as the Aeolian Company.

The player piano (also known as a pianola) was all the rage from the early 1900s until the stock market crashed in 1929. During its heyday, these devices could be found in homes, bars, restaurants, penny arcades, and many other venues. This fad was before the record and radio industry took the nation by storm, so sheet music and piano rolls were the two primary ways to deliver music to the masses at that time. To get the gadget going, someone had to pump up the bellows with a foot pump; later models included electric motors. As the paper passed through a reader, the machine depressed a corresponding key, sounding a note (or several notes at a time, depending on the number of holes punched in the paper for the melody). It was a mechanical and cultural phenomenon, giving millions of people enormous pleasure and entertainment.

In 1917, Gershwin stopped working with Standard altogether and focused on the Aeolian Company, which was located on 42nd Street between 5th and 6th Avenues right across from Bryant Park and the New York 42nd Street Public Library. The Aeolian Company released his rolls under several labels: "Duo-Art"; "Mel-O-

Dee"; "Metro-Art"; "Universal"; Universal Song Roll"; and "Universal Uni-Roll."

The Aeolian Duo-Art player piano and its rolls boasted state-of-the-art technology. This high-end machine let the piano reproduce the expression and dynamics of the music far more accurately than any other "automatic piano" before it. It was so sharp that Aeolian performed blindfold tests on music experts as a marketing tactic. Aeolian would blindfold experts and have one of their automatic pianos play a tune and then have a live musician play the same tune, or vice versa. The experts were not able to tell the difference between the live or recorded performance, thus proving time and time again, that the Duo-Art could reproduce a live performance with sterling accuracy.

In his work for Aeolian, Gershwin sometimes used pseudonyms, including Fred Murtha, James Baker, and Burt Wynn (which was a tip of the hat to his hero, the comedian Ed Wynn). Early on, he cut other composers' music on the rolls, but as the years progressed, George started to cut more and more of his own compositions. Naturally, his rolls reflected a marked progression in his own skills over time, evolving from a youthful style to a much more sophisticated one. Savvy listeners can actually hear his virtuoso improvisational skills develop as this young artist matured into the medium.

As Gershwin's fame increased, the producers gave him more and more creative freedom. He experimented with a form of overdubbing, superimposing a second piano performance onto the first rendition. This technique made for a very interesting performance that delivered more depth and a fuller sound. (There are several albums available today of the piano roll songs performed by Gershwin, and they are truly amazing. The songs have been digitally remastered, reflecting the virtuosity of Gershwin alone on the piano. These must-buy items are easily found on the Internet.) In addition, Gershwin occasionally recorded duets with other artists, including Rudolph O. Erlebach (fifteen rolls), Edwin E. Wilson (six duets), Cliff Hess (one duet), and Muriel Pollock (one duet).[2]

Over the years, player piano technology continued to improve, adding much more expression and sophistication to the music. Advanced player pianos were much more costly; the piano rolls for these instruments also cost more. The numbers will illustrate the difference:

In 1924, the cost of a traditional upright player piano was about $600 ($8,000 today); an Aeolian baby grand was $1,850 ($25,000 today). A top-of-the-line Steinway seven-foot baby grand ran a whopping $4,675 ($65,000 today)! By 1927, as the player piano craze reached its high-water mark, a Steinway player piano retailed for $7,000 ($96,000 today)—not including the cost of the individual piano rolls. The prices of rolls are harder to pin down, but they ranged from about 30 cents to $1.75 ($4 to $25 today). Still, the player piano's heyday was a short one. After the stock market crash in 1929 and the advent and popularity of records and radio, the player piano quickly lost its luster.[3]

There is much more to appreciate regarding George's piano roll inventory, but my publisher is *kvetching* to me about running short of paper and ink; therefore, I need to wrap this part of the story. Those who are interested should invest in some of the Gershwin piano rolls albums. They clearly demonstrate Gershwin's virtuosity on the piano (even though the recordings are lifted from such a mechanical source), and they include some very informative booklets that help explain both the piano roll industry as well as Gershwin's performances on the rolls. Another great source is a book by Robert Kimball and Alfred Simon, titled *The Gershwins*. It contains a

Piano Rollography of Gershwin's piano rolls compiled by Michael Montgomery.[4] A piano rollography—is that a typo? No. In the back of the book, the authors include a Gershwin Piano Rollography—in other words, a "bibliography" of all the known Gershwin piano rolls. It's an excellent reference (although since its publication in 1973, new information and piano roll discoveries should be added). The more current albums fill in some of this new important information in their descriptions.

Now that I'm on a roll, here are a few of Gershwin's most noteworthy rolls:

"Bring Along Your Dancing Shoes"—Released in January 1916, it was Gershwin's first piano roll. Cut in 1915 (the time from cutting to release was approximately three months), the song was written by Gus Kahn ("Ain't We Got Fun" and "Makin' Whoopee"). Also in January of the same year, "Kangaroo Hop" was released. Like many of Gershwin's early piano rolls, these first two songs were written by other composers.

In June 1916, the Perfection label released two piano rolls of Yiddish music with Gershwin on piano: "Das Pintele Yud" (The Jewish Spark) and "Gott un Sein Mishpet Is Gerecht" (G-d and His Judgment Are True). Both songs had been around for years and were featured in the Yiddish Theatre long before Gershwin cut the rolls. They are reminiscent of Gershwin's childhood on the Lower East Side in the heart of the Yiddish Theatre District.

"When You Want 'Em, You Can't Get 'Em, When You've Got 'Em, You Don't Want 'Em"—Released in September 1916, under both the "Metro-Art" and "Universal Uni-Record" labels, this was the first Gershwin song to be published. He recorded it on a piano roll for the Aeolian Company, making it the first ever recording of Gershwin playing Gershwin. Prior to this release, Gershwin had cut thirty-four piano rolls, but of other composers' material.

"Rialto Ripples"—This rag was the first Gershwin song that Remick ever published. It appeared in 1917, which meant that after nearly three years as a song plugger for the company, it finally broke down and published one of his tunes. Gershwin collaborated on this song with fellow Tin Pan Alley veteran Will Donaldson (who wrote the lyrics to "Do Wacka Doo"). Gershwin cut the piano roll for the Aeolian Company in 1916, and it was released in September under the "Metro-Art" and Universal Uni-Record" labels.

"Swanee"—A blockbuster hit after Al Jolson performed the tune in blackface for the Broadway show *Sinbad*. Gershwin wrote "Swanee" in 1919, and his piano roll was released in February 1920 (just one month after Jolson made his blockbuster recording) under the "Mel-O-Dee" and "Duo-Art" labels. Like his other piano rolls, this fantastic performance demonstrates his virtuosic abilities and absolute mastery of the piano.

"Waiting for the Sun to Come Out"—This roll was the very first collaboration between the Brothers Gershwin; George wrote the music and older brother, Ira, wrote the lyrics. It was Ira's first published song as a lyricist, but he used the pseudonym Arthur Francis in the credits. (Arthur Francis was an inside joke . . . a combination of their younger siblings' names.) The roll was released in October 1920 under the "Mel-O-Dee" banner.

"Rhapsody in Blue"—The song became a smash hit after it premiered at the much-acclaimed Aeolian Hall concert on February 12, 1924. (Much more on that to come.) The roll was initially released in May 1925, but oddly, only *Part II: the Andantino and Finale* was released first. Eighteen months later in January 1927, *Rhapsody* in Blue, Part I* was released. Rollologists (yes, it's a term I made up) are baffled by this strange order of release and the time lapse between the two. Both parts were cut at the same recording session in 1925. Both parts were released under the "Duo-Art" label. One thing is for sure though; hearing Gershwin personally performing his signature piece is truly a gift.

Probably the last rolls he ever cut, both released under the "Duo-Art" and "Mel-O-Dee" banners in April 1926, are "Sweet and Low-Down" and "That Certain Feeling," both of which were featured in the Broadway show *Tip-Toes*.

Before moving on, I want to thank the folks who preserved these piano rolls and then digitally remastered them, so modern audiences can hear Gershwin playing, improvising, and sharing his unique creative genius. I would also like to thank Robert Kimball and Alfred Simon, authors of *The Gershwins*, for including in their book a detailed Gershwin Piano Rollography (compiled by Michael Montgomery). Their efforts are a tremendous gift to Gershwin fans and music historians everywhere.

Wake Up, Brother, and Dance*

*Shall We Dance (Unused) (1937)

A fondness for music, a feeling for rhyme, a sense of whimsy and humor, an eye for the balanced sentence, an ear for the current phrase, and the ability to imagine oneself a performer trying to put over the number in progress . . .
—IRA GERSHWIN, ON THE QUALITIES OF A GOOD LYRICIST[1]

Morris and Rose Gershwin's firstborn son, Ira (Hebrew name Israel), was born in 1896, two years before George. These two boys were polar opposites. Ira was an introverted "good boy," known to be shy, quiet, and refined. His kid brother, George, was an extroverted juvenile-delinquent type, full of pep and vigor. Ira was dry and studious and yet also somewhat carefree; George was a hooky-playing troublemaker, always self-assured and aggressive. Ira enrolled in City College in 1914 majoring in English but then quit before getting a degree; George was a high school dropout.

Ira was *bar mitzvah'd*, but neither George nor his younger brother, Arthur, ever were. (Their youngest sibling, Frances aka Frankie, was not *bat mitzvah'd*, since it was not customary for girls at that time, as it is today.) Ira's *bar mitzvah* was quite an affair. Two hundred guests at two bucks a plate (about ten grand today) were hosted at the luxurious kosher Zeitlan's Restaurant on Grand Street, just a couple of blocks north of Canal Street.[2] Mama Rose threw one heck of a shindig, which she did not do for her other kids. I guess George could have said to Ira, "Mama always liked you better." But that's another story, and "It Ain't Necessarily So."

Unlike George, who definitely knew his future was in music, it took some time for Ira to find his passion. He eventually became a master lyricist, but it was not a straight path. As a young adult, he bounced from job to job, searching for a career he loved. He tried his hand as a desk clerk at his father's businesses—Lafayette Baths in downtown Manhattan and St. Nicholas Baths on 111th Street, but both went belly up, pun intended. He then took a job in the receiving room at the midtown Manhattan department store B. Altman and Company on 5th Avenue and 34th Street for a short stint. He even worked as the secretary-treasurer of a Midwest tent carnival called *Colonel Lagg's Great Empire Show*. In Ira's own words:

> I was lucky to get that job . . . the other treasurer had absconded. And I got $35 a week, too, only $5 less than the highest-paid man in the show—the wire-walker. But I had to put up my own tent, and that title, secretary-treasurer, is just a lot of hokum for ticket-seller.[3]

With World War I still ablaze, he nearly ended up in the army, but the day he was ordered to report for duty was November 11, 1918—the day the Armistice was signed. (George had also prepared for war, purchasing a saxophone and learning to play it, so he could join the Army Band if need be.[4])

In 1918, the Brothers Gershwin collaborated on their first song: "The Real American Folk Song (Is a Rag)." From his earliest days as a professional lyricist, Ira used a pseudonym for his credits to avoid the inevitable assumption that he was riding on his brother's coattails. "Arthur Francis," as a nod to their younger siblings (as mentioned earlier), disguised his true identity all the way to 1924, allowing him to be judged for his artistic merits instead of his familial ties.

When Ira was ready to assume his own name publicly, he put much thought into choosing the "right" professional name. Although his given name was Isidore (Israel) and everyone called him Iz or Izzy, he finally decided on Ira because it was an uncommon name at the time.

He dropped his pseudonym for the first time in 1924, not so coincidentally on a showtune titled "Be Yourself"! Also in 1924, Ira first wrote all the lyrics to his younger brother's Broadway musical *Lady, Be Good!*

Many people have wondered just how did the Gershwin brothers create their masterpieces? What was their process? Did George write down the notes and give them to Ira, or did Ira write down some lyrics and pass them to George?

Jules Meler, a reporter for a global news service, asked George, "So Mr. Gershwin, what really comes first, the music or the words? Do you punch out some notes to your brother Ira and he thinks up some catchy lyrics or does Ira feed you one of his unique phrases and you put it to music? Which is it? Music then lyrics? Or lyrics then music?"

George took a long pull on his cigar and exhaled a plume of smoke, ending with a few smoke rings. His dark brown eyes gazed deeply into his interviewer's, and after a long pause, Gershwin replied, "Ah, the old 'which came first, the chicken or egg' question? I get this all the time. What comes first, the music or the words? Or is it the words and then the music? Well Jules, the answer is . . . the contract!"

Great answer!

Actually . . . I made this story up. It never happened. It is an old generic songwriter's joke that I lifted in part from the Jablonski and Stewart biography, *The Gershwin Years*.

In truth, Gershwin asked and then answered this proverbial question in an article he wrote in 1930 for the *New York Sunday World Magazine*, as follows:

> What comes first, the words or the music? Odd, how this question is the first which enters the mind of most people when the art of writing songs is under discussion. In my own case most frequently the music is written first. Often, however, my brother Ira will write the lyric first, but always in a definite rhythm. These songs are mainly of the comedy variety.[5]

Ira, on the other hand, put it this way in his autobiography, *Lyrics on Several Occasions:*

> Every songwriter has been put this question many times, and by now nearly all interested know that no rule obtains; sometimes it's the lyric and sometimes the tune. And sometimes—more often than not these days—the words and music are written practically at the same time; this, when collaborators are at work together (in the same room, that is—though I have heard of collaboration on the telephone); and a song, sparked either by a possible title or by a likely snatch of tune, emerges line by line and section by section.[6]

In their years of collaboration, the Gershwin brothers usually started with the music first—but Ira's creative genius must not be considered an afterthought. Sometimes the long shadow cast by his younger brother, George, overshadows the recognition that Ira should have had and still have today. But make no mistake, Ira was an exceptionally gifted giant of a lyricist, and George was well aware of his older sibling's genius. Ira was indeed immersed in the creative process on every level. The two evolved a method of working together that worked for them and transformed the brothers into one of music's greatest creative teams.

Ira opined about his lyric writing technique in his own unique scientific, analytical manner:

> The important thing about a lyric to me is the title and idea. You get an idea, you put it as a theorem in your title, you prove it . . . to the listener's satisfaction in the lines that follow.[7]

Yet, he did not sacrifice everything just for the sake of the rhyme.

Ira was also the master of the contraction. He explained that it was a vaudevillian comedian who inspired him to use them:

> Hearing Walter Catlett use words like pash for passion, delish for delicious gave me the notions for half a dozen songs like *Sunny Disposish* and *'S Wonderful.*[8]

Family friend and virtuoso pianist, Oscar Levant, said of the relationship between George and Ira:

> Theirs were talents that suffused and penetrated each other, paralleled and completed each other remarkably. . . . Ira's curious whimsically and dryness, the brilliant finish and cohesion of his lyrics were a definite stimulus to George. One could not tire of the clean detail and effortless smoothness (in their final effect) of his texts . . . the brightness of Ira's thought acted as a spur to George's musical resources and produced many songs that departed from the conventions they had found. They also strongly influenced others. . . . Ira paralleled George's diversity of talents with his own skill in painting, his excellent tennis.[9]

The Brothers Gershwin soon became a hot ticket in the news. Appearing on the cover of the July 20, 1925, issue of then two-year-old news magazine, *Newsweek*, a picture of George was the first ever composer to be on a front cover. The article inside was titled, "Gershwin Bros." It was now obvious that they were very firmly joined at the hip with the news media and the American public.

Although Ira was a quiet, refined guy, he also had a sharp, dry wit as shown in the following story:

> While at a dinner party with some artsy-fartsy types, Ira accidentally dropped some beets on his freshly laundered and pressed white shirt. He became very agitated and upset, complaining to everyone at the table about his bad

misfortune. The guests attempted to console him, but to no avail. After some minutes of kvetching, Ira blurted out, "It's terrible when a songwriter drops a beet."[10]

Even though the Gershwin family's first piano was purchased with the idea of firstborn son Ira taking it up, he immediately and happily relinquished it to the talented and enthusiastic George. In fact, even though Ira is today a music legend, he never was able to read musical notation. Ira played the piano using the one-finger pecking method.

I found a contract for several songs that included both the music and lyrics and signed by both brothers. The contract stipulated that George would receive 60% of the agreed fee and Ira, the remaining 40%. Again, this contract was for several songs, so I cannot say if this was typical or not, but this sixty/forty split seems plausible to me.

The brothers loved each other and clearly admired each other's uniqueness.

George said of Ira: "Never a worry. If not today, tomorrow. That's how he always feels. Isn't it wonderful to feel that way?"[11]

And Ira said of George: "Nothing discourages him, always ready to jump into harness. Or tackle four things at a time. Isn't it wonderful to be that way?"[12]

George also opined about his gifted brother and partner:

> Now, in song lyric writing, sound is one of the most important things, and I don't think anybody surpasses my brother, Ira, when it comes to inventing song titles. He fancies abbreviation. For example, "Sunny Disposish" and "'S Wonderful." And don't ever let Ira hear you say "It's Wonderful." Just 'S Wonderful, 'S Marvelous."[13]

Pianist, composer, and conductor Alexander Steinert said of the Brothers Gershwin:

> George's relationship with his brother Ira was a most interesting one, and more than by blood. Each had a profound influence on the other; each completed the other. When they collaborated on popular music, George's understanding of the lyrics equaled his brother's feeling for music. They worked with an amazing rapidity and seemingly without effort, although those close to them knew how often they would struggle over a single phrase.[14]

In 1932, Ira Gershwin was honored to win the Pulitzer Prize for the lyrics to the Broadway hit musical "Of Thee I Sing." This was the first time a Broadway musical had won the coveted prize. But only the lyrics won the Pulitzer, not the music! George never received the Pulitzer, because at the time the prize did not include music.

Cinderrelatives*

*George White's Scandals of 1922 (1922)

I am a leading composer of unpublished songs.
—ARTHUR GERSHWIN[1]

Ira was the shy, quiet brother; George was the outgoing, energetic one; and Arthur was the funny one. Youngest of the Gershwin brothers, Arthur (1900–1981) ended up a stockbroker, but he did show some sparks of musical ability. He wrote over 100 songs, including "Invitation to the Blues," which was featured in the 1982 film *Tootsie*. In 1934, on one of George's radio programs, Arthur performed some of his music, and the youngest Gershwin sibling Frances sang some songs. The talent really was everywhere in this family.

Of the three brothers, Arthur was the only one who produced a male offspring to carry on the Gershwin name, an accomplishment that was and still is a very significant achievement for Jewish males (although, these days, nobody is willing to admit it since it is considered politically incorrect).

The pretty kid sister, Frances (1906–1999), or Frankie as she was called, was born on December 6, 1906—ten years to the day after her oldest brother, Ira. Frankie was a very talented painter (as were her brothers, Ira and George; more on that later), but that was just one of her many gifts. She became a professional singer and dancer while still a child—the first of the Gershwin kids to go on the road. In 1917, at the tender age of ten, she joined a road show, earning an astounding $40 a week ($750 today).[2] Leveraging both her talents and beauty, she continued performing on the vaudeville circuit as a singer and dancer well into the 1920s.

Later in life, she married Leopold Godowsky, Jr., son of the world-renowned concert pianist and composer Leopold Godowsky. Junior was a concert violinist, as well as the co-inventor of Kodachrome color photography ("So Mama, don't take my Kodachrome away"). They had one son and three daughters.

Rose and Morris Gershwin, parents of the Gershwin kids, were known to be detached emotionally from each other as well as from their children. Some have suggested that the four children were all emotionally detached, just like their parents. Be that as it may, one thing is for sure: George and Ira appeared to be connected at the hip all of their lives.

"Papa" Morris had a thick Yiddish accent. Once he was stopped by a police officer and tried to get out of a ticket by asking, "Do you know who mine son is? He is "Judge" Gershvin (George converts to Judge when put through the Yiddish tongue). The cop promptly let Papa off the hook. Morris always thought it was because of his son's fame. If the truth be told, however, the cop thought the fellow was the father of "Judge" Gershvin! And he did not want to mess with City Hall.

A 1929 article by S. N. Behrman in *The New Yorker* describes Mrs. Gershwin as a "level-headed and practical" woman. Behrman then continues to offer some insights on Papa Gershwin:

> He is short, rotund, inclined to literalness, and he has that singular unerring faculty which certain originals have for saying, in any situation, that final thing beyond which there is nothing left to be said . . .
>
> The family was discussing the new Einstein paper and George commented on the astonishing compactness of the scientific vocabulary:
>
> "Imagine working for twenty years and putting your results into three pages!"
>
> "Well," said Mr. Gershwin calmly, "it was probably very small print."[3]

Swanee*

*New York City revue *Demi-Tasse* (1919); *Sinbad* (1920)

*My mother is the sort of woman
for whom composers write mammy-songs.
Only—I mean them.*

—GEORGE GERSHWIN[1]

Young George achieved musical success early in his career as a Tin Pan Alley hack. His first tune, "When You Want 'Em, You Can't Get 'Em, When You've Got 'Em, You Don't Want 'Em," was published when he was eighteen, earning the fledgling composer five bucks. It was the first five bucks in his march to millions, which would happen sooner than anyone could have ever guessed. Just a short two years later, in 1919, George wrote his first blockbuster hit at the tender age of twenty. "Swanee" sold millions of copies of sheet music—the most of any song Gershwin would ever write; the phonograph record alone sold 2.25 million copies![2]

"Swanee" started as an idea from the lyricist Irving Caesar, who wanted to write a song to ride the coattails of "Hindustan," a popular one-step song that was sweeping the country. Eager to give his song an American feel, Caesar discussed the idea with George, first at a restaurant called Dinty Moore's on West 46th Street, and then on a bus heading uptown toward George's Washington Heights home. Upon entering the Gershwins' brownstone, they hurried past Papa's weekly poker game and sat down at the piano. There, in that smoke-filled parlor, they completed the song in just fifteen minutes. It was the song that would change their lives.[3]

Gershwin inserted an interesting twist in the song by reaching back to the mid-1800s to quote Stephen Foster's most famous song, "Old Folks at Home." It was a popular song on the minstrel circuit, often performed by the 19th-century blackface group Christy's Minstrels. (It is also the official state song of Florida.) If you are wondering what "Old Folks at Home," written over seventy years earlier, had to do with Gershwin's "Swanee," just consider the lyrics. "Old Folks at Home" lyrics mention, "Way down upon the Swanee River." Many people actually know the song as "Swanee River." In quoting this classic in his own 20th-century hit, Gershwin made a very clever connection to the past.

"Swanee" was first performed by the famous Arthur Pryor Band at the Capitol Theatre, but it did not win over the audience. Gershwin and Caesar hung around the theater lobby, trying to gauge the sales of the sheet music, but to their disappointment, the sales were dismal. The local music store sales fared no better. In a moment of despair, Caesar said he would sell his rights to the lyrics for $200 ($2,300 today). Fortunately, his pal George talked him out of this foolish idea.

One evening at Bessie Blood's House of Fame, a swank whorehouse where Gershwin played piano from time to time, Al Jolson heard the song and fell in love with it.[4] He added "Swanee" to his current show, Sinbad. After Jolson belted it out onstage, the song became a major hit, reaping Gershwin and Caesar over $10,000 each —more money than either had ever seen.[5] (Adjusting for inflation, $10,000 in 1919 would equal about $138,000 today.)

Gershwin said that after Jolson sang the song in Sinbad, "Swanee" penetrated to the four corners of the Earth."[6] It earned the young composer a notable degree of popularity in Europe, and at just the age of twenty, Gershwin was well on his way to becoming an international sensation.

Without a doubt, Swanee set Gershwin's career on the fast track. In 1920, he landed a gig composing for George White's Scandals, a Broadway review format show fashioned after the Ziegfield Follies (which Gershwin worked in as well). Scandals featured lots of scantily clad showgirls in dance numbers, and the shows launched many popular artists' careers (e.g., The Three Stooges and W. C. Fields). The Scandals review shows were so successful that they ran for twenty years (1919–1939). For Gershwin, they became a steady gig that lent him name recognition in his early years.

The piano rolls of "Swanee," with Gershwin on the piano, were released in February 1920 under the Mel-O-Dee and Duo-Art labels. However, Jolson had beat him to market with a blockbuster recording of the song, which probably motivated George to cut the piano rolls and thus capitalize on the Jolson hit.

Despite the enormous success of this song, George wrestled with one major problem: Jolson performed "Swanee" in blackface—something Gershwin was very much against doing. Yet because he was so young and new, he was powerless to do anything about it. In 1922, the blackface issue arose again, this time in Gershwin's one-act jazz opera, Blue Monday, performed as part of George White's Scandals of 1922. Although it was set in Harlem and written with an all-black cast of characters, the producer chose to present an all-white cast in blackface instead. Again, as a former lowly Tin Pan Alley song plugger, Gershwin was powerless and unable to convince George White to use an all-black cast, as he had written the work. Later in his career, after he gained fame and industry status, Gershwin had the power to prevent such reoccurrences—and he did when he insisted that his folk opera, Porgy and Bess, be performed by blacks (as opposed to whites in blackface).

The writer Gilbert Seldes said of "Swanee":

To have heard Al Jolson sing this song is to have had one of the few great experiences which the minor arts are capable of giving; to have heard it without feeling something obscure and powerful and rich with a separate life of its own coming into being, is—I should say it is not to be alive. The verse is simple and direct, with faint foreshadowings of the subtly divided, subtly compounded elements of the chorus where the name "Swanee," with a strong beat, long drawn and tender, ushers in the swift passages leading to the repetition, slow again, of the name . . . it has a strongly individual quality, a definite personal touch. Mr. Gershwin has progressed in his technical handling of syncopation . . . in "Swanee" he is at his highest point, for he has taken the simple emotion of longing and let it surge through his music, he has made real what a hundred before him had falsified. He should "do it again."[7]

Author's note: In ending the paragraph with "do it again," Seldes referenced a 1922 Gershwin hit song by that very name.

Blue Monday Blues*

*George White's Scandals of 1922 (1922)

Although he had matured considerably past his days of juvenile delinquency, George never really lost his deep-seated desire to push the envelope.

He partnered with lyricist Buddy DeSylva to write *Blue Monday,* a one-act operatic jazz work, for *George White's Scandals of 1922.* The two men sequestered themselves for five days and amazingly finished the entire opera in that time period.

They may have been inspired by the 1921 all-black, smash hit musical, *Shuffle Along,* which had a musical score written by the jazz piano great Eubie Blake and Noble Sissle. *Shuffle Along* featured the still-famous song, "I'm Just Wild About Harry" (Blake music with Sissle lyrics). The show ran for over 500 performances, an astonishing feat, especially for a musical written by blacks and featuring an all-black cast. Future stars like the singer/actor Paul Robeson and exotic dancer/singer/actress Josephine Baker got their starts in this show.

Perhaps producer George White sensed an opportunity to spice up his *Scandals of 1922* with some black culture. Maybe that's why he allowed a one-act black jazz opera performed by whites in blackface, set in Harlem, with music by the twenty-four-year-old Jewish George Gershwin, and performed by an all-white cast to be in his scantily-clad girlie show that featured The Three Stooges. We can only guess.

How many performances of this one-act, jazz operatic piece would George White permit? The entire season? Six months? Three months? One week? No . . . ONE PERFORMANCE! Actually, it is more accurate to say it ran for twenty minutes. That was the total timeframe of this one-act opera. The opera did not even come close to the expectations of the audience. They were paying to see half-naked wiggling girls and slapstick comedians; they did not want to be intellectually lifted by a "cultural experience." This twenty-minute operatic piece inserted into a Broadway vaudeville show was like playing Mozart as part of the Super Bowl Halftime show! A total fish out of water.

Professionally speaking, *Blue Monday* was a huge leap for Gershwin, and he knew it. A one-act opera was both daring and bold, and it seemed to suit Gershwin's style, but he was freaking out before the premiere, as stated:

> Before the opening night Gershwin began to suffer from constipation; this malady was to become chronic and since physicians were unable to put their finger on the source of the trouble, he always referred to it as his "composer's stomach."[1]

Blue Monday turned out to be a big trip-up for Gershwin, or so it seemed at the time. But that doesn't mean that the *Scandals of 1922* was a total bust for George either, because it wasn't. The first act closed with his show-stopping tune, "I'll Build a Stairway to Paradise." The tune became a popular hit and was featured in the 1951 film *An American in Paris*. "Stairway to Paradise" was also featured in classical singer Éva Gauthier's Aeolian Hall concert in November 1923.

As it turned out, Paul Whiteman and his orchestra were playing in the pit for the performance of *Blue Monday* (as well as for the entire 1922 *Scandals* season). Whiteman must have been pretty impressed by the gifted young Tin Pan Alley composer, because just over a year later, he commissioned Gershwin for *Rhapsody in Blue*.

Years later, in 1925, Whiteman dusted off *Blue Monday*, the one-night wonder and renamed it *135th Street*, thus reflecting the setting of the storyline in Harlem. Whiteman liked the one-act operatic piece very much and correctly understood that the *Scandals* venue was not the right place for it with its jiggling showgirls and all. Go figure! In December 1925, Whiteman's Orchestra performed the opera at the end of a Carnegie Hall concert, sans theater sets. Clearly, Gershwin and Whiteman shared the same risk-taking spirit. It was a spirit that has made the world a much better place.

The entire December run at Carnegie Hall that featured the new and improved one-act operetta, *135th Street*, was a smashing success. A *New York Times* review declared:

> Mr. Gershwin's' music, whether or not it proves the "grandest," was certainly the first in an opera premiere to be whistled within the hour on Broadway. . . . On a stage dedicated once to Tchaikovsky . . . and in the presence of a typical house . . . Blossom Steely and Charles Hart acted the swift tragedy of Harlem Mike's Saloon, with its "prologue" by Jack McGowan, "just like the white man's opera." The operetta and show end with the song, *I'm Goin' South in the Mornin'*. The song was sung by the crowd applauding out in front, it echoed later in the lobbies and was still in the air when a street full of limousines came surging to the carriage calls.[2]

Whiteman told Gershwin that, "he likes the themes of the black opera better than those of the *Rhapsody in Blue*."[3] But others were not so impressed. Music writer Oscar Thompson's opinion of *135th Street* was that it was a "one-act travesty on opera . . . downright insanity." He continued by saying it might be a better fit for a vaudeville stage where the audience could listen to it "as a crude and half-amateur parody on the worst features of the lyric drama."[4]

Gershwin's subsequent opera, *Porgy and Bess*, performed over a decade later, actually had its roots in *135th Street* and even further back to *Blue Monday*. They were all based on black American culture and premiered to mixed reviews by the critics. Certainly, many believe that *Porgy and Bess* was a Gershwin masterpiece.

Despite his theater critics, many top musicians of the day praised Gershwin's abilities during this early stage of his career. Tin Pan Alley cats like Jerome Kern and Irving Berlin lauded his skills, and others outside the Alley recognized his talents as well. Renowned classical pianist, composer, and child prodigy Beryl Rubinstein said George was a great composer, and his music was better than anyone's in New York at the time. In a 1922 interview (two years before *Rhapsody*), Rubinstein said:

> I am absolutely in earnest. . . . What I mean is that this young fellow George Gershwin, now at only 25, has the spark of musical genius which is definite. In his serious moods he has written some very worthwhile things . . .
>
> This young American composer has the fire of originality. . . . With Gershwin's style and seriousness he is not definitely from the popular music school, but one of the really outstanding figures in this country's serious musical efforts. . . . This young man has great charm and a most magnetic personality and I really believe that America will at no distant day honor this young man for his talent . . . and that when we speak of American composers George Gershwin's name will be prominent in the list.[5]

It seems whoever saw and heard this young man named George Gershwin immediately recognized he was someone very, very special.

Unique
Concert of Negro Music

COMPOSED AND RENDERED EXCLUSIVELY
by COLORED MUSICIANS

Carnegie :: Hall
MAY SECOND AT 8:15 P. M.

Under the Auspices and for the Benefit of
THE MUSIC SCHOOL SETTLEMENT
FOR COLORED PEOPLE

CARNEGIE HALL
Thursday Evening -- May 2, 1912
At 8.15 o'clock

CONCERT OF NEGRO MUSIC

Under the auspices of
The Music School Settlement for Colored People, Inc.

The Clef Club Orchestra
JAS. REESE EUROPE, Conductor;
WM. H. TYERS, Assistant Conductor.

Clef Club Male Chorus
WILL MARION COOK, Leader.

Choir St. Philip's Church
PAUL C. BOHLEN, Organist.

Royal Poinciana Quartette
Messrs. HILLARD, HAWKES, SUTTON and FOSTER.
By Courtesy of Reisenwebers.

Versatile Entertainers Quintette
Messrs. TUCK, MILLS, JACKSON, WHITNEY and JOHNSON.
By Courtesy of Bustanoby Bros.

J. Rosamond Johnson, Piano

Miss Elizabeth Payne, Contralto

Program continued on second page following

J. M. Gidding & Co.
564-566 AND 568 Fifth Avenue, 46TH AND 47TH STS.
WOMEN'S HIGH-CLASS OUTER APPAREL

Soon*

*Strike Up the Band (1930)

The first time "low-brow" American music was performed in a "high-brow" American venue was in 1912, when James Reece Europe and his Clef Club Orchestra performed a benefit concert for the Music School Settlement for Colored People, Inc., in none other than the classical hoity-toity capital of music, Carnegie Hall.

Europe was the son of a Washington, D.C., clergyman. He had moved to New York and put together a band of talented musicians. Europe's Clef Club Orchestra was made up of black musicians who were trained to read music—a notable skill at the time, seeing that most black musicians were still unable to read music (or even a word of English, for that matter).

Europe knew that white audiences would feel threatened by highly trained, literate, and technically excellent black musicians, so he chose to perpetuate the stereotype of the ignorant black musician who played unbelievable music due to some sort of innate gift, not the musical training white folks had. He required his excellent and highly trained musicians to memorize their songs, so when they played at the gigs, there would not be any music placed in front of them.

Using this marketing ploy, he got many gigs for his band, including some from high and mighty society folks like the Vanderbilts and the Astors.

PROGRAMME
Part I
1. Clef Club March......*Jas. Reese Europe*
Clef Club Orchestra, conducted by composer
2. Song, "Li'l Gal," Words by Paul Laurence Dunbar....*J. Rosamond Johnson*
The Composer
3. (a) Dance of the Marionettes
Hugh Woolford
(b) "You're Sweet to Your Mammy Just the Same"..........*Johnson*
Versatile Entertainers Quintette
4. (a) Tout à vous—Valse Petite
Wm. H. Tyers
(b) Panama—Characteristic dance
Wm. H. Tyers
Clef Club Orchestra, conducted by the composer
5. (a) Song "Jean"   *Henry T. Burleigh*
(b) Song "Suwanee River"   *Foster*
Miss Elizabeth Payne
6. Benedictus (from an original Mass)
Paul C. Bohlen
Choir of St. Phillip's Church, New York,
Paul C. Bohlen, Organist

Part II
7. "Swing Along," a Negro Melody
(See page 10 for words.)
Will Marion Cook
Clef Club Chorus, Will Marion Cook, Leader
8. Piano Solo, Danse Héroique
J. Rosamond Johnson
The Composer
9. (a) "Hula"—Hawaiian Dance *Europe*
(b) "On Bended Knee"......*Burleigh*
Clef Club Orchestra
10. "By the Waters of Babylon
Coleridge-Taylor
Choir of St. Phillip's Church,
Paul C. Bohlen, Organist
11. (a) Dearest Memories
(b) The Belle of the Lighthouse
(c) Take Me Back to Dear Old Dixie
(d) Old Black Joe
Royal Poinciana Quartette
12. "The Rain Song," words by Alex. Rogers
Will Marion Cook
Clef Club Chorus, Will Marion Cook, Leader
Assisted by Deacon Johnson's Martinique Quartette
13. (a) Lorraine Waltzes........*Europe*
(b) March, "Strength of the Nation,"
Dedicated to the proposed Colored
Regiment ....*Europe*
Clef Club Orchestra

Note: The performers at this concert are not pupils of the Settlement School, which has been in existence only six months, but have generously volunteered their services in aid of the School. See page 6 of this programme for information about the School.

CHICKERING PIANO USED
(By courtesy of John MacFarlane)
21 EAST 15th STREET

Although his strategy might be considered by some today to be morally questionable, his methods did serve to keep a whole slew of black musicians and their entourage well fed and well paid.

When James Reece Europe's Clef Club Orchestra played the benefit concert for the Music School Settlement for Colored People in Carnegie Hall on Thursday May 2, 1912, it was billed as a "Unique Concert of Negro Music, composed and rendered exclusively by Colored Musicians" and featuring a mix of jazz (in its earliest form), blues, ragtime, spirituals, and minstrel songs. The performance ended with a march composed by Europe and performed by his Clef Club Orchestra titled, "Strength of the Nation, Dedicated to the Proposed Colored Regiment." Although the concert occurred before the jazz era, it definitely showcased the precursors of the idiom. All of the songs in the concert were written and performed exclusively by blacks. As Carnegie Hall's website states, "Europe was among the first to translate the syncopated rhythms of African American music to a large ensemble."[1]

Although Europe led an orchestra of 125 musicians, including 10 pianos and 85 mandolins (talk about an overachiever!), the Carnegie Hall concert failed to leave a lasting impression on the public and did not lead to any follow-up concert gigs. So the genre stayed frozen in the "low culture" venues. It seems that high society was not yet ready for jazz.**

Europe's career was cut short by a stabbing during a backstage argument with one of his musicians when an angry drummer tragically stabbed and killed James Reece Europe in 1919. This event reminds me of the line my good friend and mentor, the late piano giant Eddie Higgins, used to say, "What kind of people like to hang around jazz musicians? . . . Drummers."

Although their career paths never intersected, James Reece Europe was highly influential in the musical development of George Gershwin. As the story goes, when George was a young boy:

> One day, while roller-skating in Harlem, he heard jazz music outside the Baron Wilkins Club where Jim Europe and his band performed regularly. The exciting rhythms and raucous tune made such an impression on him that he never forgot them. From then on he often skated up to the club and sat down on the sidewalk outside to listen to the music. He later told a friend that his lifelong fascination for Negro rags, blues, and spirituals undoubtedly began at this time, that Jim Europe's music was partially responsible for his writing works like "135th Street" and parts of "Porgy and Bess."[2]

James Reece Europe and his Clef Club Orchestra made history on that eventful Thursday evening. It marked the first time that jazz, or more accurately, the predecessors of jazz music, was heard in those hallowed halls. It took over eleven more years for jazz to be heard again at Carnegie Hall—not played by black cats, but rather performed by Éva Gauthier a classically trained prima donna and her surprising Jewish piano accompanist, George Gershwin.

Author's note: Regarding the program at the beginning of this section, I would like to thank the Carnegie Hall Trust for generously granting me permission to publish the original program of the concert. I would also like to give special thanks to Carnegie Halls' Gino Francesconi, Director, Archives & Museum for locating the program and helping me to obtain the rights. THANKS!

Oh, Lady, Be Good!*

Lady, Be Good! (1924)

In the July 1917 issue of *Seven Arts*, Kelly Moderwell wrote a piece titled, "A Modest Proposal." In the article, she sang the praises of ragtime music and proposed a concert of Negro spirituals and ragtime songs with the final segment of the concert to feature three Irving Berlin songs and one Jerome Kern tune. She challenged the serious music establishment to hold this concert in Aeolian Hall, the bastion of all things civilized. (This was seven years before *Rhapsody in Blue* premiered at Aeolian Hall.) Moderwell's "A Modest Proposal" fell on deaf ears and was ignored for seven years. Although one can say that Moderwell was quite the prognosticator predating *Rhapsody*, she seemed to have some memory failure since she did not mention James Reece Europe's concert in Carnegie Hall five years earlier. How quickly people forget! Now back to Aeolian Hall.

Aeolian Hall was located on 42nd Street, between 5th and 6th Avenues, across from Bryant Park and the 42nd Street Library. Built in 1912 for the Aeolian Company, which sold Pianolas (player pianos), the seventeen-story building stretched the entire block, from 42nd Street all the way to 43rd Street. It housed the Aeolian Company product showroom, corporate offices, and a 1,500-seat concert hall.

Seven years after Moderwell's "A Modest Proposal," someone picked up the gauntlet she had dropped. On November 1, 1923, Aeolian Hall hosted the "Recital of Ancient and Modern Music for Voice by Éva Gauthier." Madame Gauthier was a classically trained and highly regarded opera singer. Tickets were sold at the Aeolian Box Office (sorry, no Ticketmaster sales in those days), and ranged in price from 75 cents to $2; boxes were $15 ($10, $28, and $209, respectively today). All tickets carried a 10 percent war tax. (That's how we helped pay for our involvement in World War I.)

The program was pretty straightforward with tunes one would expect to hear in this type of venue. Songs by Béla Bartók, Darius Milhaud, Vincenzo Belinni, Arnold Schönberg, and other similar composers filled Parts I, II, IV and V of the program. But what about Part III?

Was there a gap in the middle of the show? No. Did the program proofreader mess up? No. Why am I even bringing it up then? What happened in Part III? The answer is that Part III was clearly included in the playbill and was a daring and groundbreaking segment of the performance.

Let's explore an interesting footnote here that has been all but forgotten in jazz history because, sometimes, even footnotes are crucially important (I call them Bigfoot notes). This Éva Gauthier performance was one of those seminal, yet forgotten, footnotes, in particular Part III of this concert.

In the spring of 1923, critic, photographer, and writer Carl Van Vechten suggested that Gauthier add some jazz songs to her fall concert. French composer Maurice Ravel (the "Bolero" guy) repeated the same idea to her. She then asked Van Vechten for suggestions on who should accompany her in this daring gamble. Who would dare to bring jazz into a bastion of "serious" music? Van Vechten could only think of one man who would fill the bill. It was our fearless hero, George Gershwin!

What did Gershwin know? And when did he know it? These are tough questions to answer about a concert that happened some ninety years ago, but I hold in my hands a copy of the playbill—and more to the point, the program page.

Part III had five American songs, composed by three different Jewish Tin Pan Alley song-plugger veterans. The first tune was "The Siren's Song" by Jerome Kern, followed by Irving Berlin's "Everybody Step." The final three songs were composed by none other than George Gershwin—"Innocent Ingénue Baby," "Stairway to Paradise," and "Swanee." At the bottom of this section of the playbill, in capital letters, is text that reads: "GEORGE GERSHWIN AT THE PIANO."

So, exactly 103 days before he would debut *Rhapsody in Blue* in that same exact venue, Gershwin was on the piano, accompanying a classical diva who was singing five tunes written by him and two other Jewish Tin Pan Alley tunesmiths (indeed three of the five songs were his).

Although Madame Gauthier was front and center and singing up a storm, Gershwin did draw attention to himself and his pianistic virtuosity, which he was always inclined to do. For the first time then, songs from the Great American Songbook were played in a highbrow, hoity-toity concert hall by a He-bro, and George Gershwin was at the center of it all.

Eva and Gershwin received a standing ovation and were coaxed into performing an encore, so the duo performed another one of Gershwin's compositions, appropriately titled, "Do It Again." He also threw in a musical quote (a jazz technique) from Rimsky-Korsakov's *Scheherazade*, which really thrilled the crowd. As stated in *Novelty Is Spice*:

> Mr. Gershwin, at the piano, provided accompaniments which were something like works of art in their own genre, and in Mme. Gauthier's encore—his own *Do It Again*—[he] raised a gale of laughter by slyly inserting a phrase from *Scheherazade* at the appropriate moment.[1]

Some sources assert Gershwin inserted the humorous musical quote into "Do It Again"; other sources indicate it was added into "Stairway to Paradise."[2] Either way, it happened at some point in the performance and drew a lot of smiles. That's really all that counts.

The audience loved the encore so much that they roared for the pair to perform "Do It Again"—again, and the pair willingly obliged. This performance was Gershwin's debut on the highbrow concert stage, and by all accounts, he was a smash hit. It was the first time a He-bro had played "modern music" (aka jazz) to the highbrows in Aeolian Hall . . . but it certainly wasn't the last.

At the end of January 1924, the Gauthier-Gershwin team repeated this program in Boston. Critic H. T. Parker wrote about Gershwin's piano playing in the *Boston Evening Transcript:* "He is the beginning of the age of sophisticated jazz."[3]

Carl Van Vechten also opined on the concert, saying:

> I consider this one of the very most important events in musical history. . . . I suggest we get up a torchlight procession headed by Paul Whiteman to honor Miss Gauthier, the pioneer.[4]

Van Vechten then continued with almost uncanny prognostication: "I prophesy that the Philharmonic will be doing it in two years." Almost exactly two years later, Van Vechten's prediction was realized when the conductor and composer Walter Damrosch, Director of the New York Symphony Orchestra, conducted the world premiere of Gershwin's symphonic piece, *Concerto in F.* (Good call, Carl!)

American composer and music critic Deems Taylor wrote a review of the concert in *The World,* saying:

> The six jazz numbers stood up amazingly well, not only as entertainment but as music. Some of them had their vulgar moments. . . . What they did possess was melodic interest and continuity, harmonic appropriateness, well-balanced, almost classically severe form, and

subtle and fascinating rhythms—in short, the qualities that any sincere and interesting music possesses.[5]

Taylor continued on about Part III, the modern music section of the concert, saying:

> The singer reappeared, followed by a tall, black-haired young man [Gershwin] who was far from possessing the icy aplomb of those to whom playing on the platform at Aeolian Hall is an old story. He bore under his arm a small bundle of sheet music with lurid black and yellow covers. The audience began to show signs of relaxation; this promised to be amusing.... Young Mr. Gershwin began to do mysterious and fascinating rhythmic and contrapuntal stunts with the accompaniment.[6]

This concert was a great achievement for Gershwin. He had fulfilled two very important and distinctive roles—composer and piano accompanist in a major concert hall. Not only did the modern music section showcase three of Gershwin's compositions, but the encore was one of his compositions as well.

Much was also said of Gershwin's piano playing since it was his debut performance as a pianist in a concert hall setting. That evening, he played with a jazz touch and jazz improvisation and polyrhythms, as opposed to performing like a piano pounder of the Tin-Pan tradition. The music critic Henry Taylor Parker (H.T.P.) wrote in the *Boston Evening Transcript*:

> Gershwin's playing improved the jazz songs. ... He diversified them with cross-rhythms; wove them into a pliant and outspringing counterpoint; set in pauses and accents; sustained cadences; gave character to the measures wherein the singer's voice was still.... In America, and above Mr. Berlin, he is the beginning of the age of sophisticated jazz.[7]

Actually, the concert turned out to be more of a tour de force for the little-known Gershwin than for the famous diva, Gauthier, elevating him to the official spokesman of jazz to the cultural elites. In the audience that evening, listening intently to Madame Gauthier singing and Gershwin playing modern music for an audience of society muckety-mucks was the one and only Paul Whiteman. He was absorbing each and every note!

Whiteman was a great businessman, and he knew that the person who performed the first all-modern music concert would get the most bang for the buck. So he nearly *plotzed* (fainted) on hearing that his archrival bandleader, Vincent Lopez, was planning a concert of modern music at an esteemed concert venue in New York City. That's when Whiteman put his music machine in motion. He immediately booked Aeolian Hall, shelling out $7,000 ($97,000 today) of his own loot and started working feverishly to produce and deliver the first full-length concert of modern music.

Whiteman's friends objected to this concert, fearing it could ruin his new reputation as "King of Jazz" and turn him into the "Clown of Aeolian Hall." Some even dubbed the plan "Whiteman's Folly." He had much to lose, but that risk did not dissuade him from pursuing his dream—and he knew just the guy to ask to join him in this colossal gamble/venture.

What's the Big Idea?*

*(Unused) (1920s)

There had been so much talk about the limitations of jazz, not to speak of the manifest misunderstanding of its function. . . . Jazz, they said, had to be in strict time. It had to cling to dance rhythms. I resolved, if possible, to kill that misconception with one sturdy blow. Inspired by this aim, I set to composing. I had no set plan, no structure, to which my music could conform. The Rhapsody, you see, began as a purpose, not a plan . . .

—GEORGE GERSHWIN[1]

Imagine three twentysomethings, shooting pool and smoking cigars at a midtown Broadway pool hall and probably downing a beer or two as well into the wee hours. Two of these men were brothers. The older brother was sitting out a game, reading the early edition of the newspaper. Suddenly, he jumps off his stool and excitedly yells to his kid brother, "Your name is in the paper!"

The younger brother drops his pool cue, rushes over, and grabs the paper to see for himself and make sure his older brother is not yanking his chain or, more important, that his name is not just in the obits. Lo and behold, there's his name in the *New York Tribune*. They both erupt in a chorus of cheers, knowing full well that that if you can make it in New York, you can make it anywhere.

It may seem like a far-fetched story, but this scenario is precisely what happened to George, his older brother, Ira, and their lyricist friend, Buddy DeSylva (who wrote the lyrics for Gershwin's one-act opera, *Blue Monday*).

They were shooting a game of three-cushion billiards (which George lost, by the way) at the Ambassador Billiards Parlor on Broadway and 52nd Street, late in the evening of January 3, 1924. Over to the side, perched on a stool sat the quiet brother, Ira, reading the early edition of the *New York Tribune*. Ira's eye caught a small article on the amusement page: "Whiteman Judges Named." The subtitle read, "Committee Will Decide 'What Is American Music.'" Ira jumped up and interrupted the game, now reading aloud. The article publicized an upcoming Paul Whiteman concert at the Aeolian Hall.

As the article stated, "George Gershwin was at work on a jazz concerto" that the Whiteman Orchestra would play at the February 12, 1924, Valentine's Day Concert in Aeolian Hall. It also noted that a panel of distinguished musicians would determine what constituted American music. The panel consisted of Sergei Rachmaninoff, Jascha Heifetz, Efrem Zimbalist, and Alma Gluck. The Editor of the *Musical Courier*, Leonard Liebling, would be the Chairman of these U.S. leading critics and would form a committee to answer the question, "Just what is American music?"[2]

The article also stated that Victor Herbert would compose some music for the concert and Irving Berlin would create a "syncopated tone poem." Keep in mind that Gershwin and Whiteman had already worked together in *George White's Scandals of 1922*. (That's where Whiteman conducted his orchestra for Gershwin's song "Stairway to Paradise," as well as the then flop one-act opera, *Blue Monday*.)

After hearing the news, Gershwin frantically got in touch with Whiteman (not on Facebook obviously) and asked why Whiteman had sent out a press release before talking to him. Whiteman replied in purely business language that it was a matter of market position. His rival bandleader, Vincent Lopez, had gotten wind of Whiteman's idea and had already booked another venue to perform a similar concert of "modern music."

Lopez had been born in Brooklyn, and his parents were Portuguese immigrants. He was a huge competitor of Whiteman's—with a gigantic completive edge, a weekly ninety-minute radio show that was broadcast from Newark, New Jersey.

As soon as Whiteman discovered his rival's plans, he set out to beat Lopez to the punch, knowing that he who struck first would get the fame and fortune commensurate with taking the risk. Nobody remembers the guy who comes in second. As Whiteman told it:

> Another leader got word of it, and reports came to me that he was going to do the thing

we had been talking about. I certainly didn't want to see a brainchild of mine ruined, so I called up Aeolian Hall and made arrangements for a concert within 24 days.

George came running to me. "What's this I hear, Paul? You're going to do this thing in 24 days? I'd planned to take six months with it. But if it's 24 days, it's 24 days, and I'll do it.[3]

Here's a little-remembered fact—Lopez actually conducted his concert of modern music two days *before* Whiteman's Aeolian Hall gig. Lopez conducted his Pennsylvania Orchestra at the Anderson Galleries, with Harvard music professor Edward Burlingame Hill leading a discussion. Lopez and his Pennsylvania Orchestra later performed his "modern music" concert in a formal concert setting at the Metropolitan Opera House on April 27, 1924 (two and a half months after the Gershwin/Whiteman Aeolian success). Its goal was "to demonstrate the scope of the modern jazz instrument." He increased the orchestra to fifty musicians and included twenty saxophones! Lopez also included the very old "Old Folks at Home" aka "Swanee River" in the program as a poke in the eye to Gershwin and his greatest hit, "Swanee." Bottom line, however, was that Lopez evaporated into a footnote of history.

Still, all of Vincent Lopez's maneuvers did not detract from the program being created by the "King of Jazz." Whiteman had booked Aeolian Hall, the home of classical music, for $7,000 out of his own pocket. Adding the extra expense of rehearsals, additional musicians (twenty-three in all), plus comp'ing the best seats in the house to celebrities and adding all the glamorous frills, he drove the total cost of the gig into the rafters.

In the end, the concert grossed $11,000 ($153,000 today), making it a huge financial bust for Whiteman. Ticket sales didn't even come close to covering his expenses—even though it was a full house, and the box office personnel said they could have sold out the show several times over. Whiteman lost $7,000 ($97,000 today) . . . but in the long run, this concert made his name and his career. It also put George Gershwin on the map. So I guess we can call the whole deal an investment in both their futures.

Eager to give the program both panache and respectability, Whiteman was hungry for fresh, new songs. Who better to turn to than the founder of the American Society of Composers, Authors and Publishers (ASCAP) and its first president, Whiteman's old friend and former boss (from the 1915 San Francisco Fair), Victor Herbert?

Herbert was a perfect choice—and his inclusion in the event gave Whiteman the tacit support of the very important ASCAP. Herbert's participation also lent Whiteman's program the respectability and acceptance he was striving for and needed.

So, let's get back to the complicated Gershwin/Whiteman relationship.

In late 1923, Whiteman approached Gershwin to compose a piece for his "experiment" concert, but Gershwin felt compelled to decline since he had both hands full with a show called *Sweet Little Devil* that was opening in Boston.

In Gershwin's mind, the invitation was done and all but forgotten—until that fateful day in Ambassador Billiards Parlor, when his brother read the press release in the newspaper. Life was about to change hugely for both Gershwin and Whiteman, and very quickly I might add.

Up to this point, Gershwin had written at least 125 songs; Ira had written the lyrics to at least 40 songs, 18 with his brother.[4] George's tunes included the blockbuster hit, "Swanee," and the showstopper, "I'll Build a Stairway to Paradise," so twenty-five-year-old George's career was already off and running. There was absolutely no need for him to gamble his budding reputation on a cockamamie "experiment in modern music" concert. Some were saying, however, that Gershwin was "breaking his neck trying to starve to death."

Why did Gershwin choose the title *Rhapsody in Blue*? Why not *Symphony in Silver*? Or *Concerto in Chartreuse*? Or *Opera in Ochre*? Why a rhapsody? Why blue? Why not cyan or violet or indigo or some other shade of blue?

George had sophisticated motives for choosing a rhapsody for his first extended work. A rhapsody is a loose form of a musical composition, ungoverned by strict rules, so it gave him tremendous freedom to express his original musical ideas. Even though conventional wisdom tells us that Gershwin chose the rhapsody for its flexibility in weaving various unrelated themes together, some very distinguished musicologists would beg to differ. Music professor, pianist, and music critic Steven E. Gilbert wrote in his book, *The Music of Gershwin*:

> In short, *Rhapsody in Blue* is not nearly as rhapsodic as it may first seem. Its themes are joined by a multiplicity of motivic relationships. It has a coherent fundamental structure.[5]

Gilbert asserted that both *Rhapsody in Blue* and Gershwin were actually quite formidable.

Rhapsody in Blue is at once Gershwin's most famous and possibly his least understood composition. Easily dismissed as a piece of popular music, or at the very least as a youthful work by one not exactly steeped in formal musical training, it turns out to be a better-written piece than anyone could first imagine it to be. *Rhapsody* already displays Gershwin's technical gifts—of counterpoint, of rhythmic invention, and of a large-scale structure of melody and harmony which succeeds with against-all-odds bravado—which would only get better as time went on. In short, *Rhapsody in Blue* is a work of achievement and promise.[6]

So it seems that the *Rhapsody* was indeed a perfect foundation for Gershwin to build his musical reputation.

As Gershwin was riding the train to Boston for the premiere of *Sweet Little Devil*, the rhythmic clickety-clack of the train actually gave him the inspiration for *Rhapsody*.

Gershwin once told an interviewer that the *Rhapsody* started out as a purpose, not a plan. Here are Gershwin's own words' describing the creation of the *Rhapsody*:

> It was on the train, with its steely rhythms, its rattle-ty-bang, that is so often stimulating to a composer, that I suddenly heard—even saw on paper—the complete construction of the *Rhapsody* from beginning to end. No new themes came to me, but I worked on the thematic material already in my mind, and tried to conceive the composition as a whole. I heard it as a sort of musical kaleidoscope of America—of our vast melting pot, of our incomparable national pep, our blues, our metropolitan madness. By the time I reached Boston, I had the definite plot of the piece, as distinguished from the actual structure.
>
> The middle theme came upon me suddenly ... It was at the home of a friend, just as I got back to Gotham, I must do a great deal of what you must call subconscious composing, and this is an example. Playing at parties is one of my notorious weaknesses. As I was playing, without a thought of the *Rhapsody*, all at once I heard myself playing a theme that must have been haunting me inside, seeking [an] outlet. No sooner had it oozed out of my fingers than I realized I had found it. Within a week of my return from Boston I had com-

pleted the structure in the rough of the *Rhapsody in Blue*.[7]

Although Gershwin says the *Rhapsody* was a completed work, I must add an asterisk here. He wrote the music for 60 percent of the piece, but about 40 percent still remained unwritten for the concert.

Gershwin was booked as the pianist for *Rhapsody*, so his plan was to improvise the remaining 40 percent. Gershwin acknowledged the fact he would be improvising much of the piece in concert by writing on the original score, "Wait for nod," thus telling the conductor, Whiteman, when his own improvisation was over and to cue in the orchestra to resume the piece. This young, self-assured musical genius and piano virtuoso's plan was to wing it—yes, spontaneously wing it through the "make it or break it" show! Whatever you may think of such a venture, if the truth be told—THAT'S JAZZ!

Things would never be the same for Gershwin, Whiteman, or jazz after that fortuitous *New York Tribune* article. Gershwin said that January 7, 1924, was the first day he began working on the manuscript for two pianos of *Rhapsody in Blue*. Eighteen days later, on January 25, he completed the two-piano manuscript of *Rhapsody in Blue*. Yes, he wrote this masterpiece in only two and a half weeks. Yet this eighteen-day time period is actually contradicted later in an article that Gershwin himself wrote. In a June 1926, article titled "Jazz Is the Voice of the American Soul," which appeared in *Theatre Magazine*, Gershwin said, "I wrote it in ten days." So who are we going to believe as far as the total number of days it took Gershwin to write *Rhapsody in Blue*? Eighteen or ten? George Gershwin or George Gershwin? You decide.

Ferde Grofé finished orchestrating the piece on February 4th, a mere eight days before the concert! Grofé was the perfect man to score work for Whiteman's orchestra, since he had been doing so for several years and was completely familiar with the instrumentation of the group. This time it was even more important, given the compressed timeframe required to finish the work, rehearse it, and tweak it. Grofé was the right man, at the right time, in the right place for such a unique job. I cannot stress enough that it was not just that he was there, doing the orchestration of *Rhapsody*; he was also a hugely brilliant musical genius (not just a well-placed guy doing a typical job).

Grofé and Gershwin worked out a system to expedite the completion of the piece at breakneck speed. Grofé would stop by Gershwin's apartment every day and pick up the page or pages that Gershwin had completed that day. While George was busy working on the piece on an old upright piano in the back room, Grofé sat with George's mother, Rose, waiting for the day's installment. Grofé would then take the new material and scurry downtown to his own workspace to orchestrate George's new work. Here is how Grofé described the scene at the Gershwins:

> He lived with his parents and brothers and sister, all of them children, except Ira, and I practically lived too at their uptown Amsterdam Avenue and 110th Street apartment, for I called there daily for more pages of George's masterpiece, which he originally composed in two-piano form. He and his brother Ira had a back room where there was an upright piano, and that is where the *Rhapsody* grew into being. During that time I learned to value the atmosphere of George's home, and the sweet hospitality of his mother and father. Mrs. Gershwin watched our labors with loving interest, and taught me to appreciate Russian tea, which she brewed for us when we rested.[8]

Grofé was certainly the right man to orchestrate this piece. First off, he was a genius musician/orchestrator; so let's check that off the list. Next, since the timeframe for the creation and performance of the piece was so short (just weeks!), having him orchestrate the piece freed up valuable time that Gershwin could use to create the work.

Another reason was that Grofé was intimately familiar with the unique instrumentation and sound of the Whiteman Orchestra, since he had been the unit's orchestrator for several years. He knew the players as well as their capabilities, including those musicians who doubled on other instruments. He was able to extract the most from each individual musician as well as the entire orchestra en masse.

Because Whiteman was known to pay top dollar, it is not surprising that he attracted and kept the best in the business, including Grofé. Money talks! Although there are several opinions about the dates when Gershwin started writing the piece and its completion date, one thing is certain—IT WAS REALLY, REALLY FAST!

So let's get back to the actual creation of *Rhapsody in Blue*.

Because Grofé was so familiar with Whiteman's band, on some of the handwritten scores he did not write the name of the instrument (i.e., trumpet), which is the industry standard; instead, he wrote the name of the cat who was to play it (i.e., Ross . . . signifying Ross Gorman on clarinet or sax). On Gershwin's personal handwritten score, George wrote *Rhapsody in Blue, For Jazz Band and Piano*.

George's original title for the work was *American Rhapsody*, but under the astute advice of Ira, he changed it to *Rhapsody in Blue*. Following a visit to an art gallery one afternoon, after viewing an exhibition of melancholy paintings by Whistler, Ira was inspired by Whistler's "Nocturne in Blue and Green." It sealed the word "blue" in his mind. Although George's title, *American Rhapsody*, was a good one, Ira's suggestion of the word "blue" was a stroke of genius. It perfectly encapsulated the exact sense of jazz and "modern" into the name. Score this one for the master wordsmith, Ira!

What's in a name? Well, everything! "Blue" put George's jazz piece in touch with its roots, the blues, to which it was deeply indebted. But let it be known as well that this name change came late in the game. An article in the February 1924 issue of *Sheet Music Review* mentioned the première performance as Gershwin's *American Rhapsody*.

In a letter to *Singing* magazine, which was published in October 1926, Gershwin quoted musicologist and music critic, Ernest Newman, on the *Rhapsody*:

> But is it really jazz? The *Rhapsody* certainly begins as jazz, and every now and then, in its later course it behaves as such. But it seems to me to forget to live up to its name for a great part of the time. Jazz, in fact, is now obeying a universal law of musical evolution. Why did so many passages in the *Rhapsody* sound so Brahms-like?[9]

In *The Gershwins* by the experts Robert Kimball and Alfred Simon, the authors incorrectly (in my very humble opinion) say of the *Rhapsody*:

> The *Rhapsody in Blue*, however, is not jazz, not even jazz dolled up. For George Gershwin, eclectic as he was, was not really a composer of jazz music. Although he indicated that the *Rhapsody* was scored for "jazz band and piano," even the most cursory examination of the *Rhapsody* reveals it to be a work of symphonic music that owes far more to the influence of Tchaikovsky and Liszt, both unquestionably

skilled syncopators, than of Buddy Bolden or King Oliver.

Ironically, the barnyard simulations in the *Livery Stable Blues*, which opened the concert, were much closer to the essence of jazz than the *Rhapsody in Blue* was, although Whiteman mistakenly presented *Livery Stable* as a grotesque burlesque of the "real jazz" of the *Rhapsody*. It is true that there is real jazz in the stunning 17-note opening clarinet glissando that clarinetist Ross Gorman hurled at the Aeolian Hall audience. And it is true that *Rhapsody* has occasional bursts of syncopation, polyrhythm, exotic instrumental effects, and even blue notes—flattened thirds, fifths, and sevenths. Yet these are really ornamentations to a work whose audacity, verve, and above all, gorgeous melodies are akin in spirit and quality to the Russian music George Gershwin heard in his formative years.[10]

I respectfully submit that Kimball and Simon are way off course in their assessment that the *Rhapsody* was not a jazz piece. It was a groundbreaking work in a new genre called "symphonic jazz," as Paul Whiteman dubbed it. The authors had to exclude so many features of the work, like syncopation, polyrhythms, and blue notes, as merely incidental in order to force their point.

We should not dissect *Rhapsody in Blue* into miniscule data points and individual notes be they red, white, or even blue, because then we will miss the big picture. When one zooms in so close, as these people have done, the picture becomes a bunch of individual pixels instead of a beautifully integrated artistic masterpiece.

Now, it is my turn to ask George Gershwin an important question: "So, George, where did the idea for the *Rhapsody in Blue* come from?"

George puffs on his big cigar, slowly exhaling a plume of smoke, and then politely responds to my question: "Thanks for asking such a brilliant and insightful question, Richie."

The idea for the *Rhapsody in Blue* came to me quite suddenly. The vivid panorama of American life swept through my mind—its feverishness, its vulgarity, its welter of love, marriage and divorce, and its basic solidity in the character of the people. All of the emotional reactions excited by contemplating the American scene, with all its mixtures of races . . . were stuffed into the first outline of the *Rhapsody*, with a dominant theme derived from the fashionable "blue" or melancholy rhythm.

"Does that answer your superb question, Richie?"

Yes, George, it does. Thanks. Actually, I knew the answer before I asked it. You wrote it in an article entitled, "Making Music" which appeared in the May 4, 1930, issue of *New York World Sunday Magazine*[11]

The following quote by Ira tells the filmmaker Paul Schrader (for a film that was never made) some interesting details about the creation of *Rhapsody in Blue*. The words in parenthesis are stage directions for the screenplay. Ira (Iz) explained how his little brother, George, described the idea to him:

GEORGE: You start with an ice-breaker, an ascending clarinet to get attention, to start the engine. Just after the first theme, four bars in, I stress an unaccented beat. First bump in the road (gesture). . . . Same thing two bars later but fool with the harmony too. The second bump is also the first turn! With the second theme five bars later you're on your way with the scenery all blue and jazzy—but where are you headed? Keep changing keys, turn, detour seven times before hitting straightaway A Major, like the cycle of fifths rag players use (*George dashes to the keyboard, demonstrates*). . . . Meantime I'm pitting four notes against three so you feel like you're accelerating all the time. Add a few classical conventions and you think you're listening to Tchaikovsky or Liszt. It's a rhythm for our time, Iz. Not just pep. Our pulse (a beat). . . . And Grofé will orchestrate.[12]

What a fantastically insightful description!

In my personal copy of the Harms sheet music for *Rhapsody in Blue*, printed in the 1920s, the score reads, "Dedicated to Paul Whiteman." I don't want to get too technical here, but I would like to add that the piece begins in the key of Concert Bb. It then moves into twelve different signature changes before the final six bars, like those "bumps in the road" mentioned above.

Then, suddenly, in the final six bars, Gershwin switches back to the original starting key of Bb and ends on the Bb note. It is as if he has completed a circle. After *Rhapsody in Blue* was completed by Gershwin and scored by Grofé on February 4, 1924, Paul Whiteman invited about three dozen "guests" to attend the first rehearsal at noontime in the Palais Royal, where his orchestra was the house band. Of course, the usual movers and shakers of New York were there—the music critics, composers, conductors, musicians, and many others as well.

The reactions to this first rehearsal run-through were mixed. They ranged from: "It opened up a new era for American music," to "I was frankly uncertain whether I liked it or not," and" I was not enamored of the themes or the workmanship, but the thing had zip and punch."[13]

So, at this lunchtime rehearsal for the hoi polloi, the reaction was lukewarm at best . . . with a possible foreshadowing of disaster.

George's father, Morris, gave his son some valuable advice while George was working on the *Rhapsody*. Papa Gershwin, in his very dry sense of humor, warned his son: "Make it good, George. It's liable to be important."[14]

Boy, did Papa have that one right!

Tonight's the Night*

*Show Girl (Unused) (1922)

*Would the critics decide I was trying to be smart
and succeeding in being only smart-alecky?*
—PAUL WHITEMAN[1]

Paul Whiteman had positioned the concert at Aeolian Hall as a game changer, an "experiment," something new and unique. He wrote:

> My idea for the concert was to show these skeptical people the advance which has been made in popular music from the day of discordant early jazz to the melodious form of the present . . . that they went on flaying modern jazz without realizing that it was different from the crude early attempts—that it had taken a turn for the better.[2]

But in the days leading up to *An Experiment in Modern Music* concert, Paul Whiteman was also awash in anxiety and self-doubt—and he had plenty of reasons.. There was a lot of buzz on the streets. Many jazz aficionados were waiting to pass judgment, and yet their expectations were running high, hoping Whiteman and Gershwin would officially legitimize the historically uncouth genre of jazz music. They even dubbed the concert as an attempt to "Make an Honest Woman out of Jazz," a reference to the early years of jazz and its roots in the New Orleans whorehouses and the women prostitutes who worked there.

In an effort to prevent negative reviews, Whiteman started an educational outreach program to the highbrows, snobs, artsy-fartsy, hoity-toity, hoi polloi, and critics in the days preceding the concert. A true public relations master, he hosted lunches at The Tavern (a restaurant/bar close by the Palais Royal), invited the intelligentsia to rehearsals, and actively campaigned for "The Experiment." To his astonishment (and sheer panic), they all accepted his lunch invitation.

At one of these preshow performances, Whiteman and Gershwin asked the music critic editor of the *Musical Courier,* Leonard Liebling, how he liked the *Rhapsody*. As Liebling later described their exchange:

I answered with the caution of a professional critic: "Well, it's the sort of music one ought to hear at least twice before making up one's mind."

"Shall we play it again?" said George to Paul, and they did. The second try fixed me. "Fine! Splendid!" was my honest reaction.[3]

Whiteman was getting these buy-ins, one critic at a time, but his self-doubt still persisted. In a surge of courage, he then extended concert invitations to the reigning cultural elite. Again, to his utter astonishment (and sheer panic), many of these invitations were accepted.

The concert audience would include members of the upper echelon of classical music, such as Walter Damrosch, Sergei Rachmaninoff, Jascha Heifetz, and Leopold Stokowski; opera singer Amelita Galli-Curci; patron of the arts Otto Kahn; and Cartier executive Jules Glaenzer. Highly esteemed members of the literary world also accepted his invitation, including Carl Van Vechten, Deems Taylor, Gilbert Seldes, Fannie Hurst, S. Jay Kaufman, and Frank Crowninshield. Even stride piano legend Willie "The Lion" Smith, attended the gig.

This loaded audience was filled with high-culture representatives of music, art, and literature—potentially all there to look down their noses at some low-life culture "noise." Whiteman well knew his reputation and career were on the line. His finances were as well, as he had personally bankrolled the show to the tune of $11,000. His nerves were screaming, but the die was cast . . . there was no turning back now.

"An Experiment in Modern Music" was scheduled for February 12, 1924, at 2:45 in the afternoon. Falling on Lincoln's birthday, the concert was cleverly dubbed, "The Emancipation Proclamation of Jazz." Ticket prices ranged from 55 cents to $2.20 (about $7.50 to $30 in today's bucks). It was priced that moderately because

Whiteman was desperate to ensure a full house; a half-empty room would make a bad impression on the already skeptical critics. He had to hedge his bets the best way he could.

When the fateful day finally arrived, it was a cold, snowy, and miserable Tuesday in New York City. Just fifteen minutes before the curtain rose, Whiteman yielded to an overwhelming wave of anxiety. Donning an overcoat, he slipped out to the front of Aeolian Hall to get a sense of the crowd. In his own words:

> It was snowing, but men and women were fighting to get to the door, pulling and mauling each other as they do sometimes at a baseball game, or prize fight, or in the subway. Such was my state of mind by this time that I wondered if I had come to the right entrance. And then I saw Victor Herbert going in . . . the next day the ticket office people said they could have sold out the house 10 times over.[4]

The 1,500-seat Aeolian Hall was indeed completely sold out . . . standing room only. (Quite a draw for a miserably cold, snowy Tuesday afternoon in Gotham!) In this overpacked hall, "high society" rubbed elbows with the riffraff as orchestra conductors, composers, Broadway stars, music critics, and classical musicians mingled with song pluggers, jazz aficionados, and gamblers, all under one roof that day. Whiteman later described the crowd as a "strange audience" with "vaudevillians, concert managers . . . Tin Pan Alley-ites, composers, symphony and opera stars, flappers, cake-eaters, all mixed up higgledy-piggledy."[5] Everyone was there to hear the work of an up-and-coming He-bro. Without a doubt, it was a groundbreaking cultural event that wanted to "make an honest woman out of jazz."

The stage was set with huge, colorful Japanese screens, enhanced by expert lighting, and the orchestra was set up on a three-step platform, arranged in a semicircle. Aeolian Hall looked more impressive than ever.

Whiteman had expanded his Palais Royal Orchestra by nine musicians, bringing his usual group of fourteen to twenty-three for this special performance. These were the highest-paid musicians in the biz, and each one was dressed in gray spats to heighten the theatrical effect.

The orchestra featured two trombones, two French horns, eight violins, two trumpets, one tuba, another tuba who doubled on the upright bass, drums, piano and four woodwinds. We also can't forget Whiteman's long-time sidekick and banjo man extraordinaire, Mike Pingatore, who had been a member of Whiteman's band since the good old San Francisco days.

These twenty-three musicians played more than sixty instruments. The phenomenal Ross Gorman played fourteen by his lonesome! (Of course, not all at once.) Three woodwind/reed men doubled on all sorts of instruments, including saxophones and clarinets, flutes, and some exotic instruments like the double-reed heckaphone and more. Other doublers played tuba, octavion, flugelhorn, euphonium, celesta, and more. The drummer even had a set of frying pans to bang on. They were hanging in front of his traps.

Whiteman's musicians were breaking new musical ground that day and creating novel "instrumental tricks" to match. As Edmund Dorset states in *Mr. Whiteman and the Fox Trot*:

> Ross Gorman's clarinet-glissade, for instance, would have been declared impossible 10 years ago; Henry Busse's weird lippings of his instrument, his skillful changes and manipulations of mutes inserted into its bell, are being copied, and in most cases vainly, by thousands of trumpet and coronet players all over the world; Pingatore, by extemporizing a new rhythm with his marvelous fingers, developed a new banjo-technique. . . . To sin-

gle out these three pioneers of Whitemanism, is perhaps to work injustice to other. . . . It is out of them that the new music has grown.[6]

The concert was teeming with innovation. Having marketed "An Experiment in Modern Music" as an educational event, Whiteman had his manager, Hugh C. Ernst, give an introductory lecture before the concert started. He explained to the audience that:

> The experiment is to be purely educational. Mr. Whiteman intends to point out . . . the tremendous strides which have been made in popular music from the day of discordant Jazz, which sprang into existence about ten years ago from nowhere in particular, to the really melodious music of today.[7]

Mr. Ernst then went on to introduce each subsequent song, and the audience followed along in their programs.

The program itself is a fascinating piece of history, so let's take a moment to consider it in more detail. Thanks to Maestro Maurice Peress, a foremost expert on this concert, I received a copy of the original 1924 Aeolian Hall Program.

The cover states:

An Experiment in Modern Music
Aeolian Hall

Inside, Whiteman arranged twenty-three songs into ten distinct categories, as shown on the facing page.

The program also included a brief bio on four of "Mr. Whiteman's Associates"—Victor Herbert, George Gershwin, Zez Confrey, and Irving Berlin. Whiteman's manager, Hugh C. Ernst, used the last page of the program to invite the audience to share their feedback and opinions of the concert, as follows:

> Questions, criticisms and suggestions pertaining to this Experiment in Modern Music addressed to Mr. Whiteman will be most welcome and will be given serious consideration.
> Paul Whiteman
> 160 W. 45th Street
> New York City[9]

The first number, *Livery Stable Blues,* is a twelve-bar blues song played by a quintet with drums, cornet, clarinet, trombone, and piano. It was a fun number to open with because, as the name suggests, the musicians imitated the sounds of barnyard animals, using various musical props like a wood block being tapped like hoofs sound, a cowbell, a large tin can, and a bowler hat to create animal sounds. The audience loved the song and its comical musical antics. Music editor/critic for *The New York Times* Olin Downes noted:

> The "Livery Stable Blues" was introduced apologetically as an example of the depraved past from which modern jazz has risen. The apology is herewith indignantly rejected, for this is a gorgeous piece of impudence, much better in its unbuttoned jocosity and Rabelaisian laughter than other and more polite compositions that came later.[10]

"Livery Stable Blues" was a perfect choice to open the concert. Not only was it appealing and amusing, but it also had a rich history. First performed and recorded in 1917 by trumpeter Nick LaRocca's all-white Original Dixieland Jass Band, it was the first jazz record and a blockbuster hit, selling over a million copies! Later, it got tangled up in a famous court case that decided whether "Livery Stable Blues" was stolen from another song, "Barnyard Blues." The case was eventually dismissed, but not before various musical experts were called to testify. One of

AN EXPERIMENT IN MODERN MUSIC
AEOLIAN HALL

FIRST HALF

True Form of Jazz

a. Ten Years Ago—"Livery Stable Blues"
   ....La Rocca
b. With Modern Embellishment—
   "Mama Loves Papa" ....Baer

Comedy Selections

a. Origin of "Yes We Have No Bananas"
   ....Silver
b. Instrumental Comedy—
   "So This Is Venice" ....Thomas
   (Featuring Ross Gorman)
   (*Adapted from "The Carnival of Venice"*)

Contrast–Legitimate Scoring vs. Jazzing

a. Selection in True Form
   "Whispering" ....Schonberger
b. Same Selection with Jazz Treatment

Recent Compositions with Modern Score

a. "Limehouse Blues" ....Braham
b. "I Love You" ....Archer
c. "Raggedy Ann" ....Kern

Zez Confrey (Piano)

a. "Medley Popular Airs"
b. "Kitten on the Keys" ....Confrey
c. "Ice Cream and Art"
d. "Nickel in the Slot" ....Confrey
   (*Accompanied by the Orchestra*)

Flavoring a Selection with Borrowed Themes

"Russian Rose" ....Grofé
   (*Based on the* Volga Boat Song)

Semi-Symphonic Arrangement of Popular Melodies

a. "Alexander's Ragtime Band" ....Berlin
b. "A Pretty Girl Is Like a Melody" ...Berlin
c. "Orange Blossoms in California" ...Berlin

SECOND HALF

A Suite of Serenades ....Herbert

a. Spanish   c. Cuban
b. Chinese   d. Oriental

Adaptation of Standard Selections to Dance Rhythm

a. "Pale Moon" ....Logan
b. "To a Wild Rose" ....McDowell

c. "Chansonette" ....Friml

George Gershwin (Piano)

"A Rhapsody in Blue" ....Gershwin
   (*Accompanied by the Orchestra*)

In the Field of Classics

"Pomp and Circumstance" ....Elgar"[8]

these experts was black musician and blues composer Professor "Slaps" White. As reported in the October 19, 1917, issue of *Variety*, the headline read: "BLUES ARE BLUES, THEY ARE," SAYS EXPERT IN "BLUES" CASE. It goes on to say:

"Just what are blues?" asked Judge Carpenter. (Author's note: And the Professor answered as only a true jazz cat would:)

"Blues are blues, that's what blues are," replied the professor. The answer was written into the records and will stand as the statement of an expert.[11]

Thanks to Professor "Slaps" White, the proverbial question "Just what are the blues?" had been settled in a United States Court of law for evermore. Next case!

"Livery Stable Blues" was followed by "Mama Loves Papa," a hit song at the time, and played by Whiteman's fourteen-piece Palais Royal Orchestra. It was a smart move to juxtapose these two songs, so the audience could compare a seven-year-old hit to a current one.

After Whitman's Palais Royal Orchestra played the first five numbers . . . additional musicians were added, bringing the total to twenty-three.[12] Coincidentally, in addition to having twenty-three musicians in the orchestra, there were also twenty-three songs on the program.

Next came the section of Comedy Selections, starting with "Yes! We Have No Bananas"—another song with some interesting history.

There is a close relationship between this comedy tune and Handel's *Messiah*, specifically the "Hallelujah Chorus." To hear them both, one after the other, it becomes clear that "Bananas" was derived from "Hallelujah." (Perhaps, we should refer to it as "Hallelujah, We Have No Bananas!")

Although the music was lifted from Handel, the phrase came straight from the streets of New York City. As J. W. T. Mason explained in a New York edition of the *London Daily Express*:

The phrase originated in the fruit shops kept in New York by Greeks, Italians, and Jews, whose knowledge of the English language is limited in verbiage, but not in volubility, nor in willingness to try.

These ancient races come to the New World for profit, and never like to turn a customer away. So they have evolved a curious positive and negative for the same sentence. Why the slangmakers hit on bananas has not been discovered. It might as well have been any other commodity. But the phrase means that one having asked for bananas in a fruit shop where there are none, the anxious proprietor, seeking to be ingratiating and not desiring to displease, answers: 'Yes; we have no bananas.' Thereupon he may seek to sell a cabbage or a bunch of beets instead, since most fruit shops in New York are vegetable establishments as well.

The phrase is a tribute to the optimism of the newly arrived immigrant; to his earnest fight to master the language of his temporary country, and so, somehow, is supposed to take on the American characteristic of "getting there," even though by way of an affirmative in a negative sentence.[13]

As the son of an immigrant grocer and former owner of natural foods supermarkets, I was raised with this "never say 'no' to a customer" philosophy. In fact, I trained my employees to never say we were out of an item, but rather, "Absolutely, it will be in stock on (x) day." Products were either in stock or on order, NEVER OUT OF STOCK. My father taught his son well. Thanks, Dad!

"Bananas" was followed by "So This Is Venice," which featured the woodwind virtuoso

Ross Gorman juggling instruments on variations of the "Carnival of Venice" and calling them "So This Is Venice." Gorman played eight or nine instruments during his variations, making him one hell of a busy cat.

After the Comedy Selections came Contrast—Legitimate Scoring vs. Jazzing. In this section, Paul Whiteman's smash hit song "Whispering" is played in two different ways: straight and then with a "jazz treatment." In 1920, Paul Whiteman and his Ambassador Orchestra recorded this song for Victor, and it quickly became a national hit, selling over 2 million copies and becoming the number-one song on the national charts for eleven weeks. A funny jazz quirk was that in 1945 Bebop jazz innovator Dizzy Gillespie based his hit song, "Groovin' High" on "Whispering's" chord changes.

The next section of the program was Recent Compositions with Modern Score. Here, Whiteman's band played three songs: "Limehouse Blues," "I Love You," and "Raggedy Ann." Maestro Peress later wrote about "Raggedy Ann":

> The arrangement is the most brilliant of those for the dance band alone. It features a sweet sax trio, a humoresque-like interlude modulating to D minor, and surprise . . . a pure *klezmorim* chorus for cornet and clarinet, worthy of Tevye.[14]

Section Five featured four songs composed and performed by the piano great Zez Confrey. He had built his reputation on novelty songs with a cute twist. His 1921 hit, "Kitten on the Keys," sounded like a cat frolicking on a piano's keys, and his "Nickel in the Slot" is just as amusing. The song slows down in time, begging someone to feed the slot of a nickelodeon (a public player piano that would play portions of a popular song for a nickel), and then add another nickel to speed the song up again. It was an inspired piece of music.

The next-to-last section in the first half of the program was Flavoring a Selection with Modern Themes. It included a Ferde Grofé song entitled "Russian Rose," which was based on "The Volga Boat Song." In his reconstructed and conducted album of the concert, Maestro Peress later said of this song:

> Pretentious potpourri, includes music by Tchaikovsky and Rimsky-Korsakov, the Volga Boat Song, and a quote from Rachmaninoff's Prelude in C-sharp Minor (with the composer in the audience in 1924). . . . Somehow it is hard to believe that Russian Rose was not done tongue in cheek![15]

The last section of the first half of the concert, the Semi-Symphonic Arrangement of Popular Melodies, was a showcase of three popular Irving Berlin songs. Whiteman knew that adding Berlin's name to the gig would stir up interest, publicity, and credibility for the concert. But he also knew that this genius composer could neither read nor write a lick of music and would be unable to deliver the "syncopated tone poem" mentioned in the concert's press release. So, to keep Berlin's panache attached to the "Experiment," Whiteman put his brilliant arranger, Ferde Grofé, to work orchestrating "Alexander's Ragtime Band," "A Pretty Girl Is Like a Melody," and "Orange Blossoms in California." In this way, Whiteman was able to deliver Irving Berlin's music to concertgoers in a fresh, new style.

At the time of this concert, "Alexander's Ragtime Band" was still causing a stir, even thirteen years after it was a major hit (in 1911). Gershwin wrote in the November 22, 1929, issue of *The American Hebrew*:

Irving Berlin was the first to free the American song from the nauseating sentimentally which had previously characterized it, and by introducing and perfecting ragtime he had actually given us the first germ of an American musical idiom; he had sowed the first seeds of an American music. The first real American musical work is "Alexander's Ragtime Band." Berlin had shown us the way; it was now easier to attain the ideal.[16]

Some may remember "A Pretty Girl Is Like a Melody" as the pre-1955 theme song of the Miss America Pageant, before it was replaced by "There She Is, Miss America." The last of the Berlin pieces was "Orange Blossoms in California," thus ending the first half of this concert. As you can well imagine, by this point, the audience was starting to get restless.

So let's head out to the lobby and stretch our legs before the second half.

The second half of the program began with the section entitled A Suite of Serenades. It showcased four songs composed by Whiteman's former orchestra leader boss, Victor Herbert. Herbert had been commissioned by Whiteman to compose this suite especially for the concert, and Herbert delivered an exceptional and culturally diverse selection of music: Spanish, Chinese, Cuban, and Oriental serenades. According to Maestro Maurice Peress:

"The Suite of Serenades" is the most challenging work on the entire program. Masterfully scored for the unusual dance-band-plus ensemble, it introduces many sophisticated instrumental touches and totally fresh harmonic and melodic ideas.[17]

(Unfortunately, these were the last pieces Herbert ever wrote. He died less than three months following this performance.)

The serenades were followed by Adaptation of Standard Selections to Dance Rhythm, which featured three songs: "Pale Moon" (based on an American Indian melody); "To a Wild Rose"; and "Chansonette."

Throughout the concert, the tension continued to build at Aeolian Hall. The general feeling of the crowd was that, thus far, there had been nothing extraordinary in the show. Yet, anticipation stayed high because, as the program promised:

Mr. Gershwin has written a "Rhapsody in Blue," which he has consented to play, accompanied by the orchestra. He is capable of everything, from "Swanee" to "A Stairway to Paradise"; from "Ingenue Baby" and "Virginia" to "Do It Again." Delicacy, even dreaminess, is a quality he alone brings into Jazz music. Gershwin's sense of variation in rhythm of shifting accents, of emphasis and color is faultless. He has, moreover, an insatiable curiosity about everything connected with his work and, for that matter, with music in general. He is learning and he is not forgetting, and being one of the youngest of the composers he is actually one of the brightest hopes of our popular music.[18]

The audience was still growing fidgety and antsy, however, showing signs of fatigue during this marathon concert. But all that changed the moment Ross Gorman began his now signature glissando introduction to *Rhapsody in Blue*.

The air electrified with his opening clarinet solo, which transformed both the auditorium and the sound of jazz, and defined the sound of the Roaring Twenties from that moment on. The opening clarinet solo was so spectacular and innovative that I have devoted the entire section "Stiff Upper Lip" to exploring its technical and artistic genius.

During this performance of the *Rhapsody*, Gershwin demonstrated the full range of his exceptional abilities to the fully engaged, highbrow, lowbrow, and He-brow audience. With years of experience as a Tin Pan Alley song plugger and Broadway musical-review performer, Gershwin had developed quite a bag of performance tricks to "wow" a crowd with—and "wow" them he did. His piano improvisation was a full 40 percent of the piece! When the *Rhapsody* finally concluded, the audience went wild with a roaring ovation.

As a writer who attended the concert observed:

Applause varied from moderate ("To a Wild Rose") through hearty (the Herbert pieces), enthusiastic (the Gorman antics in "So This Is Venice") and stormy (Zez Confrey's imitation of a decrepit automatic piano), to wild and even frantic (Gershwin). In a word, the mixed public present was considerably more than satisfied.[19]

Urban legend would have us believe that the concert ended with the *Rhapsody*, but it actually ended with "Pomp and Circumstance"—as if the audience had just completed their higher education course study in jazz music. One might say of course that they had just received their diploma from the Doctor of Jazz himself, Professor George Gershwin!

On a side note, which is an interesting bit of trivia, on that same day, just a few hours later, Gershwin's musical, *Sweet Little Devil*, was playing at the Astor Theatre several short blocks away. One could have attended the ivory-towered, hoity-toity Aeolian Hall concert in the afternoon and then walked over to Broadway's Theatre District to catch a Gershwin musical that evening. New York City was all Gershwin, all the time that day and from then forward!

Carnegie Hall Program

FIRE NOTICE
Look around NOW and choose the nearest Exit to your seat. In case of fire walk (not run) to THAT Exit. Do not try to beat your neighbor to the street.

THOS. J. DRENNAN, Fire Commissioner

CARNEGIE HALL
Monday Evening, April 21, 1924

Concert by

PAUL WHITEMAN
and
HIS ORCHESTRA

for

THE AMERICAN ACADEMY IN ROME

PROGRAM

1. True Form of Jazz
   (a) Dixie Land One Step....La Rocca
   (b) Medley One Step

2. Comedy Selection
   (a) Origin of "Yes, We Have No Bananas"............Silver
   (b) Instrumental Comedy—
       "So This Is Venice"....Thomas
       (Featuring Ross Gorman)
       (Adapted from "The Carnival of Venice")

3. Contrast—
   Legitimate Scoring vs. Jazzing
   (a) Selection in true form, "Japanese Sandman"............Whiting
   (b) Same Selection with Jazz Treatment

Program continued on second page following

Program Continued

4. Recent Compositions with Modern Score
   (a) "Limehouse Blues".......Braham
   (b) "Linger Awhile"..........Rose
   (c) "Shanghai Lullaby" ......Jones

5. Zez Confrey (Piano)
   (a) Medley Popular Airs
   (b) "Ice Cream and Art"
   (c) "Kitten on the Keys".....Confrey
   Accompanied by the Orchestra

6. Adaptation of Standard Selections to Dance Rhythm
   a. Pale Moon ....Logan
   b. To a Wild Rose.........MacDowell
   c. Chansonette ....Friml

7. Flavoring a Selection with Borrowed Themes
   "Russian Rose" ....Grofé
   (Based on the Volga Boat Song)

INTERMISSION

8. A Suite of Serenades........Herbert
   (a) Spanish
   (b) Chinese
   (c) Cuban
   (d) Oriental

8. George Gershwin (Piano)
   Rhapsody in Blue..........Gershwin
   Accompanied by the Orchestra

Chickering Pianos Used

For special announcement see second page following
See top next page for important Concert Announcements.
(See page inside back cover)

INFORMATION BUREAU FOR LOST AND FOUND ARTICLES AT SUPERINTENDENT'S OFFICE

J. M. Gidding & Co.
Incorporated
37 and 39 WEST 57th STREET, NEW YORK

Somebody Loves Me*

*George White's Scandals of 1924 (1924)

Of course it's great; doesn't it take 15 minutes to play?
—A COMMENT BY GEORGE GERSHWIN'S FATHER, MORRIS,
WHEN ASKED IF RHAPSODY IN BLUE WAS A GREAT SONG

So, what did the critics have to say about Whiteman's "An Experiment in Modern Music"? Did his risks pay off . . . or tank his career forever?

As *Musical Digest* described it, the press was divided, but it leaned toward the positive. In fairness, let's consider what both sides had to say, starting with the fans.

Music critic, W. J. Henderson, of the *Herald* said of the concert:

> One of the most interesting of a busy season. Mr. Herbert's music was delightful. Mr. Gershwin's composition proved to be a highly ingenious work, treating the piano in a manner calling for much technical skill. . . . If this way lies the path toward the development of American modern music into a high art form, then one can heartily congratulate Mr. Gershwin on his disclosure of some of the possibilities.[1]

Henderson went on to say that Zez Confrey had "captivating cleverness and should not be forgotten." He then gave a tip of his hat to woodwind genius Ross Gorman, calling him "a supreme virtuoso who played 10 reed instruments." Henderson also congratulated Whiteman on his adventurous spirit and called him a born conductor, saying, "Paul Whiteman is to be congratulated on his adventure and the admirable results he obtained in proving the euphony of the 'Jazz orchestra.'"[2]

Conductor Walter Damrosch "enjoyed every minute of it," and Lawrence Gilman of the *Tribune* called the performance an "uproarious success."[3]

Deems Taylor, writer for the *World*, found Gershwin's *Rhapsody*, "in a way the most interesting offering, despite its short-comings. . . . Certainly the experiment was worth the trouble." He went on to say it revealed a "genuine melodic gift and a piquant individual harmonic sense to lend significance to its rhythmic ingenuity. . . . It is genuine jazz music not only in its scoring but in its idiom."

In *The New York Times*, Olin Downes wrote:

> There were the incredible gyrations of that virtuoso and imp of the perverse, Ross

Gorman. And then there was Mr. Whiteman. He does not conduct. He trembles, wabbles, quivers—a piece of jazz jelly conducting the orchestra with the back of the trouser of the right leg, and the face of a mandarin the while. . . . Mr. Gershwin's composition shows extraordinary talent. . . . In spite of technical immaturity, he has expressed himself in a significant and on the whole highly original manner. This is fresh and new and full of promise. . . .

There was tumultuous applause for Mr. Gershwin's composition. There was realization of the irresistible vitality and genuineness of much of the music heard on this occasion, as opposed to the pitiful sterility of the average production of the "serious" American composer.[4]

The *Evening Sun*'s music critic and Williams College grad (where his archives are housed), Gilbert W. Gabriel, said of the concert:

It was one long strong musical cocktail . . . Mr. Whiteman has some amazing musicians under him and he shines out as an extraordinarily well-rounded musician.

Gershwin's *Rhapsody* impressed Gabriel:

The beginning and ending of it were stunning . . . Mr. Gershwin has an irrepressible pack of talents.[5]

The editor of *Musical Courier*, Henry O. Osgood, wrote: "The *Rhapsody* is a more important contribution to music than Stravinsky's *Rites of Spring*." And Henry T. Finck insisted that Gershwin was "far superior to Schönberg, Milhaud, and the rest of the futurist fellows."[6]

With an ear on the concert and an eye on the future, writer, music critic, and cultural visionary Carl Van Vechten made an uncanny prediction, telling George:

The concert . . . was a riot, and you crowned it . . . the foremost serious effort by any American composer. . . . I think something might be done in the way of combining jazz and the moving-picture technique. Think of themes as close-ups, flash-backs, etc.![7]

Van Vechten wrote these words three years before the first talkie, *The Jazz Singer*, appeared in 1927. He was quite the prognosticator, indeed!

Certainly, many people "in the know" realized that *Rhapsody in Blue* and George Gershwin were both quite special. But alas, not everyone had such a rosy perspective.

Although Lawrence Gilman called the performance an "uproarious success," he also offered some sharp criticisms. Of the *Rhapsody*, he wrote, "Recall the most ambitious piece on yesterday's program and weep over the lifelessness of its melody and harmony, so derivative, so stale, so inexpressive." He continued, saying the *Rhapsody* and other works on the program contained "trite and feeble conventional . . . tunes" and "sentimental and vapid harmonic treatment."[8]

Oscar Thompson, an author of several books on music, wrote in 1926, "Even the *Rhapsody* is second rate as jazz. As anything else it scarcely merits consideration. . . ."[9]

Another Thomson, this one named Virgil, was a composer and music critic. In his article, "The Cult of Jazz," published in the June 1925 issue of *Vanity Fair*, he said of Gershwin's *Rhapsody*:

Just some scraps of bully jazz sewed together with oratory and cadenzas out of Liszt. . . . The *Rhapsody* is at best a piece of aesthetic snobbery. That, and no more, is its raison d'être.[10]

Music critic Pitts Sanborn said the *Rhapsody*, "was applauded stormily . . . Although to some ears this *Rhapsody* begins with a promising theme well stated, it soon runs off into empty passage work and meaningless repetition."[11]

Not to be outdone as far as kicking Gershwin around, music critic Paul Rosenfeld wrote, "*Rhapsody in Blue* is circus-music, pre-eminent in the sphere of tinsel and fustian."[12] (Of course, as history has indeed proven, this so called "circus-music" had much more staying power than Paul Rosen-what's his name.)

Many musical experts gave the concert mixed reviews, both immediately and for years to come. Famed music author and Gershwin biographer David Ewen wrote:

> This program . . . was a strange, almost indiscriminating, potpourri of the good and the bad in popular music; and none of it was real jazz . . . the similarity of style and orchestral coloring in the various numbers and the lack of any genuine sustaining musical interest made the concert... a bore. But for the Gershwin Rhapsody in Blue, the event might well have been a failure. Up to the moment the Gershwin *Rhapsody* appeared on the long program, the audience showed increasing signs of fatigue and restlessness. Then came the opening clarinet trill of the *Rhapsody in Blue* and the audience was magnetized to attention. This was something definitely new—a refreshing, even exciting, change from the dull routines that had preceded it. The opening clarinet yawp plunged into the first theme—a brash, impudent, saucy subject that not only set the mood for the entire work but was the voice for the entire era of the frenetic and convention-shattering 1920s. Other ideas, no less infectious, followed, culminating in the broad rhapsodic slow section for the strings which has since become one of the most celebrated melodies in serious American music, and Whiteman's signature music. The *Rhapsody* came to a close with a brief and dramatic coda.
>
> The *Rhapsody in Blue* gave point and meaning to an otherwise dull and poorly organized program . . . Single-handed, the *Rhapsody* converted Whiteman's concert from an exotic novelty, to be forgotten a day later, into a musical event of historic importance.[13]

I respectfully disagree with Mr. Ewen's harsh criticism of the concert as a whole. Although there may have been a few clunkers in the program, on the whole many of the songs as well as their performances were very entertaining. Ewen was correct in his assessment that the program was quite long and did drag a bit, causing some distraction in the audience, but many of the tunes received hearty applause.

Having listened carefully to a recording of Maestro Maurice Peress's painstaking recreation of the entire "Experiment," I personally found it exceptional. On the other hand, I wholeheartedly agree with Mr. Ewen's opinion that the opening clarinet solo of the *Rhapsody*, as well as the rest of the piece, set the mood for the Roaring Twenties. On that point, he was spot on.

In more recent years, jazz critic Leonard Feather discussed the *Rhapsody* in his massive book, *The New Edition of the Encyclopedia of Jazz*:

> Paul Whiteman, busy trying to "make a lady out of jazz," introduced George Gershwin's *Rhapsody in Blue*. . . . Much of the harmonic and melodic quality but little of the rhythmic content of jazz could be detected in the ambitious Gershwin work. Like so many pseudo-jazz concert works that were later introduced in European concert halls and Hollywood movie studios and on New York radio shows, the *Rhapsody* lacked the blend of orchestration and individual improvisation that has

long been a part of every real jazz performance. It has the surface characteristics but few of the basic elements that had already established jazz as an internationally successful, if unladylike, musical innovation.[14]

I must respectfully, yet wholeheartedly, disagree once more with these comments from the esteemed Leonard Feather. He either ignores, disregards, or is ignorant (which seems highly unlikely) of the fact that large portions (40%) of the *Rhapsody* were completely improvised, on the spot. The score clearly stated that Gershwin would nod to the conductor when his improvised solo was finished. If that's not jazz, Mr. Feather, then what is? (*Hmmm . . . since Mr. Feather died in 1994, please consider this a rhetorical question!*)

For decades, and even to this day, Gershwin has received a bad rap from some of the music intelligentsia for not writing "true" or "real" jazz—even though Gershwin's "I Got Rhythm" is the second most often used chord pattern in jazz (the twelve-bar blues being the tops). In 1933, nine years after the debut of *Rhapsody in Blue*, British jazz musician and composer Spike Hughes wrote a piece for London's *Daily Herald*, in which he praised the jazz chops of Duke Ellington and pooh-poohed those of George Gershwin. In the article, Hughes asserted:

In common with many other musicians, I have long been bewildered by the almost universal and distressing acceptance of the *Rhapsody in Blue* as the apotheosis of Jazz. George Gershwin is surely first and foremost a composer of "light" music that can be, and is, "arranged" for performance by anything from male quartets to harmonica bands. (*Author's Note: "Harmonica bands" was Hughes' dig at Gershwin for harmonica virtuoso Larry Adler's performances of his concert works.*) The mere fact that a Gershwin "number" is incidentally used for dancing does not mean that it is Jazz.

Ellington's music, on the other hand, cannot be sung in revues or cabarets. It needs no Broadway love lyrics. It is not "about" anything—except Duke himself.[15]

Give me a break, Spike . . . you've gotta be kidding. Gershwin was the foremost composer of tunes used by jazz musicians globally, and he was a magnificent improviser. I don't mean to overshadow Duke Ellington's contributions to jazz, but we certainly shouldn't minimize Gershwin's either. One is not mutually exclusive of the other. Both Duke and Gershwin were masters. Nuff said!

Conductor Leonard Bernstein gave a surprising opinion of the *Rhapsody* in later years. (Author's note, Bernstein conducted *Rhapsody in Blue* many times during his career.) He stated:

The *Rhapsody* is not a composition at all . . . but a string of separate paragraphs stuck together—with thin paste of flour and water. . . . One could cut out parts of it without affecting the whole in any way. . . . You can't just put four tunes together, God given though they may be, and call them a composition.[16]

Say what they will, the critics and naysayers can't really argue much with public opinion. Perhaps Paul Whiteman said it best:

The idea struck nearly everybody as preposterous at the start. Some hold to the same opinion still. But the list of pessimists was a little shorter, I believe, when at half-past five, on the afternoon of February 12, 1924, we took our fifth curtain call.[17]

"An Experiment in Modern Music" concert proved to be so popular that Whiteman presented another Aeolian Hall show on March 7th. He followed that with a Carnegie Hall performance on April 21, 1924, a benefit concert for the American Academy in Rome. (Please see the original program on page 152. My thanks go to Carnegie Hall Trust and Gino!)

In the months that followed, Whiteman took the show on the road for a thirty-concert tour throughout the United States and Canada, featuring Gershwin on the bill for most of it. My copy of the original souvenir program of the 1924 tour, with its cover price of 25 cents, notes that impresario F. C. Coppicus is the tour producer. (Coppicus's booking agency was the Metropolitan Musical Bureau, which was housed in the Aeolian building.)

However, in subsequent performances, "Pomp and Circumstance" was dropped from the program. It was only played that one time, at that first Aeolian Hall performance. As Maestro Peress said:

> Whiteman decided to end the 1924 concert program with *Pomp and Circumstance* following *Rhapsody in Blue,* but realized this was an anticlimax and dropped it from subsequent concerts and the tour.[18]

Immediately after the whirlwind tour, Victor Records recorded *Rhapsody in Blue* with the Whiteman Orchestra. (Those Victor executives knew how to strike when the iron was hot!) This recording was a shortened version, due to the limited amount of recording time on the 78 RPM records. (Other recordings of *Rhapsody* followed, but you always remember your first! It went down in history.)

The sheet music and licensing rights brought Gershwin a hefty sum of money. Some experts estimate it exceeded $250,000 (about $3.5 million today) in just a couple of years. In addition, in 1925, Gershwin cut two piano rolls of *Rhapsody in Blue* for Aeolian. The recordings are still available for purchase, and it's a real treat to hear the great Gershwin performing his own material.

A decade later, for the 10th anniversary of *Rhapsody in Blue,* Gershwin went on tour with the Leo Reisman Orchestra, traveling across the United States and Canada from January 13 to February 10, 1934. It was a grueling twenty-nine-day tour of twenty-eight cities.

Also in 1934, Gershwin signed on with NBC radio to play fifteen minutes of his music on Mondays and Fridays for a whopping two grand a week ($35,000 today), but I am getting ahead of myself a bit here.

Fifty years later, in 1984, Maestro Maurice Peress meticulously re-created the infamous "Experiment in Modern Music" in honor of its 60th anniversary. He later made a recording, which is a must-have piece for any serious collector. In "Livery Stable Blues," we can hear the clarinet wailing, as the trombone glides up and down, and the wood block, tapping like hooves to the trumpet, singing the melody. The clarinet neighs like a horse, passing it along to the trumpet, and the song ends with the clunking of a drumstick against a cowbell.

Peress conducted this concert scores of times following its 60th anniversary in 1984 well into the 1990s, effectively preserving its legacy and sharing its brilliance with the next generation and beyond. Much thanks to Maestro Peress for reconstructing and conducting Paul Whiteman's Historic Aeolian Hall Concert of 1924 for all to hear today. The recording is titled *The Birth of Rhapsody in Blue.* and it gives us a marvelous window in time and lets us hear that concert once again. Maestro Peress's liner notes are fantastic as well.

Stiff Upper Lip*

*A Damsel in Distress (1937)

Finally George Gershwin darted out on stage, took his place at the piano, glanced at Whiteman, and Whiteman signaled to Ross Gorman, his virtuosic clarinetist, whose skill with a glissando had inspired George to open his Rhapsody with an electrifying, rising sweep on the clarinet. Gorman produced the required electricity. The audience was suddenly all interested attention. At the conclusion of the piece, they burst into enthusiastic, sustained applause.[1]

THE GLISSANDO HEARD AROUND THE WORLD

The signature glissando at the beginning of *Rhapsody in Blue*, performed by woodwind virtuoso Ross Gorman, was actually an improvisation on Gershwin's original score.

At a rehearsal, Gorman had been tinkering around with the stiff, written clarinet opening by Gershwin, and in a moment of sheer genius, he pulled a low-register G to a high A, lipping it sharp all the way, especially in the final third of the segment. It was a fresh, daring, technically complicated and unique sound, never before heard from a clarinet.

Gorman used several techniques to achieve this new sound, including a muscular lip and sliding his fingers off the holes, plus some indescribable magic, a pinch of voodoo, and lots of *chutzpah!* At the time, there was not a single other clarinet player who could generate that sound. After this first performance, other clarinetists were able to figure out how to copy Gorman's newly created glissando. Some might go so far as to say that since *Rhapsody* is performed so often throughout the world today, many woodwind players have mastered this phrase, proving it is not that difficult after all.

Poppycock! Gorman was the innovator who paved the path for those musicians who came after him to try and conquer this glissando. Compare it to Einstein discovering the Theory of Relativity. Both were truly *aha!* moments. Once others saw the path, they merely followed the trailblazer. (In my youth, I constantly tried to imitate that passage on my clarinet. Impossible! I could never come close to achieving Gorman's smoothness and accuracy, but the pursuit alone gave me plenty of practice that helped develop my musical chops, as well as my embouchure [facial muscles and lip].)

In its upward *schmearing* glissando of notes, one note merging with another without ever stopping until it reaches the terminal high A, Gorman produced a feeling of Yiddish Klezmer. When Gershwin heard Gorman play this glissando, he loved it (possibly reminding him of his younger days growing up on the Lower East Side) and immediately wrote it into the piece as the opening line.

A word on Yiddish Klezmer music: Klezmer is a form of band music that was popular in the Jewish *shtetls* (villages and communities) of Central and Eastern Europe from the 15th through the 20th century. It featured the clarinet expressing many human-like sounds from the wail of an aching mother to yelping sarcastic laughter, weeping, and sobbing to sequels of sheer happiness and every other human emotional sound imaginable including the now famous *"kvetch."* If spirituals were Sunday Church music and the blues expressed the other six days of the week for blacks, then cantorial and prayer music was Saturday *Shul* music, and Klezmer expressed the other six days of the week for the Jews. Although Klezmer expressed the entire gamut of human emotions, much of it was also upbeat-fun music —think of the *hora* at a Jewish wedding or a bar mitzvah and you get the point. *Mazel tov!*

When looking at the score and listening to the glissando, I can clearly describe the clarinet solo as a three beat (with a hold) G/G# trill in the low register (also known as the chalumeau register), followed by a rapid seventeen-note ascent. In the musical notation, Gershwin scores each and every one of these seventeen notes, terminating the figure in the second measure by ending the upward ascent on a half note above the line Bb. But (approximately) halfway through that ascent, Gorman stopped playing individual notes and began to *schmear* the notes—a portamento (aka glissando) in musical lingo. Until that critical rehearsal, this sound technique was considered an impossible feat on a clarinet.

Let me explain this impossible (but not really), never-before-executed clarinet glissando/portamento in baseball terms. A runner on third base takes off to steal home plate. At first he is taking individual steps (notes), one after another (note after note). Then about halfway to home plate, he stops taking individual steps and proceeds to slide (glissando) toward home. Not taking individual steps anymore but rather taking a giant slide (glissando) gets him to home plate (high A). HE'S SAFE!

Technically, Gorman's opening solo could be described as a glissando or portamento solo, rising over two octaves plus—but all technicalities aside, it was simply revolutionary! This opening clarinet trill and the seventeen-note glissando has become one of the most recognizable musical quotations of all time—and some even feel that this single musical measure set the stage for the entire Roaring Twenties.

The story behind that iconic three-beat trill and its seventeen-note ascent is one of genius, talent, technicality, and strong-willed men who kept pushing each other to create something together that had never been heard before.

When Gershwin conceived the ascending clarinet glissando, he knew precisely the effect for which he was reaching: a hyperthyroid, hysterical wail, almost the voice for a hyperthyroid, hysterical era. He explained to Paul Whiteman's clarinetist, Ross Gorman, precisely how he wanted the passage to sound. At first Gorman insisted that no clarinetist could produce the effect Gershwin had in mind. The composer, however, was so intransigent that Gorman had to keep experimenting with various reeds and techniques until, at last, he brought to life Gershwin's music exactly as Gershwin had heard it with his inner ear. . . .

That opening is surely one of the unforgettable moments in contemporary music.[2]

In an interview with Henry Osgood, the author of *So This Is Jazz*, Whiteman said, "Who ever heard of a portamento on the clarinet such as Ross Gorman plays? Technically speaking, there is no such thing on the clarinet—but there it is." Osgood also said:

> [*The*] technical standard required of the player in a good jazz band is higher than that demanded from the same kind of instrumentalist in a symphony orchestra. Clarinets play portamenti that are theoretically impossible.[3]

Clearly, Whiteman hired the greatest musicians of the day, and Gershwin leveraged their exceptional talents to the limit to achieve a new perfection.

Later, Osgood added:

> Will anyone who heard Ross Gorman play the solo clarinet forget the astonishment he created in the very first measure when, half way up that seventeen-note run, he suddenly stopped playing separate notes and slid for home, on a long portamento that nobody knew could be done on a clarinet? It's not in any of the books. Ross spent days and days hunting round for a special reed that would allow him to do it. Days and days. That's the spirit that has made jazz what it is. By the way, what is it?[4]

In a September 1924 article entitled "Current Opinion," the music critic for the *New York Herald Tribune*, W. J. Henderson, said of Gorman's electrifying glissando:

> And now at last we have such a wizard as Ross Gorman, who can evoke the laugh of a hyena from a clarinet and the bark of a dog from the heckelphone . . . Portamento effects on wind instruments are the real jazz.[5]

There is no question in my mind or in the minds of many distinguished musicologist that *Rhapsody in Blue* carries in it an abundance of Eastern-European Jewish Klezmer-sounding passages. (Right from the beginning, with its signature clarinet glissando, we fall into a kind of Klezmer Blues fantasy world; anyone familiar with Klezmer music will relate to the variety of sounds and emotions that can emanate from the clarinet.) It's Jewish-black music, clearly reflecting the influence of Gershwin's early years on the Lower East Side and his exposure to the Yiddish Theatre. He also drew on his Upper West Side experience in Harlem afterhours clubs.

This Yiddish Klezmer flavor surfaces in other parts of the *Rhapsody* as well. Apparently, you can take the boy out of Brooklyn, but you can't ever take Brooklyn out of the boy. From the Lower East Side to the streets of Brooklyn to the Upper West Side, Klezmer is the soul music of the Jewish people. Even legendary jazz piano great Dick Hyman heard it in the glissando, stating, "Gorman's sound was very much in the East European-Jewish Klezmer tradition."[6]

Although this story is an often-repeated one, some believe otherwise. In his book, *George Gershwin: A New Biography*, William Hyland shared some alternative thoughts on the creation and inclusion of this famous clarinet intro:

> Some accounts claim that the opening clarinet glissando, or "smear," was clarinetist Ross Gorman's idea. In one account, he and Gershwin supposedly worked for an hour to get it right. Another version claimed that Gorman supposedly experimented with different clarinet reeds before he mastered the sound. One writer even claimed that this achievement was impossible before the *Rhapsody*.

All of this is nonsense. The glissando was similar to an exercise written in Gershwin's notebooks from his studies with Kilenyi. There are also examples in the standard text on orchestration by Cecil Forsyth, which Gershwin owned. Even a cursory acquaintance with the jazz clarinetists of the day would demonstrate the very same techniques. Such a phrase in the key of concert B-flat (C for a clarinet) is not that difficult.[7]

I sincerely appreciate Hyland's addition to the story, but I think he oversimplifies the facts. If this type of phrase was so accessible to musicians and composers, why did this particular version of the glissando by the Gershwin-Gorman team make such a lasting impact?

As one critic claimed in a February 23, 1924, article in *Musical America*:

> One should not neglect to mention the astonishing performances of Ross Gorman, who in a symphony orchestra would be called the concertmaster. This young virtuoso does things with reed instruments of every size, shape and color which are positively breathtaking.[8]

In a 1926 article titled, "Where Jazz Comes From," author Earl Chapin May wrote:

> I once spent an evening with Ross Gorman, of the Paul Whiteman organization, inventorying his stock in trade. Ross was primarily a saxophonist. But all jazz artists must specialize in effects. Ross was getting his with equipment valued at $3,540. . . . Ross makes about $400 a week.[9]

Let's do the math—$3,540 invested in musical instruments in 1926 equates to about $47,500 in today's dollars. His weekly salary of $400 would be about $5,400 a week today or a yearly salary of $280,000! Both the instruments and the musician were top of the line in every respect.

Ira Gershwin shared some interesting color on the glissando and its inclusion found in one of George's old notebooks. Ira said, "George had notated the glissando in one of his theme books for possible future use and instantly thought of it as an opening for the work [*Rhapsody in Blue*]."[10]

He also said of the glissando:

> His brother had long been impressed by the two-octave-plus glissando that Ross Gorman, Whiteman's clarinetist, could draw from his instrument. Before Gorman, such a long slide was thought to be technically impossible; Gorman not only played it effortlessly, but in such a way as to make the clarinet sound as if it were laughing or mocking itself.[11]

Olin Downes, chief critic for *The New York Times,* wrote of the glissando, "An outrageous cadenza on the clarinet . . . a flutter-tongued drunken whoop of an introduction which had the audience rocking."

Maybe part of the glissando's greatness and its unique memorability is that it means so many different things to so many people.

In an article, published in the June 1923 edition of *The Etude* magazine, titled "The Jazz Fiddler," the author is not very keen on the glissando technique (also called slides):

> The art of the jazz violinist, if art it can be called, is founded on the continual use of the glissando, that is, unbroken one-finger slides, *ad nauseum*. . . . Primitive people and savages like this sliding.[12]

This piece was published just seven months before Ross Gorman's historic glissando.

(Yes, I did just devote an entire section to the first bar of *Rhapsody in Blue* and its historic seventeen-note glissando. I promise, I will not examine the remaining 451 bars of the piece in such great detail.)

* * *

The Paul Whiteman Archives are held at Williams College in Williamstown, Massachusetts. My son was a student there, and we were thrilled to be able to spend some time poring through this material. To get to it, we descended the narrowest stairway I have ever seen into a basement jammed full of Whiteman-related materials. The archivist handed me the original file containing all of the orchestra parts to *Rhaposdy in Blue*. Low and behold, the first score in the file was the clarinet's.

There I stood with my wife, Julie, and our son, Isaac (also a sax player), holding the original musical charts that Gershwin created and Ross Gorman actually performed. What a rich and humbling moment. (A couple of days later, with great pride, I watched my son, Isaac, graduate from Williams College while the band played *Pomp and Circumstance* in the background, once again connecting me to the original 1924 Aeolian Hall "Experiment" concert.) The circle had completed.

Could You Use Me?*

*Girl Crazy (1930)

Without a doubt, the Whiteman "Experiment" would not have made such a lasting impression on American culture without *Rhapsody in Blue*. Simply put, this music is one of the most celebrated and performed symphonic works of the 20th century. The *Rhapsody* has been broadcast over the radio, performed as a ballet, and made into a movie; it's been arranged for a solo piano, two pianos, a harmonica orchestra, a mandolin orchestra, and more. In the opening ceremonies of the 1984 Olympics in Los Angeles, a group of eighty-four pianists played *Rhapsody in Blue* in unison, on eighty-four pianos, honoring the 60th anniversary of its premiere performance at Aeolian Hall. The point is: people can't get enough of *Rhapsody in Blue*. Throughout the world, piano soloists, orchestras, bands of all sizes, even pop groups perform all or parts of this remarkable piece of music. Duke Ellington, Glenn Miller, Oscar Levant, Leonard Bernstein, and Arthur Fiedler's POPs, and many others have performed *Rhapsody* over the years.

There are recordings of George Gershwin playing the piano on *Rhapsody*, both with the Paul Whiteman Orchestra and as a soloist, that are lifted from his original piano rolls.

I have an original Harms score of the piano solo, and on the title page it is noted, "Dedicated to Paul Whiteman." It also indicates there is a second piano part. A newer version of the piano solo sheet music by New World Music Corporation mentions the "Two Pianos—Four Hands (original setting)."

In 1998, the centennial year of his birth, George Gershwin was awarded a posthumous Pulitzer Prize for his distinguished and enduring contributions to American music. Believe it or not, his not-so-baby sister, Frankie Gershwin Godowsky accepted the prize! That same year, George and Ira were immortalized with a star on the Hollywood Walk of Fame. (That was certainly a long wait. In show biz terms, it was light years!)

George played the piano at his sister Frances's wedding to Leopold Godowsky, Jr., at brother Ira's penthouse apartment. He played the *Rhapsody* as a wedding march![1]

The Gershwin Estate had a momentous year in 1987 when fifty years after Gershwin's demise and sixty-three years after the *Rhapsody's* debut, the trustees signed a multi-year contract with United Airlines for the rights to use *Rhapsody in Blue* as their advertising theme song. The annual fee was (drum roll, please) $300,000 per year! EVERY YEAR! This marked the first time *Rhapsody* was ever used in commercial advertising.² *

So how did this deal work out for United Airlines? Well, as of 2015, the airline has been using *Rhapsody in Blue* as its theme song, as well as in advertising, for over a quarter of a century! In 2010, United Airlines merged with Continental Airlines to form the world's largest airline. Two years after that merger, on January 12, 2012, United issued the following statement:

> United Airlines, now officially merged with Continental Airlines, will continue using its catchy theme song *Rhapsody in Blue*.
>
> "We're going to keep that around, but whether it will be part of ad campaigns, we haven't decided," said United Holdings spokesman Rahassan Johnson. "We have the rights to use it, so we will."
>
> United Airlines purchased the rights to George Gershwin's familiar 1924 piano music in 1976 and has used it in radio and television spots since the mid-1980s.
>
> The music will also continue playing at Chicago O'Hare International Airport. "If you walk between concourses B and C, you hear it playing overhead. It will still be around," Johnson said.³

Rhapsody in Blue has been "flying the friendly skies of United" for over a quarter century. Now that's a song with legs . . . and wings!

Victor Records released a recording of *Rhapsody in Blue* on June 10, 1924, to great acclaim. That year and the next were extremely successful ones for Gershwin. The hits kept rolling in from shows like *George White's Scandals of 1924* (June 1924); *Primrose* (September 1924); *Lady, Be Good!* (December 1924); *Tell Me More* (April 1925); and *Concerto in F* and *Tip-Toes* (both by the end of 1925). That's a remarkable level of output, especially considering that each Broadway show contained multiple songs. Gershwin was a prolific workhorse, but he had even loftier goals in mind.

After the success of *Rhapsody in Blue*, Gershwin was eager to prove that he was not just a "one-hit wonder" in the concert world. His ambition drove him to sign a contract with the New York Symphony Orchestra, committing to compose a "serious" work and perform it with the orchestra at Carnegie Hall! Imagine that!

---

*The author's source of this information is *The Washington Post*, November 25, 1987. (www.highbeam.com/doc/1P2–1356228.html). However, you will notice that this endnote gives a date for the deal of 1987, which is different from the date, 1976, in the information in the excerpt quoted by Rahassan Johnson that follows (http://articles.chicagotribune.com/2012–01–05/business/chi-united-to-keep-rhapsody-in-blue-as-theme-song-20120105_1_theme-song-rhapsody-united-airlines).

Concerto in F*

*(1925)

> George always "had a very special affection for the concerto," preferring it to all his other concert pieces.
>
> —IRA GERSHWIN[1]

One of Gershwin's early fans was Walter Damrosch, a composer and also conductor, and director of the New York Symphony Orchestra. As the story goes, Damrosch was at the Aeolian Hall performance and was so impressed with the *Rhapsody* that he commissioned Gershwin to compose, orchestrate, and perform a full-scale piano concerto for the New York Symphony Orchestra.

Let's understand this situation clearly. The director of the world-renowned New York Symphony commissioned an untrained, Brooklyn-born, Jewish, Tin Pan Alley song plugger—who according to some might have gotten lucky with a one-hit wonder (*Rhapsody in Blue*)—to compose *and* orchestrate (which Gershwin did not do for *Rhapsody*) a symphonic piano concerto for one of the top symphonies in the world! It all seemed reasonable. What could possibly go wrong with such a plan?

Author's note: the original December 3, 1924, Carnegie Hall Program signed by George Gershwin. Many thanks to the Carnegie Hall Trust and Gino Francesconi, Director, Archives & Museum, Carnegie Hall

Just a smidgen over a year after *Rhapsody in Blue* premiered at Aeolian Hall, Gershwin signed the contract for the new gig, which was slated for performance in early December 1925. The deal paid Gershwin $500 (the equivalent of $6,800 today) to compose the work and perform it with the orchestra seven times (only six performances actually occurred).

Let's take a moment to consider the situation. Gershwin contractually had committed to deliver an orchestral concert work, supplying both the music as well as the orchestration, both of which he had absolutely no experience in doing. Not only that, he had agreed to deliver the goods in less than seven months, leaving enough time for the orchestra to rehearse with him on the piano. Now, that's *chutzpah*!

But wait! There's more! The piece was to premiere in, of all places, Carnegie Hall. If Gershwin was going to fail, he would do so naked and in front of the most powerful people in music and the arts at their high temple of classical music and culture: Carnegie Hall. Now, *that's* **really** *chutzpah*!

For me, that's like some Brooklyn kid pitching in a schoolyard stickball game, and a scout comes and signs him to pitch for the Brooklyn Dodgers in the seventh game of the World Series against the New York Yankees. Oh, and yes, the game starts in three hours, so make sure your Mom packs a peanut butter and jelly sandwich. (Truth be told, in my youth, I was a southpaw pitcher in the Brooklyn sandlot leagues, and that was *my* dream, but then again, it was every boy's dream in the 1950s.)

George was up for the challenge. Even though he was a proven master of the piano and a notable composer, he still felt he had something to prove to the critics. As he later told his biographer:

Many persons had thought that the *Rhapsody* was only a happy accident. Well, I went out, for one thing, to show them that there was plenty more where that had come from. I made up my mind to do a piece of absolute music. The *Rhapsody*, as its title implied, was a blues impression. The *Concerto* would be unrelated to any program. And that is exactly how I wrote it. I learned a great deal from that experience. Particularly in the handling of instruments in combination.[2]

It's hard to believe that such an accomplished master still felt the need "to show them." This comment exemplifies one of the most paradoxical aspects of Gershwin's remarkably successful career. He had a nearly superhuman drive accompanied by great insecurity.

Although his working title was *New York Concerto*, he eventually changed the name to make it sound more like a pure concerto, rather than only a popular piece. Clearly, Gershwin was striving to distance himself from his Tin Pan Alley/Broadway roots and blend in with the "serious" music world and the upper crust of Carnegie Hall.

The tale of the *Concerto in F* continues with Gershwin then embarking on a journey of classical musical self-education. He purchased books on harmony, composition, and orchestration. Yet before learning how to orchestrate, Gershwin had to figure out one very important detail—the definition of a concerto! He soon learned that a concerto is a three-movement piece written for a solo instrument (a piano, in this case), accompanied by an orchestra. This twenty-six-year-old Brooklyn-born kid actually thrived on challenges and working way outside his knowledge base.

To concentrate and devote more time to the work, he left New York City's sweltering summer heat and sequestered himself in a pianist friend's Chautauqua cabin, in Western New York State, south of Buffalo and near Lake Erie. Gershwin started working on the *Concerto* in July 1925, and finished (composing and orchestrating) on November 10, approximately four months later.

Gershwin said of the *Concerto in F*:

> The first movement employs the Charleston rhythm. It is quick and pulsating, representing the young enthusiastic spirit of American life. It begins with a rhythmic motif given out by the kettledrums, supported by other percussion instruments, and with a Charleston motif introduced by bassoon, horns, clarinet and violas. The principal theme is announced by the bassoon. Later, a second theme is introduced by the piano.
>
> The second movement has a poetic nocturnal atmosphere which has come to be referred to as the American blues, but in a purer form than that in which they are usually treated.
>
> The final movement reverts to the style of the first. It is an orgy of rhythms, starting violently and keeping to the same pace throughout.[3]

Perhaps because of Gershwin's insecurity, he hired sixty musicians to perform a dry run of his *Concerto*. He played the piano, while his pal William Daly conducted the orchestra. He then held some additional rehearsals with Walter Damrosch listening. After a few minor edits, George felt the work was ready for prime time. Carnegie Hall, here we come!

Concerto in F debuted in Carnegie Hall on the afternoon of December 3, 1925, just two months shy of the two-year anniversary of the *Rhapsody's* debut. Just like the Aeolian concert, Carnegie Hall hosted a full house, even though the weather was horrible. Once again the audience was comprised of both the highbrow classical music élite with upturned noses and lowbrow Tin Pan Alley types with runny noses. All segments of the arts and the world of music were represented that day.

Of course, the concert program was jam packed with classical works, but Damrosch saved the best for last. The audience was again overcome by the creative genius of Gershwin, not only as composer and arranger, but also as a formidable concert pianist. The show ended with earsplitting applause. Gershwin had once again redefined his personal boundaries, as well as those of jazz, in this first-ever jazz concerto. BRAVO!

Gershwin inserted modern jazz and also dance music like the Charleston into this highbrow work. Believe it or not, the blues was ironically much more a part of the *Concerto in F* than it was his *Rhapsody in Blue*. This point is clearly made in the book *Gershwin: Rhapsody in Blue* by the composer and music expert David Schiff. He wrote:

> The principal idea of the second movement is a blues, which owes more to the "race" blues of Bessie Smith than Handy. The delicate scoring for the clarinet trio and muted trumpet sounds like a transcription of the recordings Smith made with Fletcher Henderson or James. P. Johnson on piano. Although the first statement of the blues theme is 16 bars long, its structure follows the classic 12-bar design (which Gershwin had not used in the *Rhapsody*). The extra four bars in the first statement of the theme are just an echo.
>
> The "modernism" of the *Rhapsody* also returns in the Concerto, but in an updated form—as the percussive opening immediately proclaims. The powerful tune that the piano plays at its first entrance is written on the tones of an A flat blues scale, though Gershwin approaches the blues third through the downward leap of a major seventh—something he would never do in a show tune.

... The third movement, which Gershwin called an "orgy of rhythm" updates the Confreyesque cross-rhythms of the *Rhapsody* with hints of Stravinsky.[4]

Musician, music critic, and friend of Gershwin Samuel Chotzinof opined the day after hearing his friend's *Concerto in F* performance, "The truth is George Gershwin is a genius ... an instinctive artist." He went on to say:

The slow movement, a Blues whose themes closely resembled the fine Negro improvisations ... is to my mind a masterpiece. I can recall nothing in modern music so beautiful, so haunting, so "kiddingly" melancholy ... Mr. Gershwin played his concerto excellently and simply and disposed of its difficulties as if he had been a concert pianist all his life.[5]

George's boss for the *Concerto,* the conductor Walter Damrosch also noted:

Various composers have been walking around jazz like a cat around a plate of hot soup, waiting for it to cool off so that they could enjoy it without burning their tongues, hitherto accustomed only to the more tepid liquid distilled by cooks of the classical school. Lady Jazz, adorned with her intriguing rhythms, has danced her way around the world. ... But for all her travels and her sweeping popularity she has encountered no knight who could lift her to a level that would enable her to be received as a respectable member in musical circles. George Gershwin seems to have accomplished this miracle. He has done it boldly by dressing this extremely independent and up-to-date young lady in the classic garb of a concerto. Yet he has not detracted one whit from her fascinating personality. He is the Prince who has taken Cinderella by the hand and openly proclaimed her a princess to the astonished world, no doubt to the fury of her envious sisters.[6]

Walter Damrosch also said:

I still think that the second movement of this concerto, with its dreamy atmosphere of a summer night in a garden of our South, reaches a high water mark of his talent.[7]

F—the Concerto! Not everybody thought *Concerto in F* was wonderful. The Classical music critic Lawrence Gilman wrote:

We think it is only fairish music—conventional, trite, at its worst a little dull. ... We listened with uncomfortably strained ears to catch a hint of that self-confident and untrammeled Young America ... Instead we heard a facile and anxiously conformist youth stalking the stale platitudes of the symphonic concert hall—retailing exhausted clichés.[8]

Music critic and author Oscar Thompson also opined on the *Concerto* saying:

The musical comedy writer further sacrificed vigor and directness of utterance and became much more self-conscious and artificial than in the *Rhapsody*. The plain truth was that he had not the technical ability to accomplish what he set out to do. Jazz or no jazz, a concerto was beyond him, and such attempts as were made at development of themes—these, in themselves, trite, unoriginal, banal—sounded a continual call for help.[9]

Referring to Gershwin as "the musical comedy writer" was certainly an attempt to disparage him as a Tin Pan Alley/Broadway musical hack. I guess the joke is on Oscar what's-his-name, and it's one heck of a long-lasting joke!

The John Kerry "I voted for it before I voted

against it" Award goes to music author Charles L. Buchanan, who first disliked the *Concerto in F* and then changed his tune to wholeheartedly support it (as well as our golden boy, George Gershwin). In an article published in *The Outlook* on February 2, 1927, entitled "Gershwin and Musical Snobbery," Buchanan expressed his change of heart on the *Concerto*:

> I wrote about it last season. At that time it had seemed to me self-conscious, tongue-tied and partially sterile; although even at first hearing the unprecedented, queer beauty of the second movement made itself felt unmistakably. I am now inclined to assert that this work can hold its own with the finest examples of this form of composition that we have. Given a fair trial (which is precisely what one fears it will not be given), its second and third movements will go miles ahead of such outstanding and popular works as the Tchaikovsky *B-flat Minor Concerto* or the Rachmaninoff *C Minor Concerto*.[10]

Earlier in the article, he also stated of the work that it was "to be ranked the one composition of indubitable vitality, originality, and authentic progressiveness that this country has produced." The author tells us that because of Gershwin's connection with Tin Pan Alley, Broadway musicals and popular music, the "Musical Snobs" would not take him and his music seriously. At the end, he declared, "This music is rattling good fun, to begin with, and fascinating, at times exquisite music, to end with . . . There is nothing in all music quite like the second movement of this *Concerto*."

The award for the funniest statement about the *Concerto in F* goes to Gershwin's Tin Pan Alley pal Irving Berlin who sent the following telegram to Gershwin for the premiere:

> I HOPE YOUR CONCERTO IN F IS AS GOOD AS MINE IN F SHARP STOP SERIOUSLY GEORGIE I AM ROOTING HARD FOR THE SUCCESS AND GLORY YOU SO RICHLY DESERVE . . . IRVING BERLIN[11]

But not everyone was thrilled with the uncouth, uneducated, youthful Jewish Tin Pan Alley, high-school dropout upstart crashing the gates of the classical fortress. In *Hot Jazz: The Guide to Swing Music*, author Hugues Panassié wrote:

> As to the works of a Gershwin, such as *Rhapsody in Blue* and the *Concerto in F*, the less said the better. It is music which dimly resembles jazz only because of the instrumentation used and, still more dimly, by reason of certain bastard tunes distantly related to hot music. But swing, which makes all real jazz, is entirely absent from these works; such compositions are, really, most closely related to symphonic music.[12]

Musicologist, author, and lecturer Sigmund Spaeth also opined on the *Concerto* saying:

> Gershwin's *Concerto in F*, for piano and symphony orchestra, is even more significant. It is perhaps the best piece of absolute music yet composed by a native American. . . . The basic musical ideas, however, sparkle with individual genius and the jazz treatment is always legitimate.[13]

George's older brother, Ira, further proudly noted:

> In 1930 when Albert Coates, the eminent English conductor, compiled a list of Fifty Best Works in Music there was included only one American work and that was the *Concerto in F*.[14]

After *Rhapsody in Blue*, Gershwin had become the new toast of the town, as well as the entire nation. The accolades elevated his stature by leaps and bounds, and his output from *Rhapsody in Blue* at the beginning of 1924 to the *Concerto in F* at the end of 1925 was enormous and successful. The Gershwins were picking up steam on Broadway, beginning just a couple of weeks before the Aeolian Hall performance of *Rhapsody in Blue* in February 1924. From that date until the end of December 1925, they were on a tear—*Sweet Little Devil* (January 1924), *Rhapsody in Blue* (February 1924), *George White's Scandals of 1924* (June 1924), British show *Primrose* (September 1924), *Lady, Be Good!* (December 1924), *Tell Me More* (April 1925), *Concerto in F* (December 1925), and *Tip-Toes* (December 1925). That's an aggressive production schedule! And remember that between April and December 1925, not only did George have to write a concerto, but he also had to teach himself the art of orchestration. He was one busy cat indeed.

George received commissions for Broadway shows for many seasons to come, scoring hit after hit for years. *Lady, Be Good!* (1924), *Tip-Toes* (1925), *Oh, Kay!* (1926), *Strike Up the Band* and *Funny Face* (1927), *Rosalie* (1928), *Show Girl* (1929), *Girl Crazy* (1930), and many more became huge hits.

These were the years when he and Ira solidified their dominance in composition (George) and lyrics (Ira). They were an unbeatable team. The historic first-ever Pulitzer Prize for a musical, *Of Thee I Sing* (1931), was the icing on the cake. (Author's note: Although Ira and the writers received the prize, George did not, even though he was intimately involved in the show.) In 1935, George wrote the now classic songs "Summertime," "It Ain't Necessarily So," and "I Got Plenty o' Nuttin'"; indeed, all were featured in his groundbreaking opera, *Porgy and Bess*.

Cranking out Broadway musical tunes, year after year, was only one aspect of this great man's creative output. During these years, George also created many critically acclaimed "serious" musical scores, including *Preludes for Piano* (1926), *An American in Paris* (1928), *Second Rhapsody* (1931), *Cuban Overture* (1935), and the aforementioned American opera, *Porgy and Bess* (1935).

Before we venture any further, it's time to delve deeper into the man we all know as George Gershwin.

A Typical Self-Made American*

*Strike up the Band (1927 and 1930)

I feel that I was meant for hard physical work, to chop down trees, to use my muscles. This composing is indoor labor, much of it, and it takes it out of a fellow like me. . . . When I'm in my normal mood the tunes come dripping off my fingers. And they're lively tunes, full of outdoor pep.
—GEORGE GERSHWIN[1]

"The tunes come dripping off my fingers. . . ." What a perfect way to describe how easily his musical genius flowed! Although Gershwin's music career was but a short twenty years, he composed a vast amount of music in that short time. As he explained it, "I write 15 songs a day. . . . That's the way I get the bad ones out of my system."[2]

Overflowing with creativity, he kept notebooks full of music and musical ideas—a habit acquired during his days as a Tin Pan Alley song plugger. George once lost one of his prized notebooks that contained over forty songs. Rather than freaking out, he shrugged it off; he couldn't be bothered. The way Ira told it, George had so many new ideas that he didn't need to worry about lost material. His attitude as far as his music was concerned was there was always lots more where that came from.

As prolific as he was, George Gershwin was much more than a fountain of music; he was also a supremely complex man. He certainly embodied the song title "A Typical Self-Made American," and, paradoxically, he was also an *atypical* self-made American. This brilliant double entendre, written by Ira, fits George like no other.

As the son of hardworking immigrants who had fled the tyranny of Jew-hating Czarist Russia, George spent his childhood on the streets of New York—an unanchored high-school dropout, drifting from Brooklyn to Harlem to the Lower East Side of Manhattan. Wandering from place to place was a typical life for countless American Jews in the early 1900s. And yet, George grew to become a one-of-a-kind American treasure who inspired the world with his talent, artistry, innovation, and mastery. Atypical, indeed!

Beyond his background and achievements, Gershwin had many other facets. I won't pretend to address them all or capture their true depth, but I would be remiss to leave out some of the key personal characteristics that I think made him the man he was.

George Gershwin was brimming with nervous energy; indeed, many described him as a "high-energy guy." As Gershwin biographer David Ewen wrote:

> Gershwin was a human dynamo. He rarely walked on the street or the golf course—he had to run. He rarely walked slowly up a flight of stairs, but leaped a few steps at a time. He had more vitality when sick than others did in the full flush of health.
>
> He was a man of irrepressible enthusiasms, a man who had an extraordinary zest for living and for enjoying.
>
> When he found a new diversion he went after it with an incomparable intensity and passion. When it was golf (his game was in the 80s), he played it every free moment he could find, and golf dominated his conversation and thinking all the time. Then it was something else: backgammon, croquet, ping pong, photography, fishing, swimming, horseback riding, roulette. Generally he preferred pastimes that taxed his muscles. He was physically powerful, with the build of an athlete and muscles that knew the discipline of exercise. Besides participating in various sports, he was methodical about doing setting-up exercises at regular intervals. He liked baseball a great deal, but rarely played it for fear of hurting his hands.
>
> His fine muscular co-ordination that made him such a splendid pianist (and frequently without practicing), and so good an athlete, also made him an excellent dancer.[3]

An "excellent dancer" indeed! Master hoofer Fred Astaire once shared a story about Gershwin helping him create a dance routine for the song "Fascinating Rhythm":

> During final rehearsals of the "Fascinating Rhythm" number, just before we were ready to leave for the opening in Philadelphia, Adele and I were stuck for an exit step. We had the routine set but needed a climax wow step to get us off. For days I couldn't find one. Neither could dance director, Sammy Lee.
>
> George happened to drop by, and I asked him to look at the routine. He went to the piano. Ukulele Ike was doing his stuff with the "Lamb Chop," as he called it. [*Author's note: "Lamb Chop" is musician lingo for the ukulele because the instrument is shaped like a lamb chop. So Ukulele Ike "doing stuff with the 'Lamb Chop'" meant he was fartzing around on his ax. But don't ask me . . . I am a vegetarian!*]
>
> We went all through the thing, reaching the last step before the proposed exit and George said, "Now travel—travel with that one."
>
> I stopped to ask what he meant, and he jumped up from the piano and demonstrated what he visualized. He wanted us to continue doing the last step, which started center stage, and sustain it as we traveled to the side, continuing until we were out of sight off stage.
>
> The step was a complicated precision rhythm thing in which we kicked out simultaneously as we crossed back and forth in front of each other with arm pulls and heads back. There was a lot going on, and when George suggested traveling, we didn't think it was possible.
>
> It was the perfect answer to our problem, however, this suggestion by hoofer Gershwin, and it turned out to be a knockout applause puller.[4]

The fact that Gershwin taught Fred and Adele Astaire a "knockout applause puller" step is a true testament to his multifaceted genius. Music moved not only through his mind, heart, and hands, but also through the rest of his body, all the way down to his feet and toes! This cat had soul.

Despite his commitment to fitness, George was also an avid cigar smoker. This became a defining characteristic of Gershwin's public persona—big, black cigars. (Remember, as mentioned several sections back, his father once owned a cigar shop.) In photos, caricatures, and pictures of Gershwin, it's commonplace to see a cigar perched between his lips or in his hand. There are numerous photos of him smoking a pipe, as well. Being a fitness fanatic while smoking cigars demonstrates he was indeed a complex man, but at the time, the two actions hadn't yet been connected negatively.

He quit the habit in June 1931; then in a September 1931 letter to his old flame, Rosamond Walling, the cousin of brother Ira's wife, Leonore, he humorously wrote:

> I gave up smoking three months ago & not one puff of smoke has passed through these lips. I may start smoking again someday if only to live up to those caricatures of me with a corona-corona in my face.[5]

He was brutally frank and honest about others, and even more so about himself and his music.

Gershwin's pal DuBose Heyward, who wrote the novel *Porgy* in 1925 and later partnered with the Gershwin brothers to transform the story into the American folk opera, *Porgy and Bess*, said of George:

> My first impression of my collaborator remains with me and is singularly vivid. A young man of enormous physical and emotional vitality, who possessed the faculty of seeing himself quite impersonally and realistically, and who knew exactly what he wanted and where he was going. This characteristic put him beyond both modesty and conceit. About himself he would merely mention certain facts, aspirations, failings. They were usually right.[6]

Beyond both modesty and also any conceit? That's an exceptionally high mark to hit! But George was a "what you see is what you get" kind of guy.

Gershwin biographer Merle Armitage wrote:

> As a man, George Gershwin had qualities of heart and mind which were extremely ingratiating. He was entirely sincere. His ability to achieve a good bargain in a business sense resulted from his protecting his own very generous nature. He always seemed to be in balance. He had a very definite idea of his place in the world and his importance as an artist—yet he was modest. I have seen him blush at flattery. Although he often presented a somewhat cold exterior, I have known the inner warmth of his friendship. George Gershwin possessed the love of Broadway, the admiration of the motion picture industry, and the respect of the serious musical world—an unparalleled accomplishment. He had one supreme quality, without which everything else would have availed [him] little. He had style![7]

Unlike Ira, his shy, quiet brother, George was extremely gregarious and personable—always the life of the party and always eager to entertain from the piano bench. A painter of merit (which I will explore later) and a skilled photographer as well, George was one of the most sought-after bachelors on the New York City arts and society scene.

Although generally modest, even self-deprecating at times, he was also sometimes seen as a braggart by those who did not understand his frankness. As the composer, conductor, and pianist Alexander Steinert put it:

One of George Gershwin's greatest qualities was his complete belief in what he was doing, and this was not always appreciated and understood by those who did not know him well. He knew he had something to say, and he said it. He was always open to conviction, however, and frankly admitted when he felt he had fallen short of the goal he had set. He was distinctly ambitious, and no one can say what his next major work might have been... He was a great perfectionist, and whatever he undertook he did well, whether it was painting, photography, or sports.[8]

Clearly a dynamic personality, his friends and critics spoke at length about his particular quirks and *mishegas*, or craziness.

One of Gershwin's idiosyncrasies was a habit of cracking his neck. He explained this cracking habit in an article in the *New York World* May 4, 1930, edition where we learn, "his bones are dry and that he cracks them in the manner of a person cracking his fingers."[9] Spending endless hours on the piano stool might have contributed to his need to crack his stiff neck.

Gershwin differed from other celebrities in that he did not employ a press agent or a business manager, and he only used a lawyer on an as-needed basis rather than keeping one on retainer.

The conductor Walter Damrosch, who signed Gershwin to compose and perform *Concerto in F*, said, "I developed a strong affection for him personally, and for the genuineness of his musical talent. He had an almost child-like affection and pride for his own music. . . ."[10]

Ferde Grofé, Paul Whiteman's orchestrator extraordinaire, described his first meeting with the then-twenty-two-year-old Gershwin at the Palais Royal in 1920. Grofé had just arranged one of George's hit tunes for the Whiteman Orchestra. "The young composer was extremely modest and grateful, and expressed his pleasure and thanks for what I had done to his piece."[11]

Porgy and Bess director, Rouben Mamoulian, also said of Gershwin:

> George was like a child. He had a child's innocence and imagination. He could look at the same thing ever so many times and yet see it anew every time he looked at it and enjoy it . . . George was like a child . . . He was a complicated, nervous product of our age . . . an intricate and restless combination of intellectual and emotional forces . . . With all this, George had a keen and joyous sense of humor.[12]

To explain Gershwin's unique sense of humor, Mamoulian shared a conversation the two had once had:

Rouben: "Tell me, George, how much does a psycho-analyst usually charge?"

Gershwin: "He finds out how much you make and then charges you more than you can afford!"[13]

His humor was laced with unapologetic genuineness and ingenuity as Mamoulian wrote, "George was so completely naïve and innocent in his liking of his own work that it actually became one of the endearing qualities of his nature."[14]

Pianist/composer and Gershwin friend Oscar Levant told a story about sharing a sleeping compartment on a train to a concert where he and Gershwin were to appear. Gershwin immediately claimed the highly desirable lower berth. No words were spoken, but Gershwin sensed Levant's displeasure with the sleeping arrangement. So Gershwin teased, "Upper berth, lower berth—that's the difference between talent and genius."[15] The two musicians had a close, complicated, and warm/cold relationship, but George was always the top dog and never hesitated to let Levant know it.

Of course, Levant had no problem jabbing Gershwin right back. At a high-society party, where George was playing his usual role as the center of attention, Levant asked him quite pointedly, "Tell me, George, if you had to do it all over, would you fall in love with yourself again?"[16]

Paradoxically, Gershwin also had a modest and self-deprecating side to his personality. He was self-conscious about his lack of formal music training that so many other professionals did have. Those missing years of tutoring seemed to bother him. He often said, "There is so much I have to learn."

He once told composer Jerome Kern ("Ol' Man River" and "Smoke Gets in Your Eyes"), "I am a man with a little bit of talent and a great deal of *chutzpah*."[17] Yes, Gershwin actually attributed his immense success more to his *chutzpah* (nerve and confidence) than to his talent! What a revealing comment from this modest, exceptionally talented and very gentle authentic artist.

In many ways, George Gershwin was also an extremely disciplined man—especially when it came to composing. To him, writing music was a discipline, like exercise, and he needed to keep writing in order to stay in shape. At his "fittest," he could write six songs a day.

In a 1930 *New York Times* article, Ira described George's routine:

> He composes, so far as routine is concerned, at no regular hours. Sometimes he is at the piano early in the afternoon, sometimes at three in the morning. When he gets eight bars he likes, he can finish a chorus in a couple of minutes. I have known him to write four tunes in an afternoon, tunes I thought he would put down for future use, only to find next day that he had discarded them.[18]

Most of his composing was done in the afternoon or at night. He often stayed up until the wee hours and then went to bed for seven or eight hours.

> He often works far into the morning; and, if you see a tall, slender young man with thick, dark hair and large brown eyes toying with a bowl of porridge at a marble-top lunch counter on upper Broadway anywhere from 2 A.M. to 6 A.M:, you may be watching the recuperation of a popular hero from the creation of a foxtrot or a piano prelude.[19]

George described his process in more detail to his biographer Isaac Goldberg:

> My work is done almost exclusively at night, and my best is achieved in the fall and winter months. A beautiful spring or summer day is least conductive to making music, for I always prefer the outdoors to the work. I don't write at all in the mornings for the obvious reason that I am not awake at the time. The afternoon I devote to physical labor—orchestrations, piano copies, etc. At night, when other people are asleep or out for a good time, I can get absolute quiet for my composing. Not that perfect peace is always necessary; often I have written my tunes with people in the same room or playing cards in the next. If I find myself in the desired mood I can hold it until I finish the song.[20]

I find this explanation fascinating. How then should we understand songs like "Summertime" and "Sing of Spring," which were written about those particular two seasons when he was admittedly less productive?

George liked to write music while sitting at the piano; he said he always needed the piano for writing. But obviously, there were times that songs came to him while he was away from the piano. He also did not need complete solitude to compose, and on many an occasion, he would compose songs while surrounded by people. It seemed nothing could block his need to compose music.

Pianist extraordinaire Oscar Levant was fascinated by George's relationship with the piano:

> Listening to him improvise and play was enough for me. He had such fluency at the piano and so steady a surge of ideas that any time he sat down just to amuse himself, something came of it. Actually this is how he got most of his ideas—just by playing. He enjoyed writing so much because, in a sense, it was play for him—the thing he liked to do more than anything else.[21]

In an article discussing the lack of creativity in Broadway musicals, Gershwin renamed the "Great White Way" the "Great Blight Way." Discussing his own creative process, he said:

> I can think of no more nerve-wracking, no more mentally arduous task than making music. There are times when a phrase of music will cost me many hours of internal sweating. Rhythms romp through my brain, but they're not easy to capture and keep; the chief difficulty is to avoid reminiscence.

In the same article, he described his own music writing procedure:

> I sit at the piano and play. Thus I find myself most frequently at the piano while composing. . . . Like the denizens of the prize ring, the songwriter must always keep in training. He must try to write something every day. I know that if I don't do any writing for several weeks I lose a great deal of time in catching my stride again. Hence, I am always composing.[22]

George Newell wrote in his 1929 article "George Gershwin and Jazz":

> I saw Mr. Gershwin a few weeks ago, following the New York opening of "Rosalie," and I can best characterize his present condition as imminently volcanic. Something is going to happen soon. He is so calm outside that his insides must be seething. Something big is coming. Is it another *Rhapsody in Blue?* No one can say but George Gershwin himself, as he writes high up in the sound-proof studio at the top of his New York home.[23]

Newell also said:

> Every inch of this tall young man is that of a gentleman. He is poised, quiet, and well-mannered. He is genuinely polite, kind, and considerate. He is always willing to listen to the work of any other composer and advise him. The names of the men and women whom he has helped along the barbed road to success would give our typesetter a dizzy morning. Yet he is not a rail-splitter, nor is he the arrogant, temperamental qualities of a Wagner or a Debussy.
>
> As a man, I should say he is more like that kindly, naïve composer Mozart. Mozart, you will recall, was that fastidious gentleman so patently at home in either the glittering Court of Vienna or the smoky cottage of a roadside peasant.
>
> If any harassed process-server ever has occasion to search out the presence of Mr. Gershwin, I advise him to look either at Mrs. Astor's or "Pop" Connolly's lunch-wagon. If he is at the wagon, Mr. Gershwin will be the only diner whose elbows do not garnish the counter![24]

The author Gilbert Seldes described Gershwin in his 1924 book, *The 7 Lively Arts*, as follows:

Gershwin is capable of everything. . . . His sentiment is gentler than Berlin's, his "attack" more delicate. Delicacy, even dreaminess, is a quality he alone brings into jazz music. And his sense of variation in rhythm, of an oddly placed accent, of emphasis and colour, is impeccable.[25]

Later in his career, Gershwin told an interviewer:

[I] would like to be known as the "insomnia composer." I'd like my music to keep people—all kinds of people—awake when they should be sleeping. I'd like my compositions to be so vital that I'd be required by law to dispense sedatives with each score sold.[26]

For the record, in a 1930 article that appeared in the *New York World*, we learn that "George Gershwin believed that the best music he has ever written is contained in the score of *Strike up the Band*."[27] The show featured "The Man I Love" and "I've Got a Crush on You," among other jazz classics. The article goes on to say that his favorite tune for entertaining at parties was "Liza" (from *Show Girl*).

In Bennett Cerf's (the *What's My Line?* guy) 1944 book of witticisms, Cerf shared a story about George Gershwin and Florenz Ziegfeld (of "Ziegfeld Follies" fame). Ziegfeld was an ornery and difficult boss. After Gershwin signed a contract with Ziegfeld (in 1929) to write the score for *Show Girl*, Ziegfeld headed over to Carnegie Hall to see *An American in Paris*. Following the show, the master of ceremonies made a brief onstage statement that Gershwin was on his way to being considered a genius. The announcer said, "Someday he will be a genius, but geniuses must suffer, and George hasn't suffered yet." Upon hearing this, Gershwin's new boss, Ziegfeld turned to his companion, winked, and said, "He'll suffer!"[28]

The He-Man*

*Tell Me More (1925)

Meticulous about adhering to a Spartan diet during mealtimes, he could, late at night, often devour a quart of ice cream.
—GERSHWIN BIOGRAPHER DAVID EWEN[1]

As I have mentioned previously, George Gershwin was very concerned about his health, vigor, and diet. He was kind of a health nut. George had a personal trainer and a gym in his apartment complete with a heavy bag that boxers use for training. George was a huge boxing fan, but only as a spectator, never a participant for fear of damaging his million-dollar hands.

His baby sister, Frankie Gershwin, said, "It was George who brought vegetables into our house because my mother just never paid attention to these things. He became very conscious of food and what was good for one . . . George loved cornflakes."[2] She tells us that in the evenings when they all gathered in the kitchen, George would join in with his big bowl of cornflakes and milk.

Gershwin suffered from what he termed "composer's stomach" (that's constipation to us non-composers). He was constantly searching for ways, both conventional and alternative, to relieve his distress by adjusting his diet. Although suffering from this ailment for years, it did not stop him from being energetic and a sports enthusiast. He loved to play golf and tennis. He was the poster boy for an active lifestyle. Gershwin had, "The sick stomach in an athlete's body of steel."[3]

The first time the American writer, radio personality, critic, and journalist Alexander Woollcott met Gershwin in the restaurant of an Atlantic City hotel, the gifted musician's *mishegas* regarding food came shining through. Woollcott said:

> [Gershwin] began by apologizing for the eccentric dinner he would have to order.
> "You see," he explained, "I have terrible trouble with my stomach."[4]

Gershwin's longtime friend, the concert pianist Oscar Levant, described George's diet as follows:

> I felt, George would cajole me frequently to leave the wonderful savory dishes on Ira's table to share with him a menu suited to his favorite ailment—"composer's stomach." It consisted of gruel (and such variants as oat-

meal and farina) rusk, zwieback, melba toast (only on festive occasions), Ry-krisp, Swedish bread and rusk. The pièce de résistance was stewed fruit or, when he was in a gluttonous mood, applesauce.5

Gershwin also sought relief through psychoanalysis and alternative medicine. Gershwin biographer David Ewen tells us:

Despite his athletic build and his muscular physique, he suffered most of his life from a chronic constipation which sometimes induced nausea and brought acute gastric pains. He continually consulted physicians after 1923. When they failed to find a cure, he sought the help of the psychoanalyst, Dr. Gregory Zilboorg, who attended him for a little over a year between 1934 and 1935. Dr. Zilboorg has said that the source of Gershwin's trouble was a chronic neurosis . . . But Dr. Zilboorg ventured the opinion that Gershwin's ailment was not infrequent with musicians, and it was probably for this reason that Gershwin often spoke of his "composer's stomach." Psychoanalytic treatment helped Gershwin in several ways—it made him somewhat less self-centered and inhibited—but it did not relieve his physical condition, which continued to torment him until the end of his life. He took agar-agar regularly before retiring. Often he recorded in a special notebook the details of the day's diet, hoping thereby to check the origin of one of his attacks. He took to eating yeast and to drinking hot water with lemon juice, and for a time he felt they improved his condition. In 1931, after a long addiction to cigars, he gave up smoking, hoping it would "help my stomach disturbances." That sensitive stomach made him highly fastidious about his eating habits. His meals were unimaginative . . . "Nobody believes me when I say I am sick," he would complain endlessly.6

As a former health food supermarket owner/operator and licensed nutrition counselor, I'm impressed with Gershwin's diligence and resourcefulness. The additional fiber he ate put him on the right track, and his use of agar-agar was spot on. He must have been talking to the right health nuts because it is ideal for people with stomach issues. Derived from seaweed, agar-agar is high in fiber, which stimulates elimination and absorbs water in the digestive tract. My wife (also a licensed nutrition counselor) and I call it "the vegetarian's gelatin." It must have worked wonders for him, because an article that appeared in the *New York World* on May 4, 1930, noted:

He suffered from stomach trouble for a long time. That trouble went flying with the acquisition of a new house man, Dindle, who placed him on a diet of agar. George becomes positively eloquent on the subject of agar.7

It seems George's houseman Dindle sure knew his weed . . . seaweed that is!

But man cannot live by weed alone, so let there be jazz, too. In 1929, Dr. William Howard Hay wrote a book titled *Health via Food*. Dr. Hay graduated from New York University Medical School as a surgeon. After many years of practicing medicine and surgery he was diagnosed with Bright's disease, a liver ailment. After attempting to cure his ailment with conventional medical methods, he journeyed into the realm of alternative medicine. Welcome to my world!

The good doctor's thesis for achieving health was through diet as the title of his book suggests. After Dr. Hay radically changed his diet, he lost a tremendous amount of weight and his liver disease seemed to be cured. He then left conventional medicine and became the medical director of The East Aurora Sun and Diet Sanatorium in the Western part of New York State near Buffalo.

East Aurora's claim to fame was that the 13th president of the United States, Millard Fillmore, lived and practiced law and started his political career there. It is also the birthplace of the toy manufacturer Fisher-Price.

Dr. Hay developed a diet that he appropriately called "The Hay Diet" (go figure). It pioneered such nutritional concepts as "food combining" as well as dietary awareness of the interplay of "acid and alkaline" in the diet. So how does all this discussion relate to George Gershwin, you may wonder? The simple answer is—more than you think since George and other celebrities of the day, including the surreal artist Man Ray were interested in what Hay had to say.

In a 1932 letter to his mother, Rose, George wrote:

> Ask Golly [Author's note: nickname of a family friend] to get you that diet book "Health via food" by Dr. Hay. I read it & believe that if you follow it, you will never be ill again. In fact when you get back, I will go with you to his health farm & together we will take his cure. I am sure it will be beneficial to us both.[8]

George's offer to his mom to visit Hay's "health farm" (actually The East Aurora Sun and Diet Sanitorium) tells us much about his thinking on many levels. Let's explore the Hay book *Health via Food* a bit further to understand in the author's own words his concepts of disease and good health and possibly get a closer peek into the health-conscious mind of George Gershwin.

Dr. Hay was an early pioneer of the modern-day health foods movement. This cat had his hand on the pulse of natural health decades before it became popular and mainstream. Maybe some of the following concepts are not familiar to you, but take it from me, a forty-plus-year vegetarian, former organic farmer, natural foods supermarkets owner/operator, natural foods restaurant owner, nutrition counselor, and former vice president of the Florida Region for Whole Foods Markets, Dr. Hay's ideas were the foundation of the natural products industry.

Some (but not all) of the concepts discussed in Dr. Hay's book that Gershwin recommended to his mother, Rose, were to eat raw foods, avoid concentrated proteins (meat, dairy, fish and eggs), do not smoke or drink alcohol, engage the mind in positive thinking, and reduce caloric intake. He also felt that food "is THE cause of disease." Dr. Hay was also a big proponent of physical and spiritual purification through fasting and nightly enemas. He advocated nudity in order to cleanse toxins through the skin saying, "Living largely in the raw, nude state in which the skin has the opportunity to regain its natural instincts and effectiveness as the outer organ of elimination."[9]

I can go on and on about Dr. Hay's ideas, but that is another book. All of it should be taken with a grain of salt . . . but I am not sure the good doctor would approve of the additional sodium. One final note on Gershwin and *Health via Food*. The program was geared for an individual with chronic constipation, which probably got Gershwin interested in Dr. Hay's regimen in the first place because of his self-described, "composers stomach." Then again, it takes a certain kind of guy to invite his mother to a health sanatorium in Upstate New York to run around nude with him, eat raw foods, and get a daily enema. The End!

When You Live in a Furnished Flat*

*La-La-Lucille! (1919)

It was a perpetual wonder that Gershwin could do his work in the living room of this particular flat, the simultaneous stamping ground of the other members of the family and the numberless relatives and visitors who would lounge through, lean on the piano, chat, tell stories, and do their setting-up exercises. I have seen Gershwin working on the score of the Concerto in F *in a room in which there must have been six other people talking among themselves, having tea, and playing checkers.*

—S. N. BEHRMAN'S 1929 ARTICLE IN THE NEW YORKER ON THE GERSHWINS' LIVING AND WORKING CONDITIONS IN THEIR WEST 110TH STREET APARTMENT[1]

George Gershwin was connected to his family by an umbilical cord his entire life. He lived with his parents for thirty-one of his thirty-eight years of life, spending only seven years on his own—and even those seven were spent next door to, or across the street from, or sharing a house with his brother, Ira.

Gershwin wrote his first blockbuster hit "Swanee" in 1919 while living with his clan at 520 West 144th Street in the Washington Heights section of New York. Directly after hitting it big with "Swanee," the family pulled up stakes and moved to the West 110th Street and Amsterdam Avenue building mentioned in the quote at the beginning of this section. This location is where Gershwin created *Rhapsody in Blue*.

As hefty royalty checks came thundering in, it was time for the family once again to pick up the pieces. This time they settled into a building more suitable to George's newfound wealth and celebrity stature. In 1925, the family moved into a five-story, white granite (a few notches above a brownstone) house on West 103rd Street near Riverside Drive. Although the new house was more luxurious, as usual, the Gershwins' domicile was always delivering a five-act play. Here is a description of that house:

On the ground floor there was a billiard room which served as a meeting place and general hangout for the young people of the neighborhood. Some were friends of Arthur or Frances, some were neighbors; a few were total strangers. On the second floor were the living—and dining-rooms where the Gershwin, Wolpin, and Bruskin clans would congregate over cups of tea, or to play poker or pinochle. The next two floors had bedrooms.

When Ira married Leonore Strunsky on September 14, 1926, they took over the fourth floor; and the fifth floor was George's inner sanctum. The rooms in which George worked and entertained had a brick fireplace, a grand piano, and comfortable chairs. A study lined with books, music, and a specially designed and built-in cupboard for his manuscripts led to his bedroom.[2]

The house even had an elevator—a truly opulent feature, especially in 1925. But as impressive as the house was, George could usually be found in his fifth-floor hideaway, bare-chested and puffing away on his ever-present cigar while he pounded on his Steinway grand piano.

Here's how the house was described in a January 1, 1927, article in *The New Yorker*:

There is, perhaps, no harder worker in the field of music than this Gershwin. Royalties have purchased, among other bits of real estate, a house on the upper West Side, just off the Drive, where two music rooms have been set aside because one didn't seem quite enough for his energetic purposes. In one—second floor front—may be found two pianos and usually Bill Daly, who conducts many of the Gershwin shows. More often Gershwin himself chooses the silences of a top-floor studio.[3]

Because the house always overflowed with family, friends, neighbors, and even strangers at times, it became too chaotic for George to focus. So, he rented a suite at the nearby Upper West Side Whitehall Hotel to work in peace. Alas, it was to no avail. Even when he sequestered himself, all the usual (and unusual) suspects showed up anyway. Fortunately, Gershwin could still produce great work in the midst of chaos. As S. N. Behrman wrote, "Possibly his training in Tin Pan Alley, when he plugged songs for Remick, accustomed him to writing under conditions that the average creative artist would find impossible."[4]

Climb Up the Social Ladder*

Let 'Em Eat Cake (1933)

> They live next door to each other,
> not only topographically, but mentally.
> —GEORGE GERSHWIN'S BIOGRAPHER ISAAC GOLDBERG
> ON THE RELATIONSHIP BETWEEN GEORGE AND IRA[1]

In 1928, George, Ira, and Ira's wife, Leonore, moved into adjoining duplex penthouse apartments at 33 Riverside Drive, near West 75th Street. A large, shared terrace and an interior passageway connected their apartments, thereby extending their family home environment while still allowing for privacy. The brothers lived in these adjoining apartments for five years, and because they could bounce ideas off each other 24/7, living in such close proximity lubricated their wheels of creativity—as well as their social lives. During many parties, guests would flow freely from one brother's digs to the other.

The Riverside Drive apartment was Gershwin's ultimate bachelor pad. It had everything George could want: space to entertain; inspiring panoramic views of the mighty Hudson River; and even a small gym, complete with a heavy punching bag and a speed bag, which boxers use for stamina, coordination, and rhythm—traits he actively cultivated and employed in his work. George's gym also included fencing foils, a beloved Ping-Pong table, and other types of athletic paraphernalia. He even had a personal trainer. Like most athletes, he was supremely coordinated and always fit and trim. His exercise regimen gave him the stamina to play the piano and write music for hours and hours on end. It also gave him the energy to party into the wee hours, reveling in high-energy conversations about the nuances of music (of course), football, art, painting, prize fighting, and sex.

We learn much about Gershwin's apartment, perched high in the sky, from a November 1995 special issue of *Architectural Digest*, titled "Broadway at Home." It featured the homes of such Broadway notables as the playwright/theater director Moss Hart and composer Richard Rodgers (of the Rodgers and Hammerstein team), as well as George Gershwin's Riverside Drive penthouse.

Decorated in a streamlined Art Deco motif, the popular style of the day, the quarters reflected his persona as a modern man, living in the modern world. Gershwin's friend and lover, the musician and socialite Kay Swift (who was married to a powerful Wall Street banker at the time) had decorated his pad in line with the current rage—streamlined and modern, dominated by a dramatic black-and-white motif and an abundance of angularity. Terraced bookshelves housed his books along with a dramatic bust of Gershwin created by his artist/buddy Isamu Noguchi. The walls were well appointed with numerous works of art by the masters of the day. Of course, there was also a Steinway grand piano in the living room, ready for George to attack at any moment with or without notice. In the bedroom was a hand-painted screen of Gershwin's symphonic masterpiece *An American in Paris,* crafted by Gershwin's cousin Henry Botkin—or as George often called him, "My cousin Botkin, the painter."

Thanks to Swift, George's penthouse was very much in sync with his music and psyche. "Lean and streamlined, in harmony with both his appearance and his temperament, was how Gershwin's new aerie soon looked."[2] His penthouse apartment was perched high in the New York City sky, which gave him a bird's eye view of the cityscape and the river.

A little trivia about 33 Riverside Drive is in order. This particular location has an interesting history and a strong connection to the arts. In the early 1920s, the famous Russian composer and pianist Sergei Rachmaninoff lived in a five-story house at this very spot. During the 1922–23 season, the Moscow Art Theatre, under the leadership of Konstantin Stanislavsky, stayed at Rachmaninoff's house. When the property was sold, the house was torn down to make way for a seventeen-story apartment building, designed by one of New York's most respected architects, George F. Pelham. Isn't it interesting that the Gershwins, also of Russian descent, wound up in a new apartment building built on a piece of land with so many Russian music predecessors! Only in America!

In the 1974 movie *Death Wish,* Charles Bronson stars as an architect with a vigilante vendetta against criminals in New York City. When he is stopped on the street and questioned by a group of police officers, they ask him where he lives. Bronson replies, "33 Riverside." Of all the apartment buildings in the city to choose, the writers chose the home of the Gershwin brothers! It remains a storied, even legendary, location.

Today, it is a co-op building with 143 units and a doorman. A four-bedroom/four-bathroom/ 2,600-square-foot unit on the ninth floor sold in August 2009 for $4,350,000! In July 2009, Penthouse C, a four-bedroom/four-and-a-half bathroom unit rented for $8,500 per month. Penthouse C had been George's apartment. Then in August 2012, George's former pad went up for sale, priced at $2,999,000. This duplex apartment, with an entrance on the 17th floor and a circular stairway down to another living area, includes a wraparound terrace on three sides. Yet, by 2012, it was considered a fixer-upper. The apartment finally sold in April 2013 for $1.5 million. Why so low? One problem was the unit's monthly maintenance charge: an astounding $8,500!

In 1933, when George was ever more famous, successful, and now wealthy, he moved from the Riverside Drive penthouse to 132 East 72nd Street, between Lexington and Park Avenues. Ira and his wife moved to an apartment across the street, at 125 East 72nd Street. By maintaining such close proximity, the brothers were able to keep the umbilical cord between them intact, just a bit more stretched. They even installed a direct, dedicated phone line, so they could stay connected with each other across the 72nd Street divide.

Their new East Side neighborhood both then and now known as Lenox Hill was considered a much more hoity-toity, high-society neighborhood than Riverside Drive. The Brothers Gershwin were now hob-knobbing with the upper crust of New York society, the world's movers and shakers, and George was delighted to demonstrate his meteoric social gains through a classy East Side address.

For the sake of comparison, consider that current real estate values in George's building range from $1.5 to $3.5 million for a three-bedroom apartment. In 1933, George's apartment was an elegant and spacious fourteen-room duplex. Clearly, this sprawling, palatial crib on the East Side represented a massive leap up the social ladder for George Gershwin.

In addition to giving him ample space to properly display his rapidly growing art collection, George's new apartment also included an art studio where he could paint. Surprisingly, the one thing George's new bachelor pad lacked was a guestroom. Friend and composer, Oscar Levant, major talent and pain in the butt, figured Gershwin had done this intentionally, so Levant would *not* have a place to crash. (Given the fact that Gershwin, a towering musical giant at the time, was pulling in nearly $2 million a year in today's dollars, I have to agree with Levant's assumption![3])

Quite a Party*

*Sweet Little Devil (1924)

When I don't play, I don't have a good time!
—GEORGE GERSHWIN'S RESPONSE TO HIS MOTHER'S CRITICISM THAT AT PARTIES
HE PLAYED TOO MANY HOURS OF PIANO AND MOSTLY HIS OWN SONGS[1]

During the Roaring Twenties, George Gershwin was the darling of the New York high-society circuit. He was a prized guest at the parties of such notables as writer and photographer Carl Van Vechten; Edsel Ford; the banker Otto Kahn; publishers Alfred Knopf and Conde Nast; and Cartier's head honcho, Jules Glaenzer—to name just a few. George would always, without exception, end up at the piano, thus becoming the center of attention at parties. He was sure to dazzle all in the room with his virtuosic command of the instrument, as well as his crowd-pleasing personal charisma. Everyone knew that Gershwin was the "must have" go-to guy for a successful party.

At the beginning of his high-society party days, George was a bit out of place, as he had been raised in the lower-class neighborhoods of

New York. This "street kid" lacked the requisite sophistication and social airs required by the hoi polloi of the New York society scene. (He didn't even know to hold his pinky finger in the air when drinking a glass of champagne . . . how vulgar!)

Early on, his pal and major party host Jules Glaenzer described George in the following way:

> [As] naïve and as lacking in social grace as you are likely to find in anybody. Why, I had to take him aside and tell him to get the cigar out of his mouth when I introduced him to a young lady. But George learned quickly. In a short time he was as well-poised and as completely at ease on Park Avenue as he was on Broadway.[2]

In the late 1920s, George started to host his own parties at his Riverside Drive penthouse—and his parties were "the cat's meow."

In 1921, George and Ira composed a song that grew to legendary proportions on the party circuit. It was called "Mischa, Jascha, Toscha, Sascha" (the first names of four famous Russian-Jewish violinists living in New York at the time: Mischa Elman, Jascha Heifetz, Toscha Seidel, and Sascha Jacobsen). Ira wrote the lyrics (under his pen name, Arthur Francis), and his clever side was really showcased in this song—especially when Russian-Jewish violinists say that we are not highbrows or lowbrows; "We are He-brows." Excellent! This early collaboration between the Brothers Gershwin became an underground party classic. They performed this cute little ditty on a moment's notice, and it always got plenty of laughs. It remained a popular, yet unpublished, work until it was finally published in the collector's edition of the *George Gershwin's Song Book* (1932).

Rouben Mamoulian, the director of *Porgy and Bess*, said of this underground classic piece:

> [The] humorous ditty Misha, Yasha, Tasha, Sasha, which always remained one of his favorites in spite of the fact that it had never been generally published. (Curious that the first time I met George he played this ditty and he played it again the last time I saw him, which was a few days before his death).[3]

Gershwin was happiest when he was at the piano playing his own songs, which eventually numbered in the hundreds.

George was in great demand at parties. Everyone was enthralled by his virtuosity. Even the greatest composers and musicians of the day were captivated by Gershwin's command of music. Once seated at the piano, he would play for hours on end, and nobody was ever bored by his performances. Nobody! As stated in the May 25, 1929 article in *The New Yorker* entitled "*Profiles: Troubadour*":

> When he sits at the piano and plays his own songs in a roomful of people, the effect that he evokes is extraordinary. I have seen Kreisler, Zimbalist, Auer, and Heifetz caught up in the heady surf that inundates a room the moment he strikes a chord. It is a feat not only of technique, but of sheer virtuosity of personality. At the piano Gershwin takes on a new life and so do his auditors. When he comes to a line. . . . His hand flies to his tie to convey. . . . Magnanimity. Described, this sounds grotesque, but actually it is as beautifully integrated as a clever harmony. Gershwin becomes a sort of sublimated and transplanted troubadour, singing an elemental emotion, an unabashed humor.[4]

George's father, Morris, had a favorite song he would ask his son to play at parties: "Embraceable You" (1930), which included the line, "come to Papa." Of course, Morris's nickname was "Papa," and when that line was sung, the Gershwin patriarch would beam with pride.[5]

Gershwin's "life of the party" persona soon spread far and wide. More accurately stated, Gershwin WAS the party. His friend and fellow composer Richard Rodgers (of Rodgers and Hammerstein) documented this view in a Gershwin biography, writing:

> He loved to play the piano. He played marvelously—and at the least provocation. Performing was like a shot of adrenalin to George; he loved to be the life of the party, and could entertain for hours at a stretch, improvising on themes suggested by his "audience," or playing endless variations on themes of his own. Nor was his performing limited to the piano. He was a great storyteller, had a natural gift for dancing, and demonstrated no little talent as an actor. He liked being a star. . . .

If parties gave Gershwin an additional platform for his considerable talents and a forum for his original and intriguing ideas, they were also the perfect showcase for a personality that helped to give New York in the twenties so much of the character we have come to associate with those years.[6]

Another perspective on Gershwin's "life of the party" persona was expressed in an article published in the January 1, 1927, edition of *The New Yorker*, this way:

> He is invited to almost every party that is given these playful days. Usually he is asked to play and does so without the coaxing most celebrities consider essential. His informal repertoire is enormous and contains a number of songs he has written for his own amusement and which have never been published, including *Jascha, Sascha, Mischa and Toscha*, which you may have heard. On these unconventional occasions he plays with a large cigar cocked at a rakish angle, but recently he was overcome with dignity when called upon to rehearse with a symphony orchestra and appeared with a pipe.[7]

A Wonderful Party*

*Lady, Be Good! (1924)

> *There are people who will tell you that Gershwin can't write a tune and there are people who will tell you that he plays too long at parties. There are, in fact, all sorts of people. As a matter of fact, Gershwin has been exploited mercilessly by hostesses—and hosts—whose parties he has saved from irredeemable dullness.*
>
> —PLAYWRIGHT, SCREENWRITER, AND WRITER FOR *THE NEW YORKER*, S. N. BEHRMAN[1]

After Gershwin moved into his Riverside Drive penthouse, George began to host a regular Sunday-night gathering—which, of course, featured him on the piano. The food was spectacular, especially the sturgeon from the Barney Greengrass deli on West 86th Street and Amsterdam Avenue.[2] Barney Greengrass—"The Sturgeon King"—is still in operation to this very day, and yes, they truly do deserve that title.

Wherever there was a party, George Gershwin was at the piano—and whenever Gershwin was at the piano, it was an exhilarating experience. In the words of the playwright S. N. Behrman, "I felt on the instant, the newness, the humor, above all the great heady surf of vitality. The room became freshly oxygenated; everybody felt it, everybody breathed it."[3]

Friend and fellow pianist Oscar Levant said of Gershwin's Riverside Drive parties:

> There was a constant house party, with a piano playing, Ping-Pong balls bouncing across a net and a "sporadic stream of talk embracing prize fighting, music, painting, football and sex."[4]

A party animal, George made many acquaintances at these society extravaganzas, and not just people from the upper crust of white society. He also met other artists, musicians, movers and shakers, blacks as well as whites. Although at the time, black musicians were not allowed to play with whites on stage, at these private parties, those barriers were completely obliterated. Carl Van Vechten started to throw integrated parties in his apartment in the early 1920s; he invited Harlem Renaissance black writers, intelligentsia, and musicians to these blasts. It was there that Gershwin made friends with Paul Robeson, whom he often accompanied at the piano, as well as the Johnson Brothers and the blues singer Bessie Smith, to name just a few. Gershwin's long list of friends also included Fats Waller, Earl "Fatha" Hines and W. C. Handy.

One of Gershwin's favorite "uptown musicians" was blind jazz/stride pianist Art Tatum. Gershwin loved to listen to Tatum's recording of "I Got Rhythm" with the Benny Goodman Trio. Levant said of Gershwin's delight with Tatum:

> He was so enthused with Tatum's playing that he had an evening for him at his Seventy-second Street apartment before leaving for Hollywood. Among George's invited guests was Leopold Godowsky, who listened with amazement for 20 minutes to Tatum's remarkable runs, embroideries, counter-figures and passage playing ... Sometime after he arrived in California, Gershwin discovered that Tatum was playing at a local night club, and we went together to hear him. It was a small, dingy, badly lighted room—an intimate version of the too-intimate Onyx Club. We joined the group of enthusiasts clustered around the piano where the blind virtuoso was in full swing. To George's great joy, Tatum played virtually the equivalent of Beethoven's 32 variations on his tune, *Liza*. Then George asked for more.[5]

As much as he loved to hear great talent on the piano, George loved to play it even more. In Deena Rosenberg's fascinating book *Fascinating Rhythm: The Collaboration of George and Ira Gershwin*, there is a description of the party that followed *Rhapsody in Blue*'s première performance. Among other notable guests were three legendary black jazz pianists of the day: Fats Waller (the "Ain't Misbehavin'" composer), Willie "The Lion" Smith (Black/Jewish stride piano cat), and James P. Johnson (*the* "Charleston" composer). "The Lion" said of that gig:

> We all knew Gershwin because he used to come up to Harlem to listen to us and he was the one who got us invited. . . . It looked for a while as though he was going to stay seated at the piano all night himself and hog all the playing. . . . I finally went over and said to Gershwin, "Get up off that piano stool and let the real players take over, you tomato." He was a good natured fellow and from then on the three of us took over the entertainment.[6]

As the parties multiplied, with Gershwin always at the piano possibly singing or accompanying a singer, Mexican caricaturist Miguel Covarrubias would be busy "murdering" the guests with pen and paper. Many top celebrities and popular figures of the day were captured and respectfully lampooned in his line drawings. In fact, some thought that if Covarrubias did not "murder" you in a caricature then you were not an "A" list celebrity worthy of note.

It just so happens that the illustrations in this book have been penned by Señor Covarrubias, who captured the spirit of "The Jazz Age" in his unique style. Actually, the image of Whiteman at Carnegie Hall performing *Rhapsody in Blue*, which appears on the cover of this book became the inspiration for me to tell this story. Gracias, Miguel!

Writer, photographer, and patron of the Harlem Renaissance, Carl Van Vechten, asked his friend Covarrubias to draw a caricature of Gershwin for inclusion in Covarrubias's 1925 book of caricatures, *The Prince of Wales and Other Famous Americans*. In the book, Covarrubias even did a self-caricature, calling himself "The Murderer." At an extravagant Van Vechten party on March 20, 1925, Covarrubias surprised everyone with his Gershwin caricature shortly before the publication of his book.[7] This caricature of Gershwin has since morphed into iconic proportions and is included in this book on page 99.

When George got the call from the movie

moguls to move west, he jumped at the chance. Ira and wife, Leonore, moved to Hollywood with George and set up shop together. Of course George continued throwing bashes, affording him the opportunity to be the center of attention to a whole new crowd. (This move to California is discussed later.) Just as in New York, a party with George meant he would be anchored to the piano, playing and singing and performing unmatched musical acrobatics.

Gershwin was a bundle of high energy and full of pep, a trait that characterized his speed walking, his professional life, and his personal manner. He was always in a hurry to get to the next thing. Nothing could keep him down—not even an illness.

One day in 1931, as told by biographer David Ewen, when composer/screenwriter Harry Ruby and "The Clown Prince of Baseball" Al Schacht, two friends of Gershwin's, arrived at his apartment:

> George was sick in bed with a fever and a cold. Nevertheless he welcomed his visitors eagerly. He could not lie in bed idly. As he spoke to his guests, he picked up sketching paper and pencil and drew a portrait of Ruby, which he then inscribed: "I can write music, too. Remember Atlantic City?" Schacht remarked wistfully, "Some day when you feel better, George, I'd love to hear you play the piano." George jumped out of bed and, [as] sick as he was, played for a full hour, including the complete *Rhapsody in Blue*. "Never in all my many years of sojourn on this sphere," Ruby has said, "have I ever seen anything like it. His vitality and purpose were not in the least bit dimmed by his illness."[8]

My Cousin in Milwaukee*

*Pardon My English (1933)

He once told me when we were discussing the French painter, Rouault [that] "I am keen for dissonance; the obvious bores me. The new music and the new art are similar in rhythm[;] they share a somber power and fine sentiment."
—GEORGE GERSHWIN'S "COUSIN BOTKIN, THE PAINTER"[1]

Gershwin's cousin Henry Botkin was not from Milwaukee, but let's not hold that against him. He played a very important role in George's life.

Around 1929, George jumped into the world of fine arts, as both a collector and a painter, thanks to the influence of his cousin, Henry Botkin, a celebrated American Modernist painter and art connoisseur. Botkin, or as George called him, "my cousin, Botkin, the painter," became Gershwin's art mentor, helping him amass an exceptional art collection. Cousin Botkin, the painter, would search the New York and Paris galleries for great works of art, which incidentally, he had quite an eye for (as did George). At times, they went on gallery field trips together, looking for the next greatest work of art. And boy did they find them! The walls of George's Riverside Drive penthouse looked like a museum, graced with the talent of artists, such as Modigliani, Renoir, Cézanne, Derain, Gauguin, Chagall, Rouault, Kandinsky, Leger, Rousseau, Max Weber, Klee, Siqueiros, and even Picasso. A 1934 article in *Arts & Decoration* entitled, "A Composer's Pictures," stated that Gershwin buys pictures "because he gets pleasure out of them."[2]

Gershwin's collection was so extraordinary that in 1933, he loaned forty-nine oils, seventeen watercolors, numerous lithographs and drawings, and three sculptures to the Arts Club of Chicago (located at the time in the Wrigley Building) for an "Exhibition of the George Gershwin Collection of Modern Paintings."[3]

By the time of his demise, George's art collection exceeded 140 paintings. His brother, Ira, estimated that George paid about $50,000 for the whole collection (just shy of $1 million today), but its value grew exponentially over time. For example, Gershwin purchased Picasso's "The Absinthe Drinker," which was done during Pablo's "Blue Period," for $1,500 (which equates to about $25,000 today)[4]. In 2010, Christie's Auction House in London auctioned "The Absinthe Drinker" for a whopping $51.2 million!

Gershwin started to paint with watercolors in 1927, and showing amazing talent, he quickly progressed to oils. Some have commented that if he had not found success as a composer, he could have made it as a painter. That's how good he was. Ira followed George's lead and took up painting as well. He also proved to be pretty good at it, but it was George who truly excelled.

Under Cousin Botkin's tutelage, George honed his natural artistic ability and painted many wonderful canvases. Botkin had plenty to say about his talented relative and pupil:

> His painting and collecting have resulted in the assimilation of aesthetic nourishment for his musical genius. He was always interested in the various movements of art, but never allowed himself to follow the dictates of fashion. His pictures were not considered as ornaments or decorations for his walls and he was not affected by any intellectual snobbishness . . . Thus it was that nine years sufficed to bring together one of the most significant collections of modern art in America as well as a group of his own paintings. The collection consists of over a hundred examples of paintings and sculpture, drawings, prints, etc., and though it has no pretense to completeness, it contains some of the greatest examples of contemporary painting that can be found in this country . . . Besides paintings in oil by the masters, he had gathered a most varied group of important examples of Negro sculpture, together with drawings, rare watercolors and lithographs . . . The work of Rouault was especially close to him and he was constantly enthralled by the life and spirit that animated his work. He wanted his own pictures and music to possess the same breathtaking power and depth . . . I noticed especially how he tried to supply to his painting the same warmth, enthusiasm and power that characterized his music.[5]

If Gershwin had a favorite artist, it had to be Rouault.

"Cousin Botkin, the painter" hand painted a beautiful screen depicting scenes from Gershwin's tone poem, *An American in Paris*. George proudly displayed the screen in his Riverside Drive apartment bedroom.

Gershwin described his personal artistic style as "modern romantic"—a phrase he attributed to both his paintings and his music. Gershwin viewed himself personally as the ultimate modern man, who was part of and reflected the modern machine age. As for being a romantic, we can let his beautiful music speak for itself on that score. So Gershwin's self-described artistic style of a "modern romantic" is spot on. As Merle Armitage's 1938 tribute to Gershwin explained:

> If one wished to sum up George Gershwin as an artist, his own label could well be used. He spoke of himself as a "modern romantic." His music expresses it; his own painting exudes it; his collection of works of art confirms it. Perhaps nothing about George Gershwin is more revealing than his collection of contemporary paintings. He loved them, he understood them, he caressed them. He had great independence of judgment in his collecting. He had one of the finest Utrillos I have ever seen; yet it was not a "typical" example in the dealer's sense. His Modoglianis were superb, and he had fine examples by Derain, Rousseau, Pascin, John Carroll, a self-portrait by Gauguin, and was especially fond of his paintings by Sequiros, of which he had several. Musicians' being notoriously indifferent to any other art makes Gershwin's taste seem even more remarkable.[6]

Gershwin was a rare bird whose blunt honesty was at times mistaken for a lack of modesty. When a lady guest commented on the rarity that

Gershwin was extremely gifted in two creative arts, music and painting, Gershwin responded as if it was no big deal. "Look at Leonardo da Vinci," he replied nonchalantly.[7] Clearly, he recognized the magnitude of his talents by comparing himself to da Vinci, the ultimate Renaissance man.

Many top artists of the day considered themselves friends of Gershwin, and their own heightened relationship to art afforded them greater insight into his dynamic sense of artistry. Famous biomorphic sculptor/artist, the Japanese-American Isamu Noguchi met Gershwin in 1929 and sculpted a dramatic, angular sculpture of Gershwin's head, which Gershwin displayed proudly and prominently in his living room at the Riverside Drive apartment. After Gershwin's death, Noguchi said:

> That Gershwin also involved himself in the study of painting to the extent that he did, is completely astonishing to me. Did he doubt the adequacy of music as a complete expression, or was it a divertissement? Perhaps fleeing from the exorbitant expectations which are heaped upon genius in the "public eye" painting was his solace.[8]

An interesting article about Gershwin's art career appeared in the January 1934 edition of *Arts & Decoration*. Titled "A Composer's Pictures," it attempted to describe the ways that painting and music overlap, as follows:

> As Mr. Gershwin points out, music is design—melody is line; harmony is color; contrapuntal music is three or four times forming an abstraction or sometimes a definite shape; dissonance in music is like distortion in a painting, and as Alice Toklas adds, like the eggshell in the coffee.[9]

The article noted that Gershwin's favorite painting in his private collection was a huge four-foot by four-foot canvas entitled *Invocation*, painted by Max Weber in 1918. The image is of three Orthodox Jewish men sitting around a table; one is dozing off, another wearing a yarmulke is looking at a third man, who is gazing upwards to Heaven with his arms in the air, performing some sort of ritualistic invocation, as the work's title suggests. Of this painting, it is said:

> Mr. Gershwin sees in it a deeply wrought picture, tremendously felt. To him the distortion increases its feeling and adds to the design. Technically, he points out, it is a composition of triangles, and in it there is strict absence of line, only color against color. And in the whole there is great movement.[10]

It is indeed a powerful work of art, with a visual as well as a spiritual impact. Another painting in Gershwin's collection was a Chagall entitled *Rabbi*, which connected that painter of Jewish-Russian descent to this composer of Jewish-Russian descent.

Lovers of Art*

*George White Scandals of 1924 (1924)

If only I could put Rouault into music.
—GEORGE GERSHWIN[1]

One of my favorite stories about Gershwin's art collection involves the Mexican artist Miguel Covarrubias (whose illustrations grace the pages of this book) and Paul Whiteman. Covarrubias created a painting entitled *Rhapsody in Blue* (featured in Covarrubias's classic book, *Negro Drawings*, published in 1927). It is a vivid painting of a black female blues singer standing in front of the bandstand with her hands in the air, performing for a black audience seated at cocktail tables (see page 135). Whiteman bought the work, and here is the story of how this piece—the title of which was *Rhapsody in Blue*, Gershwin's very own musical masterpiece,—was twice refused by a young and naïve George Gershwin and later purchased by his older and more experienced former boss, Paul Whiteman. Covarrubias first contacted Whiteman and offered the piece to him. After Covarrubias told Whiteman the name of the work was *Rhapsody in Blue*, their conversation continued:

"Gee, I think George Gershwin ought to have it," the maestro said.
"Well, I've showed it to George," Covarrubias told Whiteman.
"Didn't he like it?" asked Whiteman.
"Oh yes, he liked it," he answered.
"Why didn't he take it?" Whiteman asked puzzled.
"We were getting along fine," Covarrubias said, "until I told him I wanted $1,250 for it. And George said no, he didn't think he wanted it."
"Well," Whiteman said, after pondering a moment, "if George doesn't want it, why I'd be very happy to have it. I'd be glad to take it."

A couple of weeks after Whiteman bought the painting, he ran into Gershwin.

"Hey, you've got that Covarrubias painting, *Rhapsody in Blue*," the composer said.
"That's right," Whiteman said.
"I ought to have that painting," Gershwin told the bandleader.
"That's what I said. You should have it," Whiteman said. "And better than that, you can have it."
"How can I have it?" George asked.
"Well," Whiteman said, "I'm not going to give it to you. You'll have to give me what I paid for it. I don't want to make any profit. I think the painting should rightfully belong to you."

"What'd you pay for it?" asked Gershwin.

"Twelve hundred and fifty dollars," answered Whiteman.

"Darned if I want the painting then," Gershwin said. So Whiteman kept the painting and thought much of it.[2]

Author's note: $1,250 in 1924 equals about $17,000 today—certainly a lot of moola at the time, but by 1924, Gershwin was a heavyweight earner, so he certainly could not have pleaded poverty. However, this incident happened before his interest in the fine arts, as in paintings, developed. Perhaps Gershwin was just being cheap; perhaps he had not yet acquired an appreciation of fine art; perhaps he just didn't like the work and/or thought it was overpriced; or perhaps his reluctance was due to something else entirely.

Whether Gershwin appreciated him or not, Miguel Covarrubias had a true gift for translating jazz onto canvas. In late 1929, months after the Carnegie Hall premiere of Gershwin's symphonic tone poem, *An American in Paris*, the Steinway & Sons piano company commissioned Covarrubias to express the musical piece in a painting. And boy, did he express it! The 26-x-36-inch *Gouache* is a masterpiece of Art Deco and Cubist technique. Steinway & Sons used the image for its own advertisements in both *Vanity Fair* and *McCall's* in 1930. The painting even earned Covarrubias a medal at the prestigious Ninth Annual Exhibition of Advertising Art in May 1930. In May 1997, Sotheby's auctioned the piece. (I actually put in the very first bid, which I admit was a low-ball attempt. The one that followed mine knocked me out of the running.) The piece sold for $250,000—about $365,000 in today's bucks!

In the mid-1930s, Gershwin moved to California and settled into a Beverly Hills mansion at 1019 North Roxbury Drive. He shared it with Ira and his sister-in-law, Leonore. But no matter how spectacular the house, George didn't feel at home unless the walls were adorned with the works of his favorite artists. In September 1936, he wrote a letter to his New York secretary, Zenna Hannenfeldt, requesting a shipment of some of his favorite paintings to his new Beverly Hills 90210 address:

Picasso's *Absinthe Drinker*

Pascin's *Girl with Cat*

Gauguin's *Self-Portrait*

Utrillo's *Fishermen Houses*

Modigliani's *Portrait of Doctor*

Modigliani's *Woman's Head*

Rousseau's *Isle De La Cite*

Derain's *Road Through the Forest*

Sequiro's *Mexican Children*

Segonzac's *Landscape*

Thomas Benton's *Burlesque*

Chagall's *Rabbi*

Max Jacob's *Religious Festival*

Chagall's *Slaughter House*

Gershwin's *Portrait of Grandfather*[3]

One could say these pieces were some of his most beloved and inspiring friends. In today's market, the value of George Gershwin's art collection would easily top out in the **HUNDREDS OF MILLIONS!** Not too shabby for a $50,000 investment.

The Matrimonial Handicap*

*Sweet Little Devil (1924)

A dapper lean shark of a man.
—HOAGY CARMICHAEL'S DESCRIPTION OF GEORGE GERSHWIN[1]

Gershwin was a very good-looking guy. He stood about five-nine with dark hair, eyes, and skin. He had thick, heavy dark bristly facial stubble that forced him to shave twice a day; indeed, in many pictures, his 5 o'clock shadow can be seen at 4 o'clock. His arms were also covered with hair, and yet he started to go bald in his late twenties. This change made him quite self-conscious, but even with a receding hairline, he was still a very handsome man. Always impeccably dressed, his favorite clothes designer was the Upper West Side Jewish fashionista, Oscar de la Yenta (no such person ever existed, this is my attempt at a joke.) Head to toe, George Gershwin was a class act.

Gershwin was a true ladies man, and being successful, famous, and handsome, he was a supremely eligible bachelor. In essence, he was the "perfect catch." George always had a woman at his side—but never one he would tie the noose, (oops) I mean knot, with. (*I've been happily married for over forty years and hope to stay that way for another forty—so, Julie, please forgive my tongue-in-cheek terminology.*)

Ever on the lookout for that perfect woman to marry, for Gershwin, she never did materialize. Some say Gershwin was so focused on music that there was no room for a woman in his life. After a breakup with one gorgeous beauty he had been dating, he told his brother, Ira, "I'd be terribly heartbroken if I weren't so damned busy."[2] That pretty much sums up his relationships with women. His life was always about him, and that was just fine—because there was always another lady who was eager to show up on his arm.

Is it possible George was a mama's boy? All of us Jewish boys look for a gal just like the gal that married dear old dad. Gershwin also showed that maternal handicap saying, "I think the reason why I've never gotten married is that I'm always looking for a woman like my mother—and there just isn't another like her."[3]

Jewess singer/actress Kitty Carlisle (of TV's *To Tell the Truth* fame) talked about a beautiful dinner date she enjoyed with George after they went to see *Porgy and Bess*. She described the dinner as a jazz version of a Passover Seder, led by the pianist/composer/actor Oscar Levant. "Fascinating, absolutely fascinating." She said:

> George was so dear. He had everything, but there was something terribly vulnerable about him. People felt very protective about him. Why, I don't know. He was successful, he was good-looking, women adored him, he had money. He had everything, but yet there was something vulnerable, childlike. He needed approval. Yes, maybe that's it. And you felt it. That was part of his charm. Enthusiasm—that was part of his charm too. And his enthusiasm was terribly boyish for a man who was that successful. He had an enormous sense of enjoyment and enthusiasm which he infused into everything he did. And enormous energy, and there's nothing quite as sexy as energy, is there? What else is there?[4]

Guys, please forgive me . . . but I am about to reveal to the ladies a secret that all of us testosterone-driven organisms share. Once men stumble onto a line or a move that ladies like, we use it over and over again. Ladies, do you remember that one line that made you swoon? He probably used it on many women before you came along (and probably with a lot of success). Men stick with what works—and Gershwin was no exception. Just like the rest of us drones, he had his own personal *"shtick"* to use to make the damsels swoon. Gershwin's pal, the publisher Bennett Cerf (from the TV show *What's My Line?*), revealed Gershwin's favorite trick. It was an unpublished song, a waltz, which he played to any woman he was on the make for. He would tell his date that she was the kind of woman who inspired him to create a new tune and then bring her to the piano in his suite. Once she was lured into his web, Gershwin would go in for the kill, telling her he was "dedicating" this well-worn but "new song" to her.[5]

Gershwin was just like the rest of us regular mortal jazz cats. We love the music, but we also love the ladies—and sometimes we aren't sure which is more important! Take it from an old jazz saxophonist. Most cats use their musical prowess to impress the fairer sex. It really works, as my wife, Julie, still swoons when I play her a sweet song. Jazz musicians are lady magnets—especially world-class cats like George Gershwin.

Although he had numerous romantic liaisons, George never married. Some say his affairs resulted in illegitimate children, although this history has never been proven, nor are any of his alleged offspring included in his estate. However, it is interesting that George's self-proclaimed bastard son, Alan Gershwin (aka Albert Schneider) and his self-proclaimed illegitimate daughter, Nancy Bloomer Deussen, both ended up writing music. I will discuss this aspect later in this book.

Only two women ever came close to filling the bill as Mrs. George Gershwin. One was the beautiful movie actress and Ziegfeld girl Paulette Goddard. She was married four times, two of which were to the Hollywood stars Charlie Chaplin and Burgess Meredith. One would think that being married four times would make her an expert on the subject, but go figure. While Gershwin was living in Hollywood, he had a fling with Ms. Goddard, but she was married to Chaplin at the time and did not want to leave the silent film star for the musical genius. So, George remained a bachelor. (If you're wondering, *What was Gershwin thinking? She was a married woman!* Remember, it was Hollywood. True then and true now.)

The other woman was the classical and popular-music composer Kay Swift. Gershwin met Swift in early 1926 at a party for the violinist Jascha Heifetz at Swift's swanky New York City apartment. Gershwin had accompanied Jascha's younger sister, Pauline Heifetz, to the party. As usual, George ended up at the piano, showboating for the crowd. Suddenly, Gershwin jumped up from the piano and exclaimed, "I've got to go to Europe."[6] Kay Swift found this comment—and him—irresistibly charming.

As a child, Swift was classically trained in music and had a very impressive intellect. George encouraged her to leave the classical music sphere and concentrate on popular music. She took his advice and became a very successful composer of popular music. In 1929, she penned the hit tune "Why Can't We Be Friends." The following year, she wrote the music for the song "Fine and Dandy" featured in a Broadway show of the same name. This success gave her the distinction of being the first woman ever to write the music for a hit Broadway musical. Her song eventually became a classic in the jazz repertoire.

Gershwin and Swift were often seen together in public—at restaurants, show openings, parties, concerts, and other places that dating and married couples would typically go. But their romance wasn't exactly a fairytale.

There were four "inconvenient" problems with their relationship. First, at the time, Swift was married to a mega-banker mogul James P. "Jimmy" Warburg. For the eight years before she met George, Kay and Jimmy had made a name for themselves among New York's social elite. Problems two, three, and four were the three small children she had with problem number one, her socially prominent husband. These entanglements cast a long shadow on her relationship with George. Kay's entire family was humiliated by and ashamed of the Gershwin-Swift love affair, but that didn't slow it down. Not one whit.

Compounding the family's embarrassment was a 1926 Broadway musical with music and lyrics by the Brothers Gershwin. The name of the show was, *Oh, Kay!*—obviously named after Kay Swift. (Because of all the *mishegas* surrounding this musical, I would here formally change the name *from Oh, Kay!* to *Oy Vey!*) Initially, the show's name was *Mayfair*, then *Miss Mayfair*, then *Cheerio*, and finally (thanks to George's insistence) *Oh, Kay!* Granted, the name was a double entendre (for "okay"), but it was clearly a below-the-belt punch to Jimmy Warburg. To add insult to injury, the leading lady was named Kay, and the leading man's name was Jimmy. Ouch!

The show featured a spectacular song that went on to become a jazz songbook classic: "Someone to Watch Over Me," a reflection of George's relationship with Kay. In his Gershwin biography, David Ewen explained:

> She looked after him with a solicitude born out of tenderness, filling his apartment with flowers, always seeing to it that his boutonniere came on time before each of his concerts. Gershwin, in turn, came as close to being completely in love with her as he did with any woman; and he remained devoted to her longer than to any other. He spoke of her in a way few other women inspired him to do. She was the only woman to whom he gave an expensive gift (two precious paintings), the only woman to whom he dedicated one of his works—the piano transcriptions of his songs published by Simon and Schuster.[7]

Kay and George remained friends until the end of his short life.

To her credit, Kay Swift was a musical force in her own right, but she was not looking for the limelight. Swift recognized Gershwin's formidable gift as a creative artist and was very comfortable being the assistant to the genius. One of her gifts was her musical recall. Speaking of her amazing musical recall ability, Ira said that Swift had, "total musical recall" and "could play from memory the entire *Porgy and Bess* vocal score of 559 pages."[8] That is one heck of an amazing feat!

After George passed, Kay's exceptional memory and familiarity with his work turned out to be a huge boon for the Gershwin archives. Because she possessed both formal music training and an uncanny memory, she was able to recall many songs they had worked on together and yet never put to paper. (At the time, some of these songs were not up to par for George's eyes and ears, so he had trashed them.) Swift recalled a slew of these "lost" songs and transcribed them for all to hear, thus adding to the Gershwin musical legacy. Kay also worked with Ira to bring some of the lost gems to the big screen, such as those used in the motion picture *The Shocking Miss Pilgrim*, starring Betty Gable (1947).

I think that George's relationship with women can be summed up perfectly in the title of his tune "A Woman Is a Sometime Thing." For George that "sometime" was just that—for some time.

Drifting Along With the Tide*

*George White's Scandals of 1921 (1921)

*Music is entering into medicine. Music sets up certain vibrations
which unquestionably results in a physical reaction. Eventually
the proper vibration for every person will be found and utilized.
I like to think of music as an emotional science.*

—GEORGE GERSHWIN, IN AN ARTICLE HE TITLED "THE COMPOSER IN THE MACHINE AGE,"
WHICH APPEARED IN *REVOLT IN THE ARTS* (1933)[1]

HOLY MOLY! Eighty years ago, George Gershwin was talking about a branch of medicine that even today we still consider alternative medicine. In addition to using specific foods to treat his "composer's stomach," Gershwin was tuning into the healing power of "good vibrations" decades before The Beach Boys and The Beatles met the "fool on the hill" in 1967, otherwise known as Maharishi Mahesh Yogi. Now, for the benefit of Mr. Kite, let me be perfectly clear: George Gershwin was no "day tripper"! He was just way ahead of the curve in his understanding of both music and health.

His declaration that "the proper vibration for every person will be found and utilized" proved to be prophetic. Decades later, Maharishi Mahesh Yogi, the Indian sage who brought Transcendental Meditation to the West, developed a healing technique known as "Maharishi Vedic Vibration Technology." Based on ancient Vedic scriptures, it operates on the principle that everything has its own, unique vibrational signature. Every person has his or her own specific vibration, and every organ of each person's body has its own vibration as well. (Many years ago, when I was dealing with some chronic health issues, I experienced several Vedic vibration treatments. The expert consultant chanted various sounds and gently breathed on the affected area and then gave me a bottle of water, which was attuned to a specific vibration.)

The healing power of vibrations has since crossed over into Western medicine. For example, Dr. Richard Gerber (no relation to me, but he must be very smart and handsome for obvious reasons) wrote a popular book titled, *Vibrational Medicine: The No. 1 Handbook of Subtle-Energy Therapies*.

A deeply esoteric man, George Gershwin lived in tune with Mother Nature and the many forms of "music" she plays. Gershwin expressed his belief in the connection between mind/body and environment in a 1930 article that he wrote entitled, "The Composer in the Machine Age." In his own words:

> Music . . . has a very marked effect on the emotions. It has the power of moving people to all of the various moods . . .
>
> . . . we have music all around us in some form or other.
>
> . . . it can have a cleansing effect on the mind, a disturbing effect, a drowsy effect, an exciting effect. . . .
>
> There is music in the wind.
>
> . . . one does not need a formal education to appreciate it. Music can be appreciated by a person who can neither read nor write and it can also be appreciated by people who have the highest form of intelligence. For example, Einstein plays the violin and listens to music.
>
> People in the underworld, dope fiends and gun men, invariably are music lovers and, if not, they are affected by it.[2]

The Man I Love*

*(Unused) (1924)

*That, my boy, is a masterpiece—a masterpiece, do you hear?
This man Gershwin beats the lot of us. He sits down and composes
one of the most original, most perfect songs, of our century. . . .
Who wants another symphony if he can write a song like that?
Perfect, my boy, perfect. This is the music of America, it will live
as long as a Schubert Lied [song] and a Brahms waltz . . .*
—ESTEEMED COMPOSER JOHN IRELAND'S COMMENTS ON GERSHWIN'S SONG
"THE MAN I LOVE" TO A YOUNG FRIEND[1]

One of the great songs of all time.
—COMPOSER/ARRANGER AND CONCERT PIANIST PERCY GRAINGER'S
OPINION OF GERSHWIN'S "THE MAN I LOVE"[2]

"The Man I Love" is considered by many to be in the top tier of the Gershwin brothers' output—and possibly one of the greatest songs of all time. The funny thing is that although it was written into at least three shows, the song never made it to a Broadway stage.

The brothers wrote it in 1924 under the initial title, "The Girl I Love," for the hit show *Lady, Be Good!* staring Fred and Adele Astaire. Unfortunately, by the time the show opened in December 1924, at New York's Liberty Theater on 42nd Street, "The Man I Love" had been cut from the show. Some said the cut was because the show was too long and this powerful ballad put more drag on the production. Strike one for "The Man I Love."

Three years later, in 1927, George resurrected the song and wanted it included in the Broadway production of *Strike Up the Band*. That show closed down during its out-of-town run, never seeing the lights of Broadway. Strike two for "The Man I Love." But wait—there's more!

The following year, in 1928, Gershwin resurrected the song once again and wanted it included in the show *Rosalie*, staring the famous stage performer Marilyn Miller. In January 1928, that show opened at Broadway's New Amsterdam, but the diva had nixed the song. Strike three for "The Man I Love." But wait—there's even more!

As the old baseball saying goes, "Three strikes and you're out"—but not so with "The Man I

Love." In 1930, a new and improved version of *Strike Up the Band* became a Broadway hit, but regrettably, "The Man I Love" was not included. Strike FOUR!

Or so it seemed.

"The Man I Love" is an undeniably powerful piece of music with lyrics that gave it a life of its own. When European high-society muckety-muck, Lady Mountbatten (no relation to Lady Gaga) heard Gershwin play the song at a party in New York, she absolutely fell in love with it. From that day forward, she did everything she could to promote the tune. Upon her return to London, she convinced the Berkeley Square Orchestra to play the song. It became a big hit in London and then crossed the channel to the continent and hit it big in Paris as well. Eventually, after years of obscurity, bands in America started to cover the song, finally launching its popularity in America. (Quite an ass backwards path to success for a great American jazz standard!)

In his wonderful autobiography, *Lyrics on Several Occasions*, Ira Gershwin addressed the song's roundabout path to fame. Apparently, when "The Man I Love" failed to launch in America, the Gershwin's publisher, Max Dreyfus, suggested that the brothers shave their royalty from six cents (three cents each to composer and lyricist) to four cents (two cents each) so he could leverage the discount when marketing the tune. They agreed, and the strategy proved to be a brilliant move. The song became an overwhelming success. Several recordings were made, and in the first six months, the sales of the sheet music exceeded 100,000 copies.[3]

This story proves that although the song was cut from several Broadway shows, it was far from flawed. In fact, many other excellent Gershwin songs were sacrificed on the Broadway chopping block. An article in the May 25, 1929, issue of *The New Yorker* addressed this circumstance by noting:

> There was talk once of making up a score of Gershwin songs which, for one reason or another, had been thrown out of shows, and the list made one feel like going out at once to raise the money. At the mercy of banal librettists and the exigencies of "show business," Mr. Gershwin has to take out songs because the prima donnas can't sing them, or because it's time for the slapstick men, or because they're too intricate for the chorus to dance. Almost anyone who knows him will tell you that much of his stuff which sounds magnificent when he plays it on the piano is dimmed and muffled by the time it reaches the theatre.[4]

"The Man I Love" is a beautiful, melancholy melody with deeply haunting lyrics by Ira. Over the years, it has become one of the most popular jazz standards, covered by a dizzying array of talented jazz cats including Billie Holiday, Miles Davis, Dizzy Gillespie, Lester Young, and John Haley "Zoot" Sims, to name just a few.

In researching the song, I stumbled upon two astute comparisons of it to *Rhapsody in Blue*. The first is in David Schiff's excellent 1997 book, *Gershwin: Rhapsody in Blue*. His discussion of the relationship between these songs was brief, so it wasn't until I read Deena Rosenberg's 1991 book, *Fascinating Rhythm: The Collaboration of George and Ira Gershwin*, that I fully realized the deep connections between the two Gershwin masterpieces.

Rosenberg devoted a great deal of ink and pulp to describing the connection and included comparative musical notations to make her point more graphic. She illustrated, in musical notation, that the hook musical phrase in "The Man I Love" virtually underlies the exact same phrase in *Rhapsody*. When one sees and hears the two musical pieces in this fashion, their sisterhood becomes crystal clear.

I dug out my trusty manuscript of the piano solo of *Rhapsody in Blue* as well as the old recording and searched both for the first appearance of this musical reference. There it was, just nineteen bars into *Rhapsody*. The piano solo first presents "The Man I Love" phrase to the listener with a muted *wah-wah* trumpet playing the figure. In fact, the piano repeats the solo phrase, adding emphasis to its importance. "The Man I Love" phrase is repeated many times throughout *Rhapsody in Blue* in various ways and by various musical voices. Finally, just three bars from the end, after a multi-bar buildup from the orchestra, the piano sings out, above the orchestra in a slow and authoritative voice, "The Man I Love" hook. Once again highlighting the importance Gershwin gave to this phrase. (Many thanks to both David Schiff and Deena Rosenberg for their spectacular insight.)

Gershwin loved "The Man I Love" so much that he used it as the theme song for his 1934 radio program *Music by Gershwin* on WJZ in New York City.

Perhaps we can best understand Gershwin's relationship to "The Man I Love" by looking through the lens of George's close friend, the playwright S. N. Behrman, who commented that Gershwin "Told me once that he wanted to write for young girls sitting on fire escapes on hot summer nights in New York and dreaming of love."[5]

Certainly, "The Man I Love" fits that bill.

Nice Work if You Can Get It*

*A Damsel in Distress (1937)

*George had no particular feeling for money per se. . . .
He was not consumed by wanting to produce hit songs;
he was only concerned with creating music of quality.*

—OSCAR LEVANT, COMPOSER, PIANIST,
AND GERSHWIN FRIEND[1]

By 1928, George Gershwin was a smoking-hot commodity, and I am not talking about his cigars. "How hot was he?" you may be asking yourself. Let's just say he was a million-dollar baby. That year, he signed a contract with the Fox Movietone Company to write the score for the new musical *Delicious*. The movie was part of the new generation of movies called "talkies." (If you ask me, these "talkies" seemed like a passing marketing fad at the time . . . but my extensive research reveals that they did, in fact, become popular. Go figure!) George received $100,000 for the musical score to *Delicious*. Adjusted for inflation, that equates to about $1.4 million! And that is just for starters. As the great Gershwin tune so eloquently states, "Nice Work if You Can Get It!"

That same year, Gershwin was paid $50,000 (the equivalent to $700,000 today) for the rights to use *Rhapsody in Blue* in Whiteman's film, *The King of Jazz*.[2] By adding the *Delicious* $1.4 million to this fee, we get an astounding $2.1 million so far for the year, and that's not counting all the other gigs, which were substantial as well, the same year.

Speaking to reporters about the *Rhapsody* deal, George said, "That's more than Beethoven or Schubert ever got for a composition, eh? I guess that would make them turn over in their graves!"[3]

With these two windfalls, in addition to the royalty checks and payments for all the other gigs the brothers performed that year, 1928 was an extremely profitable year for George and Ira. Further, at the time, the top federal tax rate was only 25 percent! The Gershwins were positively rolling in dough, almost literally.

Gershwin was averaging over $250,000 a year in income; in today's dollars, that's over $3.5 million a year. This money gave him complete freedom to decide where, when, and with whom he wanted to perform—and also to indulge one of his lesser-known facets, which was his extremely generous nature.

The avant-garde composer, pianist, and inventor George Antheil said of Gershwin's generosity:

> But George, like another composer in another time—Franz Liszt—supported a good many poor American composers; even at the time of his death in Hollywood I personally knew of four American white hopes whom George was supporting and this is the first time that this fact has been made known. Throughout the long years he never said a word about it to anyone.[4]

From head to toe, George Gershwin was a class act.

If I Became the President*

*Strike Up the Band (1930)

George was invited by FDR to play the piano at a New Year's Eve blast at the White House during FDR's first term in office.
—DEENA ROSENBERG, GERSHWIN BIOGRAPHER[1]

The influence of politics in Hollywood, and Hollywood on politics, stretches way back in our country's history.

George's first contact with a President of the United States happened when he was only twenty years old. During the week of March 4, 1918, named Preparedness Week, Gershwin accompanied Louise Dresser on the piano in a performance for none other than President Woodrow Wilson, hosted at the B. F. Keith's Theatre in Washington, D. C.

According to Gershwin biographer Deena Rosenberg, both Gershwin brothers were liberal and lifelong Democrats. In the biography *George Gershwin: A New Biography*, William G. Hyland offered some insight into the Gershwin brothers' politics:

> George Gershwin was not particularly political. But his brother was politically sensitive; along with most New York intellectuals, Ira was well to the left of center.[2]

In a rare move, George did take a public stand in the presidential campaign of 1928.

Introverted and conservative, the small-government Republican Calvin Coolidge had declined to run for a second term, thereby opening up the field for new blood. The ballot pitted California Republican Herbert Hoover against the New York Democrat Al Smith.

When *Vanity Fair* polled a slew of celebrities on whom they were voting for, the public learned that Al Smith was favored by Charlie Chaplin, Eddie Cantor, Rube Goldberg, Fred and Adele Astaire, H. L. Mencken, Edna St. Vincent Millay, Cole Porter, and John Riddell. Herbert Hoover had won the support of Robert C. Benchley, Cecil B. DeMille, and Helen Willis, among others.

So, where did George Gershwin fall on this *Vanity Fair* poll? Drum roll, please . . . his vote went to the New York Democrat Al Smith![3] Surely, he must have been disappointed when Hoover won the election by a landslide, carrying 40 of the 48 states and 444 of the Electoral College votes, compared to 87 for Smith. The popular vote was 58 percent to 40 percent in favor of Hoover. Please note that the vote appeared to be fair and square; no "hanging chads" or "pregnant chads" or "dimpled chads" that I could find in my research.

Although they generally distanced themselves (at least publicly) from American politics, the Brothers Gershwin wrote several songs for political satire musicals, including *Strike Up the Band* (1927), *Of Thee I Sing* (1931)—which won a Pulitzer Prize for Ira—and *Let 'Em Eat Cake* (1933).

An American in Paris*

*An American in Paris (1928)

. . . would like to spend the rest of his life working mornings in New York, and then spending his evenings in Paris.
—GEORGE GERSHWIN TO A FRIEND[1]

In March 1928, the four Gershwin siblings vacationed together in Europe. After touring London, they ended up in Paris. This vacation marked the fifth and final European visit for George, and his third trip to Paris. (He traveled to Paris first in 1923 and again in 1926.) This time, however, because he was not on one of his whirlwind tours, he finally had a chance to relax and enjoy the sights and sounds of *Gay Paree*.

Gershwin biographer William G. Hyland said that George absolutely fell in love with the city. It inspired him; he felt it had a "real musical atmosphere"[2]

Always eager to improve his musical chops, Gershwin sought out his friend, French composer Maurice Ravel (the *Bolero* guy), to study with while in Paris. When they got together, Gershwin played for Ravel for over an hour. Afterward, Ravel said to George, "Why be a second-rate Ravel when you are a first-rate Gershwin?"[3] Excellent point, maestro!

Some tell a different story, however. In an article entitled, "Misunderstanding Gershwin," published in the October 1998 issue of *The Atlantic Monthly*, musicologist and Gershwin expert David Schiff referred to Gershwin biographer Charles Schwartz's research on the genesis of the story. Schwartz asserted that the story traced back to the Gershwin family. He suggested that Gershwin loved to tell this story as a parlor tale at parties. In time, the story became a Gershwin legend.[4] Whether fact or fiction, nobody really knows for sure. But I, for one, caucus with the majority on the side that says that story was absolutely true!

The Gershwin family stayed at the Majestic Hotel, and according to Ira, that's where George wrote the entire blues section of *An American in Paris*. Gershwin had started the piece in January 1928, calling it a "symphonic tone poem." The five-part poem included walking themes, as well as sweet, raucous, and blues passages. The piece opens with the so-called "walking theme," which is an up-tempo light and airy recurring passage suggesting the cityscape of Paris through sounds heard by an American tourist.

Gershwin scored *An American in Paris* for a typical symphony orchestra—but he added a couple of twists, like saxophones and a celesta, which has a keyboard that resembles a piano, but the hammers hit metal plates rather than the strings on a piano. In fact, the celesta owes its name to its heavenly celestial sound. Most surprising, however, was Gershwin's decision to incorporate a sound that permeates and characterizes *Gay Paree*—taxi horns!

Gershwin had heard Paris taxi horns in his head long before he put them into musical notation. But he needed to get his hands on some. So he and his friend Mabel Schirmer (wife of the Schirmer Music Publishing Company chief) went shopping on the *Avenue de la Grande Armée*. As Mabel remembered:

> It's not a very chic street. . . . In those days it had nothing but automobile parts and all the things that you need for automobiles. And so we went, up and down. George, it turned out, was looking for taxi horns; and that shopping solved his thematic problems.[5]

They must have shopped for hours because he bought quite a few. Shortly thereafter, the composer and pianist Mario Braggiotti and his partner, Jacques Frey, showed up unannounced at Gershwin's hotel room in Paris. The two young music students noticed a collection of taxi horns strewn on top of the piano, each one with a different pitch: A, A-flat, B, G, and F-sharp. Braggiotti described the encounter with Geashwin as follows:

> He was in his dressing gown, and his hair was all kind of up in what I call the composer's style . . . He was very welcoming. There was a Steinway piano right in the middle of his room and I noticed on the piano a collection of taxi horns—from those old-fashioned taxis they used in the Bataille de la Marne. There were about 20 of them lying there . . . I thought this was some new American eccentricity or fad . . .
>
> "Oh," he said, "you're looking at these horns. Well, in the opening section of *An American in Paris* I would like to get the traffic sound of the Place de la Concorde during the rush hour, and I'd like to see if it works . . . Jacques, you take this horn—this is in A flat. Mario, you take this—it's in F sharp. Now, I'll sit down and play, and when I go this way with my head, you go 'quack, quack, quack' like that in that rhythm."
>
> So we took the horns, and there we stood, nervous and excited, and for the first time, we heard the opening bars of *An American in Paris*—a lanky American walking down the Champs-Elysees. He captured the atmosphere, the feeling, the movement, the rhythm so perfectly.
>
> Well, when we came to the horn parts, he nodded and we came in. That was the first and last time that I ever played French taxi horns accompanied by such an illustrious composer.[6]

Although he had purchased quite a few horns, he eventually selected four to use in the piece. In addition to the taxi horns, Gershwin returned from Paris with other prizes as well: a Mustel reed organ and a beautifully bound set of the works by Claude Debussy (a French composer whom he greatly admired).

By the time he returned to New York, Gershwin had completed a basic sketch of *An American in Paris*. But it was far from complete. In *George Gershwin: His Life and Work*, Howard Pollack quoted Gershwin discussing his challenges when developing this work further and the inspiration that finally brought it all together. As George put it, "As I was not a Frenchman, I knew that I was about as far as I could get with it." As he sat in his apartment on 103rd Street, gazing at the Hudson

River, however, he did suddenly find the inspiration and direction he needed. In his words:

> I love that river and I thought how often I had been homesick for a sight of it, and then the idea struck me—an *American in Paris*, homesickness, the blues. So there you are. I thought of a walk on the Champs Elysees, of the honking taxi, of passing a building which I believed was a church but which Deems Taylor, who wrote the program notes, said is the salon. There are episodes on the left bank, and then come the blues—thinking of home, perhaps the Hudson. There is a meeting with a friend, after a second fit of blues (a) decision that in Paris one may as well do as the Parisians do.[7]

Just four weeks after he finished composing it, *An American in Paris* premiered at Carnegie Hall on December 13, 1928, with Gershwin's pal Walter Damrosch conducting the New York Symphony. It was part of a classical program, and, judging from the reviews, it definitely stood out. Imagine the astonishment of the Carnegie Hall audience on hearing the honking of Paris taxi horns at the beginning of a "symphonic tone poem"! It was thrilling, exciting, unheard of, and uniquely Gershwin. Capturing the sounds and feeling of the Paris streets, as heard through an Americans ears, in the tapestry of a musical score was an exceptional feat, and those taxi horns played a critical role in delivering it.

In *The New York Times* review of the premiere titled, "Gershwin's New Score Acclaimed," music critic Olin Downes wrote:

> The evening's hero was a svelte and feted young man, who beamed from his box while the audience applauded rapturously his latest compositions, and in vain endeavored to induce him to descend and bow from the stage. This young man—need it be said?—was George Gershwin, who, to the accompaniment of four automobile horns, saxophones, and other unallowed machines of sound supposed to be taboo in serious musical circles, made his third bow as the composer of professedly symphonic intentions to a New York audience. . . . It was Mr. Gershwin's evening.[8]

In his review, Downes quoted the composer and music critic Deems Taylor's description of the work in the performance's program notes:

> An American strolls the Paris Boulevard. A "walking theme" portrays the Champs-Élysées on a blithe May morning. French taxicabs amuse the American. Their calls, played on taxi horns, sound in the orchestra. From a café comes the sound (trombones) of "La Maxixe." A clarinet "in French with a strong American accent" announces another "walking theme."[9]

Again, Gershwin has the orchestra play the "walking theme" for a third time. As the audience hears the light up-tempo passage, one is left to wonder, "*Has the American crossed to the Left Bank? Or was he walking around, "exploring the mysteries of an Anise de Lozo"?*[10] Downes continues quoting Deems Taylor's program notes:

> Enter a solo violin, of a soprano sonority and address. But sentimental colloquy does not cure the American of his "blues." His "blue" tune is one of the most characteristic in the score. The blue tune and the violin solo do much to fill the later pages. And now a final gay theme (the American having, according to Mr. Taylor, met a compatriot), and the various motives, check by jowl, jostle each other to an uproarious conclusion.[11]

Once again, the critics gave Gershwin a split decision. "Merry, rollicking music," said Liebling of the *American*. Yet, Peyser of the *Telegram* described the work as:

> [A] nauseous clap-trap, so dull, patchy, thin, vulgar, long-winded and inane that the average movie audience would be bored by it into open remonstrance. . . . Cheap and silly affair seemed pitifully futile and inept.[12]

It is ironic that Peyser spoke so poorly of the score, especially regarding a "movie audience." He would be shocked to know that, just under a quarter century later, *An American in Paris* was made into a movie—and the New York City Ballet performed it on May 4, 2005. In fact, throughout the years, *An American in Paris* turned out to be one of Gershwin's most celebrated works. It appears that Mr. Peyser ended up inserting his foot into his own "nauseous clap-trap."

An American in Paris—
The Movie

Sheerly enchanting . . . The most imaginative original, chic and dazzling musical of the year, or of last year and probably of next year and the next.

—LOS ANGELES REVIEWER'S COMMENTS ON THE MOVIE
AN AMERICAN IN PARIS[1]

An *American in Paris* was made into a film in 1951 and starred Gene Kelly and Leslie Caron. (Gershwin's old pianist pal, Oscar Levant, played a strong supporting actor role.) It was codirected by Gene Kelly and Vincente Minnelli (Liza's daddy and one of Judy Garland's five hubbies).

With help from the well-paid consultant Ira Gershwin, Minnelli and Kelly sifted through the massive inventory of Gershwin music, searching for songs that best fit into the song-and-dance script for the silver screen. Lucky for them, the enormous inventory was full of wonderful songs that were perfect for the project. In the end, the film featured some of the greatest songs in the Gershwin songbook: "I Got Rhythm"; "'S Wonderful"; "Nice Work if You Can Get It"; "Embraceable You"; "I'll Build a Stairway to Paradise," as well as, of course, *An American in Paris*. (They did not include *Rhapsody in Blue*, but they did have Oscar Levant play the third movement of *Concerto in F* in the movie, and that was a real treat.) The flick ended on a high note, with a stunning seventeen-minute ballet featuring Impressionist sets and Gene Kelly's choreography telling an incredible story of *An American in Paris* through dance. Very powerful indeed!

The flick premiered in New York City on October 4, 1951, and it was an immediate smash hit. It won six(!) Academy Awards: Best Picture, Best Musical Score, Best Cinematography, Best Costume Design, Best Screenplay, and Best Set Decoration. It also chalked up nominations for Best Director and Best Editing. They sure don't make movies like that nowadays, except for maybe *Teenage Mutant Ninja Turtles* . . . not!

This blockbuster movie brought Gershwin's music to a new generation of music lovers, also driving an increase in interest (sales and profits) in the Gershwin songbook. Fourteen years after his death, Gershwin was still a top seller, both at the box office and in the music business. That's what I call a true legacy!

In 1973, over two decades after the movie's release, Donald Knox wrote a revealing book on the movie titled, *The Magic Factory: How MGM Made An American in Paris*. According to the book, the movie producers did not want the movie to be a biography of Gershwin's life, so they designed a story around his music. As producer Arthur Freed explained:

> Ira Gershwin is one of my closest friends, and I grew up with George Gershwin in New York when I was first writing songs. I used to spend a lot of time over at the Gershwins. I still spend every Saturday night with Ira at his house, and we either play poker or pool. So one night I was with Ira Gershwin playing pool and afterwards, it was about two in the morning, we sat talking about pictures and I said, "Ira, I've always wanted to make a picture about Paris. How about selling me the title *An American in Paris?*" He said, "Yes, if you use all Gershwin music." I said, "I wouldn't use anything else; that's the object." This was the start of the idea. Now, I didn't know what I wanted to do. The only thing I said to Ira was I wanted to use George's compositions and his title *An American in Paris* and maybe do a ballet. I didn't even know who was going to be in it, but I knew it would have to be a dancer, either Fred Astaire or Gene Kelley.[2]

Freed connected the dots after reading an article about postwar GI's studying in Paris under the GI Bill. He thought that since Gershwin had spent time studying in Paris, the male lead (Gene Kelly) should be a GI studying in Paris as a Gershwin-like model so to speak. The movie moguls began a script that was loosely based on Gershwin studying art in Paris, but since it was not meant to be a biography, that's where the parallels ended. The final script revolved around an ex-GI aspiring painter practicing his art with Gershwin music intertwined.

The movie was a big-budget production. According to Freed, the studio paid $300,000 (over $2.75 million in today's bucks) for the title *An American in Paris* plus the other songs used in the movie, and an additional $50,000 (just shy of a half-million dollars today) to Ira to consult on the project.[3] A studio executive said that the cost of the production, $3 million (approximately $27.5 million today), exceeded twice the average cost of their pictures.[4] In fact, the seventeen-minute ballet scene cost over $500,000[5] (about $5 million today)—just for that one scene! Big budget indeed!

In the August 18, 1951, issue of the *New Statesman and Nation,* one reviewer wrote:

> By far the most original and successful ballet the cinema has devised will be found in the last 20 minutes of *An American in Paris*. Let me emphasize that the new screen ballet is not merely a bit of film ingenuity . . . it attains a genuine art of its own.[6]

In the end, the investment paid off. *An American in Paris* was a blockbuster hit, breaking attendance and revenue records in theaters around the country. And the movie had legs—and I don't mean dancers legs (although it had plenty of them, too). It enjoyed long runs in the theaters and it never died on the shelf; to the contrary, it was revived over and over again. And now for:

YOUR NOT-SO-HUMBLE AUTHOR'S REVIEW OF AN AMERICAN IN PARIS: THE MOVIE

I purchased the DVD online. It was easy to find and inexpensive, so I did not have to break my research budget. The trailer touts eleven Gershwin songs featured in the movie, but many more songs are included as snippets.

In the two-hour flick, starving painter and ex-GI Jerry Mulligan (not to be confused with jazz bari-sax great Gerry Mulligan) falls head over heels for a beautiful nineteen-year old, played by

French actress Leslie Caron (who at the time was only seventeen years old and making her big-screen debut). Not to give away too much of the plot, I can say the story is the usual Hollywood formula (rejection, love, rejection, love, ending in a seventeen-minute impressionistic ballet scene), but this typical script does not detract from the overall musical production.

Oscar Levant, who delivers a splendid performance, played Jerry's best friend, neighbor, and starving concert pianist. (After reading Levant's autobiography, *A Smattering of Ignorance*, it seems plausible that he was not really acting—just being his sharp, quick-witted, sarcastic self.) His piano playing is fantastic, especially in the dream sequence in which he plays the third movement of *Concerto in F* with a full orchestra. Both his piano skills and his wit contribute greatly to this serious piece.

One especially memorable scene is set in a nightclub, with a black jazz combo playing in the background. The leader of the band is none other than jazz alto-sax/trumpet legend Benny Carter (two-time Grammy Award winner). Other highlights include a costume ball and the Busby Berkeley-esque number revolving around Gershwin's hit "I'll Build a Stairway to Paradise."

The movie proved, beyond a shadow of a doubt, that Gene Kelly was an awesome choreographer as well as an immensely talented dancer. He gave a standout performance, capped by the ballet finale danced to the music of *An American in Paris*. The ballet's set designs are excellent, and the translation of music into movement is exceptional. The ballet scene alone makes the movie a must-see, but in its entirety, I give it my highest rating, the coveted . . . 'S Wonderful!

The Dybbuk

Extra! Extra!
READ ALL ABOUT IT!
*GEORGE GERSHWIN QUITS JAZZ!
SIGNS DEAL WITH METROPOLITAN OPERA TO WRITE
AN OPERA ABOUT JEWISH ZOMBIES! OY VEY!*

Okay, I know you may be thinking I went off the deep end here, just grandstanding to get attention. Fair enough, I have been known to do that occasionally—but not so fast. Let me tell you why. Yes, I admit the above headline is a factitious attention grabber, offered tongue in cheek . . . but really it's not too far from the truth! Here are some actual October 1929 newspaper headlines that all seemed to spring from an Associated Press story:

"GERSHWIN ATTUNED TO WRITE AN OPERA" *New York Evening Post* (October 16, 1929)

"GERSHWIN PLANS NEW OPERA" *Los Angeles Examiner* (October 17, 1929)

"GEORGE GERSHWIN PLANS NEW OPERA" *Los Angeles Examiner* (November 6, 1929)[1]

"PLANS TO QUIT JAZZ IN ORDER TO WRITE OPERA" *Geneva Daily Times* (October 16, 1929)

The front page of the *Geneva Daily Times* announced:

George Gershwin, one of Broadway's foremost musical comedy composers, plans to quit jazz temporarily to write a full-length grand opera for the Metropolitan Opera Company.[2]

So far, my so-called factitious attention grabber headline seems to be based on the truth reported in actual newspapers. Gershwin planned to temporally stop writing jazz tunes and devote himself completely to composing an opera for the Metropolitan Opera Company. I am only halfway there, however.

What am I missing? OH! . . . The ZOMBIES! No, I didn't forget. That's the easy piece, which I will get to shortly. Just bear with me . . . there's a true story here! Let me add one more fact to our story. George Gershwin would not be caught dead writing a ZOMBIE opera about your everyday, run-of-the-mill, *Night of the Living Dead* ZOMBIES. If George Gershwin were to write an opera about ZOMBIES, they had to be:

JEWISH ZOMBIES!

First, there is the backstory, then the JEWISH ZOMBIES. Really, I promise. On October 30, 1929, George Gershwin inked a deal with the Metropolitan Opera Company to compose the music for an opera that would premiere sometime before April 1, 1931. (No, it was not an April Fool's joke!) The contract called for Gershwin to compose a full-blown piano and vocal score, written and orchestrated for both orchestra and voice, plus a conductor's score. It also required Gershwin to play four performances. For that effort, he would receive $1,000 ($15,000 today). At first blush, it doesn't seem like much of a payday for such an accomplished composer, but this man was on a much larger mission.

By this time, Gershwin was known as an enormously successful composer of Broadway musicals with numerous blockbuster tunes and lots of cash in the bank (so he was not in this project for the money). He was also known for his orchestral works: *Rhapsody in Blue* (1924), *Concerto in F* (1925), and *An American in Paris* (1928). However, George's big dream was to compose an American opera—something more than *Blue Monday* (his one-act opera that was performed only once—in George White's *Scandals* in 1922).

Long before *Porgy and Bess*, which he wrote in the 1930s, George had struck a deal with the Metropolitan Opera Company in which he would compose an opera based on the popular Jewish mystical play, *The Dybbuk*.

(Look out! Here come the JEWISH ZOMBIES!)

According to Jewish tradition, a *dybbuk* is the displaced soul of a deceased person, a restless soul, or evil spirit that possesses a living person for a period of time, overtaking the host's body, speaking through his or her mouth and acting through his or her body. (Think of the young girl in *The Exorcist*—but instead of being Catholic, she is a Jew. Instead of being named Regan, she is named Rivkele, and then trade in the priest collar for a rabbi in a yarmulke.)

The term *dybbuk* first appeared in the 1600s. It means, "to cling to," so the evil entity "clings to" a living person and causes strange behavior and mental illness—at least from where we regular folks see it. It became infamous through acts of the 17th-century false messiah Shabbetai Zvi, who performed many sexually deviant and sinful acts.

The great 18th-century Talmudist and Kabbalist, Rabbi Jonathan Eybeschutz (an ancestor of my wife, Julie), secretly created amulets to protect pregnant women from evil spirits. In 1903, a famous *dybbuk* possession was reported in Bagdad and was treated by a Hasidic rabbi who performed an exorcism of that evil spirit. My European-Jewish mother used to pull my ear and spit to the side of my head to ward off "the evil one." Because it was believed that *dybbuks* were after little boys and were not interested in little girls, my mother also let my curly hair grow very long so I would be mistaken by "the evil one" for a girl and thus be left alone. They thought young boys were much easier pray for the evil spirit than girls, who were believed to have a stronger resistance to the evil one. Really, this belief was very common among the European-Jewish community, and they brought that belief over to America. But now, let's get back to Gershwin and the JEWISH ZOMBIES.

The Dybbuk, or Between Two Worlds was a story written by S. Ansky in 1914. Ansky's story was turned into a play, which then became very successful. It was translated from Yiddish into English and kept the audiences in the Lower East Side Yiddish Theatre District coming back for more. Here is a short review of the play that appeared in *The New Yorker* (January 23, 1926):

> THE DYBBUK ... Miss Mary Ellis seen at the Neighborhood Playhouse ... Practically all of the spirit of mysticism and beauty of a sensitive race is caught in this Anglacized [sp] production of the Hebraic masterpiece, and thereby is provided a valid reason for getting lost on Grand Street these evenings. David Vardi, the director, it is respectfully suggested, should take curtain calls with the cast.[3]

George immediately started working on some of his ideas for turning *The Dybbuk* play into an opera. In *George Gershwin: A Study in American Music,* Isaac Goldberg wrote the following regarding *The Dybbuk*:

> Pointing to a few melodic phrases unsupported by any harmonic structure; they suggested a slow lilt and might have been anything from a buck-and-wing to a dirge. He glanced at the notes and was soon constructing not only music but a scene. This slow lilt gradually assumed a hieratic character, swinging in drowsy dignity above a drone. The room became a synagogue, and this was the indistinct prayer of those to whom prayer has become a routine such as any other. The lilt had acquired animation; it was the swaying bodies of the chanters.
>
> An upward scratch in the note book suddenly came to life as a Khassidic dance. And those who know what Khassidic tunes can be like in their wild, ecstatic abandon, know also that the Khassid, like his brother under the skin, can grow wings and walk all over God's heaven.[4]

Gershwin abruptly had to stop his work when he found out that the Italian composer Lodovico Rocca had already purchased the rights to *The Dybbuk*, thereby nixing any chance for a Gershwin opera. Both the Metropolitan Opera Company and Gershwin just had to lick their wounds and unravel the contract, which must have been a great disappointment to all. Yet, as we know now, this setback didn't destroy Gershwin's dream of one day composing an American opera. Gershwin had an opera in him, and its birth could not be denied, just delayed for a few years.

As they say, the best is yet to come! Shalom!

Strike Up the Band*

*Strike Up the Band (1927)

> *I see him in the orchestra pit conducting one of his musical comedies, swinging the baton with the lightness and authority of an experienced conductor, and the orchestra played for him with enthusiasm. It was the first time he had ever conducted or held a baton in his hand.*
>
> —MUSICIAN, CONDUCTOR, AND COMPOSER SERGE KOUSSEVITZKY ON GERSHWIN'S CONDUCTING SKILLS[1]

We all know Gershwin played piano with many symphony and Broadway orchestras, but a lesser-known fact is that he also had aspirations to conduct. Sure, he had conducted songs of his own numerous times, but never a whole show. After a short spin at the baton, he would hand it back to the conductor and return to the piano or the audience for the remainder of the show.

But Gershwin always pushed himself to greater and greater heights, so in the summer of 1929, he finally got his first opportunity to lead an orchestra for an entire program at the Lewisohn Stadium in New York City.

Before that performance, he sought out a mentor to give him some baton lessons. That mentor was his former teacher from the good old days, Edward Kilenyi. Kilenyi coached Gershwin on baton technique and had him practice conducting while listening to records. One might say that Gershwin was the greatest conductor on record!

The Lewisohn Stadium concert was a smash, and George did a more than splendid job. The crowd of 15,000 was fortunate to witness yet another side of this unique musical genius at that event. After his debut conducting performance, Gershwin conducted many later orchestra concerts and radio performances.[2]

As a conductor, Gershwin was unique. I would describe his technique as "holistic." Here is what biographer Isaac Goldberg said on his style:

> George cherishes no ambitions to surpass Stokowski, Toscanini, and Koussevitzky. But let it not be imagined that there is anything perfunctory about his conducting. To watch him at rehearsals is to see with what ease he gets the most out of the men under his baton. Baton, did I say? George conducts with a baton, with his cigar, with his shoulders, with his hips, with his eyes, with what not. Yet without any antics for the eyes of the audience. It is, rather, a gentile polyrhythm of his

entire body—a quiet dance. He sings with the principles and the chorus; he whistles; he imitates the various instruments of the orchestra; nothing but a sense of propriety, indeed, keeps him from leaping over the footlights and getting right into the show himself.[3]

However, let's give Gershwin the last word on his own conducting:

> There is one great difficulty, however, in the employment of jazz that is extremely difficult for the composer to overcome. It is almost impossible to write down definitely exactly the effects wished, with the result that the musicians are only too apt to exaggerate their expression, and, allowed to have their way, to twist the composition utterly away from the composer's intention. This is, of course, up to the conductor, who must be continually on the lookout and who must rule his musicians' fancy with an iron hand. Indeed, when a conductor undertakes to direct a work in which jazz plays an important part, he must be even more jealous of the composer's intention than if he were conducting a classical symphony. Once give the musicians their head with jazz, and in a short while they will evolve something which the author himself will fail to recognize as his own offspring.[4]

Gershwin's words on conducting carry a lot of weight since he lived on all sides of music as composer, musician, and conductor. So he knew all the forces at play in a show. But the part I find most fascinating is that when he picked up the baton, his loyalty and devotion was unquestionably to express and respect the composer's voice. As a composer himself, he always assumed this task with the upmost seriousness.

Cuban Overture*

*(1932)

I dedicate this section to my wonderful wife of more than four decades. Julie was born in Havana, Cuba. Fortunately, after several years of living under the totalitarian Castro regime, she escaped that brutal Communist dictator's rule and found exile in the United States of America. Thank G-d for me, she ended up in Brooklyn. Coincidentally, the first American school she attended was George Gershwin Junior High School in the East New York Section of Brooklyn!

In my composition I have endeavored to combine the Cuban rhythms with my own thematic material. The result is a symphonic overture which embodies the essence of the Cuban dance. . . . The conclusion of the work is a coda featuring the Cuban instruments of percussion.

—GEORGE GERSHWIN[1]

Gershwin was known to have helped many musicians along the way, one of which was the bandleader Xavier Cugat. Cugat was a great showman, the self-proclaimed "Emperor of the Rumba." (He called himself emperor because "The King of the Rumba" was already taken.)

When Cugat was first getting started in New York, Gershwin pulled some strings to get the unknown a "significant" gig.[2]

Gershwin had become a regular customer at the swank Sert Room (named after Jose Maria Sert, whose murals adorned the space) in the luxurious Waldorf Astoria. In 1930, Xavier Cugat and his band became the house band at the Sert Room. Upon getting the gig, Cugat renamed his group the Waldorf-Astoria Orchestra. Gershwin was infatuated with the rhythms and music of Xavier Cugat and his Waldorf-Astoria Orchestra, and so night after night, he would come and savor the compelling Cuban sound.

In his autobiography, *Rumba Is My Life,* Cugat remembered Gershwin:

> Several times he invited the boys in the band and me to his Riverside Drive apartment. There, as we had done before with Cole Porter, we would have a jam session, with George sitting at the piano, alternating with my own pianist, Nilo Menéndez, a talented composer who did, among other hits, "Green Eyes." It was Gershwin, I remember, who first suggested to Lucius Boomer, in a well-worded letter, that after three years of steady employment at the Waldorf-Astoria, I was entitled to a vacation. The fertile field becomes sterile without rest.[3] [*Author's note: Lucius Boomer was co-owner and manager of the Waldorf-Astoria*]

In February 1932, Gershwin took a two-week vacation in Havana, Cuba, "The Pearl of the Antilles," with several of his mover-and-shaker society pals: Everett Jacobs, Bennett Cerf, Adam Gimbel (the Macy's vs. Gimbel's guy), Danny Silverberg, and Emil Mosbacher. It was on this trip that Gershwin became enamored of the unique music of the Caribbean Pearl.

Like many Americans, Gershwin was becoming familiar with the sounds of Cuban music. The 1930 hit song "The Peanut Vendor," introduced in the United States by Don Azpiazu's orchestra as well as the 1931 hit movie *The Cuban Love Song,* had raised America's awareness of, and infatuation with, all things Cuban. Americans became particularly enamored with Afro-Cuban music, especially the rumba (which predates the mambo and the conga). Part of the rumba's appeal was its use of a percussion section (as opposed to the single drummer, which was commonly used in popular music of the time). The percussion section had numerous percussionists' playing bongos, conga drums, timbales, maracas, claves, guiros, and more. This Afro-Cuban sound created a unique, multilayered, polyrhythmic feel to this newly "discovered" music. It was enormously infectious, inspiring a strong urge to dance, and it fueled the dance craze that was sweeping the country.[4]

While in Havana, Gershwin and his crew stayed at the Hotel Almendares. The hotel's advertising offered guests, "every opportunity for pleasant recreation; ocean bathing, swimming, sailing, golfing, tennis playing, polo tournaments, motor-boating, deep-sea fishing, motoring, and races of international importance." But there was one special feature the ad did not mention—a wee-hours serenade outside Gershwin's window by a sixteen-piece rumba band. This personal rumba tribute inspired Gershwin to compose an orchestral piece that incorporated the sound and instrumentation of this beautiful, tropical island paradise.

Gershwin returned from his Cuban vacation with a slew of percussion instruments (reminiscent of his return from Paris with taxi horns), and he began writing the score of his *Cuban Overture*, which at first was titled just *Rumba*. Since bongos, maracas, sticks, and gourds were not well known at the time, Gershwin (ever the artist) drew little drawings of the instruments on the score to ensure that everyone knew what was what.[5] On a facsimile of the title page of *Rumba*, which was written in Gershwin's hand, there was a "conductor's note" at the bottom that read, "The Cuban instruments should be placed right in front of the conductor's stand."[6] Directly under that note, Gershwin drew labeled images above each percussion instrument: Cuban sticks, bongo, gourd, and maracas. The man wasn't taking any chances!

On August 16, 1932, at an all-Gershwin program held at Lewisohn Stadium, the *Rumba* piece inspired by Havana, Cuba, was performed. Gershwin relied heavily on the Cuban percussive instruments he had discovered in Havana.[7] He was unhappy with the sound of *Rumba*, however, because the percussive effects of the Cuban instruments lost some of their power in an outdoor concert setting. Nonetheless, the concert was still a blockbuster show that broke all existing attendance records.

George wrote to a friend:

Last night was the most exciting I ever had. First, because the Philharmonic Orchestra played an entire program of my music (this was the first time that an all-Gershwin program was given anywhere), and second, because the all-time record for the Stadium Concerts was broken. I have just gotten the figures: 17,845 people paid to get in, and just 5,000 were at the closed gates trying to fight their way in—unsuccessfully.[8]

When future attendance records were broken at the stadium—as happened in 1937 and again in 1941—it was due to all-Gershwin concerts.[9]

Gershwin changed the name of *Rumba* to *Cuban Overture* when it was performed at the Metropolitan Opera House in a concert to benefit the Musicians Symphony Orchestra. From that point on, the song was always called *Cuban Overture*.

The *Rumba* was widely acclaimed as a unique and celebrated addition to American music. Gershwin's brother, Ira, said that music critic Pitts Sanborn found the *Cuban Overture* to be "superior to Ravel's 'Bolero' in musical body." I guess Pitts gave the Cuban Overture a "10" in more ways than one!

In his 1948 autobiography, *Rumba Is my Life*, Cugat claimed he was the inspiration for Gershwin's *Cuban Overture*.

I became very friendly with the immortal George Gershwin, who often visited the Sert

Room. Deep in thought, he would listen to my band as if he were making mental notes. Which indeed he was. For later, he flattered me by saying my music inspired him to do his famous "Cuban Concerto."[10]

[Author's note: Cugat was referring to *Cuban Overture*]

Yet, the *Cuban Overture* had deeper roots than Cugat even knew. Shortly before Gershwin's Cuban vacation in early 1932, he had begun four years of study on music composition and theory with the renowned musical composer, teacher, and theorist Joseph Schillinger. A very interesting and controversial cat, Schillinger had developed a system of musical composition that was based on mathematical principles and formulas. George's notebooks were filled with Schillinger's esoteric concepts, exercises, and lessons—for example, "Rhythmic Groups Resulting From the Interference of Several Synchronized Periodicities" and "Groups With the Fractioning Around the Axis of Symmetry." It was a purely analytical system for composing that replaced emotion, feeling, and inspiration with the steely precision of a cold, hard slide rule.

Today, in the modern age of computers, the marketplace is full of computer programs that can generate an infinite number of songs, harmonies, and chord progressions. These programs utilize mathematical algorithms, just like Schillinger was teaching Gershwin to do in the 1930s. With a click of the mouse, today's software generates a melody that can be saved or overwritten. Once the user settles on a melody, the program can generate a chord structure and even corresponding harmonies. These modern conveniences are solidly rooted in Schillinger's techniques.

In a Gershwin biography, author David Ewen wrote:

Schillinger once showed how a polyphonic composition in the style of Bach could be manufactured by tracing on graph paper the fluctuations of a business curve in the *New York Times*, and then translating the units of the graph into proportionate values in melodic and harmonic intervals.[11]

Imagine the music that Schillinger could have written for the stock market crash (October 28 and 29, 1929) in the style of Tiny Tim's rendition of "Tip-Toe Through the Tulips" (coincidentally, also written in 1929)!

Cuban Overture marked the first time Gershwin applied some of Schillinger's theories to a published piece. Some say that Gershwin's song "Mine," which he wrote in 1933 for the show *Let 'Em Eat Cake*, was the result of an exercise in which Gershwin utilized the Schillinger template. (Ira staunchly refuted this theory.) During the Gershwin/Schillinger period, Gershwin wrote *Cuban Overture* (1932), "Variations on I Got Rhythm" (1934) and *Porgy and Bess* (1935), among others.

After Gershwin's untimely death, Schillinger claimed that Gershwin had told him he had run out of ideas and inspiration and needed Schillinger's system to help him create new songs, including the songs for *Porgy and Bess*. Although some musicologists acknowledge a limited use of some of Schillinger's theories in a few of Gershwin songs, it is widely accepted that Schillinger retroactively inflated his own significance in Gershwin's creative process.

Money, Money, Money*

*La-La-Lucille! (1919)

The stock market in the Roaring Twenties was a true speculator sport, riddled with the irrational exuberance of high-margin players—until the fateful day it crashed on Tuesday, October 29, 1929.

Before "Black Tuesday," the genesis of the Great Depression, investors could use their existing stock as collateral for loans to purchase even more stock. Many investors could borrow up to 90 percent on their stocks. So, if you owned 100 shares of XYZ Inc., valued at $1 per share (total shares worth $100), you could borrow $90 from your broker to buy more stock in XYZ Inc. or some other company. Thus, you were leveraging your original $100 into $190 worth of stock.

This system worked swell—as long XYZ traded above the $1 mark. If the share price went "underwater" and dropped below $1, then your broker would demand the difference. If you couldn't (or wouldn't) pay it, he would sell some of your shares to pay the difference. This scenario was known as a "margin call."

When the market started slipping into a vicious downward cycle, however, brokers flooded the market with stock, which lowered the share prices, which triggered more sell orders, and on and on it went, all the way down the rabbit hole. Vast fortunes vanished in just a few hours, and soon, Americans were jumping out of high-rise buildings in despair.

Wall Street's crash impacted everyone in the country from the fat cats at the top of the food chain to the average joe schmo on the street. High rates of unemployment severely impacted global trade, and farming, manufacturing, and many other segments of the economy ceased. Breadlines and food shortages became common throughout the land. Taxes and personal incomes plunged to previously unseen lows. The nation and the world were now in uncharted waters. The Roaring Twenties had crashed and crashed hard, and the new decade's theme song, written in 1930 by Gershwin's long-time pal, lyricist Yip Harburg, was a truthful "Brother, Can You Spare a Dime?"

During those dark days, my father and his brother owned a grocery store in Brooklyn. He told my brothers and me that one of the main reasons he had a grocery store was he was the one guy in the neighborhood who could always feed his family. Memories of people lining up outside the store, early in the morning, waiting for bread and canned goods left a mark on him that he never forgot.

As you might imagine, New York's Theater District was decimated by the fiscal collapse of

1929. Both the number of shows and the gross receipts tumbled. Many shows closed, and of those that remained open, average ticket prices plummeted from $6 (about $83 today) to between 25 cents and a dollar ($3.50 to $14 today). About half of the theaters were shuttered, and an estimated 25,000 theater workers, mostly from the Great White Way in New York, found themselves without work, including actors and actresses, stagehands, musicians, box-office personnel, and all sorts of ancillary workers. Restaurants and other businesses in the Theater District also fell on hard times. Nobody was spared, and almost no one was prepared for the sudden and dramatic turn of events.

In desperation, actors and producers experimented with repertory productions to keep as much of the talent working as possible, but they didn't find much success. During that time, the best way to empty a room of rich folks was to announce, "I'm seeking investors for a new Broadway musical!" Investors were as rare as a dodo bird in Central Park.

So, how did our hero, George Gershwin, fare during the early years of the Great Depression? Well, like all Americans, he certainly felt the cold wrath of hard times. Biographer William G. Hyland assessed Gershwin's finances as follows:

> In 1932 he sold his stocks, valued at $81,000 [*$1.4 million today*], for $19,000 [*$330,000 today*]; accordingly, his net income for that year was only about $4,700 [*$82,000 today*]. His losses on stocks were paper losses, however, and his income from royalties was over $65,000 [*$1.1 million today*]. Nonetheless, even royalties declined in the 1930s, and the Gershwins were kept afloat by their ASCAP earnings. On the other hand, their prospects were potentially quite bright. George and Ira were about to burst forth with a major Broadway achievement, *Of Thee I Sing* . . .[1]

Even during the hardest times, the Gershwins were able to find opportunities and new successes.

Delishious*

*Delicious (1931)

As previously noted, the Brothers Gershwin signed a contract with Fox Movietone Company in 1929, agreeing to write the music and lyrics for a new movie musical. The movie industry had discovered its voice with the first "talkie," *The Jazz Singer*, just a couple years earlier, and the studios were hungry for top-notch music to showcase in these new movies. The contract gave George $70,000 for the music (just shy of $1 million today) and Ira $30,000 ($417,000 today) for the lyrics. This marked the first time the brothers would write all the music for a "talkie" movie—but it would not be their last. In November 1930, George, Ira, and Ira's wife, Leonore, shipped out to Beverly Hills and rented the Greta Garbo house on Chevy Chase Drive, which the three then shared.

The movie was called *Delicious* and stared the silent movie blockbuster team of Janet Gaynor and Charles Farrell (Gale Storm's dad, Vern Albright, in the 1950s TV show *My Little Margie*) in their first "talkie" musical. Indeed, the pair made a total of twelve movies together. In 1928, Gaynor won the first-ever Academy Award for best actress for three movies; *7th Heaven* (1927), *Sunrise* (1927), and *Street Angel* (1928). This was the first and last time an actress won the Oscar for multiple roles. (A few years later, the Academy changed its rules to ensure this unique situation would never happen again.)

By 1931, the United States was still in the throes of the Great Depression. Industrial production was severely cramped, and capital remained tight. The 1930 Smoot-Hawley Tariff Act had dramatically increased tariffs on over 20,000 imported items. These incredibly high tariffs froze the economy, further fueling the Great Depression. A second wave of bank failures then occurred, unemployment remained very high, and the downward spiral continued. It was during that period that Congress approved "The Star Spangled Banner" as our National Anthem.

In the midst of this debacle, America was graced with the movie *Delicious*, a love story between two people from very different classes. It's a rags-to-riches story interwoven with a Cinderella story, the perfect fantasy for Americans held in the grip of an economic collapse. He (Charles Farrell) was a millionaire, polo-playing, Westbury socialite, courting a gold-digging lady, who was accompanied at all times by her gold-digging mother. The other woman (Janet Gaynor) was a dirt-poor Scottish illegal immigrant. On a ship from Europe to New York City, the illegal (stow away) sneaks up to the higher decks, where the hoi polloi are situated and folks of her standing are not allowed. She meets the aforementioned rich, almost-but-not-quite, engaged bachelor and they feel electricity between them. Then all sorts of obstacles get in their way. The plot is basically the 1931 version of an ICE officer chasing an undocumented illegal, hoping to send her back home to her country of origin. No wet foot/dry foot here!

The weirdest scene in the film was a kind of foreshadowing of Gershwin's life several years in the future. The scene features Farrell, with his head all bandaged, in his darkened bedroom after a polo accident. (Further on in this book, you will see why this scene is so spooky.)

The Gershwins' music props up the movie, helping to offset the weak plot. The title song, "Delishious," which is a takeoff on the lead female's Scottish accent. Another song, "Blah-Blah-Blah," is a clever rib on cliché love songs. Ira's lyrics for both of these tunes really stand out. The movie was supposed to include the brothers' 1921 underground party hit, "Mischa, Jascha, Toscha, Sascha," but unfortunately and to the disappointment of many, it did not survive the final cut.

One famous scene, known as the "Dream Sequence," is a surreal five-minute piece of cinematography that features Gershwin's *Welcome to the Melting Pot* orchestra piece. But in my mind, the real high point of the movie is another surreal six-minute piece, backed by the Gershwin orchestra piece, in which Sascha (the piano player in the movie) names *New York Rhapsody*, also known as *Manhattan Rhapsody*—which later morphed into an extended Gershwin orchestral work titled *Second Rhapsody* (although Gershwin first called that work *Rhapsody in Rivets*). Did I lose you there? That is not surprising because it is quite convoluted.

Therefore, let's take a closer look at the story behind the *Second Rhapsody* to clear things up.

Second Rhapsody*

*(1931)

Why not call it "Rhapsody in Blue No. 2"
—THIS WAS PAPA GERSHWIN'S SUGGESTED TITLE...
BUT AS WE ALL KNOW, IT DIDN'T STICK. NICE TRY, PAPA.

The title of Gershwin's *Second Rhapsody* evolved over time. As I mentioned previously, the tune first appeared in the movie, *Delicious*, under the name *Manhattan Rhapsody*. In the dialogue that led up to this song, piano man Sascha explains to the illegal immigrant Heather (Gaynor) that the music represents the New York skyscrapers, towering up to the sky, while the people on the ground are like seeds growing toward the light. Loaded with noise, the piercing sound of rivets gives way to the night, which silences the noise. Sascha then bursts into song, as Gaynor dreamily walks through a series of New York City streetscapes, first getting help from a good Samaritan (in NYC, of all places!), then struggling through the crowds leaving the subway, then on to the New York City docks, where the dockworkers are busy at work. It is a beautiful orchestral piece, coupled with excellent, surreal cinematography and images.

Gershwin first worked on the song in California, using the working title of *Rhapsody in Rivets*. Incorporating the staccato sound of rivets into the piece, Gershwin illustrated the fast pace of construction through the sound of riveters' working on skyscrapers. The rivets perfectly express Gershwin's sense of the nervous energy of those times and also the "staccato pace" of modernity.

Movie executives nixed the name *Rhapsody in Rivets*, changing it to *New York Rhapsody*, and later to *Manhattan Rhapsody* for the movie's release. After the movie's debut in New York City on December 25, 1931, followed the next day with an opening in 162 theaters nationwide, the reviewers were underwhelmed (although some did say that Gershwin's music helped save the flick from total oblivion).

Gershwin kept working on the six-minute song, however, refining and expanding it into a full-blown fourteen-minute orchestral and piano symphony work. He named it *Second Rhapsody*, not to be confused with his first *Rhapsody in Blue*.

In late January 1932, this *Second Rhapsody* premiered in Boston; the concert was repeated in Carnegie Hall less than a week later on February 6, 1932. It was performed by the Boston Symphony Orchestra, with Gershwin as the solo pianist, ably led by the conductor Serge Koussevitzky. Unlike *Rhapsody in Blue*, which had been orchestrated by Grofé eight years earlier, Gershwin had orchestrated this new composition himself.

The critics recognized the technical development and evolution of Gershwin's skills, as well as his virtuosity on the piano. However, to summarize the general consensus of the critics, "Gershwin's *Second Rhapsody* was fine as far as music was concerned, but it was no *Rhapsody in Blue*." As far as Gershwin rhapsodies were concerned, the *Second Rhapsody* was appropriately named in more ways than one.

Of Thee I Sing*

*Of Thee I Sing (1931)

The Gershwins wrote phenomenal music, time and time again. So, despite the crushing economic climate of the times, their fortunes got a shot in the arm in 1931 with the smash hit musical *Of Thee I Sing*, which opened on Broadway and had a long run of 441 performances.

The show was a political satire that poked fun at the stupidity of corrupt politicians and included beautiful women, a buffoon vice president, corrupt politicians, talk of impeachment, insulting France to the brink of war, and did I mention corrupt politicians? (Actually, it sounds a bit like current events today.)

The show opened to great reviews in late December 1931. People liked to laugh at the incompetent government characters, especially when the economic times were horrible (a popular theme also today).

It was the first musical to win a Pulitzer Prize for drama. The award went to Ira for the lyrics and the playwright team of George S. Kaufman and Morrie Ryskind. Why did the prize go to the wordsmiths and not to the composer of the music? As I explained much earlier in the book, it wasn't because George did not deserve it! The Pulitzer Prize for Music did not come into existence until a dozen years *after* this music was composed.

The Pulitzer Prize Board made the following statement regarding the award for the music, er . . . words:

This award may seem unusual, but the play is unusual. Not only is it coherent and well knit enough to class[ify] as a play, aside from the music, but it is a biting and true satire on American politics and the public attitude toward them.[1]

Papa Gershwin offered a very succinct summary: "That Pulitzer must be a smart man."[2]

Several years later, the Gershwin brothers signed on with the winning Kaufman/Ryskind team for another Broadway political satire musical. It was titled *Let 'Em Eat Cake*, referencing the line once spoken by the infamous (and eventually, headless) Queen of France, Marie Antoinette. The show advanced the storyline of the previous show, but it had a darker edge. It even had a dictatorship and a revolution in it just for laughs. Unfortunately, it failed to hit the mark that its predecessor had set. In fact, the critics tore it apart. No Pulitzer Prize for this pooch! It opened in October 1933 and shut down after only 89 performances. Clearly, sequels were tough to pull off—even for the Gershwins. But please don't worry, that won't deter me from writing a sequel to this fabulous book!

I Got Rhythm*

*Girl Crazy (1930)

*He could play I've Got Rhythm (sic.) for the thousandth time,
yet do it with such freshness and exuberance as if
he had written it the night before.*

—ROUBEN MAMOULIAN, DIRECTOR OF PORGY AND BESS[1]

Let's get one thing clear from the start of this section—the name of this tune is *not* "*I've* Got Rhythm." George Gershwin's favorite song was called "I Got Rhythm."

It first appeared in the Broadway show *Girl Crazy*, which opened at the Alvin Theatre on October 14, 1930. Ginger Rogers was the star, and the jazz greats Benny Goodman, Gene Krupa, and Glenn Miller were playing in the orchestra pit—but it was twenty-one-year-old Broadway newcomer, Ethel Merman, who really stole the show. At the end of the first act, right before the intermission, she belted out "I've Got Rhythm" oops!—"I Got Rhythm" like she was born to perform that song. She held the final note for an unbelievably long time, an astounding sixteen bars, which brought the crowd to a tumultuous standing ovation and catapulted Merman into an overnight sensation. As Gershwin said, "She can hold a note longer than the Chase Manhattan Bank."

In her autobiography, *Who Could Ask for Anything More* (a line from "I Got Rhythm"), Merman wrote about her audition with the world-famous composer/pianist George Gershwin at his Upper West Side Riverside Drive penthouse.

It was the first time I'd met George Gershwin, and if I may say so without seeming sacrilegious, to me it was like meeting God. Imagine the great Gershwin sitting down and playing his songs for me. . . . When he played "I Got Rhythm," he told me, "If there's anything about this you don't like, I'll be happy to change it." There was nothing about that song I didn't like. But that's the kind of guy he was. . . . I smiled and nodded, but I didn't say anything. Gershwin seemed puzzled at my silence. Finally he said again, "If there's anything about these songs you don't like, Miss Merman, I'll be happy to make changes." . . . I was so flabbergasted. Through the fog . . . I heard myself say, "They'll do very nicely, Mr. Gershwin."[2]

Reaching far beyond Broadway, the song quickly took center stage in the jazz world. As harmonica virtuoso Larry Adler wrote in his autobiography, *It Ain't Necessarily So:*

Gus Edwards took me with him to a spectacular event in the Waldorf-Astoria ballroom in 1932, in aid of some charity. On the stage there were about two dozen concert grand pianos. At center stage front was one concert grand. When the curtain went up, there were the great composers of the day, two at each piano. One would go to the central grand and play a chorus of his best-known melody, and on the second chorus all the composers at the other pianos would join him. I've never seen anything like it. Imagine, George Gershwin plays "I Got Rhythm" and on the second chorus is joined by Jerome Kern, Sigmund Romberg, Noel Coward, Irving Berlin, Hoagy Carmichael, Harold Arlen, Sammy Fain, Johnny Green, Arthur Schwartz, Burton Lane, Harry Revel, J. Fred Coots, Benny Davis, Gus Edwards, Richard Rodgers, Jimmy McHugh, W. C. Handy, Duke Ellington, "Fats" Waller—and at that I know I'm leaving out some.[3]

"I Got Rhythm" was quickly elevated to legendary status in the jazz world, largely because of its signature musical structure. The chord changes follow a specific pattern: A A B A^1, where:

A = statement of melody
B = bridge or release
A^1 = restatement of melody (A)

Other than the twelve-bar blues chord progression, "I Got Rhythm" is the most widely used chord form in jazz. Music professor/historian and former president of the scholarly American Musicological Society, Richard Crawford wrote that "the song's harmonic design summoned jazz performers' inventiveness, both melodic and harmonic, to a degree matched by only one other structure in the history of jazz; the twelve-bar blues."[4] Hundreds of jazz tunes are based on its chord changes. In musical terms, this "borrowing" is called a contrafact, or creating a new melody around an existing harmonic structure.

Jazz cats often utilized "Rhythm's" ("I Got Rhythm") chord changes and substituted their own melodies to circumvent paying royalties. Among many others, bebop legend Charlie Parker used contrafact extensively in his compositions and improvisation. Charlie Parker's *Omnibook* has at least fourteen tunes that Parker composed around the "Rhythm" structure. Every jazz sax cat has a copy of that book. The easy part is owning it; the hard part is playing it!

Here is a *very* short list of tunes based on the "Rhythm" chord structure: "Salt Peanuts"; "Moose the Mooche"; "Flintstones Theme" (Really! Yabba, dabba doo!); "Red Cross"; "Steeplechase"; Duke Ellington's "Cotton Tail"; "Chasin' the Bird"; "Dizzy Atmosphere"; "An Oscar for Treadwell"' Sonny Rollins' "Oleo"; and Charlie Parker's "Anthropology." Clearly, a fundamental universality appears in the chord progression of "I Got Rhythm."

In Dizzy Gillespie's memoirs, *To Be, or Not . . . to Bop,* he quotes drummer Max Roach, who was addressing the practice of bebop cats using "Rhythm" chord changes to circumvent royalties as it gave them an opportunity to copyright the resulting tunes as different tunes. Roach is quoted as follows:

Of course there are about ten million tunes written on the changes of "I Got Rhythm." . . . That was our thing in bebop, putting in substitutions. . . . This wasn't pilfering. In cases where we needed substitute chords for these tunes, we had to create new melodies to fit them. If you're going to think up a melody, you'd just as well copyright it as a new tune, and that's what we did. We never did get any lawsuits from publishers.[5]

Jazz is a rich and colorful art form, and its improvisational nature continually delivers many surprises. On the bandstand, a cat might call out to the group, "'Rhythm' changes with a Sears-Roebuck bridge." Or he might shout out, "'Rhythm' changes with a Montgomery-Ward bridge." I kid you not. This happens, and the rest of the band knows exactly what this "call out" means. I refrain here from offering all the details, but the point is that "Rhythm" is jazz shorthand and code, and jazz cats everywhere know exactly what to do with it.

Ironically, many jazz historians have largely ignored Gershwin's contribution to jazz. Perhaps the most glaring example is in *The New Edition of the Encyclopedia of Jazz*. Written and compiled by jazz composer/pianist/writer/expert Leonard Feather, the book has over 500 pages on jazz (two columns per page!) and features introductory notes by Duke Ellington, Benny Goodman, and John Hammond. It's more than two inches thick and weighs nearly three and a half pounds; there was no scrimping on paper and ink for this tome. And yet, the space afforded to George Gershwin is positively puny, *a smidgen less than three column inches!* Even Texas trombone player Mathew Gee, Jr., exceeded that, and alto sax man Herb Geller has almost four inches of text.

Why do they get more ink than the internationally, but apparently somewhat infamous George Gershwin? Another pianist/composer of his same era, Duke Ellington, gets almost 40 inches—thirteen times more space than Gershwin. With all due respect, the jazz snob intelligentsia (and Feather is a card-carrying member of that group) refuses to acknowledge George Gershwin's tremendous contribution to jazz.

I am certainly not the first to figure our that many jazz "experts" have snubbed Gershwin in the annals of history. Over the years, I have wracked my brain trying to understand why a group of jazz cats keep devaluing Gershwin's contribution to jazz. Was it because he was a Jew and they held a hidden anti-Semitic tic? Or was it because he was not a black man? Or was it merely because of jealously? I think possibly it is a combination of some or all of these explanations and more. Be that as it may, Gershwin has been undeservedly ignored. In a 1998 article appropriately titled "Misunderstanding Gershwin," the composer and musicologist David Schiff wrote:

> Jazz historians barely mention the composer of "I Got Rhythm," whose harmonic progression supports nearly as much jazz improvisation as the blues; and most accounts of 20th Century classical music treat Gershwin as a speck compared with giants like Stravinsky, Ravel, and, more recently, Ives. At the same time, though, Gershwin concerts invariably sell out; the all-Gershwin concert by the San Francisco Symphony and Michael Tilson Thomas that opens the Carnegie Hall season this fall is the hottest ticket in New York.[6]

As Schiff readily acknowledged, Gershwin has indeed been unfairly ignored in both the jazz world and the classical world, even though Gershwin's compositions remain ironically extremely popular in both realms. Quite schizophrenic! In the same article, Schiff explains that jazz cats love to use Gershwin songs as their launching point for improvisation because Gershwin wrote tunes with "strong harmonic structures." They would throw out the original melody and wrote their own songs based on the underlying Gershwin chord changes. As far as George Gershwin goes—jazz can't live with him and jazz can't live without him!

Legendary jazz pianist great Dick Hyman spoke for all jazz cats (okay . . . maybe not Leonard Feather) when he said, "Gershwin songs appeal to us . . . because they suggest infinite variations and endless interpretations."[7]

Variations on "I Got Rhythm"*

*(1934)

> *George wrote this [song] partly because he had become rather sick of playing the* Rhapsody *or the* Concerto.
> —KAY SWIFT ON "VARIATIONS ON 'I GOT RHYTHM'"¹

As far as "endless interpretations" go, apparently George had that same thought and wanted to keep things fresh for himself and his audience.

Late in 1933, while vacationing at George's high-society pal Emil Mosbacher's home, in Palm Beach, Florida, Gershwin began to work on "Variations on 'I Got Rhythm.'" It showcased Gershwin's remarkable ability to improvise. The tune is based on the pentatonic scale, a five-tone scale with a strong Asian feel to it. He finished the work in early 1934, and in an act of brotherly love, he dedicated the song to his brother/partner, Ira.

After premièring "Variations" in Boston on January 14, 1934, George then took it on tour to celebrate the 10th anniversary of his masterpiece, *Rhapsody in Blue*. The Reisman Symphonic Orchestra accompanied Gershwin, performing twenty-eight concerts in twenty-eight days, with George on the piano the entire time—quite a testament to his stamina. The last show of the tour was held on Saturday, February 10th at the famous Brooklyn Academy of Music.

"Variations on 'I Got Rhythm'" was the one and only popular song Gershwin used as the core for a symphonic work, perhaps reflecting his particular affection for this song.

There is an actual recording of Gershwin playing "Variations" on his radio show, *Music by Gershwin* (broadcast on April 30, 1934), that really showcases his stellar piano skills. The recording also includes his introduction to the song, which is a real treat to hear. His sweet voice and the unique way he describes each variation provides a rare glimpse into this musical genius's creative process. Also, on the web is rare video footage of Gershwin playing "Variations on 'I Got Rhythm'." Truly Amazing!

George Gershwin's Song Book

In these pages any pianist of average ability will find several evenings of entertainment for himself and his friends.[1]

—NEW YORK TIMES, FROM THE BACK COVER
OF GEORGE GERSHWIN'S SONG BOOK

In 1929, the book publisher Simon & Schuster contracted with Gershwin for him to put on paper some of his sophisticated improvisations and the variations of his most famous songs. Gershwin's tremendous reputation as a party improviser *par excellence* had spread throughout the country and beyond, and many were eager to learn the secrets of improvisation directly from the master. The book was released in 1932 with the title *George Gershwin's Song Book,* and it quickly sold out.

It contained eighteen of his most famous songs, including his own special arrangements for the piano, starting with his 1919 blockbuster hit, "Swanee," and progressing chronologically to his 1931 song, "Who Cares!" It also included "I'll Build a Stairway to Paradise" (1922); "Fascinating Rhythm" (1924); "Oh, Lady Be Good!" (1924); "Somebody Loves Me" (1924); "The Man I Love" (1924); "'S Wonderful" (1927); "I Got Rhythm" (1930); and more.

Much more than a standard songbook, this publication included sophisticated piano variations and improvisations after each song. These transcriptions of actual Gershwin solos were for advanced piano players. On the back cover of the dust jacket of my 1941 edition is the following quote from *The New York Times*:

> The real gold of the book is to be found in the inimitable treatments of his best songs, his uncanny mastery of the piano, especially in matters of rhythm and modern color, all of which have evolved into a brilliant and radically individual style which at once becomes identified with Gershwin and with no one else.[2]

In his introduction, Gershwin wrote:

> Sheet music, as ordinarily printed for mass sales, is arranged with an eye to simplicity. The publishers cannot be blamed for getting out simplified versions of songs, which since the majority of the purchasers of popular music are little girls with little hands, who have not progressed very far in their study of the piano. . . .
>
> Gradually, with the general increase of

technical skill at the piano, there has arisen a demand for arrangements that shall consider that skill. Playing my songs as frequently as I do at private parties, I have naturally been led to compose numerous variations upon them, and to indulge the desire for complication and variety that every composer feels when he manipulates the same material over and over again. It was this habit of mine that led to the original suggestion to publish a group of songs not only in the simplified arrangements that the public knew, but also in the variations that I have devised.

Hence, in this book, [are] the transcriptions for solo piano of each chorus, after its appearance in the regular sheet-music form. Some of these are very difficult; they have been put in for those good pianists, of whom there is a growing number, who enjoy popular music, but who rebel at the too-simple arrangements issued by the publishers with the average pianist in view.[3]

The original songbook was dedicated to Gershwin's friend, lover, and musical assistant, Kay Swift, who helped George with the transcriptions of his exceptional and sophisticated variations.

Tune In (to Station J.O.Y.)*

*George White's Scandal's of 1924 (1924)

> *In his own radio programs, George devoted a certain amount of time to introducing some of the younger composers and playing their music or having them play their own music. And it was not just to encourage these young composers, but to let the radio audience know that he considered them clever writers and liked their work.*
>
> —HAROLD ARLEN (WHO COMPOSED OVER THE RAINBOW AND MANY MORE STANDARDS)[1]

Gershwin was certainly no stranger to radio. He was a featured guest on many shows over the years. He appeared as a guest on shows hosted by Rudy Vallee, Ted Weems, Walter Damrosch, and also on the American Telephone and Telegraph's *The Telephone Hour*. According to Gershwin biographers Jablonski and Stewart, his first radio appearance was on the NBC's *The Eveready Hour* (WEAF) on December 14, 1926, then two weeks later again on the same program.[2] This was followed by many more performances and interviews, but unfortunately, none of these appearances were recorded for posterity.

On February 19, 1934, Gershwin began hosting his own radio show. *Music by Gershwin* was broadcast on WJZ, the Blue Network, and aired on Monday and Friday nights from 7:30–7:45. In addition to hosting the show, George was also master of ceremonies, conductor, composer, and pianist. He talked about his music, interviewed popular composers of the day, played the piano, and conducted the in-studio orchestra. He also generously shared his airtime with a number of unknown up-and-comers. He received $2,000 per week.[3] (In today's dollars, that would be $35,000 per week—$1.8 million per year!) His show ran for nearly four months (which meant he was paid almost $600,000 in today's bucks!) and featured "The Man I Love" as its theme song. The announcer was Don Wilson, who later became the sidekick, announcer, and foil for comedian Jack Benny.[4] The radio band included jazz heavyweights of the day, including The Dorsey Brothers, Tommy and Jimmy. The radio show ended in June when George decided to travel to South Carolina with his Cousin Botkin, the painter, to study the Gullah Negro community and devote himself to writing *Porgy and Bess*. Later that year (from September 30, 1934, through year's end), *Music by Gershwin* ran on CBS and WABC as a weekly half-hour spot. Gershwin biographers Kimball and Simon wrote that the Feen-A-Mint sponsored show was fifteen minutes at first, and then expanded to thirty minutes later in the year.

The show sponsor Feen-A-Mint was a laxative gum. Although this detail seems a bit of divine comedy for a man with "composer's stomach" (aka chronic constipation), Gershwin was not happy about the show being sponsored by a laxative company. The great American composer Harold Arlen wrote:

> George was famous, but he was also strongly criticized in his time. One day when I walked him home, he kept complaining, "What do they want me to do? What are they criticizing me for?" This was at the time of the radio shows he did for Feen-A-Mint. People forget that was in 1934, and the Depression was still on. Those were bad times, and what George was doing on his radio show was helping all of us.[5]

DuBose Heyward, author of *Porgy* and Gershwin's partner in the masterpiece opera, said in 1935:

> Statistics record the fact that there are 25 million radios in America. Their contribution to the opera was indirect, but important. Out of them for half an hour each week poured the glad tidings that Feen-A-Mint could be wheedled away from virtually any drug clerk in America for one dime—the tenth part of a dollar. And with the authentic medicine-man flair, the manufacturer distributed his information in an irresistible wrapper of Gershwin hits, with the composer at the piano.
>
> There is, I imagine, a worse fate than that which derives from the use of a laxative gum. And, anyhow, we felt that the end justified the means, and that they also served who only sat and waited.[6]

When people chided George for having a show sponsored by a laxative, he replied, "Without Feen-A-Mint, I would not have been able to write *Porgy and Bess*."[7] (I can clearly hear him say, "Radio's been berry, berry good to me.")

Gershwin's last radio gig was broadcast on WOR on July 9, 1936. It was a live performance at one of his favorite venues, New York's Lewisohn Stadium, and he performed three of his most celebrated works: *Rhapsody in Blue*, *Concerto in F*, and *An American in Paris*.[8]

I Loves You, Porgy*

*Porgy and Bess (1935)

If, say, an opera like Die Meistersinger *was given about six times a season at the Metropolitan Opera, then the 124 performances of* Porgy and Bess *represented a run of over 20 years for a great opera house.*
—GEORGE GERSHWIN[1]

George was known for his relentless desire to challenge himself. Never resting on his laurels, he constantly pushed himself beyond his comfort zone. He did so over and over again, from the very beginning of his career all the way to its untimely conclusion. He wrote two rhapsodies, a concerto, a symphonic tone poem, an overture, a one-act black opera, and then, of all things, a full-blown opera! And a jazz opera, at that. And that's not counting the never completed Jewish Zombie Opera. This output was in addition to the hundreds of show tunes and hit songs he composed. He was perpetually stretching the limits of his knowledge and experience. "I am a man without traditions!" was a favorite declaration of Gershwin's.[2] And indeed, this perspective freed him from the creative constraints of his past and his contemporaries as well.

After Gershwin wrote the ill-fated one-act opera, *Blue Monday* (later renamed *135th Street*), he had a burning desire to do a full-blown operatic work. We saw this desire flare up in his (later jettisoned) contract to write an operatic work based on the Jewish folklore tale, *The Dybbuk*, as mentioned previously.

Gershwin was not the only one at the time feeling the urge to produce an American-made opera. His friend, banker, financier, one percenter, patron of the arts and Metropolitan Opera Company chairman, Otto H. Kahn, sent out a challenge to the musical world in November 1924, announcing his plan to produce a jazz opera at the Metropolitan Opera House. Game on!

In the early 1930s, Kahn offered Gershwin a $5,000 bonus (about $90,000 today) to do *Porgy and Bess* with the Metropolitan Opera Company. Gershwin's response is cited at the beginning of this section, implying that he believed the opera would have very little exposure. Gershwin was also opposed to Kahn's offer because it included the prospect of using white performers in blackface, something Gershwin had sworn against doing. He insisted on black performers in his black opera —no compromises, whatsoever! That is why, on October 26, 1933, Gershwin signed a contract to do *Porgy and Bess* with the Theatre Guild, which had originally produced the play back in the 1920s. And yes, the performers would be blacks.

An interesting piece of history is that Al Jolson put in a bid to do *Porgy* in blackface. Jolson, as you may recall, gave Gershwin his first big break in 1919, performing Gershwin's "Swanee" in blackface. However, Gershwin would not let that happen again on his watch.

Gershwin's desire to compose a jazz opera grew even stronger after he read DuBose Heyward's novel *Porgy*. Heyward, a sickly kid who had contracted polio as a teenager, was an interesting cat with deep American roots. A descendant of Southern aristocracy, one of his ancestors was a signatory to the Declaration of Independence. When his father died, his mother, Janie, moved the family to Charlestown, South Carolina, where she encountered a black subculture known as the Gullah. The Gullah were descendants of African slaves, and they maintained strong cultural, religious, and traditional customs, including their own dialect. At the time, the majority of Charleston blacks were Gullah, and Janie Heyward was fascinated by them. She eventually became an expert and a lecturer on the subculture, and her interest and expertise clearly rubbed off on her son.

DuBose Heyward wrote *Porgy* in 1925. It is a novel loosely based on a Charleston beggar named Samuel Smalls, whom Heyward had often seen begging on Charleston's King Street in an area called Cabbage Row. Heyward set *Porgy* here and renamed the street Catfish Row. Smalls had lost the use of his legs, so he got around town in a small goat-drawn cart, earning him the nickname "Goat Sammy." When Heyward saw a notice in the newspaper, announcing that Smalls had been arrested for attempting to shoot a woman, he wondered what could have driven the man to such violence. This story became the impetus for his novel *Porgy*.

Gershwin read the novel in 1926 and contacted Heyward about doing a project based on the book. Heyward's wife, Dorothy, then adapted the book into a play in 1927, which was produced by the Theatre Guild. But the Gershwin opera seemed to fall by the wayside until the Gershwin/Heyward team finally started working on it in 1934.

After signing on with Heyward, Gershwin reached into what he called "the icebox," a large notebook where he kept random musical ideas he had developed over the years.[3] The first song he composed for the opera was the now classic "Summertime." There was much more work to do of course, but that was a pretty strong start!

In 1934, Gershwin and Cousin Botkin, the painter, spent July and August in South Carolina. Gershwin was doing his research, learning about the culture of the Gullah, while his cousin painted. George did some painting as well. It was a hot, humid, uncomfortable time of year, and the two shared a small wooden shack on Folly Island, a small barrier island just a few miles from Charleston. The accommodations were very primitive. "Their rooms were crude, with an old iron bed, a small wash basin, and decaying furniture. Their drinking water had to be brought in from Charleston."[4] But the shack did have one basic necessity—an upright piano for George to create his music.

To prepare himself to write a folk opera about the unique Gullah community, George immersed himself in their music, spirituals, dialect, and culture. He spent a lot of time in the black Macedonia Church, where he learned one specific aspect of Gullah culture exceptionally well. As Heyward described one of Gershwin's encounters with the locals:

> The Gullah Negro prides himself on what he calls "shouting." This is a complicated rhythmic pattern beaten out by feet and hands as an accompaniment to the spirituals, and is indubitably an African survival. I shall never forget the night when, at a Negro meeting on a remote island, George started "shouting" with them. And eventually to their huge delight stole the show from their champion "shouter." I think he is probably the only white man in America who could have done it.[5]

A New York Jewish guy out-shouting the champion shouter of the Gullah! Luckily they didn't play the "Horah"! *Mazel tov!*

The black communities in the south Atlantic states were known for their "ring shouts," a carry-over tradition from an old African dance. In 1867, just a short two years after the end of the Civil War, *Slave Songs of the United States* was published. The book was the work of three Northerners, William Francis Allen, Charles Pickard Ware, and Lucy McKim Garrison. The trio did the research in South Carolina. Here is how the authors described the ring shout:

> Old and young, men and women, sprucely dressed young men, grotesquely half-clad field-hands—the women generally with gay handkerchiefs twisted about their heads and with short shirts—boys with tattered shirts and men's trousers, young girls barefooted, all stand up in the middle of the floor, and, when the "sperichil" is struck up, begin first walking and by and by shuffling round, one after the other, in a ring. The foot is hardly taken from the floor, and the progression is mainly due to a jerking, hitching motion, which agitates the entire shouter, and soon brings out streams of perspiration. Sometimes they dance silently, sometimes as they shuffle along they sing the chorus of the spiritual, and sometimes the song itself is also sung by the dancers. But more frequently a band, composed of some of the best singers, and of tired shouters, stands at the side of the room to "base" the others, singing the body of the song and clapping their hands together or on the knees. Song and dance are alike extremely energetic, and often, when the shout lasts into the middle of the night, the monotonous thud, thud of the feet prevents sleep within half a mile of the praise house.[6]

Musician, author, civil rights activist, and one-time leader of the NAACP, James Weldon Johnson described his own childhood memories of the ring shout:

As the ring goes around, it begins to take on signs of frenzy. The music, starting, perhaps, with a spiritual, becomes a wild, monotonous chant. The same musical phrase is repeated over and over, one, two, three, four, five hours. The very monotony of sound and motion produces an ecstatic state. Women, screaming, fall to the ground prone and quivering. Men, exhausted, drop out of the shout. But the ring closes up and moves round and round.[7]

On a different occasion, Heyward and Gershwin shared another road trip, this time to a Negro Holy Roller meeting. As Heyward described that experience:

Another night, as we were about to enter a dilapidated cabin that had been taken as a meeting house by a group of Negro Holy Rollers, George caught my arm and held me. The sound that had arrested him was one to which, through long familiarity, I attached no special importance. But now, listening to it with him, and noticing his excitement, I began to catch its extraordinary quality. It consisted of perhaps a dozen voices raised in loud rhythmic prayer. The odd thing about it was that while each had started at a different time, upon a different theme, they formed a clearly defined rhythmic pattern, and that this, with the actual words lost, and the inevitable pounding of the rhythm, produced an effect almost terrifying in its primitive intensity. Inspired by the extraordinary effect, George wrote six simultaneous prayers producing a terrifying primitive invocation to God in the face of the hurricane.[8]

Maestro Maurice Peress bridges this prayer to Gershwin's Jewish roots by saying:

The "simultaneous prayers" remind me of a davening minyan, a Jewish prayer group, something Gershwin was familiar with. Each davener (worshipper) picks up the mode or key center established by the cantor or prayer leader and takes off on his own, embellishing the text, emphasizing an important phrase or word with raised voice. On musical cues from the leader, the whole congregation comes together for special tunes that mark a particular passage or the end of a section. This is precisely how Gershwin scored the storm scene.[9]

The musical score of *Porgy and Bess* took Gershwin eleven months to compose and an additional nine months to orchestrate. He finished the entire score, both music and its orchestration, on August 23, 1935. It was a huge body of work with the vocal score running 560 pages and the orchestral manuscript a whopping 700 pages![10] Gershwin considered *Porgy and Bess* the greatest work of his entire career. It was also the one he loved most.

Gifted baritone singer Todd Duncan was handpicked by Gershwin to play Porgy, and over the years, he performed this role over 1,800 times. Recalling his audition with George, he said:

So I went to New York and went up to his apartment at one P.M. He came to the door himself and he asked, "Where's your accompanist?" I didn't know anything about New York ways. I said, "Accompanist? Can you play?" "Well, I play a little," he said. He blinked his eyes. "If you can't play it, I'll play it for myself," I told him. "I'll try to play for you, I'll try," he finally said.[11]

Duncan handed Gershwin a classical piece, which surprised him, since most other singers brought black spiritual music to audition. According to Duncan, Gershwin memorized the entire piece almost instantaneously.

After hearing Duncan sing, Gershwin immediately offered him the role of Porgy. Duncan then coyly answered, "Maybe." First, he had to hear the music before committing to the gig. What a charming and unique interaction that must have been between the naïve newcomer and the old pro.

While rehearsing for the premiere, everyone's nerves were on edge. George suggested a three-day weekend getaway to help them blow off some steam, clear their heads of *Porgy and Bess,* and be able to come back to rehearsals renewed, revived and refreshed. A few folks agreed, and so off they went to Long Beach, Long Island.

Upon their return, Rouben Mamoulian (the producer of this production as well as the original stage play that played to crowds for over two years) was asked what the entourage did during their forget-all-about-*Porgy*-get-away-three-day-weekend. He answered, "Can't you guess? From morning to night, for the three days, George was at the piano, playing the music from *Porgy.*"[12]

The opera premiered in Boston on September 30, 1935, commanding a thunderous ovation and rave reviews. Boston Symphony Orchestra conductor, Serge Koussevitzky, said, "It's a great advance in American Opera . . . and one of the greatest." The Boston press was ablaze with glittering reviews as well. One reviewer wrote of Gershwin, "He has traveled a long way from Tin Pan Alley to this opera. He must now be accepted as a serious composer." L. A. Sloper reported in the *Christian Science Monitor,* "Easily Gershwin's most important contribution to music."[13] And New England Conservatory of Music alumnus and noted black singer/composer J. Rosamond Johnson (who played the humorous lawyer, Frazer, in the original production of *Porgy and Bess*) said to Gershwin, "George, you've done it—you're the Abraham Lincoln of Negro music."[14]

The opera then moved to New York for its opening on October 10, 1935, at the Alvin Theatre (now the Neil Simon Theatre) on West 52nd Street. All the usual suspects were in attendance. The highbrow elite arrived in their chauffeur-driven limos, and the lowbrow denizens of Tin Pan Alley and Broadway came any way they could. The audience loved the opera, but as in the past, the critics delivered a split decision on Gershwin's work.

Brooks Atkinson wrote, "Mr. Gershwin has contributed something glorious to the spirit of Heyward's community legend." And from John Mason Brown, "Unless my untrained ears deceive me, it contains some of the loveliest music he has written." Robert Garland called it a "modern masterpiece."

But, according to Olin Downes, "It does not utilize all the resources of the operatic composer. . . . The style is at one moment of opera and another of operetta or sheer Broadway entertainment." And composer/critic Virgil Thomson characterized the opera in *Modern Music* as "crooked folklore and halfway opera."[15]

Thomson wrote a blistering review, complete with some anti-Semitic comments:

> Gershwin has not and never did have any power of sustained musical development. . . . The material is straight from the melting pot. At best it is a piquant but highly unsavory stirring-up together of Israel, Africa and the Gaelic Isles. . . . His lack of understanding of all the major problems of form, of continuity, and of serious or direct musical expression is not surprising in view of the impurity of his musical sources and his frank acceptance of the same. Such frankness is admirable. At 25 it was also charming. Gaminerie of any kind at 35 is more difficult to stomach. So that quite often *Porgy and Bess,* instead of being pretty, is a hoydenish. . . . It is clear, by now,

that Gershwin hasn't learned the business of being a serious composer, which one has always gathered to be the business he wanted to learn.... His efforts at recitative are as ineffective as anything I've heard.... I do not like fake folklore, nor fidgety accompaniments, nor bittersweet harmony, nor six-part choruses, nor gefilte-fish orchestration.[16]

Once again we see this critic going right for Gershwin's Jew-gular vein. Thomson's career was always shadowed by his anti-Semitic comments, which were many. For example, he renamed the League of Composers "The League of Jewish Composers." In an article about the composer Aaron Copland, Thomson could not help but stereotype him with references to his Israeli and Hebrew ancestry. Thomson opined on a score written by the composer Kurt Weill ("Mack the Knife"), saying he "evoked the Jewish Underworld of Berlin.... Anyway it had something international about it and maybe the Jewishness was what was so goddamned international."[17] Thomson of course denied being anti-Semitic, insisting that some of his best friends were Jews.

NOTE TO SELF: DO NOT INVITE VIRGIL THOMSON TO MY NEXT PASSOVER SEDER!

Gershwin thankfully and wisely paid his detractors little heed. In his words:

I have created a new form, which combines opera with theatre, this new form has come quite naturally out of the material.... Come naturally from the Negro. They make for folk music. Thus, *Porgy and Bess* becomes a folk opera—opera for the theater, with drama, humor, song and dance.[18]

Gershwin was a man of the people, and that is how he approached this work. In a 1935 *New York Times* piece entitled "Rhapsody in Catfish Row," he wrote:

The reason I did not submit this work to the usual sponsors of opera in America was that I hoped to have developed something in American music that would appeal to the many rather than to the cultured few.[19]

Gershwin biographer Isaac Goldberg opined on Gershwin's *Porgy and Bess* composition in an article that he penned for *Stage Magazine's* December 1935 issue. It was titled "Score by George Gershwin." He wrote:

This fellow has plenty of somethin', and it ain't only old man rhythm! His new attitude toward opera promises to discover a new public for it. In that public, as in himself, will be symbolized the victorious clash of healthy instinct with conventional formula. It is all part of a personal and a national growth that happily coincide.[20]

In this same article, Goldberg highlighted the "melting pot" aspect of *Porgy and Bess*, as follows:

Why the Jew of the North should, in time, take up the song of the Southern Negro and fuse it into a typically American product is an involved question. Perhaps, underneath the jazz rhythms and the general unconventionality of musical process lies the common history of an oppressed minority, and an ultimately Oriental origin. In any case, the human focus of this particular type of musical Americanism has been, from his very first notes, George Gershwin.[21]

A great controversy arose after an interview between the broadcast journalist Edward Morrow and jazz legend Duke Ellington, titled "Duke Ellington on Gershwin's 'Porgy.'" It published in the December 1935 issue of the left-wing magazine *New Theatre*. Morrow asked Ellington what he thought of *Porgy and Bess*, and the Duke replied, "Grand music and a swell play." So far so good, right? Not so fast.

Morrow inquired why the Duke said the music was "grand." Ellington shot back, "Why shouldn't it be? It was taken from some of the best and a few of the worst. Gershwin surely didn't discriminate: he borrowed from everyone, from Liszt to Dickie Wells' kazoo band."[22] (Author's note: The "Dickey Wells' Shim Shammers" recorded a few sides for Columbia in 1933.) This obvious put-down of Gershwin implied that the music in *Porgy and Bess* was "borrowed" from others, including, of all things, a kazoo band!—and it was quite out of character for the usually laid-back Duke.

Morrow wrote that Ellington played some snippets of *Rhapsody in Blue* and compared them to some Negro songs. Duke then played his own music and explained that his was not "borrowed," saying, "I have taken the method, but I have not stolen or borrowed."

Later in the article, Morrow exposed his own slant, which could lead the reader to attribute his personal perspective to being that of Ellington. Sharing his opinion on Rouben Mamoulian's directing of the folk opera, Morrow wrote:

> No Negro could possibly be fooled by *Porgy and Bess*. . . . His Negroes still wave their arms in shadowed frenzy during the wake. The production is cooked up, flavored and seasoned to be palmed off as "authentic" of the Charleston Gullah Negroes—who are, one supposes, "odd beasts."

Morrow went on to say, "But the times are here to debunk such tripe as Gershwin's lamp-black Negroisms, and the melodramatic trash of the script of *Porgy*." It was easy to read these comments as the Duke's, but in fact, they came from Morrow.

The Duke's booking agent, Mills Artists, did damage control by having their representative, Richard Mack, write a response to the interview. Published in the May 1936 issue of *Orchestra World*, in an article titled "Duke Ellington—In Person," Mack wrote:

> [Ellington] hates being misquoted in interviews. Very often a reviewer will ask Duke to express his opinion on some subject, and in the reviewer's elaboration of Duke's statements, the writer will add ideas of his own. The Ellington *Porgy and Bess* interview is an example of this.

Mack also stated that some of the comments were supposed to be off the record, and yet they turned up in the printed article. Mack insisted:

> [Ellington] felt that Gershwin's music, though grand, was not distinctly or definitely negroid in character. The reviewer then proceeded to add pet notions of his own and credited them to Duke, finally appearing with a so-called statement by Ellington accusing Gershwin of being everything from a bad musician to an obvious plagiarist. Duke was very unhappy over these uncalled-for misquotations. . . . Duke feels the injustice of it to this date and constantly expresses the hope that "Gershwin didn't take any stock in those things I was supposed to have said."[23]

Ellington was known to be a very diplomatic cat—an ambassador of jazz, if you will—so the statements attributed to him by Morrow do seem out of character. On the other hand, Morrow was an award-winning journalist with a reputation for getting the facts straight. Who ever heard of a journalist misquoting someone to create controversy? Oh, my! So who are we to believe? Maybe Brian Williams can help us get to the truth.

The editor of *The Duke Ellington Reader*, Mark Tucker, offered his take on the credibility of the Duke's statements. "Are the quotes attributed to Ellington in Morrow's article genuine? While the frank tone is surprising, the manner of delivery would seem to be Ellington's own." I pose the following question. In the interview, what was actually said by Ellington, the diplomat, and what was Morrow, the firebrand journalist trying to pin on him? I am of the belief that Morrow was on a mission to discredit the greatness of Gershwin's masterpiece, so perhaps he heard what he wanted to hear even if he had to embellish the interview to fit his agenda. It wouldn't be the first time a journalist stretched the truth to "create" a story that was controversial.

Let us not draw the wrong conclusions, however, regarding the Gershwin-Ellington relationship. They were both men of high character and were not known for demeaning others, including each other. In 1929, Ellington led his Cotton Club Orchestra in the Gershwin Broadway Musical *Show Girl*, produced by Florenz Ziegfeld. The show stared Ruby Keeler and Jimmy "The Great Schnozzola" Durante and was a flop with only 111 performances. The two great composers must have had many professional interactions during this time period. Decades later, Ellington wrote in his 1973 autobiography, *Music Is My Mistress*:

> [Gershwin] once told Oscar Levant that he wished he had written the bridge to "Sophisticated Lady," and that made me very proud.[24]

Reading that Ellington was "very proud" that Gershwin appreciated his song so much puts to rest for me any thought of a wedge between these two great artists, making me more apt to think that Morrow was stirring up dissension.

In his 1939 article Oscar Levant said Gershwin, "greatly admired Duke Ellington records for their rich effects and fine tonal originality—mood pieces like the 'Creole Love Song,' 'Swanee Rhapsody,' and 'Daybreak Express.'"[25]

* * *

Getting back to *Porgy and Bess*.... In the short run, it was a financial train wreck, losing all of its initial $70,000 ($1.2 million today) investment, including $5,000 each ($86,000 today) from George, Ira, and DuBose Heyward. Even counting their royalties, it was a bust ... but over time, the opera turned into a perpetual money machine, unfortunately after the demise of both Gershwin and Hayward. It has been performed thousands and thousands of times to sold-out crowds around the world. Recordings and the movie earned huge sums of cash for the Gershwins as well as DuBose and Dorothy Heyward. All in all, *Porgy and Bess* was a multi-multi-million-dollar baby.

Porgy and Bess has been performed in opera houses, concert halls, theaters, cafes, and countless other venues. (I once campaigned to have it performed in one of my health food supermarkets, near the seafood case to promote a special on catfish in honor of Catfish Row. That idea never got approval from upper management—Julie!)

One of the most memorable and historic performances of *Porgy and Bess* occurred in our nation's capital on March 31, 1936. The lead, Todd Duncan, led a protest by the troupe, saying they would not perform unless the theater was desegregated. This kind of protest at the National Theatre had never happened before. Every performance at the National Theatre, up until that time, always and without exception had a segregated, separate-but-equal (Jim Crow) audience. However, thanks to the brave artists who stood up to prejudice, a precedent occurred. Blacks were, for the first time ever, granted permission to attend the National Theatre of Washington, D.C., in an unsegregated audience. George Gershwin's music thus officially staked a viable and important claim in the Civil Rights Movement, helping to break down the barriers and indignities that have scarred our nation's character. It also highlights the importance of Jews' coming to the aid of a fellow oppressed minority who were in search of equality and the American Dream.

In addition to these segregation-busting performances in Washington, D.C., the opera also scored a hit against the Nazis. As you might imagine, *Porgy and Bess*, an opera about black life in the South, written by a Jew, was not appreciated by the Nazis. In early 1943, the opera was performed at the Danish Royal Opera in Copenhagen during the Nazi occupation of Denmark. The show was delivered to sold-out crowds, and that really pissed the Nazis off. The Third Reich could not tolerate a show written by a Jew about blacks. After several sold-out performances, the Nazis threatened to blow up the theater. Rather than lose the building, the Danes closed down the show.

But that didn't stop the work continuing, because, as they say in show business—the show must go on! There were over forty underground performances of the opera during the war, which angered the Nazis even more. But their storm troopers never got to any of these clandestine performances in time to do any real damage.

The Danish underground resistance used "It Ain't Necessarily So" (one of the greatest songs in *Porgy and Bess*) as a symbol of defiance against the Nazi occupiers. When the Germans broadcast over the airwaves, touting their announcements about the Third Reich's victories and such, the Danish Resistance would break into the broadcast and play Gershwin's "It Ain't Necessarily So." Had he known, this presentation would have made Gershwin immensely proud, as he was an outspoken critic of the Nazi regime. He would have also liked the fact that the opera, written by an "inferior" Jew about "inferior" blacks served as a unique weapon against the supposedly "superior" Aryan Nation.

Both George Gershwin and Heyward died before *Porgy and Bess* gained the fantastic recognition it deserved and eventually did receive. Some of its songs, like "Summertime" and "It Ain't Necessarily So," did garner popular success early on, but it would be many more years before the critics turned and appreciated Gershwin and Heyward's remarkable work.

In January 1942, *Porgy and Bess* experienced a Broadway revival at the Majestic Theatre, featuring the original leads, Todd Duncan and Anne Brown. The critics now began to give the work unanimous rave reviews. Even Virgil Thomson (previously mentioned) recanted his earlier comments and declared the opera, "a beautiful piece of music and a deeply moving play."[26]

I guess it took a bit of time for the critics to understand what *Porgy and Bess* was really all about. It truly is a masterpiece with songs like "Summertime," I Got Plenty o' Nuttin'," "It Ain't Necessarily So," and others as alive and vibrant today as the day Gershwin wrote them.

During the Jim Crow era of the 1950s, the U.S. Department of State sponsored a smashing European tour of *Porgy and Bess* to demonstrate our nation's support of black arts and culture. It seems very curious that the State Department would sponsor this tour during the Jim Crow era, but it's a perfect example of our nation's split personality regarding race. The government of the United States sponsored a show featuring a group of people who, at that time, still could not eat in the same restaurant or go to the same school as whites in many parts of the country.

In 1935, George formed the Gershwin Publishing Corporation (a subsidiary of Chapell and Company) with his pal and former publisher, Max Dreyfus. This new company published all of the music of *Porgy and Bess*. It was a big deal for Gershwin to see his name as publisher, and he was thrilled about it.

Until 1927, all of Gershwin's songs had been published under Harms. Dreyfus and his brother Louis were running Harms when Dreyfus "discovered" Gershwin and signed him to an exclusive publishing deal. In 1927, Harms formed a subsidiary to publish Gershwin's music called New World Publishing Company.

After the blockbuster first movie with sound, *The Jazz Singer*, Warner Brothers went on a buying binge, gobbling up music publishers. They spent the unbelievable sum of $10 million (about $140 million today) to purchase the Tin Pan Alley giants—including Remick, Whitmark, Harms, and New World Publishing. That was in 1929. Gershwin stayed with Warner Brothers until the formation of the Gershwin Publishing Corporation in 1935. From that point forward, Gershwin's company published all of his music.

The bottom line of course and the main question is: What did Gershwin think of his music in *Porgy and Bess*?

The director of the opera, Rouben Mamoulian, received a phone call from Gershwin after the first rehearsal—which Mamoulian had described as, "awkward, disorganized, almost hopeless." Gershwin simply said to him:

> I am so thrilled and delighted over the rehearsal today. . . . I always knew that *Porgy and Bess* was wonderful, but I never thought I'd feel the way I feel now. I tell you, after listening to that rehearsal today, I think the music is so marvelous—I really don't believe I wrote it![27]

The Senatorial Roll Call*

*Of Thee I Sing (1931)

I am going to interest myself in politics.
—GEORGE GERSHWIN, 1935[1]

At the end of 1935, George went on a vacation to Mexico. Still smarting from the financial failure of his *Porgy and Bess*, he wanted to clear his mind and find new inspiration elsewhere . . . maybe even come home with a Mexican musical brainchild, like he had for his *Cuban Overture* after visiting Cuba several years earlier.

Although the trip failed to produce that musical inspiration, it did inspire his new interest in politics. While in Mexico, George spent a great deal of time with the infamous Communist painter Diego Rivera. Speaking of his newfound interest in politics, Gershwin acknowledged, "It is true that in Mexico I talked a great deal with Diego Rivera, and with his radical friends, who discussed at length their doctrines and their intentions."[2] Let me be perfectly clear, however, by no means should we interpret this statement as Gershwin ever being or supporting the Communist cause since there is no evidence at all of this direction for him.

Apparently, George was a bit of an activist though. Months later, in February 1936, Gershwin and some of his ASCAP buddies (Rudy Vallee, Irving Berlin, and Gene Buck) testified before the House Committee on Patents in Washington, D.C., on a copyright bill pending in Congress. ASCAP opposed the bill, claiming it would reduce the incomes of composers and writers. For once in his life, George here was campaigning to keep the status quo instead of challenging it.

Apparently, principles and politics ran deep in the Gershwin blood because in September 1947 (a decade after George's untimely demise), Ira also joined a political activism group. The Committee for the First Amendment included influential celebrities like Humphrey Bogart, Lauren Bacall, Henry Fonda, Groucho Marx, Lucille Ball, and Frank Sinatra, to name just a few. In October, they went to Washington, D.C., in support of another group called the Hollywood Ten to protest the House Un-American Activities Committee hearings (not to be confused with the McCarthy hearings).

Ostensibly because of his support for the Hollywood Ten, Ira was later called before the California anti-Communist Tenney Committee. Jack B. Tenney was a bulldog politician who saw a Commie under every tree. Tenney also authored several anti-Semitic books. As fate would have it, he also composed several popular songs. Put all these pieces together, and Ira was forced to testify before a committee headed by a Commie-hating, Jew-hating songwriter politician. Hardly an enviable position! (I can just imagine Tenney heading home that night to write his next hit song: "Hey There, Little Red Riding Jew!")

(I've Got) Beginner's Luck*

*Shall We Dance (1937)

After the disappointing run of *Porgy and Bess*, Gershwin told his agent, Arthur Lyons, at the beginning of 1936 that he wanted a movie deal—something similar to his 1930 contract with Fox Studios, which had earned him $100,000 ($1.7 million today) plus a percentage of the profits.

While Gershwin had been absorbed in writing *Porgy and Bess* for nearly two years, the world around him had changed, both on Broadway and in Hollywood. It's hard to believe today, but some producers now felt Gershwin had become irrelevant.

When Lyons promoted the Brothers Gershwin to the Hollywood studios, he faced rumors and concerns that, since he had ventured into highbrow work like opera, Gershwin could no longer write hits—and hits were what the studios needed. Lyons sent George a cable saying:

> "They are afraid you will only do highbrow songs." Gershwin indignantly replied, "Rumors about highbrow music ridiculous. Am out to write hits." In New York, Gershwin was being lauded for having demonstrated that Tin Pan Alley could produce a serious composer (*Porgy and Bess*), while in Hollywood this was considered a liability.[1]

Eventually, the Gershwin brothers entered into negotiations with RKO Pictures, one of the Big Five studios during Hollywood's Golden Age. It produced numerous box office hits, including *King Kong* and the series of famous musicals starring Fred Astaire and Ginger Rogers. The movie company wanted Gershwin to write the music for the next Astaire/Rogers musical. As you might remember, Gershwin and Astaire were pals from the time they both started out in show business, so that proposal must have been quite appealing to George. Yet, I do wonder if he had any reservations about partnering with RKO, given the character of one of its owners.

A little history about RKO is in order. Radio-Keith-Orpheum (RKO) was formed in a 1928 merger between Radio Corporation of America (RCA), the Keith-Albee-Orpheum (KAO) chain of theaters, and Joseph P. Kennedy's Film Booking Offices of America (FBO). If the name Joseph Kennedy sounds familiar, it should, because he was President John F. Kennedy's father. Daddy Kennedy made a fortune on this deal, causing some members of Congress to cry foul, manipulation, racketeering, and the like. But Kennedy was always comfortable with controversy; indeed, his career was riddled with it, from running booze during Prohibition to being a staunch Jew-hating Hitler supporter. (Not to worry . . . he would always says that some of his friends were Jewish.) It appears Daddy Kennedy passed on his Jew-hating gene to his oldest son, Joe Jr. (JFK's older brother), who was a Hitler admirer like dear old dad. But perhaps I digress a bit too much here.

The RKO/Gershwin deal closed with Gershwin accepting $55,000 ($941,000 today) for sixteen weeks, just shy of $3,500 a week ($60,000 a week today). The deal included an option to write the music for a second movie for the ridiculously low sum of $70,000 ($1,200,000 today). Of course, true to his word, Gershwin did indeed write several hits. After the film was completed, George commented that the studio must have finally realized that "Gershwin can be a low brow."[2]

What Causes That?*

Treasure Girl (1928)

He will try the latest remedy with all the confidence of a neophyte. . . . He will listen to old wives' wisdom, or to the latest theories of the consultation room, with avidity. . . . And when all has been said and undone he reverts to his earliest explanation: "I guess I have Composers' Stomach."
—GEORGE GERSHWIN'S BIOGRAPHER ISAAC GOLDBERG[1]

Although George was very athletic and vibrant, his "composer's stomach" kept him on a perpetual quest for better health. He tried various remedies, both conventional and alternative, all to no avail. In 1934, Kay Swift convinced him to see a psychoanalyst, Dr. Gregory Zilboorg, to ascertain if his chronic constipation had a psychosomatic connection. George went through extensive therapy with the doctor, but his condition did not improve. Biographer Isaac Goldberg later wrote:

> I should call it a health-complex. . . . The athlete in him struggling with the artist. . . . Gershwin never had any uncommon ailments. Always he has enjoyed rare strength, yet he cannot remember when he has been without some slight illness. . . . He has a weakness for dietary novelties, and at times will pick his way through a meal with the daintiness of the princess who could feel the pea beneath seven layers of bed-sheets.[2]

George was kind of a *nebbish* when it came to his health, but he did complain of stomach issues for years, even while living in sunny California with his brother, Ira, and Ira's wife, Leonore, at 1019 North Roxbury Drive in Beverly Hills. Yet aside from his digestive troubles, George was a vibrant, strong, and active man. He enjoyed all sorts of outdoor activities, such as tennis and pool parties, and in many ways, he was the picture of health to many—slim and energetic, and sporting a bronze California tan. In a January 1937 letter (just months before his untimely death), Gershwin wrote to his friend Emily Paley about how great he was feeling:

> Recently my masseur suggested a hike in the hills. I acquiesced & have become a victim to its vigorous charm. For the past week, every day, hot or cold, we walked back in the hills & really Em, I feel as tho (sic) I have discovered something wonderful. It is so refreshing & invigorating. Better than golf, because it elim-

inates the aggravation, that inevitably comes with that pastime.[3]

In a photo from that time period, George appears every bit a man's man—a lean guy with large, pumped-up, veiny arms. He looks very impressive; clearly, his trainer was doing a superb job.

Then, quite suddenly, things began to change. Frequent headaches led him back to the psychotherapist, but when he failed to find relief there, he sought the help of a medical doctor. In an article that appeared in the May 1958 (twenty years after his death) edition of *Eye, Ear, Nose & Throat Monthly*, the doctor noted:

> Gershwin's major complaints were early morning headaches and daily momentary dizzy spells, the latter covering a three-month period. There was also the strange, disagreeable sense of smell. A physical examination showed no abnormalities, but it was decided nonetheless to call in a neurologist for consultation. Except for finding that the sense of smell of one nasal passage was impaired, all other tests proved normal.[4]

Subsequent tests and x-rays revealed nothing abnormal. However, within weeks, George started to exhibit stronger symptoms of illness. In addition to frequent, severe headaches and a new sensitivity to sunlight, he developed a short temper and moodiness, even depression. He started stumbling and dropping things, and as his coordination failed, his once crisp and nuanced piano playing became sloppy and tedious.

His longtime friend and colleague Oscar Levant recalled the first night he noticed a significant change in George:

> Though he had played the "Concerto" dozens of times in public with great fluency I noticed that he stumbled on a very easy passage in the first movement. Then, in the andante, in playing the four simple octaves that conclude the movement above the sustained orchestral chords, he blundered again. When I went backstage he greeted me with a curious remark,
>
> "When I make those mistakes I was thinking of you . . ." concluding with some gruffly uncomplimentary characterization.
>
> At the second concert of the series, on the following night, he afterward remarked that he had experienced a curious odor of some undefined burning smell in his nostrils as he was conducting one number, and a sudden dizzy headache. Nobody considered it to be anything of moment, including George himself. He was so completely the personification of vitality and resonant health that a physical or mental breakdown seemed altogether unthinkable, particularly to George. The care of his physical being was almost a mania with him, a pursuit which he cultivated with considerable success.[5]

> The night George had a memory lapse while playing the Concerto in F . . . I went backstage and said, "George, what happened? Did I make you nervous or was Horowitz in the audience too?" He said, and he was very serious and he looked very tired, "Oscar, I blacked out for a minute. I felt dizzy. I don't know. Was it noticeable?" I said, "To me it was. You've been playing so many concerts and traveling so much you need a rest and maybe a checkup." So he had the checkup and it proved nothing conclusive, but when the headaches and other symptoms got worse, he wouldn't allow a spinal tap.[6]

Not allowing a spinal tap seemed in keeping with Mr. Natural, George Gershwin, and his health-conscious beliefs. I bring you back to his interest in Dr. Hay's book *Health via Food* in which the good doctor writes:

> To be sick is to fall into the maw of the scientific medical machine, with its diagnostic clinic, its various specialties, its operations... finds himself the center of a great scientific interest.
>
> He is x-rayed, his blood is analysed, his stomach contents, his urine, his stool are all examined, even his spine is punctured in the frantic search.[7]

Of course we can only guess the reasons why Gershwin did not want to have a spinal tap even though the rest of his battery of tests proved fruitless and that was the next logical test since his symptoms were indeed worsening. Maybe he saw himself falling deeper and deeper into the maw of the "scientific medical machine," which he had read about in Dr. Hay's book a few short years earlier. I feel the idea is significant enough to bring up and ponder further.

The virtuoso harmonica player Larry Adler shared his own observations as well:

> Gershwin had other warnings. I was in the audience when he played and conducted a program of his music with the Los Angeles Philharmonic. In the third movement of the *Concerto in F* Gershwin stopped playing for a few bars, looked out at the audience, then resumed. It was a weird moment. At an after-concert party at Ira's house on Roxbury Drive in Beverly Hills, I asked George what had happened that caused him to stop playing for a few moments.
>
> "Well," he said, "suddenly during the third movement of the concerto, I could have sworn I smelled burning rubber: I thought maybe the place was on fire. I stopped, looked around, but there was no panic anywhere, so I went on playing."

What we didn't know at the time was, if someone smells burning rubber when there is no burning rubber that is another possible clue to a brain tumor.[8]

Even though the people around him noticed these changes and incidents, they had a hard time imagining that the most vibrant and health-conscious man they knew could be seriously ill.

Fred Astaire remembers that while working with George on the film *A Damsel in Distress* (1937):

> I noticed, at that point, that George Gershwin had not been around to see us as often as usual during the shooting of the picture.
>
> I called him on the phone, saying we missed him, and asked why we hadn't seen him. He explained that he had been painting at home—that he was getting more and more interested in it—and asked me to come to his house and see some of his work. It was that day I first heard of his being ill. He told me that several times while working on the score of *Damsel*, he had suffered terrible headache attacks and that on one occasion his hands would not function—he could not play the piano. I had never known George to be ill. It seemed incredible.[9]

A short time later, when the composer Harold Arlen ("Over the Rainbow," "That Old Black Magic") and the lyricist Yip Harburg ("Over the Rainbow," "April in Paris") visited Gershwin just days before his death, they were utterly shocked by his appearance. Arlen said, "Just two weeks before... He looked so vital.... Pale? He looked strange."[10]

Then, one day in July 1937, George collapsed outside the home he shared with Ira and Leonore (some accounts say he collapsed in the bathroom). He sat on the curb, holding his head in his hands, and he was rushed to the hospital. He fell into a coma, and a neurosurgeon offered a dire diagnosis. It was brain cancer. Emergency surgery was the only possible treatment.

It was decided that the surgery should be done by the then best neurosurgeon in the country, Dr. Walter Dandy of Johns Hopkins in Baltimore. Unfortunately, Dr. Dandy could not be reached because he was on a yacht somewhere in Chesapeake Bay. One of Gershwin's pals contacted the White House, which dispatched two U.S. Navy destroyers to locate Dr. Dandy. By that time, Gershwin had been in a coma for two days. The government escorted Dr. Dandy back to land, and he boarded a plane in Baltimore. When he arrived at Newark Airport for his connecting flight to California, Dr. Dandy was told that Gershwin's condition had deteriorated and the operation could not wait. A California neurosurgeon would perform the operation, supported by a team of local doctors.

The surgery revealed that Gershwin's tumor was very advanced and deeply embedded. After five hours in the operating room, thirty-eight-year-old George Gershwin succumbed to a rare form of brain cancer at 10:35 AM on Sunday, July 11, 1937.

IRRESISTIBLE SPECULATION

Brain cancer in a thirty-eight-year-old is a rare occurrence, averaging just 6.5 cases per 100,000 people (and even less frequently in thirty-eight-year-old men) according to the National Cancer Institute website. Many still find it strange that such a young and vibrant man died of such a virulent, uncommon disease.

George went from the picture of health to death's doorstep in just days . . . what could have caused it? Of course, there are no definitive answers, but there are some interesting things to consider. Before going further, I must acknowledge that **the following link between George Gershwin's fatal illness and external factors is pure conjecture on my part—just a theory offered by a long-time health nut**. I just present it for your consideration.

Let's start with the modern discussion of a possible link between cell phones and brain cancer. (Yes, it is a leap to relate modern electronics to an event that occurred half a century before cell phones! But bear with me.) According to the National Cancer Institute, cell phones emit a form of electromagnetic radiation called radiofrequency energy (radio waves). Although no direct link between radio waves and brain cancer has yet been scientifically proven, there are many studies currently underway, due to a pervasive suspicion. It's also worth noting that a division of the World Health Organization (WHO) recently classified radio-frequency energy as potentially carcinogenic to humans. Based on these findings of the WHO, the American Cancer Society acknowledged the possibility of some associated risks. Officially, the jury is still out on this one, but there is significant concern that putting electromagnetic contraptions on or near one's head could possibly cause health problems.

How is this knowledge related to our hero, George Gershwin? Believe it or not, it has to do with hair! Yes, hair (and I am not talking about the 1960s Broadway musical of the same name either), but more precisely, Gershwin's increasing lack thereof. You see, George had inherited the gene for male-pattern baldness, and in his late twenties and early thirties, his full head of hair started to recede. He was very aware of his appearance, in public and in private, and took great pride in his reputation as the ultimate bachelor of his day. So, he started searching for solutions to his hair loss.

Around the same time, Dr. Andre Alexis

Cueto of Cincinnati developed and patented a machine that he claimed grew hair. The machine came in two parts. First, there was a console on wheels about three feet high by two feet wide and two feet deep, which housed the electrical and mechanical components of the machine. Attached to the console was a rubber hose that led to a dome hood, which went over one's head like the hair dryers in a beauty salon. Designed to alternate positive and negative pressure on the head, this Rube Goldberg "Frankenstein" doohickey was purported to stimulate the scalp and bring much-needed blood and nutrients to the head's "starving" hair follicles. It alternately created a strong sucking vacuum and reversed so as to apply strong pressure on the head, scalp, and ultimately the brain.

In 1936, Dr. Cueto sold the rights to his contraption to Lewis and Powel Crosley, two brothers with a business empire that included the Crosley Radio Company (which is still around today), radio and home appliance product lines, and the Cincinnati Reds baseball team (which then played at Crosley Field). The Crosleys marketed the machine nationwide, calling it the Crosley Xervac. Their national media campaign moved the machine into the hands of individuals, beauty parlors, and barbershops. One also landed in the hands of the actress Lillian Gish, who claimed to have given the contraption to her friend George as a gift.[11] Apparently, Gershwin started to use the Crosley Xervac hair-growing Franken-machine just months before his untimely demise.

While in Los Angeles, Gershwin wrote to a New York City friend, Mabel Schirmer (wife of Robert Schirmer, owner of the Schirmer Music Company), and mentioned the Franken-thingamajig. In the letter dated April 20, 1937, just shy of three months before his death, he wrote:

I am lying comfortably on a chaise longue with a new gadget, which I have just bought, on my head. You would probably scream with laughter if you could see me. The machine is a new invention put out by the Crosley Radio Company and has been recommended by several people out here as a positive grower of hair. It's an entirely new principle and you know me for new principles.[12]

Some were not as excited about the newfangled doohickey. Gershwin's valet and chauffeur, Paul Mueller, said of the hair-growing gizmo, "it looked like a football helmet with steel bands that were clamped around his head." Gershwin biographers Jablonski and Stewart continued with more of Paul Mueller's story:

The new device, he had been convinced, would electronically produce miracles. Inside the "helmet" were various electrodes which sent shocks into the scalp; at the same time the entire thing vibrated, apparently massaging George's head. But what disturbed Paul most of all was the tight band around his head which he was certain was cutting off the blood supply.

Disturbed, Paul gave George a speech about cutting off the blood to the brain. "You are doing yourself harm," he argued. "You don't know what you're talking about," George replied and continued with his strange treatment for baldness.[13]

Gershwin biographer David Ewen also noted:

He began to grow sensitive about the way he was losing his hair. He purchased a machine as large as a refrigerator in which a hose connected a motor pump to a metal cask. The cask was to be adjusted to the scalp of the head. For half an hour each day, he subjected himself to rigorous scalp treatment which brought a rush of blood to his head through electric suction; at the end of each treatment his scalp was so callous that it could not feel anything if a pin were stuck into it. What effect this treatment had upon his then dormant brain tumor is hard to say, but it certainly could not have been salutary.[14]

A search for information on why the Crosley Xervac was taken off the market produces no answers. Research regarding the frequency of brain tumors during the height of the Crosley Xervac rig's popularity also failed to produce any results. Yet, today, the machine rightly holds a place of honor in the Museum of Questionable Medical Devices at the Science Museum of Minnesota![15]

AND BEYOND

I'll Build a Stairway to Paradise*

*George White's Scandals of 1922 (1922)

GEORGE GERSHWIN, COMPOSER, IS DEAD; *Master of Jazz Succumbs in Hollywood at 38 After Operation for Brain Tumor.*
—THE FRONT-PAGE HEADLINE OF *THE NEW YORK TIMES* ON JULY 12, 1937

Gershwin's body was transported from Los Angeles to New York by train, and funeral services were held on July 12, 1937, at Temple Emanu-El on 5th Avenue and 65th Street. There was inclement weather that day, but thousands of folks still turned out to pay their final respects to this great master of music. Celebrities like George M. Cohan, W. C. Handy, and Mayor Fiorello La Guardia, along with thousands of fans, paid tribute. Rabbi Stephen S. Wise delivered the eulogy, saying in part:

> The singer of the songs of America's soul. . . . There are countries in Central Europe which would have flung out this Jew. America welcomed him and he repaid it with the gusto of a child and the filial tenderness of a son.[1]

Classical music was played during the solemn service, which ended with the pallbearers carrying out the coffin to the slow section of *Rhapsody in Blue*.

Upon hearing of George Gershwin's death, the novelist John O'Hara wrote, "George Gershwin is dead but I don't have to believe it if I don't want to."[2] Éva Gauthier, the first artist to feature George Gershwin in concert, agreed, saying, "George Gershwin will live as long as music lives. . . . He will never be forgotten, and his place will never be filled."[3]

As one of George's countless raving fans, I sincerely hope she's right. Sadly, time has a way of intruding on even our most cherished memories.

I will always remember the George Gershwin Theatre at Brooklyn College, where I was a student for a year and from where my lovely wife, Julie, graduated. The first performance at the George Gershwin Theatre was in 1953; today, it is shuttered and slated for demolition to make room for an expansion of the Brooklyn Center for the Performing Arts complex. Sadly, the Gershwin name will not grace the new building. In my humble opinion, the leadership of the college has done a disservice by erasing the name of George Gershwin from the school. How quickly we do forget.

In the East New York section of Brooklyn where George lived as a young boy is Junior High

School (JHS) 166 (aka George Gershwin Junior High School). In my younger days as a member of my junior high school's basketball and softball teams, I spent a lot of time playing ball against the Gershwin team. Today the school fares miserably. English and math test results for Gershwin JHS compared to New York State JHS students in general show 95% of 8th graders in New York State do better than the Gershwin kids do. It is a sad testament to know that the school bearing a musical genius's name, George Gershwin, is one of the worst junior high schools in the state of New York. When my wife, Julie, first arrived in the United States after escaping from the brutal Communist Castro regime, the first school she attended was JHS 166 George Gershwin Junior High School! It's a small world, indeed!

Another tribute that has come and gone is the SS *George Gershwin*. The Liberty ship was christened on April 22, 1943, as part of the 1936 American Merchant Marine Act. The ships were built to assist in the war effort. The SS *George Gershwin* survived the war and remained in service until 1975, when it was decommissioned. Today, it is a reef off the coast of Mississippi on the floor in the Gulf of Mexico.

> **The Gerber-Gershwin New York Challenge:**
> My personal challenge is to address the lack of respect and honor due George Gershwin vis-à-vis New York City. I call it the Gerber-Gershwin New York Challenge. I hereby challenge the leadership of New York to honor the memory of one of their greatest New Yorkers, George Gershwin. They should rename a street or avenue after him or erect a statue in his honor. Let's do something for this famous native son!

New York has honored many notable people over the years by naming streets, such as Delancey Street and Fulton Street; avenues like Madison Avenue and Lenox Avenue; places like Astor Place and Irving Place; circles like Columbus Circle; squares as in Madison Square (Garden) and Tompkins Square Park and Washington Square Park; Plazas i.e., Grand Army . . . and many more after its famous citizens. Not all of these namings are for people from long ago. There are many from our recent past—i.e., Martin Luther King Jr. Boulevard and Malcolm X Boulevard and Juan Pablo Duarte (from the Dominican Republic) Boulevard. All three of these are in Harlem. There is also Duke Ellington Way in the theater district and Duke Ellington Boulevard uptown in Harlem and Miles Davis Way on West 77th Street. We can visit Thelonious Sphere Monk Circle on the Upper West Side at 63rd Street; Damrosch Park and its Guggenheim Bandshell located in the park in the Lincoln (another naming) Center Arts Complex. In Brooklyn, we have Jamaica-born Bob Marley Boulevard; and Central Park has a memorial to the Liverpool, England, Beatles star John Lennon from one of his tunes, "Strawberry Fields Forever." Imagine that! Even Paris has a Rue George Gershwin, but alas, for New York native son, George Gershwin, there is only the postage-sized George Gershwin Way—located on 50th Street between 8th & 9th Avenues. The only way to find this tiny slice of the "Big Apple" is to mistakenly stumble upon it. Let's get down to business and change this injustice by properly honoring one of the greatest New Yorkers!

Now that Brooklyn College has torn down the George Gershwin Theatre and does not plan to rename the new building after Gershwin, the last public acknowledgment to the master musician/composer in New York City is only a failing junior high school in Brooklyn that bears his name. What a shame. Two private buildings bear the Gershwin name. One is a midtown hotel and the other is the Gershwin Theatre on West 51st Street.

So here is the **Gerber-Gershwin New York Challenge**. I challenge the leadership of New York to search for a street, avenue, boulevard, square, park, plaza, or even rue and place the Gershwin name on it. It is most important that the site reflect the proper gravitas that the Gershwin name deserves by the City of New York, not a way out of the way "way." I offer my help free of charge to help in that search since I have a working knowledge of New York as an ex-New York City cab driver. I do know my way around that town and am available at any time. The ball is in your court. Let's work together to honor the man named George Gershwin. Let's also do it well before February 12, 2024, which is the 100-year anniversary of *Rhapsody in Blue*. I respectfully also ask the mayor and city council of New York a question on Gershwin's behalf. It is the title to a 1924 Gershwin song, so in Gershwin's stead, I simply ask, "Will You Remember Me?" I hope so.

I Found a Four Leaf Clover*

*George White's Scandals of 1922 (1922)

George's drive had nothing to do with money or the lack of it. He never knew how much money he had in the bank. He was really doing what he did because he felt he had to do it, whether or not it would bring him success.

—IRA GERSHWIN[1]

The sole beneficiary of Gershwin's estate was his mother, Rose Gershwin, who was living at that time at 25 Central Park West. The headline in the *New York Herald Tribune*, dated September 27, 1938, declared: "Gershwin Left $341,089 Estate to His Mother; 'Rhapsody in Blue' Appraised at 'Greatest Value' and Opera Rights of 'Nominal Interest' to the Residue."

According to a Surrogate Court filing, the Gershwin's estate was valued at $430,841 gross ($7.25 million), which netted out to $341,089 ($5.75 million today) after taxes. The filing valued the residuary value of his musical works at $50,125 ($850,000 today). *Rhapsody in Blue* was appraised at $20,000 ($340,000 today); *An American in Paris* came in at $5,000 ($85,000 today); "Of Thee I Sing" was valued at $4,000 ($67,000 today); and *Concerto in F* was appraised at $1,750 ($29,000 today).[2] (Author's note: At that time, the same as today, it was common to understate values so as to pay less to Uncle Sam. Shocking!) Gershwin also had about $228,000 (just shy of $4 million today) in cash and insurance as well as $41,000 ($700,000 today) in United States Treasury notes and about $100,000 ($1.7 million today) in securities. Administrative expenses including funeral expenses and final debts totaled about $38,000 ($650,000 today).[3]

Rose outlived George by a decade, dying of a heart attack in 1948. She left her estate to her three remaining children: Ira, Arthur, and Frances. Ira received 20 percent, and Arthur and Frances got 40 percent each.

Since his passing over three-quarters of a century ago, George's royalties have continued to flow, creating a vast fortune for his descendants. Consider these interesting facts from the Warner Music Group's *Annual Report* (2008):

- Warner Music Group has ownership or control of the rights to more than 1 million musical compositions, from over 65,000 songwriters and composers.

- George and Ira Gershwin were counted among its "representative songwriters" such as Madonna, Led Zeppelin, and The Ramones

- In a list of "representative songs," including the "Star Wars Theme," "Viva Las Vegas," and "Moondance," the Gershwin evergreen, "Summertime" appears.

- *Rhapsody in Blue* is included on a top-10 list of revenue-producing songs for the last ten years, bringing in somewhere between $1 million and $2 million a year (or more, considering the list reflects the average revenue over ten years).

Yes, ninety years after its creation, *Rhapsody in Blue* is a year-in, year-out multimillion-dollar seller! And that's just one song. Many of George's hundreds of songs also bring in piles of dough.

In an article in *The Telegraph* titled "Method in the Rhythm Madness," dated February 19, 2002, its author, Maureen Paton, gives some very interesting facts on the royalty income of the Gershwin estate. Paton states that the estimated income for the estate was between $5 and $10 million a year ($6.5 and $13 million today). She goes on to say that *Rhapsody in Blue* was the largest source of that revenue and "I Got Rhythm" was the most recorded song in the Gershwin song catalogue.[4]

David Ewen's 1956 biography indicated that Gershwin was one of the "five or six highest-paid members of ASCAP, the American Society of Composers, Authors, and Publishers." (ASCAP protects the intellectual property of its members and regulates the use of their works in public performances, records, radio, television, and other venues.) Ewen also notes that Gershwin's life was abruptly cut short at thirty-eight, which stunted his numbers.[5] George's career lasted only about twenty years, but during that time, he wrote about 900 songs. Even with his short career, thirty years after his demise, he remained a top ASCAP earner. So, year after year, millions upon millions rolled into the coffers of the Gershwin family.

They Can't Take That Away From Me*

*Shall We Dance (1937)

When many millions of dollars are involved, you can be sure that problems also arise. Over the years, various people who thought they were due some of the Gershwin scratch have waged a number of legal battles. Claims and counterclaims have flown back and forth like the swallows of Capistrano. Let's start with a more recent lawsuit.

GERSHWIN VS. WARNER MUSIC

On January 15, 2013, *Billboard* published an article titled, "Warner Music Sued for Millions by George Gershwin Heirs." Apparently, the heirs conducted an audit in 2007 and found that Warner Music failed "to protect and preserve Gershwin's copyright interests both domestically and abroad." They also allege that Warner was taking excessive commissions and fees, and in some cases, paying monies due to the Gershwin heirs up to four years late. The plaintiffs declared that Warner used "misleading royalty statements, failed to monitor affiliates, and abandoned territories like Asia and Australia."

How much money is in dispute? The heirs claim over $4.4 million, plus interest. The article ended by stating:

They are now demanding at least $5 million in compensatory damages for breach of contract and at least $5 million in compensatory damages and another $5 million in punitive damages for breach of fiduciary duty. Warner Music declined comment.[1]

If awarded, this $15 million would be in addition to the money already paid by Warner Music to the Gershwin heirs during the time period in question. Nice scratch, if you can get it!

GERSHWIN VS. GERSHWIN

Despite the close-knit nature of the Gershwin family throughout George's life, recent generations have not been quite as amicable. In a Supreme Court Filing in the State of New York, dated February 10, 2011, Todd Gershwin, a great-nephew of George Gershwin, sued The Frances Gershwin Godowsky Revocable Trust, the George Gershwin Family Trust, and others for breach of contract with him and his brother, Adam Gershwin. That filing declared:

The interests in G. Gershwin's music are currently held by the children of his brother, A. Gershwin, and sister, F. Godowsky, both individually and through separate trusts, to wit:

Marc George Gershwin ("M. Gershwin"), Godowsky, three additional issue of F. Godowsky who are not parties to this litigation (Alexis Gershwin Godowsky, Georgia Keidan and Nadia Natali), the George Gershwin Trust, the Arthur Gershwin Testamentary Trust (the "Arthur Gershwin Trust," which is not party to this litigation) and the Frances Godowsky Trust. Under the foregoing ownership arrangement, the issue, per stirpes, of Arthur Gershwin and F. Godowsky share equally in the income generated by the musical assets created by G. Gershwin. M. Gershwin is a trustee of both the George Gershwin Trust and Arthur Gershwin trust and the nephew of G. Gershwin.

The filing went on to say that Todd and his brother, Adam Gershwin, signed a management agreement regarding the intellectual property, effective September 1, 2008, through December 31, 2011, which detailed the management and licensing fees to be paid to the brothers.

Then it notes a letter from the Godowsky family attorney, which curiously claims that the management agreement was "unilaterally terminated" by the Godowsky family, effective January 1, 2010, and demanded the return of all compensation previously paid to the two brothers because of "material violations of the trust confided . . . and the fiduciary nature . . . pursuant to the Agreement. These have caused irreparable injury to the Godowsky Family as well as damages and costs."

The brothers claimed this was a wrongful termination and a breach of the agreement by the Godowsky family. They also lay claim to monies owed them because they were not paid any management or licensing fees from 2009–2010. In the filing, the brothers cite three causes of action and request payment for each, as well as damages. The minimum for each action is $300,000. The total adds up to over $900,000, plus whatever the jury deems reasonable for damages.

A letter attached to the filing described the Agreement, providing an insider's view of the cash flow into the estate. The base income for the intellectual property was just under $4 million a year. Even seventy-five years after his death, Gershwin is still a bankable star! It's indeed a fitting legacy for a man who lived large, played hard, and left a stunning musical contribution to the world. Not just the music world—the entire world.

One final note, years ago when I was doing research on the poster "Whiteman at Carnegie Hall" by Miguel Covarrubias, which is the image on the cover of this book, I contacted the Gershwin Family Trust. In my phone message, I stated I had some information regarding Gershwin's *Rhapsody in Blue* Carnegie Hall performance of 1924 that they might not be aware of and would like to share it with the trust. Some time passed, but then I received a phone call from Marc Gershwin, the son of George's younger brother, Arthur. My jaw hit the ground, and I was totally flabbergasted that such a busy and important guy would actually call me on the phone, but it shows how important any new information that could be added to the Gershwin legacy was to him.

He was very polite and extremely interested in the information. He was aware of the relationship Covarrubias had with George, but he was under the understanding that the relationship happened years later than the poster suggests. He also liked the fact that the poster depicted Covarrubias and George in the audience chatting.

The bottom line is that Marc Gershwin was a well-mannered and polite professional who gave of his time freely to talk to a stranger about some new information regarding his wonderful uncle. Thank you, Mr. Gershwin. Like your uncle George, you are a class act!

Overflow*

*Porgy and Bess (1935)

What do Elvis Presley and George Gershwin have in common? Two things. If you answer that they were both Jewish musicians, you would be absolutely correct on count one. Elvis Aron Presley's mother, Gladys Love Presley (née Smith), was of Jewish descent. According to Talmudic Law, this made Elvis a Jew as well. Upon Gladys's death in 1959, Elvis made sure her headstone had a Star of David engraved on it. Elvis, aka the King of Rock 'n' Roll later shortened to The King, wore a *Chai* (a Hebrew symbol) as well as the Star of David around his neck at various times during his career. Elvis may have been a hound dog, but at least he was a Hebrew National Kosher Canine who answered to a higher authority. Such a *mensch*!

Secondly, if you said that Elvis and Gershwin were both successful composers of music, you would be absolutely wrong. Elvis did *not* write the songs he made famous; rather, he retained the rights through tough negotiations with the composers, unlike Gershwin who was a real composer. So what was the second thing these two musicians had in common? Give up? Okay, I'll tell you.

A small Netherlands publisher owned by a Dutch pension fund manages many of Gershwin's and Elvis's songs, as well as the songs of many other artists. The name of this company is Imagem Music Group. It bills itself as "the world's largest independent music publisher." It manages diverse segments of the music universe, from classical to jazz and everything else one might imagine. It licenses songs for use in commercials, TV shows, advertising, and all sorts of other applications.

Imagem issued a press release on May 23, 2013, announcing a multi-year agreement with the Arthur Gershwin Testamentary Trust. The deal granted Imagem the rights to administer any works that George Gershwin created in his final three years. This includes songs from *Porgy and Bess* and many other works, including, "Nice Work if You Can Get It" and "They Can't Take That Away From Me," to mention a couple of favorites. The trustee of the catalogue, Marc George Gershwin, is the son of George's younger brother, Arthur.

It seems that George's nephew made the move from Warner/Chappell to Imagem because he "felt neglected." He said that Warner/Chappell was too huge, and his catalogue was not getting the attention he felt it deserved. Interestingly, he added that he only moved a small portion of the trust's catalogue to Imagem; indeed, the bulk of the inventory remained at Warner/Chappell.[1]

The 1926 Gershwin classic can easily fit here when referring to nephew Marc and his stewardship of the Gershwin intellectual property—"Someone to Watch Over Me."

Boy Wanted*

*A Dangerous Maid (1921)

George was widely known as a ladies' man, always showing up at parties and events with beautiful women and showgirls in tow. When asked about this propensity, he was known to say, "Why should I limit myself to only one woman when I can have as many women as I want?"

Although we know Gershwin never married, many have speculated that George may have been a father. An article titled, "I Am George Gershwin's Illegitimate Son," written by Brooklyn-raised Alan Gershwin and published in the February 1959 issue of *Confidential Magazine*, gave this alleged descendent the chance to tell his story.

In the article, Alan Gershwin claimed that George Gershwin sired a son (him) with a beautiful chorus girl who went by the stage name of Margaret Manners. She performed in Broadway musicals, including George White's *Scandals* in the early 1920s, and when she met George, they fell in love and had an affair. Alan was born sometime around May 18, 1926, in Altadena, California, but because it was a home birth, he has no birth certificate. (I hope the Obama birthers don't get too excited over this.) His mother died while he was quite young, so his mother's sister and her husband, Fanny and Ben Schneider, took him in. They changed his name to Albert Schneider, which he later changed to Alan Gershwin.

Alan wrote that his Uncle Ben was a carpenter who did not work much due to health issues, and yet, somehow, the family always had plenty of money. Albert even had a private tutor instead of attending public school. So, how could an underemployed carpenter have afforded private tutoring? For Albert, the answer was obvious; he assumed the dough came from Daddy George. He also claimed he had seen George give his mother money, and that George's personal driver picked him up and took him to George for visits. When any of George's friends saw the two together, however, George never acknowledged the boy as his son.[1]

After George's death, the Schneider family moved from California to Brooklyn, and Albert enrolled in Erasmus Hall High School in Flatbush, Brooklyn. He claims to have visited Ira a few times in California and to have been given sums totaling a few hundred dollars, but he never got any real confirmation of his relationship to the Gershwin family. The article in *Confidential* was Albert's way of reaching out to anyone who could corroborate his claims. As you might imagine, the allegations caused quite a ruckus between the Gershwin clan and Albert.

Joan Peyser's biography, *The Memory of All*

That: The Life of George Gershwin (1993), provided additional detail on this sordid, but puzzling tale. It included stories from George's valet, who confirmed that the mother and son met regularly with George, and that he gave her money. Peyser also pointed out certain discrepancies in the story.

Today, the jury is still out on the issue of George's illegitimate son. But while we're talking about illegitimate children, let's consider one more, this time of the opposite gender.

The Illegitimate Daughter*

*Of Thee I Sing (1931)

In the 1931 Broadway hit musical and Pulitzer Prize–winning political satire *Of Thee I Sing*, politicians devise a plan to hold a beauty contest; the winner will marry the new president. Lo and behold, the winner was (get this!) the illegitimate daughter of the illegitimate son of the illegitimate nephew of Napoleon Bonaparte. In Act II, the French ambassador belts out a song, aptly titled, "The Illegitimate Daughter" (words and music by George and Ira Gershwin). Although Ira's lyrics were quite clever, the timing and title of this song did raise an eyebrow or two—especially since 1931 was the year that Nancy Bloomer Deussen was born.

Deussen claimed to be the lovechild produced from a relationship between her mother, Julia Thomas Van Norman, and George Gershwin. George did indeed have a decade-long relationship with Julia Thomas Van Norman. It stretched from the mid-to-late twenties until George's untimely demise in 1938; Ms. Bloomer Deussen was born in 1931, which makes the numbers certainly plausible. But was she really the product of this relationship?

The Gershwin/Van Norman relationship was also documented in Joan Peyser's Gershwin biography, *The Memory of All That: The Life of George Gershwin.* In the book, Peyser cites quite a bit of correspondence between Gershwin and Ms. Van Norman (much of which was donated to the Library of Congress). She also suggests that, as far as Gershwin was concerned, Ms. Van Norman was a bit of an obsessed groupie. (I could be wrong, but that's how I read it.)

Like Gershwin's alleged illegitimate son, Alan/Albert, Gershwin's alleged illegitimate daughter, Nancy Bloomer Deussen, also became a talented musician and composer. Perhaps they both inherited the Gershwin music gene. Go figure!

Do It Again!*

*The French Doll (1922)

Ninety years after *Rhapsody in Blue* and more than seventy-five years after George Gershwin's death, one would think there should be no more surprises about this great man . . . but that is not the case. Surprises and treasures are still out there hiding and waiting to be discovered. Case in point: the discovery of a huge trove of musical material in Secaucus, New Jersey—an event I've dubbed:

"The Secaucus Caper"

Before we get too far into this story, a bit of background is in order.

Some musicologists have likened this event to the opening of King Tut's tomb, finding the Ark of the Covenant, or discovering the mythological elephant graveyard (popularized in the *Tarzan* movies). However, there is one important difference to note here. In the case of "The Secaucus Caper," no one was searching for this treasure trove or even knew it existed! Through sheer luck, it was stumbled upon, "discovered" by someone with enough sense to realize the significance of his monumental find.

So, what was in that Secaucus warehouse? Eighty crates, jam-packed with "lost and forgotten" music by George Gershwin, Jerome Kern, Cole Porter, Victor Herbert, Vincent Youmans, and other composers! The trove yielded over ninety Gershwin manuscripts and about seventy of his heretofore "lost" songs, many with Ira's lyrics, as well as original scores and missing parts of Gershwin's musicals, *Primrose* (1924), *Tip-Toes* (1925), and *Pardon My English* (1933).

How did this cache of compositions by these early 20th-century musical masters end up in an old warehouse in Secaucus, New Jersey? Glad you asked . . . here's the story behind the story or as one famous radio commentator, Paul Harvey, used to say, "And now, the rest of the story."

The map to this musical treasure trove began with the advent of "talkie" movies in the late 1920s, which were pioneered by the Warner Brothers (Albert, Sam, Harry, and Jack L.). Warner Bros. Studios started producing movies in 1923, and then branched out into theater ownership as well. The Warner Brothers' groundbreaking talkie blockbuster movie, *The Jazz Singer* (1927), led them to follow up with several other hugely popular "talkies," also known then as "synchronized sound" movies.

Now, as the founders of one of the biggest and most powerful movie studios in Hollywood, the Warner brothers were obviously rolling in dough. They also realized the potential of radio stations, which they started to acquire with their newfound riches and started buying music-publishing houses, eventually forming Warner Bros. Records.

In the late 1920s, Warner Bros. Records went on a shopping spree, snapping up music publishers to produce the music in their movies. They bought Remick, where Gershwin first launched his career, as well as T. B. Harms (which Gershwin also worked for), and M. Witmark & Sons, plus others. In buying these publishers, Warner acquired the substantial inventory of music held by each publishing house.

In the 1920s and 1930s, it was common practice for musicians to rip up the music of shows that tanked. However, just because a show flopped didn't mean the music from it was also horrible. In fact, some of the greatest music of the day was featured in shows that failed. Usually these scores were destroyed, but in the case of "The Secaucus Caper," some of the original music from these failed shows was preserved. Although Warner had no interest in these scores, they were quietly stashed away and forgotten. Over the following decades, these dusty boxes and boxes jam-packed with discarded music were moved from warehouse to warehouse, finally ending up in, of all places, Secaucus, New Jersey.

Enter Robert Kimball, a music-theater historian and real-life Indiana Jones, if you will. With the support of Ira Gershwin and the trustee of the Cole Porter Music Trust, Kimball gained access to the crates in 1982.

Surprisingly, the discovery did not garner much popular attention or much press. However, five years later, on March 10, 1987, an article titled, "Broadway Song Trove Tops Original Hopes," was published in *The New York Times*. It detailed the amazing discovery and generated much excitement (as well as a fortune in legal fees). The story was even featured on the *McNeil-Lehrer News Hour*. Here is how that article explained "The Secaucus Caper."

Kimball got wind of eighty crates of old music that had been discovered in a Warner Bros. Secaucus warehouse and, because of their value, were then moved to a vault in Manhattan. (That move had occurred five years earlier, but the trove was not available to anyone until the vast amount of material was fully inventoried, appraised, and copyrighted.) Although Kimball viewed the material at the Secaucus warehouse in 1982, it was still in such disarray that it would be years before he finally grasped the significance of the material on hand.

"It's like opening the tomb of King Tut," offered John McGlinn, composer, conductor, and music theater historian. "There are major works here that had been presumed lost forever; shows that were never revived and were assumed to have vanished off the face of the Earth."[1]

"These manuscripts are worth millions to collectors and libraries," said John M. Ludwig, executive director of the National Institute for Music Theatre, "but their value to our profession and to the American public is inestimable."[2]

Kimball explained:

Jerome Kern's daughter, Betty Kern Miller, asked Warner Communications to return her father's music. They refused. For more than three years, discussions have gone on between attorneys for Mrs. Miller and the music company. Mrs. Miller wants to keep the material together and donate it to the music division of the Library of Congress, where the Gershwin and Rodgers material has already been deposited. Without access to this music, it is impossible to perform a large number of Kern's stage works as he conceived them.

'These are not leftovers."[3]

What a wonderful and noble gesture it would be to donate these works, so this important facet of our national history and its music can be preserved for all to enjoy forever!

As noted on the Warner Bros. website:

The vast Warner Bros. library, one of the most prestigious and valuable in the world, consists of more than 61,000 hours of programming, including nearly 6,500 feature films and 3,000 television programs comprised of tens of thousands of individual episodes.

How many more Secaucus surprises are yet out there, just waiting for discovery? "Maybe" someday "Soon" somebody like "Mischa, Jascha, Toscha, Sascha," wearing a "High Hat" can "Do It Again" and discover another musical treasure trove near the "Swanee" on "A Foggy Day" in the "Summertime"?

That said . . . "It Ain't Necessarily So"!

Life is a lot like jazz . . . it's best when you improvise.
—GEORGE GERSHWIN, 1929

Love Is Here to Stay*

*The Goldwyn Follies (1938)

He was full of music and even at the dinner table would drum out a rhythm . . .
—FRANCES GERSHWIN GODOWSKY
ON HER OLDER BROTHER GEORGE[1]

The very last song that Gershwin wrote was "Love Is Here to Stay."

Although the title of this book is *Jazz: America's Gift*, it would not be far off for the title to be *Jazz: America's Gift to the World*. That is because America shared her gift with everyone, and as we see so often today, her reception has been overwhelming. People in countries all over the world have embraced America's unique art form. Folks from all walks of life, religions, races, socioeconomic, and even differing ideologies gravitate to America's jazz. Republicans and Democrats, communists and capitalists, friends and foes of the United States love Jazz. What is its universal appeal based on? Slavery? Capitalism? Freedom? Oppression? White? Black? Jews? Christians? Emotions? Opportunity? Desperation? Surprise? Feelings? Hope? Hopelessness? LOVE?! The absence of love? What are the reasons for this overwhelming global attraction to Jazz? Nobody can answer this question, but one thing is for sure; it is true that Jazz has something for everybody. Jazz has universal appeal.

Jazz found its fountainhead in a medley of slavery simmered in the same cauldron with freedom and the American Dream. A mixture of conflicting opposites marinated for years and finally ended up as a gourmet delicacy. It defies all odds! Impossible! But so true! Who would have thunk it?!

Then again, why America? Why not England? France? Spain? Brazil? Greece? Sub-Sahara Africa? Germany? Slavery thrived in all of these areas, but alas, no Jazz. The Egyptians enslaved the Hebrews for two hundred years and not one jazz tune appeared. Slavery was not unique to the United States. It started thousands of years before America even existed. In fact, the United States came late to the game of buying and selling human beings as property (as a colony of another slave-trading country, Great Britain, at the start). But quite differently than other countries around the world, slavery still haunts both our collective conscience and our consciousness. America is still battling memories and scars of those past days. Although slavery was part of the American past, it was just that, "part." Not more. America is much, much more than our slave-associated past. Much more!

Of course we can slice and dice jazz into multiple individual components, such as rhythm, syncopation, blue notes, and more. But music from other countries always has these properties. Jazz stands out from them all because it is based on improvisation. Much like the American Experiment I would suggest—maybe because America is also a newer society than the old ones in Europe and Asia and other regions of the world. The performer spontaneously thus becomes a composer. I think this aspect is based on the purely and unique American quality of rugged individualism. Today this comment may sound overtly political, and maybe it is or maybe it isn't. However, I report, and you decide.

In the early 1970s I moved to Maine and started an organic farm. I moved a barn three miles to my property and, with my wife, Julie, converted the barn it into a house. I admired the people of Maine because they were rugged. Living in a place where it gets down to forty-degrees below zero makes you rugged real fast, and the Maine-iacs there had this "can-do" attitude. Jazz cats have this "can-do" attitude as well. They are ready and willing to bear their hearts and souls in front of perfect strangers and express their innermost secrets through their music. Only a rugged individual will be crazy enough to do that: make up a song on the spot.

Something else sets America apart from every other country in the world: freedom and independence. America was founded on these basic principles. Our country and our people have thrived and flourished against incredible odds and so has our music. Jazz had to free itself from the shackles of the past, but let's not forget where it originated. Jazz musicians had to feel free and independent in order to create. Without freedom and independence, there would be no jazz. Sometimes I even feel that without jazz, we would be less free as a people.

We have an America that is the melting pot of the world. It simmers people from every corner of the globe into our unique American concoction. George Gershwin felt this way while he was composing *Rhapsody in Blue* saying of that work, "I heard it as a musical kaleidoscope of America—of our vast melting pot." He expressed this melting pot concept once again in the title of one of his songs, "Welcome to the Melting Pot," written for the movie *Delicious*.

Gershwin was proud to be an American who had a *carpe diem* jazz attitude:

My people are Americans. My time is today. . . . I am sure of one thing: that the essence of future music . . . derided yesterday . . . accepted today and which perhaps tomorrow will be exalted—jazz.[2]

Furthering his seize-the-moment attitude toward life and jazz, Gershwin gave some advice to a group of young singers: "Don't condemn jazz on the say-so of any old fogy. Avoid musical snobbery. Think for yourself. Live in the present. . . ."[3]

Beyond the America melting pot, however, Gershwin searched for the soul of our great country and found it by expressing it through jazz: "And what is the voice of the American soul? It is jazz . . . "[4]

George Gershwin was not an angry guy. His music was neither bitter nor acrid It was inspiring, romantic, entertaining, exciting, exhilarating, beautiful, and sweet. These are just some of the attributes of his music; there are many more.

He wasn't learned in the "school" sense, but he knew how to educate himself. His virtuosity was acquired over the years through self-study, studying with great masters and mentors of the art and craft, as well as having a huge set of ears. He listened and learned from the best with a thirst for knowledge.

On one radio broadcast in memory of George Gershwin, the Austrian composer Arnold Schönberg said:

> Music to him was the air he breathed, the food which nourished him, the drink that refreshed him. Music was what made him feel, and music was the feeling he expressed. . . . there is no doubt that he was a great composer. What he achieved was not only to the benefit of a national American music, but a contribution to the music of the world.[5]

"Rhythm is the very life of music" for George Gershwin.[6]

"The truth is that George Gershwin is a genius" said famed pianist Samuel Chotzinoff.[7]

For me, George Gershwin was and still is the embodiment of the American Dream. His rags to riches life story lives on through his music played in every corner of the world. Somewhere, at this very moment as you read these words of mine, one of his songs is being played. The truth is that the sun never sets on the music of George Gershwin, and that is a testament to the music he gave us all that still lives on and always will.

My sense is that Gershwin was very important to the history of jazz because he was a connecting bridge between the early years when jazz was starting out and perhaps not widely known, and the later years after Gershwin, when due to his immense popularity, jazz became much more of a household name.

Jazz started in the whorehouses and among some of the "down and out," then moved into clubs in places like Chicago and New York, then eventually to the mainstream and even into the concert halls. Gershwin and his life and work strike me as the important link that ties all of this together.

Notes

You Can't Unscramble Scrambled Eggs

1. Paul Whiteman and Mary Margaret McBride, *Jazz* (New York: J. H. Sears & Company, Inc., 1926), 3

2. Henry E. Krehbiel, *Lafcadio Hearn and Congo Music* (*The Musician*, November 1906). Karl Koenig ed. *Jazz in Print (1856–1929): An Anthology of Selected Early Readings in Jazz History* (Hillsdale, New York: Pendragon Press, 2002), 79

3. Merle Armitage, Edited and Designed, *George Gershwin* (New York: Longmans, Green & CO, 1938), 5

Hooray for the U.S.A!

1. Thomas Jefferson, Notes on the State of Virginia (1784)

Dead Men Tell No Tales

1. *Fact Sheet*. New York Historical Society

2. John F. Watson, *Annals of Philadelphia and Pennsylvania in the Olden Time* (Philadelphia: J. B. Lippincott & CO., 1870), 23. Eileen Southern, *The Music of Black America*, 1st. ed. (New York: W. W. Norton, 1971), 54. Maurice Peress, *Dvorak to Duke Ellington: A Conductor Explores America's Music and Its African American Roots* (New York: Oxford University Press, 2004), 10

O Land of Mine, America

1. *The Lilliputian Musicians* (*Charleston Mercury*, November 22, 1856). Karl Koenig ed. *Jazz in Print (1856–1929): An Anthology of Selected Early Readings in Jazz History* (Hillsdale, New York: Pendragon Press, 2002), 3

2. John Fordham, *Jazz* (New York: Dorling Kindersley, 1993), 126

3. Dizzy Gillespie with Al Fraser, *To Be, or Not . . . to Bop* (Originally published: New York: Doubleday Books, 1979). This quote from Minneapolis: First University of Minnesota Press ed., 2009), 483

4. Dizzy Gillespie with Al Fraser, *To Be, or Not . . . to Bop* (Originally published: New York: Doubleday Books, 1979. This quote from Minneapolis: First University of Minnesota Press ed., 2009), 490

Follow the Minstrel Band

1. Merry, Paul (2013-06-21). *How Blues Evolved Volume One* (Kindle Locations 564–565), Kindle Edition.

2. Merry, Paul (2013-06-21). How Blues Evolved Volume One (Kindle Locations 684–690). Kindle Edition.

3. P. T. Barnum, *Life of P. T. Barnum* in a speech he gave on May 26, 1865 (Buffalo: The Courier Company, Printers, 1888), 237

Black and White

1. Michael Rogin, *Blackface, White Noise: Jewish Immigrants in the Hollywood Melting Pot* (Berkley: University of California Press, 1996), 197

2. James Brown, *James Brown: The Godfather of Soul* (New York: Thunder Mouth Press, 1986. Reprinted Macmillan Publishing Company 1997), Introduction xxii

3. Source: Beverly Hills Lodge of B'nai Brith's tribute to its "Man of the Year" in 1976

4. John F. Callahan ed., *The Collected Essays of Ralph Ellison* (New York: Modern Library Paperback Edition, 2003), 366–367

5. John F. Callahan ed., *The Collected Essays of Ralph Ellison* (New York: Modern Library Paperback Edition, 2003), 173

6. James Baldwin, *Notes of a Native Son* (New York: Dial Press, 1963), 67

7. Miles Davis with Quincy Troupe, *Miles: The Autobiography* (New York: Touchstone, Simon & Schuster, Inc., 1989), 321

8. Gene Lees, *Cats of Any Color: Jazz Black and White* (New York: Da Capo Press, 1995), 195

9. Jeffrey Melnic, *A Right to Sing the Blues: African Americans, Jews, and American Popular Song* (Cambridge: Harvard University Press, 1999); In Dr. Harold Brackman, *Let's Face The Music And Dance: African Americans, Jews, And The Creation Of Modern Popular Music,* for The Simon Wiesenthal Center, October 2010, p. 2

10. Charles Edward Smith with Fredric Ramsey, Jr., Charles Payne Rogers and William Russell, *The Jazz Record Book* (New York: Smith & Durrell, 1943), 91

We Go to Church on Sunday

1. Leviticus 25:10

Dixie Rose

1. Orrin Keepnews and Bill Grauer, Jr., *A Pictorial History of Jazz, People and Places From New Orleans to Modern Jazz* (New York: Crown Publishers, Inc., 1955), 3

2. Nat Shapiro & Nat Hentoff, *Hear Me Talkin' to Ya: The Story of Jazz as Told by the Men Who Made It* (New York: Dover Publications, Inc., 1966), 63

3. Dave Dexter, Jr., *Jazz Cavalcade: The Inside Story of Jazz* (New York: Criterion, 1946), 23

4. Nat Shapiro & Nat Hentoff, eds. *Hear Me Talkin' to Ya: The Story of Jazz as Told by the Men Who Made It* (New York: Dover Publications, Inc., 1966), 391

Pay Some Attention to Me

1. Alan Lomax, *Mister Jelly Roll: The Fortunes of Jelly Roll Morton, New Orleans Creole and "Inventor of Jazz"* (New York: Duell, Sloan and Pearce, 1950), 260

2. Louis Armstrong, Thomas Brothers ed., *Louis Armstrong, In His Own Words* (New York: Oxford University Press, 1999), 24

3. Gunther Schuller, *Early Jazz: Its Roots And Musical Development* (New York: Oxford University Press, 1968), 135

4. Alan Lomax, *Mister Jelly Roll: The Fortunes of Jelly Roll Morton, New Orleans Creole and "Inventor of Jazz"* (New York: Duell, Sloan and Pearce, 1950), 236–237

The Real American Folk Song (Is a Rag)

1. Marc Ambinder and D. B. Grady, *Deep State: Inside the Government Secrecy Industry* (Hoboken: John Wiley & Sons, Inc., 2013), 246–247

2. *Musical Courier*, September 13, 1899

3. David Ewen, *Panorama of American Popular Music* (Englewood Cliffs, N.J.: Prentice-Hall Inc., 1957), 175

4. *War On Ragtime* (American Musician, July 1901). Karl Koenig ed. *Jazz in Print (1856–1929): An Anthology of Selected Early Readings in Jazz History* (Hillsdale, New York: Pendragon Press, 2002), 63

5. Isaac Goldberg, *Tin Pan Alley, A Chronicle of the American Popular Music Racket* (New York: The John Day Company, 1930), 141

6. Isaac Goldberg, *Tin Pan Alley, A Chronicle of the American Popular Music Racket* (New York: The John Day Company, 1930), 139

7. Gunther Schuller, *Early Jazz: Its Roots And Musical Development* (New York: Oxford University Press, 1968), 19

8. Gilbert Seldes, *The 7 Lively Arts* (New York: Harper & Brothers Publishers, 1924), 71

9. *Ragtime* (The Musician, March 1900). Karl Koenig ed. *Jazz in Print (1856–1929): An Anthology of Selected Early Readings in Jazz History* (Hillsdale, New York: Pendragon Press, 2002), 60

10. Alec Wilder, *American Popular Song: The Great Innovators, 1900–1950*, James T. Maher ed. (New York: Oxford University Press, 1972), 7

11. Jeannette Robinson Murphy, *The True Negro Music and Its Decline* (Independent, July 23, 1903) Karl Koenig ed. *Jazz in Print (1856–1929): An Anthology of Selected Early Readings in Jazz History* (Hillsdale, New York: Pendragon Press, 2002), 74

12. Alec Wilder, *American Popular Song: The Great Innovators, 1900–1950*, James T. Maher ed. (New York: Oxford University Press, 1972), 7

Trumpeter, Blow Your Horn

1. Nat Shapiro & Nat Hentoff, eds. *Hear Me Talkin' to Ya: The Story of Jazz as Told by the Men Who Made It* (New York: Dover Publications, Inc., 1966), 46

2. Thomas Brothers ed., *Louis Armstrong, In His Own Words*, Selected Writings of Louis Armstrong (New York: Oxford University Press, 1999), 8

3. Thomas Brothers ed., *Louis Armstrong, In His Own Words*, Selected Writings of Louis Armstrong (New York: Oxford University Press, 1999), 9

4. Thomas Brothers ed., *Louis Armstrong, In His Own Words*, Selected Writings of Louis Armstrong (New York: Oxford University Press, 1999), 11

5. Thomas Brothers ed., *Louis Armstrong, In His Own Words*, Selected Writings of Louis Armstrong (New York: Oxford University Press, 1999), 19

6. Thomas Brothers ed., *Louis Armstrong, In His Own Words*, Selected Writings of Louis Armstrong (New York: Oxford University Press, 1999), 9

7. Thomas Brothers ed., *Louis Armstrong, In His Own Words*, Selected Writings of Louis Armstrong (New York: Oxford University Press, 1999), 6

8. Martin Williams, *Where's the Melody?: A Listener's Introduction To Jazz* (New York: Pantheon Books, 1966), 77–78

9. Gunther Schuller, *Early Jazz: Its Roots and Musical Development* (Oxford University Press, New York. 1968), 89

Show Me the Town

1. *Variety*, October 27, 1916, David Ewen, *Men of Popular Music* (Chicago-New York: Ziff-Davis Publishing Company, 1944), 51.

I'd Rather Charleston

1. F. Scott Fitzgerald, writing about the 1920's in his 1931 essay *Echoes of the Jazz Age*

2. Charles Edward Smith with Fredric Ramsey, Jr., Charles Payne Rogers and William Russell, *The Jazz Record Book* (New York: Smith & Durrell, 1943), 58

New York Rhapsody

1. David Ewen, *Men of Popular Music* (Chicago-New York: Ziff-Davis Publishing Company, 1944), 85–86

Changing My Tune

1. Isaac Goldberg, *Tin Pan Alley, A Chronicle of the American Popular Music Racket* (New York: The John Day Company, 1930), vii

2. Isaac Goldberg, *Tin Pan Alley, A Chronicle of the American Popular Music Racket* (New York: The John Day Company, 1930), 219

3. Deena Rosenberg, *Fascinating Rhythm: The Collaboration of George and Ira Gershwin* (New York: Dutton Books, 1991), 25

4. Henry Ford, *Jewish Jazz—Moron Music—Becomes Our National Music—the Story of Popular Song Control in the United States* (The Dearborn Independent, August 6, 1921)

I Love to Rhyme

1. George Gershwin, *American Hebrew*, November 22, 1929; Robert Wyatt and John Andrew Johnson, eds. *The George Gershwin Reader* (New York: Oxford University Press, 2004), 116

2. Carl Van Vechten, *George Gershwin, An American Composer Who Is Writing Notable Music in the Jazz Idiom* (*Vanity Fair*, March 1925), 40

3. Robert Kimball & Alfred Simon, *The Gershwins* (New York: Atheneum, 1973), 20

4. David Ewen, *A Journey to Greatness: The Life and Music of George Gershwin* (New York: Henry Holt and Company, 1956), 74

5. Isaac Goldberg, *George Gershwin: A Study in American Music* (New York: Frederick Ungar Publishing CO., 1958), 91

6. David Ewen, *A Journey to Greatness: The Life and Music of George Gershwin* (New York: Henry Holt and Company, 1956), 180

7. George Gershwin, *American Hebrew*, November 22, 1929; Robert Wyatt and John Andrew Johnson, eds. *The George Gershwin Reader* (New York: Oxford University Press, 2004), 116; David Ewen, *The Story of George Gershwin* (New York: Henry Holt And Company, 1945), 50

8. George Gershwin, *American Hebrew*, November 22, 1929; Robert Wyatt and John Andrew Johnson, eds. *The George Gershwin Reader* (New York: Oxford University Press, 2004), 116; David Ewen, *Men of Popular Music* (Chicago-New York: Ziff-Davis Publishing Company, 1944), 45

Harlem Serenade

1. Nat Shapiro & Nat Hentoff, eds., *Hear Me Talkin' to Ya: The Story of Jazz as Told by the Men Who Made It* (New York: Dover Publications, Inc., 1966), 176

2. Ibid.

Blue, Blue, Blue

1. Quote by W. C. Handy, *Hear Me Talkin' to Ya: The Story of Jazz as Told by the Men Who Made It*, Nat Shapiro & Nat Hentoff (Dover Publications, Inc. New York, 1966), 252

2. Merry, Paul (2013-06-21). *How Blues Evolved Volume One* (Kindle Location 91). Kindle Edition.

3. Merry, Paul (2013-06-21). *How Blues Evolved Volume One* (Kindle Locations 116–117). Kindle Edition.

4. Washington Irving, *Salmagundi*, 1807, reprinted 1871

5. *Suppression of "Ragtime,"* American Musician, July 1901; Karl Koenig ed. *Jazz in Print (1856–1929): An Anthology of Selected Early Readings in Jazz History* (Hillsdale, New York: Pendragon Press, 2002), 63

6. Walt Weiskopf in Jamey Aebersold, *Nothin' But Blues* (New Albany, Indiana: Jamey Aebersold Jazz, INC., 2nd Revised Edition, 1981), v

7. Hayden Carruth, *Sitting In: Selected Writings on Jazz, Blues, and Related Topics* (Iowa City: University of Iowa Press, 1986), 55

8. Larry M. Sanborn, *The Chordal Evolution of the American Jazz Art Form: The Twelve Bar Blues*, 11–12

9. Larry M. Sanborn, *The Chordal Evolution of the American Jazz Art Form: The Twelve Bar Blues*, 20–22

10. Dorothy Scarborough, *The "Blues" As Folk-Songs* (Journal of the Folklore Society of Texas, 1916); Karl Koenig ed. *Jazz in Print (1856–1929): An Anthology of Selected Early Readings in Jazz History* (Hillsdale, New York: Pendragon Press, 2002), 112

11. Ornette Coleman, *Honkers and Screamers* (New York: Arista Records, Inc., 1979), Album liner notes

12. Larry M. Sanborn, *The Chordal Evolution of the American Jazz Art Form: The Twelve Bar Blues*, 9

13. Abbe Niles, *A Treasury of the Blues*, W. C. Handy, ed. (New York: Charles Boni, Inc., 1949), footnote page 18

14. Henry O. Osgood, *So This Is Jazz* (Boston: Little, Brown, And Company, 1926), 65

15. Nat Shapiro & Nat Hentoff, eds., *Hear Me Talkin' to Ya: The Story of Jazz as Told by the Men Who Made It* (New York: Dover Publications, Inc., 1966), 246–247

16. Isaac Goldberg, *George Gershwin: A Study in American Music* (New York: Frederick Unger Publishing CO., 1958), 40

Midnight Blues

1. Nat Shapiro & Nat Hentoff, eds., *Hear Me Talkin' to Ya: The Story of Jazz as Told by the Men Who Made It* (New York: Dover Publications, Inc., 1966), 252

2. Abbe Niles, *Blues: An Anthology*, W. C. Handy ed. (New York: Albert & Charles Boni, New York, 1926), 10

3. Isaac Goldberg, *Tin Pan Alley, A Chronicle of the American Popular Music Racket* (New York: The John Day Company, 1930), 241

4. W. C. Handy, *Father of the Blues: An Autobiography* (New York: Macmillan, 1941), 99

Blah, Blah, Blah

1. Anne Shaw Faulkner, *Does Jazz Put the Sin in Syncopation?* (*Ladies' Home Journal*, August 1921); Karl Koenig ed. *Jazz in Print (1856–1929): An Anthology of Selected Early Readings in Jazz History* (Hillsdale, New York: Pendragon Press, 2002), 152–153

2. Anne Shaw Faulkner, *Does Jazz Put the Sin in Syncopation?* (*Ladies' Home Journal*, August 1921); Karl Koenig ed. *Jazz in Print (1856–1929): An Anthology of Selected Early Readings in Jazz History* (Hillsdale, New York: Pendragon Press, 2002), 153

3. Anne Shaw Faulkner, *Does Jazz Put the Sin in Syncopation?* (*Ladies' Home Journal*, August 1921); Karl Koenig ed. *Jazz in Print (1856–1929): An Anthology of Selected Early Readings in Jazz History* (Hillsdale, New York: Pendragon Press, 2002), 153

4. *Both Jazz Music and Jazz Dancing Barred From All Louisville Episcopal Churches* (*New York Times*, September 19, 1921)

5. Terry Teachout, *Pops: A Life of Louis Armstrong* (Boston: Houghton Mifflin Harcourt, 2009), 16

6. John R. McMahon, *Unspeakable Jazz Must Go!*, *Ladies' Home Journal*, December, 1921. Karl Koenig ed. *Jazz in Print (1856–1929): An Anthology of Selected Early Readings in Jazz History* (Hillsdale, New York: Pendragon Press, 2002), 160

7. John R. McMahon, *Unspeakable Jazz Must Go!*, *Ladies' Home Journal*, December, 1921. Karl Koenig ed. *Jazz in Print (1856–1929): An Anthology of Selected Early Readings in Jazz History* (Hillsdale, New York: Pendragon Press, 2002), 161–162

8. John R. McMahon, *Unspeakable Jazz Must Go!* (*Ladies' Home Journal*, December, 1921). Karl Koenig ed. *Jazz in Print (1856–1929): An Anthology of Selected Early Readings in Jazz History* (Hillsdale, New York: Pendragon Press, 2002), 163

9. John R. McMahon, *Unspeakable Jazz Must Go!* (*Ladies' Home Journal*, December, 1921). Karl Koenig ed. *Jazz in Print (1856–1929): An Anthology of Selected Early Readings in Jazz History* (Hillsdale, New York: Pendragon Press, 2002), 162

10. *Primitive Savage Animalism, Preacher's Analysis Of Jazz* (*New York Times*, March 3, 1922)

11. *Musician Is Driven To Suicide By Jazz; Wouldn't Play It, Couldn't Get Employment* (*New York Times*, April 7, 1922)

12. *Queen Mary Bars Jazz: She Dances a Fox Trot at Goodwood—The King Only a Spectator*, *Chicago Tribune*, July 27, 1922

13. Rev. Percy Stickney Grant, *Some Further Opinions on "Jazz" By Prominent Writers* (*Metronome*, August, 1922)

14. *Shady Dance Steps Barred By Police* (The *New York*

Times, December 10, 1922) Accessed online on July 1, 2013 from *The New York Times* archives

15. A. E. Guilliams, *Jazz in Print Detrimental Effects of Jazz on Our Younger Generation* (Metronome, February 1923); Karl Koenig ed. *Jazz in Print (1856–1929): An Anthology of Selected Early Readings in Jazz History* (Hillsdale, New York: Pendragon Press, 2002), 230

16. *Representatives of 2,000,000 Women, Meeting In Atlanta, Vote To Annihilate Jazz* (Music Courier, May 31, 1923. Reprinted in, *Jazz in Print (1856–1929): An Anthology of Selected Early Readings in Jazz History*, Edited by Karl Koenig, Pendragon Press, Hillsdale, New York, 2002), 238

17. Merle Armitage, *George Gershwin*, Merle Armitage ed. (New York: Longmans, Green & CO, 1938), 7

Little Jazz Bird

1. Paul Whiteman and Mary Margaret McBride, *Jazz* (New York: J. H. Sears & Company, Inc., 1926), 115

2. Larry M. Sanborn, *Musicianship for the Jazz Performer*, A dissertation submitted in partial satisfaction of the requirements for the degree Doctor of Philosophy in Music: Jazz Studies, May 1992, p. 2

3. Larry M. Sanborn, *Musicianship for the Jazz Performer*, A dissertation submitted in partial satisfaction of the requirements for the degree Doctor of Philosophy in Music: Jazz Studies, May 1992, p. 4

4. George Gershwin, *The Composer in the Machine Age.* "Revolt In The Arts," Oliver M. Saylor ed. (New York: Brentano's, 1930); reprinted in *George Gershwin*, Merle Armitage, ed. (New York: Longmans, Green & Co., 1938), 227

5. George Gershwin, *Fifty Years of American Music . . . Younger Composers, Freed from European Influences, Labor Toward Achieving a Distinctive American Musical Idiom* (American Hebrew, November 22, 1929) reprinted in *The George Gershwin Reader*, Robert Wyatt and John Andrew Johnson, eds. (New York: Oxford University Press., 2004), 116

6. Isaac Goldberg, *Tin Pan Alley, A Chronicle of the American Popular Music Racket* (New York: The John Day Company, 1930), 32

7. Isaac Goldberg, *Tin Pan Alley, A Chronicle of the American Popular Music Racket* (New York: The John Day Company, 1930), 268

8. George Gershwin, *Our New National Anthem* (Theatre Magazine, May 1925 p. 30)

9. Leonard Feather, *The New Edition of The Encyclopedia of Jazz* (New York: Bonanza Books, 1960), 21

10. Leonard Feather, *The New Edition of The Encyclopedia of Jazz* (New York: Bonanza Books, 1960), 22–23

11. George Gershwin, *Theatre Magazine*, June 1926

12. George Gershwin, *The Composer in the Machine Age.* "Revolt in the Arts," Oliver M. Saylor ed. (New York: Brentano's, 1930); reprinted in *George Gershwin*, Merle Armitage, ed. (New York: Longmans, Green & Co., 1938), 227

13. George Gershwin, *The Relation Of Jazz To American Music*, from *American Composers on American Music* (1933), edited by Henry Cowell; reprint Gregory R. Suriano ed., *Gershwin in His Time: A Biographical Scrapbook, 1919–1937* (New York: Gramercy Books, 1998), 97

14. Nat Hentoff, *Jazz Is* (New York: A Ridge Press Book, Random House, 1976), 25

15. Martin Williams, *Where's the Melody?: A Listener's Introduction To Jazz* (New York: Pantheon Books, 1966), ix

16. Henry O. Osgood, *So This Is Jazz* (Boston: Little, Brown, and Company, 1926), 7

17. Henry O. Osgood, *So This Is Jazz* (Boston: Little, Brown, and Company, 1926), 19

18. Paul Whiteman and Mary Margaret McBride, *Jazz* (New York: J. H. Sears & Company, Inc., 1926), 152

19. Quote—Orson Welles, *Jazz Cavalcade: The Inside Story of Jazz*, Dave Dexter (New York: Criterion, 1946), vi

20. Bill Crow, *Jazz Anecdotes* (New York: Oxford University Press, 1990), 21

21. J. A. Rogers, *Jazz at Home*, in *The New Negro*, Alain Locke, ed. (New York: Albert and Charles Boni, March, 1925), 666

22. George Newell, *George Gershwin and Jazz* (The Outlook, February 29, 1928); reprint edited by Gregory R. Suriano, *Gershwin In His Time: A Biographical Scrapbook, 1919–1937* (New York: Gramercy Books, 1998), 54

23. Charles Edward Smith, Frederic Ramsey, Jr., Charles Payne Rogers and William Russell, *The Jazz Record Book* (New York: Smith & Durrell, 1943 p. 32

24. George Antheil, *Jazz Is Music* (Forum, July 1928); Reprinted and Edited by Karl Koenig, *Jazz in Print (1856–1929): An Anthology of Selected Early Readings in Jazz History* (Hillsdale, New York: Pendragon Press, 2002), 538

25. Hayden Carruth, *Sitting In: Selected Writings on Jazz, Blues, and Related Topics* (Iowa City: University of Iowa Press, 1986), 24

26. Hayden Carruth, *Sitting In: Selected Writings on Jazz, Blues, and Related Topics* (Iowa City: University of Iowa Press, 1986), 29

27. Jerry Coker, *Listening to Jazz* (Englewood Cliffs, New Jersey: Prentice-Hall, INC., N.J. 1978), 4

28. Gunther Schuller, *Early Jazz: Its Roots And Musical Development* (New York: Oxford University Press, 1968), 58

29. Quote—Dave Brubeck, *Hear Me Talkin' to Ya: The Story of Jazz as Told by the Men Who Made It*, Nat Shapiro & Nat Hentoff, eds. (New York: Dover Publications, Inc., 1966), 387

30. Quote—Dave Brubeck, *Hear Me Talkin' to Ya: The Story of Jazz as Told by the Men Who Made It*, Nat Shapiro & Nat Hentoff, eds. (New York: Dover Publications, Inc., 1966), 408–409

31. Hayden Carruth, *Sitting In: Selected Writings on Jazz, Blues, and Related Topics* (Iowa City: University of Iowa Press, 1986), 100

32. Robert George Reisner, *Bird: The Legend of Charlie Parker* (New York: Citadel Press, 1962), 27

33. Dizzy Gillespie, *To Be or Not . . . to Bop* (New York: Doubleday Books), 1979

34. Gene Lees, *Cats of Any Color: Jazz Black and White* (New York: Oxford University Press, 1994), 40

35. Quote—Billie Holliday, *Hear Me Talkin' to Ya: The Story of Jazz as Told by the Men Who Made It*, Nat Shapiro & Nat Hentoff, Dover Publications, Inc. New York, 1966 p. 201

36. Orrin Keepnews and Bill Grauer, *A Pictorial History of Jazz, People and Places From New Orleans to Modern Jazz* (New York: Crown Publishers, Inc., 1955), 1

37. Gilbert Seldes, *The 7 Lively Arts* (New York: Harper & Brothers Publishers, 1924)

38. David Ewen, *Men of Popular Music* (Chicago-New York: Ziff-Davis Publishing Company, 1944), 115–116

39. Wilfrid Sheed, *The House That George Built: With a Little Help from Irving, Cole, and a Crew of About Fifty* (New York: Random House, 2008), 8

40. Isaac Goldberg, *Aaron Copland and His Jazz* (American Mercury, September 1927), 63

41. Isaac Goldberg, *Aaron Copland And His Jazz* (American Mercury, September 1927), 63

42. Wilfred Sheed, *The House That George Built: With a Little Help from Irving, Cole, and a Crew of About Fifty* (New York: Random House, 2008), 8–9

43. *Jazz Music And The Modern Dance*, Melody, December 1920; Reprinted and Edited by Karl Koenig, *Jazz in Print (1856–1929): An Anthology of Selected Early Readings in Jazz History* (Hillsdale, New York: Pendragon Press, 2002), 149

44. Nat Hentoff, *Jazz Is* (New York: A Ridge Press Book, Random House, 1976), 128–129

45. Nat Hentoff, *Jazz Is* (New York: A Ridge Press Book, Random House, 1976), 129

46. Nat Hentoff, *Jazz Is* (New York: A Ridge Press Book, Random House, 1976), 48

47. Nat Hentoff, *Jazz Is* (New York: A Ridge Press Book, Random House, 1976), 197

You Started It

1. Paul Whiteman and Mary Margaret McBride, *Jazz* (New York: J. H. Sears & Company, Inc., 1926), 132–133

2. Paul Whiteman and Mary Margaret McBride, *Jazz* (New York: J. H. Sears & Company, Inc., 1926), 32–34.

3. Paul Whiteman and Mary Margaret McBride, *Jazz* (New York: J. H. Sears & Company, Inc., 1926), 37

4. Paul Whiteman and Mary Margaret McBride, *Jazz* (New York: J. H. Sears & Company, Inc., 1926), 26

5. Paul Whiteman and Mary Margaret McBride, *Jazz* (New York: J. H. Sears & Company, Inc., 1926), 20

6. Duke Ellington, *Music Is My Mistress* (New York: Da Capo Press 1973), 103

7. Alec Wilder; James T. Maher ed., *American Popular Song: The Great Innovators, 1900–1950* (New York: Oxford University Press, 1972), 453

8. Hugues Panassié, *Hot Jazz: The Guide To Swing Music* (New York: M. Witmark & Sons, 1936), 19–20

9. Abbe Niles, W. C. Handy, ed., *A Treasury of the Blues* (New York: Charles Boni, 1949), 30

10. Orrin Keepnews and Bill Grauer, *A Pictorial History of Jazz, People and Places From New Orleans to Modern Jazz* (New York: Crown Publishers, Inc., 1955), 117

11. Henry O. Osgood, *So This Is Jazz* (Boston: Little, Brown, And Company, 1926), 86

12. Howard Pollack, *George Gershwin: His Life and Work* (Berkeley and Los Angles: University of California Press, 2006), 308–309

Who's the Greatest?

1. Isaac Goldberg, *George Gershwin: A Study in American Music* (New York: Frederick Ungar Publishing Co., 1958), xv-xvi

2. Edward Jablonski and Lawrence D. Stewart, *The Gershwin Years* (New York: Doubleday & Company, INC., 1973), 32

3. Isaac Goldberg, *George Gershwin: A Study in American Music* (New York: Frederick Ungar Publishing Co., 1958), 55–56

4. Henry O. Osgood, *So This Is Jazz*, (Boston: Little, Brown, and Company, 1926) 172

5. Robert Kimball & Alfred Simon, *The Gershwins* (New York: Atheneum, New York, 1973), 2–4

I'm Somethin' on Avenue A

1. Robert Kimball & Alfred Simon, *The Gershwins* (New York: Atheneum, New York, 1973), 3

2. David Ewen, *A Journey to Greatness: The Life and Music of George Gershwin* (New York: Henry Holt and Company, 1956), 34–35

3. Robert Kimball & Alfred Simon, *The Gershwins* (New York: Atheneum, New York, 1973), xxii

Official Resume

1. Joan Peyser, *The Memory of All That: The Life of George Gershwin* (New York: Simon & Schuster, 1993), 26

2. Isaac Goldberg, *George Gershwin: A Study in American Music* (New York: Fredrick Ungar Publishing CO., 1958), 61

3. George Gershwin, *Jazz Is the Voice of the American Soul* (*Theatre Magazine*, June 1926), 52; Robert Wyatt and John Andrew Johnson, eds., *The George Gershwin Reader* (New York; Oxford University Press, 2004), 92; Deena Rosenberg, *Fascinating Rhythm: The Collaboration of George and Ira Gershwin* (New York: Dutton Books, 1991), 15

4. Deena Rosenberg, *Fascinating Rhythm: The Collaboration of George and Ira Gershwin* (New York: Dutton Books, 1991), 13–15

5. Edward Jablonski and Lawrence D. Stewart, *The Gershwin Years* (New York: Doubleday & Company, 1973), 83

6. Merle Armitage, *George Gershwin: Man And Legend* (New York: Duell, Sloan and Pearce, 1958), 74

7. Steven E. Gilbert, *The Music of Gershwin* (New Haven: Yale University Press, 1995, p. 4; Original Source in notes: Ira Gershwin, *My Brother's Manuscript*, preface to the first published edition of *Lullaby for String Quartet* (New York: New World Music Corporation, 1968), p. 2

8. Howard Pollack, *George Gershwin: His Life and Work* (Berkley and Los Angeles: University of California Press, 2006), 25

9. *The New Yorker*, January 1, 1927. P. 9

10. *The New Yorker*, January 1, 1927, p. 9–10

I'm on My Way

1. Robert Kimball & Alfred Simon, *The Gershwins* (New York: Atheneum, 1973), 23

2. Fred Astaire, *Steps in Time* (New York: Harper & Brothers, 1959; this quote from: New York: itbooks, 2008), 55

3. Robert Kimball & Alfred Simon, *The Gershwins* (New York: Atheneum, 1973), xxiii

4. Howard Pollack, *George Gershwin, His Life and Work* (Berkley-Los Angeles: University of California Press, 2006), 76

5. Isaac Goldberg, *George Gershwin: A Study in American Music* (New York: Fredrick Ungar Publishing, 1958), 85

6. George Newell, *George Gershwin And Jazz* (Outlook, February 22, 1928); Reprinted and Edited by Karl Koenig, *Jazz in Print (1856–1929): An Anthology of Selected Early Readings in Jazz History* New York: Pendragon Press, 2002), 529

7. David Ewen, *A Journey to Greatness, The Life and Music of George Gershwin* (New York: Henry Holt and Company, 1956), 68

Any Little Tune

1. Howard Pollack, *George Gershwin: His Life and Work* (Berkeley-Los Angeles: University of California Press, 2006), 22

2. Robert Kimball and Alfred Simon, *The Gershwins* (New York: Atheneum, 1973), 286

3. Richard Dowling, *Kickin' The Clouds Away: Gershwin at the Piano*, CD Liner notes (Boca Raton: Klavier Music Productions, 2000)

4. Robert Kimball and Alfred Simon, *The Gershwins* (New York: Atheneum, 1973), 286

Wake Up, Brother, and Dance

1. Deena Rosenberg, *Fascinating Rhythm: The Collaboration of George and Ira Gershwin* (New York: Dutton Books, 1991), 132

2. Edward Jablonski and Lawrence D. Stewart, *The Gershwin Years* (New York: Doubleday & Company, 1958, 1973), 31

3. George Newell, *George Gershwin and Jazz* (Outlook, February 22, 1928); Reprinted in Karl Koenig, ed., *Jazz in Print (1856–1929): An Anthology of Selected Early Readings in Jazz History* (New York: Pendragon Press, 2002), 529

4. Edward Jablonski and Lawrence D. Stewart, *The Gershwin Years* (New York: Doubleday & Company, 1958, 1973), 51

5. George Gershwin, *Making Music*, New York "Sunday World Magazine" May 4, 1930; reprinted in Gregory R. Suriano, ed., *Gershwin In His Time: A Biographical Scrapbook, 1919–1937* (New York: Gramercy Books, 1998), 76

6. Ira Gershwin, *Lyrics on Several Occasions* (New York: The Viking Press, 1959. I used the 1973 version), 41–42

7. Isaac Goldberg, *George Gershwin, A Study in American Music* (New York: Frederick Ungar Publishing Co., 1958), 193

8. Isaac Goldberg, *George Gershwin, A Study in American Music* (New York: Frederick Ungar Publishing Co., 1958), 195

9. Oscar Levant, *A Smattering of Ignorance* (Garden City, New York: Garden City Publishing CO., INC., 1942), 203–204

10. Michael Feinstein, *Nice Work If You Can Get It: My Life in Rhythm and Rhyme* (New York: Hyperion, 1995), 100

11. Merle Armitage, *George Gershwin: Man and Legend* (New York: Duell, Sloan and Pearce, 1958, 124–125

12. Merle Armitage, *George Gershwin: Man and Legend* (New York: Duell, Sloan and Pearce, 1958, 125

13. Robert Kimball & Alfred Simon, *The Gershwins* (New York: Atheneum, 1973), 80

14. Alexander Steinert 1938, In Merle Armitage ed., *George Gershwin* (New York: Longmans, Green & Co., 1938), 46

Cinderelatives

1. David Ewen, *A Journey to Greatness: The Life and Music of George Gershwin* (New York: Henry Holt and Company, 1956), 32

2. Edward Jablonski and Lawrence D. Stewart, *The Gershwin Years* (New York: Doubleday & Company, 1958, 1973), 40

3. S. N. Behrman, *Profiles: Troubadour* (*The New Yorker*, May 25, 1929), 28

Swanee

1. Merle Armitage, *George Gershwin* (New York: Longmans, Green and CO., 1938), 205

2. Isaac Goldberg, *George Gershwin: A Study in American Music* (New York: Fredrick Ungar Publishing CO., 1958), 99

3. Edward Jablonski and Lawrence D. Stewart, *The Gershwin Years* (New York: Doubleday & Company, 1958, 1973), 67

4. Michael Feinstein, *Nice Work if You Can Get It: My Life in Rhythm and Rhyme* (New York: Hyperion, 1995), 60

5. David Ewen, *A Journey to Greatness: The Life and Music of George Gershwin* (New York: Henry Holt and Company, 1956), 84

6. Deena Rosenberg, *Fascinating Rhythm: The Collaboration of George and Ira Gershwin* (New York: Dutton Books, 1991), 39

7. Gilbert Seldes, *The 7 Lively Arts* (New York: Harper & Brothers Publishers, 1924), 74–75

Blue Monday Blues

1. David Ewen, *A Journey to Greatness: The Life and Music of George Gershwin* (New York: Henry Holt and Company, 1956), 92

2. *Paul Whiteman Gives 'Vivid' Grand Opera; Jazz Rhythms of Gershwin's '135th Street'* (*New York Times*, December 30, 1925), 10

3. Isaac Goldberg, *George Gershwin: A Study in American Music* (New York: Fredrick Ungar Publishing CO., 1958), 218

4. Oscar Thompson, *Jazz, As Art Music, Piles Failure On Failure* (Musical America; February 13, 1926)

5. Dolly Dalrymple, *Pianist, Playing Role of Columbus, Makes Another American Discovery: Beryl Rubinstein Says This Country Possesses Genius Composer* (*New York World*, September, 16, 1922); Robert Wyatt and John Andrew Johnson, eds., *The George Gershwin Reader* (New York; Oxford University Press, 2004), 42; Isaac Goldberg, *George Gershwin: A Study in American Music* (New York: Fredrick Ungar Publishing CO., 1958), 133–134; *Men of Popular Music* by David Ewen Ziff-Davis Publishing Company, Chicago-New York, 1944 p. 131

Soon

1. 1912 James Reece Europe and his Clef Club Orchestra perform. http://www.carnegiehall.org/History/Timeline/Timeline.aspx?id=4294968751 (Accessed on the web on August, 5, 2013)

2. David Ewen, *A Journey to Greatness: The Life and Music of George Gershwin* (New York: Henry Holt and Company, 1956), 41

Oh, Lady Be Good!

1. *Novelty Is Spice* (Musical America, November 10, 1923); Reprinted in Karl Koenig, ed., *Jazz in Print (1856–1929): An Anthology of Selected Early Readings in Jazz History* (New York: Pendragon Press, 2002), 263

2. *The Gershwins*, Robert Kimball & Alfred Simon. Atheneum, New York. 1973 p. xxx

3. David Ewen, *A Journey to Greatness: The Life and Music of George Gershwin* (New York: Henry Holt and Company, 1956), 98

4. Isaac Goldberg, *George Gershwin: A Study in American Music* (New York: Fredrick Ungar Publishing CO., 1958), 127–128

5. Isaac Goldberg, *George Gershwin: A Study in American Music* (New York: Fredrick Ungar Publishing CO., 1958), 130–131

6. David Ewen, *Panorama of American Popular Music: The Story of Our National Ballads and Folk Songs—The Songs of Tin Pan Alley, Broadway and Hollywood—New Orleans Jazz, Swing, and Symphonic Jazz* (Englewood Cliffs, N. J., Prentice-Hall, 1957, 1962), 210

7. Henry Taylor Parker, *Boston Evening Transcript*, January 30, 1924; Isaac Goldberg, *George Gershwin: A Study in American Music* (New York: Fredrick Ungar Publishing CO., 1958), 131

What's the Big Idea?

1. David Ewen, *Men of Popular Music* (Chicago-New York; Ziff-Davis Publishing Company, 1944), 133

2. New York Tribune, January 4, 1924; Edward Jablonski and Lawrence D. Stewart eds., *The Gershwin Years* (Garden City, New York: Doubleday & Company, INC., 1958, 1973), 89; Joan Peyser, *The Memory of All That: The Life of George Gershwin* (New York; Simon & Schuster, 1993), 74

3. Merle Armitage, ed., *George Gershwin* (New York; Longmans, Green & Co., 1938), 26

4. Deena Rosenberg, *Fascinating Rhythm: The Collaboration of George and Ira Gershwin* (New York; Dutton Books, 1991), 45

5. Steven E. Gilbert, *The Music of Gershwin* (New Haven; Yale University Press, 1995), 68

6. Steven E. Gilbert, *The Music of Gershwin* (New Haven; Yale University Press, 1995), 71

7. David Ewen, *Men of Popular Music* (Chicago-New York; Ziff-Davis Publishing Company, 1944), 133–134

8. Merle Armitage, ed., *George Gershwin* (New York; Longmans, Green & Co., 1938), 28

9. George Gershwin, "Mr. Gershwin Replies to Mr. Kramer" (Singing, October 1926), 17–18; Reprinted in Robert Wyatt and John Andrew Johnson, eds., *The George Gershwin Reader*, New York; Oxford University Press, 2004, 2007), 99

10. Robert Kimball & Alfred Simon, *The Gershwins* (New York; Atheneum, 1973), 36

11. *Making Music*: George Gershwin, *New York World Sunday Magazine*. May 4, 1930; Reprinted in Robert Wyatt and John Andrew Johnson, eds., *The George Gershwin Reader*, New York; Oxford University Press, 2004, 2007), 134

12. Joan Peyser, *The Memory of All That: The Life of George Gershwin.* (New York; Simon & Schuster, 1993), 81

13. David Ewen, *A Journey to Greatness: The Life and Music of George Gershwin* (New York: Henry Holt and Company, 1956), 106

14. David Ewen, *A Journey to Greatness: The Life and Music of George Gershwin* (New York: Henry Holt and Company, 1956), 35

Tonight's the Night

1. Paul Whiteman and Mary Margaret McBride, *Jazz* (New York; J. H. Sears & Company, Inc., 1926), 97

2. Paul Whiteman and Mary Margaret McBride, *Jazz* (New York; J. H. Sears & Company, Inc., 1926), 94

3. Quote-Leonard Liebling; Merle Armitage, ed., *George Gershwin* (New York; Longsmans, Green & Co., 1938), 123–124

4. Paul Whiteman and Mary Margaret McBride, *Jazz* (New York; J. H. Sears & Company, Inc., 1926), 98

5. Paul Whiteman and Mary Margaret McBride, *Jazz* (New York; J. H. Sears & Company, Inc., 1926), 99

6. Edmund Dorset, *Mr. Whiteman and the Fox Trot* (Paul

Whiteman Souvenir Program, Transcontinental Concert Tour, Season 1924–1925 (New York; Townsend & McNerney, 1924), 15

7. Hugh C. Ernst, *The Why of This Experiment* (Introductory notes to original program "An Experiment in Modern Music, Aeolian Pianos, Inc.), 1

8. Hugh C. Ernst, *The Why of This Experiment* (Introductory notes to original program "An Experiment in Modern Music, Aeolian Pianos, Inc.), 8–10

9. Hugh C. Ernst, *The Why of This Experiment* (Introductory notes to original program "An Experiment in Modern Music, Aeolian Pianos, Inc.), Last page

10. Olin Downes, *A Concert of Jazz* (*New York Times*, February 13, 1924) 16; Robert Wyatt and John Andrew Johnson, eds., *The George Gershwin Reader* (New York; Oxford University Press, 2004), 50; Henry O. Osgood, *So This Is Jazz* (Boston; Little, Brown, And Company, 1926), 149–150

11. "Blues Are Blues, They Are" Says Expert in "Blues" Case", *Variety*, October 19, 1917; Reprinted in Karl Koenig, ed., *Jazz in Print (1856–1929): An Anthology of Selected Early Readings in Jazz History* (New York: Pendragon Press, 2002), 120–121

12. Henry O. Osgood, *So This Is Jazz* (Boston; Little, Brown, And Company, 1926), 136

13. Gilbert Seldes, *The 7 Lively Arts* (New York; Harper & Brothers Publishers, New York, 1924; Dover Publications, Inc. Mineola, 2001), 367–368

14. Maurice Peress, *The Birth of Rhapsody in Blue: Paul Whiteman's Historic Aeolian Hall Concert Of 1924* (Liner notes, Musical Heritage Society, Inc., 1987)

15. Maurice Peress, *The Birth of Rhapsody in Blue: Paul Whiteman's Historic Aeolian Hall Concert Of 1924* (Liner notes, Musical Heritage Society, Inc., 1987)

16. George Gershwin, *Fifty Years of American Music . . . Younger Composers, Freed from European Influences, Labor Toward Achieving a Distinctive American Musical Idiom* (American Hebrew, November 22, 1929); Robert Wyatt and John Andrew Johnson, eds., *The George Gershwin Reader* (New York; Oxford University Press, 2004), 116

17. Maurice Peress, *The Birth of Rhapsody in Blue: Paul Whiteman's Historic Aeolian Hall Concert Of 1924* (Liner notes, Musical Heritage Society, Inc., 1987)

18. Gilbert Seldes, *Seven Lively Arts*, Reprinted in the original program "An Experiment in Modern Music, Aeolian Pianos, Inc., 1924), 2

19. Henry O. Osgood, *So This Is Jazz* (Boston; Little, Brown, And Company, 1926), 147

Somebody Loves Me

1. Paul Whiteman and Mary Margaret McBride, *Jazz* (New York; J. H. Sears & Company, Inc., 1926), 106–107

2. Paul Whiteman and Mary Margaret McBride, *Jazz* (New York; J. H. Sears & Company, Inc., 1926), 107

3. Paul Whiteman and Mary Margaret McBride, *Jazz* (New York; J. H. Sears & Company, Inc., 1926), 106–107

4. Olin Downes, *A Concert of Jazz* (*New York Times*, February 13, 1924)

5. Paul Whiteman and Mary Margaret McBride, *Jazz* (New York; J. H. Sears & Company, Inc., 1926), 110–111

6. David Ewen, *Men of Popular Music* (Chicago-New York; Ziff-Davis Publishing Company, 1944), 119–120

7. Carl Van Vechten: *Letter to George Gershwin* (February 14, 1924, Library of Congress George Gershwin Archives); Robert Wyatt and John Andrew Johnson, eds., *The George Gershwin Reader* (New York; Oxford University Press, 2004), 52; Isaac Goldberg, *George Gershwin: A Study in American Music* (New York: Fredrick Ungar Publishing CO., 1958), 154

8. Joan Peyser, *The Memory of All That: The Life of George Gershwin.* (New York; Simon & Schuster, 1993), 84

9. Oscar Thompson, *Jazz, As Art Music, Piles Failure on Failure* (Musical America, February 13, 1926)

10. Virgil Thompson, *The Cult of Jazz* (Vanity Fair, June 1925)

11. Isaac Goldberg, *George Gershwin: A Study in American Music* (New York: Fredrick Ungar Publishing CO., 1958), 152

12. David Schiff, *Gershwin: Rhapsody in Blue* (Cambridge, U. K., Cambridge University Press, 1997), 82

13. David Ewen, *Panorama of American Popular Music: The Story of Our National Ballads and Folk Songs—The Songs of Tin Pan Alley, Broadway and Hollywood—New Orleans Jazz, Swing, and Symphonic Jazz* (Englewood Cliffs, N. J., Prentice-Hall, 1957, 1962), 216

14. Leonard Feather, *The New Edition of The Encyclopedia of Jazz* (New York; Bonanza Books, 1960), 25

15. Spike Hughes, *Meet the Duke!* (London's Daily Herald, June 13, 1933; Mark Tucker, ed., *The Duke Ellington Reader* (New York; Oxford University Press, 1993), 74.

16. Leonard Bernstein, *The Joy of Music* (Pompton Plains, New Jersey; Amadeus Press LLC, 1959, 2004), 57–58

17. Paul Whiteman and Mary Margaret McBride, *Jazz* (New York; J. H. Sears & Company, Inc., 1926), 87

18. Maurice Peress, *The Birth of Rhapsody in Blue: Paul Whiteman's Historic Aeolian Hall Concert Of 1924* (Liner notes, Musical Heritage Society, Inc., 1987)

Stiff Upper Lip

1. Robert Kimball & Alfred Simon, *The Gershwins* (New York; Atheneum, 1973), xxxi

2. David Ewen, *A Journey to Greatness: The Life and Music of George Gershwin* (New York; Henry Holt and Company, 1956), 23

3. H. O. Osgood, *The Jazz Bugaboo* (The American Mercury, November 1925); Reprinted in Karl Koenig, ed., *Jazz in Print (1856–1929): An Anthology of Selected Early Readings in Jazz History* (New York: Pendragon Press, 2002), 429

4. Henry Osborne Osgood, *The Anatomy of Jazz* (The American Mercury, April 1926); Reprinted in Karl Koenig, ed., *Jazz in Print (1856–1929): An Anthology of Selected Early Readings in Jazz History* (New York: Pendragon Press, 2002), 473

5. J. W. Henderson, *Current Opinion* (*New York Herald Tribune*, September 1924)

6. Deena Rosenberg, *Fascinating Rhythm: The Collaboration of George and Ira Gershwin* (New York; Dutton Books, 1991), 56

7. William G Hyland, *George Gershwin: A New Biography* (Westport, Connecticut; Praeger, 2003), 57

8. *Capacity House Fervently Applauds As Jazz Invades Realm Of Serious Music* Musical America, February 23, 1924; Reprinted in Karl Koenig, ed., *Jazz in Print (1856–1929): An Anthology of Selected Early Readings in Jazz History* (New York: Pendragon Press, 2002), 279

9. Earl Chapin May, *Where Jazz Comes From* (Popular Mechanics, 1926; Reprinted in, *Jazz in Print (1856–1929): An Anthology of Selected Early Readings in Jazz History*, Edited by Karl Koenig, Pendragon Press, Hillsdale, New York, 2002 p. 505–506

10. Deena Rosenberg, *Fascinating Rhythm: The Collaboration of George and Ira Gershwin* (New York; Dutton Books, 1991), 56

11. Deena Rosenberg, *Fascinating Rhythm: The Collaboration of George and Ira Gershwin* (New York; Dutton Books, 1991), 56

12. *The Jazz Fiddler* (The Etude, June 1923); Reprinted in, *Jazz in Print (1856–1929): An Anthology of Selected Early Readings in Jazz History,* Edited by Karl Koenig, Pendragon Press, Hillsdale, New York, 2002 p. 240

Could You Use Me?

1. Isaac Goldberg, *George Gershwin: A Study in American Music* (New York: Fredrick Ungar Publishing CO., 1958), 163

2. David Schiff, *Gershwin: Rhapsody in Blue* (Cambridge, U. K., Cambridge University Press, 1997), 1

3. "United to keep 'Rhapsody in Blue as theme song", United Airlines Press Release, January 5, 2012, http://articles.chicagotribune.com/2012-01-05/business/chi-united-to-keep-rhapsody-in-blue-as-theme-song-20120105_1_theme-song-rhapsody-united-airlines

Concerto in F

1. Deena Rosenberg, *Fascinating Rhythm: The Collaboration of George and Ira Gershwin* (New York; Dutton Books, 1991), 124

2. Isaac Goldberg, *George Gershwin: A Study in American Music* (New York: Fredrick Ungar Publishing CO., 1958), 205

3. Douglas Lee, *Masterworks of 20th-Century Music: The Modern Repertory of the Symphony Orchestra* (New York; Routledge, 2002), 157

4. David Schiff, *Gershwin: Rhapsody in Blue* (Cambridge, U. K., Cambridge University Press, 1997), 73–74

5. Samuel Chotzinoff, *New York Symphony at Carnegie Hall* (*New York World*, December 4, 1925), 16; Robert Wyatt and John Andrew Johnson, eds., *The George Gershwin Reader* (New York; Oxford University Press, 2004), 83–84

6. Lawrence Gilman, *Mr. Gershwin Plays His New Jazz Concerto* (New York Herald Tribune (December 4, 1925), 19

7. Walter Damrosch, Merle Armitage, ed., *George Gershwin* (New York; Longmans, Green & Co., 1938), 32

8. Lawrence Gilman, *Mr. Gershwin Plays His New Jazz Concerto* (New York Herald Tribune (December 4, 1925), 19

9. Oscar Thompson, *Jazz as Art Music, Piles Failure on Failure, Musical America* (February 13, 1926)

10. Charles L. Buchanan, *Gershwin and Musical Snobbery, The Outlook* (February 2, 1927)

11. Edward Jablonski and Lawrence D. Stewart, *The Gershwin Years* (New York; Doubleday & Company, 1958, 1973), 102

12. Hugues Panassié, *Hot Jazz: The Guide To Swing Music* (New York; M. Witmark & Sons 1936), 20

13. Sigmund Spaeth, *Jazz Is Not Music—A Reply to George Antheil in the July Forum* (Forum, August 1928); Reprinted in Karl Koenig, ed., *Jazz in Print (1856–1929): An Anthology of Selected Early Readings in Jazz History* (New York: Pendragon Press, 2002), 543

14. Ira Gershwin, Merle Armitage, ed., *George Gershwin* (New York; Longmans, Green & Co., 1938), 21

A Typical Self-Made American

1. Isaac Goldberg, *George Gershwin: A Study in American Music* (New York: Fredrick Ungar Publishing CO., 1958), 11–12

2. Gerald Clarke, *Broadway Legends: George Gershwin: The Celebrated Composer's Manhattan Penthouse* (Architectural Digest, November 1995), 192)

3. David Ewen, *A Journey to Greatness: The Life and Music of George Gershwin* (New York; Henry Holt and Company, 1956), 183–184

4. Fred Astaire, *Steps in Time* (New York; Harper & Brothers, 1959, itbooks, 2008), 134–135

5. Robert Kimball & Alfred Simon, *The Gershwins* (New York; Atheneum, 1973), 139

6. Dubose Heyward, *Porgy and Bess Return on Wings of Song* (Stage Magazine, October, 1935)

7. Merle Armitage, ed., *George Gershwin* (New York; Longmans, Green & CO, 1938), 14–15

8. Merle Armitage, ed., *George Gershwin* (New York; Longmans, Green & CO, 1938), 45–46

9. Arthur Kober, *Some Things About a Young Composer* (*New York World*, May 4, 1930)

10. Merle Armitage, ed., *George Gershwin* (New York; Longmans, Green & CO, 1938), 32

11. Merle Armitage, ed., *George Gershwin* (New York; Longmans, Green & CO, 1938), 27

12. Merle Armitage, ed., *George Gershwin* (New York; Longmans, Green & CO, 1938), 54–56

13. Merle Armitage, ed., *George Gershwin* (New York; Longmans, Green & CO, 1938), 56–57

14. Merle Armitage, ed., *George Gershwin* (New York; Longmans, Green & CO, 1938), 52

15. Oscar Levant, *Variations on a Gershwin Theme* (*Town and Country*, November 1939)

16. Oscar Levant, *Variations on a Gershwin Theme* (*Town and Country*, November 1939)

17. David Ewen, *A Journey to Greatness: The Life and Music of George Gershwin* (New York; Henry Holt and Company, 1956), 182

18. Ira Gershwin, *Words and Music* (*New York Times*, November 9, 1930)

19. *Celebrity* (*The New Yorker*, January 1, 1927), 10

20. Isaac Goldberg, *Tin Pan Alley, A Chronicle of the American Popular Music Racket* (New York; The John Day Company, 1930), ix

21. Oscar Levant, *A Smattering of Ignorance* (New York; Garden City Publishing CO., INC., 1942), 160

22. George Gershwin, *Making Music* (New York Sunday World Magazine, May 4, 1930)

23. George Newell, *George Gershwin and Jazz* (Outlook, February 22, 1928)

24. George Newell, *George Gershwin and Jazz* (Outlook, February 22, 1928)

25. Gilbert Seldes, *The 7 Lively Arts* (New York; Harper & Brothers Publishers, 1924), 92–93

26. Edward Jablonski and Lawrence D. Stewart, *The Gershwin Years: George and Ira* (New York; Doubleday & Company, Inc., 1958, Da Capo Press, 1973), 271

27. Arthur Kober, *Some Things About a Young Composer* (*New York World*, May 4, 1930)

28. Bennett Cerf, *Try and Stop Me: A Collection of Anecdotes and Stories, Mostly Humorous* (New York; Simon And Schuster, 1944), 213

The He-Man

1. David Ewen, *A Journey to Greatness: The Life and Music of George Gershwin* (New York; Henry Holt and Company, 1956), 186

2. Robert Kimball & Alfred Simon, *The Gershwins* (New York; Atheneum, 1973), 48

3. David Ewen, *A Journey to Greatness: The Life and Music of George Gershwin* (New York; Henry Holt and Company, 1956), 186

4. Alexander Woollcott, *George the Ingenuous* (Hearst's

International-Cosmopolitan, November 1933) 32; Robert Wyatt and Andrew Johnson, eds., *The George Gershwin Reader* (New York; Oxford University Press, Inc., 2004), 180

5. Oscar Levant, *A Smattering of Ignorance* (Garden City, New York: Garden City Publishing CO., INC., 1942), 158

6. David Ewen, *A Journey to Greatness: The Life and Music of George Gershwin* (New York; Henry Holt and Company, 1956), 185–186

7. Arthur Kober, *Some Things About a Young Composer* (*New York World*, May 4, 1930)

8. George Gershwin: *Letter to Rose Gershwin* (*June or July 1932*), Gershwin Archival Collection, Library of Congress, Washington, D.C; Robert Wyatt and Andrew Johnson, eds., *The George Gershwin Reader* (New York; Oxford University Press, Inc., 2004), 179

9. William Howard Hay, M.D., *Diet via Food* (East Aurora, New York; Sun-Diet Health Service, 1929, 1932)

When You Live in a Furnished Flat

1. S. N. Behrman, *Profiles: Troubadour* (*The New Yorker*, May 25, 1929), 27

2. David Ewen, *A Journey to Greatness: The Life and Music of George Gershwin* (New York; Henry Holt and Company, 1956), 129–130

3. *The New Yorker*, January 1, 1927, p. 9

4. S. N. Behrman, *Profiles: Troubadour* (*The New Yorker*, May 25, 1929), 27

Climb Up the Social Ladder

1. Isaac Goldberg, *George Gershwin: A Study in American Music* (New York: Fredrick Ungar Publishing CO., 1958), 198

2. Gerald Clarke, *Broadway Legends: George Gershwin: The Celebrated Composer's Manhattan Penthouse* (Architectural Digest, November 1995), 193–194

3. David Ewen, *A Journey to Greatness: The Life and Music of George Gershwin* (New York; Henry Holt and Company, 1956), 234–235

Quite a Party

1. Edward Jablonski, Liner notes, *George Gershwin Plays The Rhapsody in Blue* (20th Century Fox, 1958)

2. David Ewen, *A Journey to Greatness: The Life and Music of George Gershwin* (New York; Henry Holt and Company, 1956), 98–99

3. Merle Armitage, ed., *George Gershwin* (New York; Longmans, Green & CO, 1938), 47

4. S. N. Behrman, *Profiles: Troubadour* (*The New Yorker*, May 25, 1929), 28

5. Ira Gershwin, *Lyrics on Several Occasions* (New York; The Viking Press, 1959, 1973), 31

6. Robert Kimball & Alfred Simon, *The Gershwins* (New York; Atheneum, New York, 1973), xii

7. *The New Yorker* (January 1, 1927), 10

A Wonderful Party

1. S. N. Behrman, *Profiles: Troubadour* (*The New Yorker*, May 25, 1929), 29

2. Bennett Cerf, *Try and Stop Me: A Collection of Anecdotes and Stories, Mostly Humorous* (New York; Simon And Schuster, 1944), 213

3. Gerald Clarke, *Broadway Legends: George Gershwin: The Celebrated Composer's Manhattan Penthouse* (Architectural Digest, November 1995), 192

4. Gerald Clarke, *Broadway Legends: George Gershwin: The Celebrated Composer's Manhattan Penthouse* (Architectural Digest, November 1995), 270

5. Oscar Levant, *A Smattering of Ignorance* (New York; Garden City Publishing CO., INC., 1942), 195–196

6. Deena Rosenberg, *Fascinating Rhythm: The Collaboration of George and Ira Gershwin* (New York; Dutton Books, 1991), 118

7. Edward Jablonski and Lawrence D. Stewart, *The Gershwin Years* (New York; Doubleday & Company 1958, 1973), 25; in Carl Van Vechten's Introduction 1958

8. David Ewen, *A Journey to Greatness: The Life and Music of George Gershwin* (New York; Henry Holt and Company, 1956), 183

My Cousin In Milwaukee

1. Merle Armitage, ed., *George Gershwin* (New York; Longmans, Green & CO, 1938), 141

2. "A Composer's Pictures" (Arts & Decoration, January, 1934)

3. Robert Wyatt and Andrew Johnson, eds., *The George Gershwin Reader* (New York; Oxford University Press, Inc., 2004), 254 footnote 3

4. David Ewen, *A Journey to Greatness: The Life and Music of George Gershwin* (New York; Henry Holt and Company, 1956), 190

5. Merle Armitage, ed., *George Gershwin* (New York; Longmans, Green & CO, 1938), 137–140

6. Merle Armitage, ed., *George Gershwin* (New York; Longmans, Green & CO, 1938), 13–14

7. Gerald Clarke, *Broadway Legends: George Gershwin: The Celebrated Composer's Manhattan Penthouse* (Architectural Digest, November 1995), 270

8. Merle Armitage, ed., *George Gershwin* (New York; Longmans, Green & CO, 1938), 210

9. "A Composer's Pictures" (Arts & Decoration, January, 1934)

10. "A Composer's Pictures" (Arts & Decoration, January, 1934)

Lovers of Art

1. Gerald Clarke, *Broadway Legends: George Gershwin: The Celebrated Composer's Manhattan Penthouse* (Architectural Digest, November 1995), 195

2. Don Rayno, *Paul Whiteman: Pioneer In American Music, Volume 2: 1930–1967* (Maryland; Scarecrow Press, Inc., 2013), 180–181

3. Robert Wyatt and Andrew Johnson, eds., *The George Gershwin Reader* (New York; Oxford University Press, Inc., 2004), 253

The Matrimonial Handicap

1. Gerald Clarke, *Broadway Legends: George Gershwin: The Celebrated Composer's Manhattan Penthouse*, Architectural Digest (November 1995), 193

2. David Ewen, *A Journey to Greatness: The Life and Music of George Gershwin* (New York; Henry Holt and Company, 1956), 176

3. David Ewen, *The Story of George Gershwin* (New York; Henry Holt And Company, New York, 1943, 1945), 116

4. Robert Kimball & Alfred Simon, *The Gershwins* (New York; Atheneum, 1973), 168

5. Bennett Cerf, *Try and Stop Me: A Collection of Anecdotes and Stories, Mostly Humorous* (New York; Simon and Schuster, 1944), 215

6. William G. Hyland, *George Gershwin: A New Biography* (Westport, Connecticut, Praeger, 2003), 103

7. David Ewen, *A Journey to Greatness: The Life and Music of George Gershwin* (New York; Henry Holt and Company, 1956), 178

8. Ira Gershwin, *Lyrics on Several Occasions* (New York; The Viking Press, 1959, 1979), 70

Drifting Along With The Tide

1. George Gershwin, The *Composer In the Machine Age*, appeared in Oliver M. Saylor, ed., *Revolt in the* Arts (Coward-McCann, Inc., 1933); reprinted in Merle Armitage, ed., *George Gershwin* (New York; Longsmans, Green & Co., 1938), 229

2. George Gershwin, The *Composer In the Machine Age*, appeared in Oliver M. Saylor, ed., *Revolt in the* Arts (Coward-McCann, Inc., 1933); reprinted in Merle Armitage, ed., *George Gershwin* (New York; Longsmans, Green & Co., 1938), 225–230

The Man I Love

1. John Longmire, *John Ireland: Portrait of a Friend* (London; John Baker, 1969), 51; Howard Pollack, *George Gershwin: His Life and Work* (Berkley; University of California Press, 2006), 138

2. Walter Rimler, *A Gershwin Companion: A Critical Inventory & Discography, 1916–1984* (Ann Arbor; Popular Culture, Inc., 1991), 118

3. Ira Gershwin, *Lyrics on Several Occasions* (The Viking Press, New York, 1959). (I used the 1973 version), p. 7

4. S. N. Behrman, *Profiles: Troubadour* (*The New Yorker*, May 25, 1929), 28

5. Deena Rosenberg, Fascinating Rhythm: The Collaboration of George and Ira Gershwin *(New York; Dutton Books, 1991)*, 70

Nice Work if You Can Get It

1. Oscar Levant, *The Memoirs of an Amnesiac* (Hollywood, CA, Samuel French, 1965), 130

2. "George Gershwin Accepts $100,000 Movietone Offer; Fox to Pay That Sum for Film Version of Musical Comedy—Composer Gets Bid of $50,000 for Rhapsody in Blue Rights" (New York Evening Post, August 14, 1928), 1–2; David Ewen, *A Journey to Greatness: The Life and Music of George Gershwin* (New York; Henry Holt and Company, 1956), 115; Isaac Goldberg, *George Gershwin: A Study in American Music* (New York: Fredrick Ungar Publishing CO., 1958), 22

3. *George Gershwin: A Study In American Music*, Isaac Goldberg, Frederick Ungar Publishing Co. New York, 1958 p. 22

4. Merle Armitage, ed., *George Gershwin* (New York; Longsmans, Green & Co., 1938), 116

If I Became President

1. Deena Rosenberg, *Fascinating Rhythm: The Collaboration of George and Ira Gershwin* (New York; Dutton Books, 1991), 203

2. William G. Hyland, *George Gershwin: A New Biography* (Westport, Connecticut; Praeger, 2003), 112

3. "Smith Far In Lead With Writers, Actors," (*Vanity Fair*, 1928); Robert Kimball & Alfred Simon, *The Gershwins* (New York; Atheneum, 1973), 105

An American in Paris

1. George Gershwin, Library of Congress; William G. Hyland, *George Gershwin: A New Biography*, Praeger, Westport, Connecticut, 2003, p. 125

2. George Gershwin, Library of Congress; William G. Hyland, *George Gershwin: A New Biography*, Praeger, Westport, Connecticut, 2003, p. 125

3. David Summers, Ruth O'Rourke-Jones, *Music: The Definitive Visual History* (New York; DK Publishing, 2013), 233

4. David Schiff, *Misunderstanding Gershwin*, The Atlantic Monthly, October 1998, p. 100; accessed online on 8/6/2014, http://www.theatlantic.com/past/docs/issues/98oct/gershwin.htm

5. Edward Jablonski and Lawrence D. Stewart, *The Gershwin Years* (Garden City, New York; Doubleday & Company, 1958, 1973), 110

6. Robert Kimball & Alfred Simon, *The Gershwins* (New York; Atheneum, 1973), 95

7. Howard Pollack, *George Gershwin: His Life and Work* (Berkeley; University of California Press, 2006), 431

8. Olin Downes, "Gershwin's New Score Acclaimed" (*New York Times*, December 14, 1928), 37; Reprinted in Robert Wyatt and John Andrew Johnson, eds, *The George Gershwin Reader* (Oxford/New York: Oxford University Press, 2004), 112

9. Ibid

10. Ibid

11. Olin Downes, "Gershwin's New Score Acclaimed," (*New York Times*, December 14, 1928), 37; Robert Wyatt and John Andrew Johnson eds., *The George Gershwin Reader* (Oxford/New York; Oxford University Press, 2004), 112–113

12. Isaac Goldberg, *George Gershwin, A Study in American Music* (New York; Frederick Ungar Publication Co., 1958), 238

An American in Paris—The Movie

1. Los Angeles Examiner, November 19, 1951; Donald Knox, *The Magic Factory: How MGM Made An American In Paris* (New York; Praegar Publishers, 1973), 183

2. Donald Knox, *The Magic Factory: How MGM Made An American In Paris* (New York; Praegar Publishers, 1973), 37

3. Donald Knox, *The Magic Factory: How MGM Made An American in Paris* (New York; Praegar Publishers, 1973), 44

4. Donald Knox, *The Magic Factory: How MGM Made An American in Paris* (New York; Praegar Publishers, 1973), 146

5. Donald Knox, *The Magic Factory: How MGM Made An American in Paris* (New York; Praegar Publishers, 1973), 147

6. New Statesman and Nation, August 18, 1951; Donald Knox, *The Magic Factory: How MGM Made An American in Paris* (New York; Praegar Publishers, 1973), 183

The Dybbuk

1. Howard Pollack, *George Gershwin: His Life and Work* (University of California Press, 2006), 776

2. *Plans to Quit Jazz in Order to Write Opera*, Geneva Daily Times, October 16, 1929, p. 1

3. *The New Yorker*, January 23, 1926, p. 22

4. Isaac Goldberg, *George Gershwin: A Study in American Music* (New York; Fredrick Unger Publishing CO. New York, 1958), 39–40; first published by Simon and Schuster, Inc. 1931

Strike Up the Band!

1. Quote, Serge Koussevitzky, 1938, Merle Armitage ed., *George Gershwin* (New York; Longsmans, Green & Co., 1938), 114

2. David Ewen, *A Journey to Greatness: The Life and Music of George Gershwin* (New York; Henry Holt and Company, 1956), 208–209

3. Isaac Goldberg, *George Gershwin: A Study in American Music* (New York; Fredrick Unger Publishing CO. New

York, 1958), 247; first published by Simon and Schuster, Inc. 1931

4. George Gershwin, *Our New National Anthem* (*Theatre Magazine*, May 1925), 30

Cuban Overture

1. Quote, George Gershwin, Edward Jablonski and Lawrence D. Stewart, *The Gershwin Years* (Garden City, New York; Doubleday & Company, Inc., 1958, 1973), 181–182

2. David Ewen, *A Journey to Greatness: The Life and Music of George Gershwin* (New York; Henry Holt and Company, New York, 1956), 182

3. Xavier Cugat, *Rumba Is My Life* (New York; Didier, Publishers, 1948), 123

4. Howard Pollack, *George Gershwin: His Life and Work* (Berkeley, University of California Press, 2006), 534–535

5. Isaac Goldberg, *George Gershwin: A Study in American Music* (New York; Fredrick Unger Publishing CO. New York, 1958), 309; first published by Simon and Schuster, Inc. 1931

6. Edward Jablonski and Lawrence D. Stewart, *The Gershwin Years* (Garden City, New York, Doubleday & Company, Inc., 1958, 1973), 183

7. Robert Kimball & Alfred Simon, *The Gershwins* (New York; Atheneum, 1973), xxxix

8. David Ewen, *A Journey to Greatness: The Life and Music of George Gershwin* (New York; Henry Holt and Company, 1956), 231

9. Ibid

10. Xavier Cugat, *Rumba Is My Life* (New York; Didier, Publishers, 1948), 123

11. David Ewen, *A Journey to Greatness: The Life and Music of George Gershwin* (New York; Henry Holt and Company, 1956), 244

Money, Money, Money

1. William G. Hyland, *George Gershwin: A New Biography* (Praeger, Westport, Connecticut, 2003), 140

Of Thee I Sing

1. William G. Hyland, *George Gershwin: A New Biography* (Praeger, Westport, Connecticut, 2003), 143

2. Ibid

I Got Rhythm

1. Rouben Mamoulian 1938 in Merle Armitage, ed., *George Gershwin* (New York; Longsmans, Green & Co., 1938), 54

2. Ethel Merman, *Who Could Ask for Anything More* (Garden City, New York; Doubleday & Co., 1955), 78–79

3. Larry Adler, *It Ain't Necessarily So* (Grove Press, 1984), 32

4. Richard Crawford, *The American Musical Landscape: The Business of Musicianship, From Billings to Gershwin* (Berkeley, Los Angeles; University of California Press, 1993, 2000), 226

5. Dizzy Gillespie with Al Fraser, *To Be, or Not . . . to Bop* (Garden City, New York; Doubleday and Company, 1979), 207

6. David Schiff, *Misunderstanding Gershwin* (*The Atlantic Monthly*, October 1998), 100–101

7. Quote—Dick Hyman; Deena Rosenberg, *Fascinating Rhythm: The Collaboration of George and Ira Gershwin* (New York; Dutton Books, 1991), 136

Variations on "I Got Rhythm"

1. Edward Jablonski and Lawrence D. Stewart, *The Gershwin Years* (Garden City, New York; Doubleday & Company, Inc., 1958, 1973), 369

George Gershwin's Song Book

1. Quote from *The New York Times*, *George Gershwin's Song Book* (New York; Simon And Schuster Inc., 1941, back of cover jacket

2. Quote from *The New York Times*, *George Gershwin's Song Book* (New York; Simon And Schuster Inc., 1941, back of cover jacket

3. George Gershwin, *George Gershwin's Songbook* (New York; Simon & Schuster, Inc, 1932 & 1941) Introduction by George Gershwin

Tune In (to Station J.O.Y.)

1. Quote by Harold Arlen 1937 in Merle Armitage, ed., *George Gershwin* (New York; Longsmans, Green & Co. London, 1938), 122

2. Edward Jablonski and Lawrence D. Stewart, *The Gershwin Years* (Garden City, New York; Doubleday & Company, Inc., 1958, 1973), 386

3. David Ewen, *A Journey to Greatness: The Life and Music*

of George Gershwin (New York; Henry Holt and Company, 1956), 249

4. John Dunning, *On The Air: The Encyclopedia of Old-Time Radio* (New York; Oxford University Press, 1998), 471

5. Robert Kimball & Alfred Simon, *The Gershwins* (New York; Atheneum, 1973), 167

6. Dubose Heyward, *Porgy and Bess Return on Wings of Song* (Stage, October, 1935); reprinted in Gregory R. Suriano, ed., *Gershwin in His Time: A Biographical Scrapbook, 1919–1937* (New York; Gramercy Books, 1998), 105

7. Robert Kimball & Alfred Simon, *The Gershwins* (New York; Atheneum, 1973), 171

8. Edward Jablonski and Lawrence D. Stewart, *The Gershwin Years* (Garden City, New York; Doubleday & Company, Inc., 1958, 1973), 387

I Loves You, Porgy

1. David Ewen, *A Journey to Greatness: The Life and Music of George Gershwin* (New York; Henry Holt and Company, 1956), 270

2. Isaac Goldberg, *George Gershwin: A Study in American Music* (New York; Fredrick Unger Publishing CO. New York, 1958), 273; first published by Simon and Schuster, Inc. 1931

3. Edward Jablonski and Lawrence D. Stewart, *The Gershwin Years* (Garden City, New York; Doubleday & Company, Inc., 1958, 1973), 233

4. David Ewen, *A Journey to Greatness: The Life and Music of George Gershwin* (New York; Henry Holt and Company, 1956), 257

5. Isaac Goldberg, *George Gershwin: A Study in American Music* (New York; Fredrick Unger Publishing CO. New York, 1958), 322; first published by Simon and Schuster, Inc. 1931

6. Henry O. Osgood, *So This Is Jazz* (Boston; Little, Brown, And Company, 1926), 61–62; William Francis Allen, Charles Pickward, Lucy McKim Garrison, eds., *Slave Songs of the United States* (New York; A. Simpson & CO., 1867)

7. Henry O. Osgood, *So This Is Jazz* (Boston; Little, Brown, And Company, 1926), 62

8. Dubose Heyward, *Porgy and Bess Return on Wings of Song* (Stage, October 1935); reprint edited by Gregory R. Suriano, *Gershwin In His Time: A Biographical Scrapbook, 1919–1937* (New York; Gramercy Books, 1998), 105–106

9. Maurice Peress, *Dvo?ák to Duke Ellington: A Conductor Explores America's Music and Its African American Roots* (Oxford, New York; Oxford University Press, 2004), 71

10. Isaac Goldberg, *George Gershwin: A Study in American Music* (New York; Fredrick Unger Publishing CO. New York, 1958), 325; first published by Simon and Schuster, Inc. 1931

11. Robert Kimball & Alfred Simon, *The Gershwins* (New York; Atheneum, 1973), 179

12. David Ewen, *A Journey to Greatness: The Life and Music of George Gershwin* (New York; Henry Holt and Company, 1956), 262–263

13. David Ewen, *A Journey to Greatness: The Life and Music of George Gershwin* (New York; Henry Holt and Company, 1956), 267–268

14. J. Rosamond Johnson 1938 in: Merle Armitage ed., *George Gershwin* (New York; Longsmans, Green & Co. London, 1938), 65

15. Isaac Goldberg, *George Gershwin: A Study in American Music* (New York; Fredrick Unger Publishing CO. New York, 1958), 327; first published by Simon and Schuster, Inc. 1931

16. Joan Peyser, *The Memory of All That: The Life of George Gershwin* New York; Simon & Schuster, 1993), 248

17. Foster Hirsch, *Kurt Weill On Stage: From Berlin to Broadway* (New York; Alfred A. Knopf, 2002), 42

18. George Gershwin, *Rhapsody in Catfish Row* (*New York Times*, October 20, 1935); reprint edited by Gregory R. Suriano, *Gershwin in His Time: A Biographical Scrapbook, 1919–1937* (New York; Gramercy Books, 1998), 112 & 114

19. George Gershwin, *Rhapsody In Catfish Row* (*New York Times*, October 20, 1935); reprint edited by Gregory R. Suriano, *Gershwin In His Time: A Biographical Scrapbook, 1919–1937* (New York; Gramercy Books, 1998), 112

20. Isaac Goldberg, *Score by George Gershwin* (Stage, December 1935), 38

21. Isaac Goldberg, *Score by George Gershwin* (Stage, December 1935), 36

22. Edward Murrow, *Duke Ellington on Gershwin's 'Porgy'* (New Theatre, December 1935), 5–6; reprinted in Mark Tucker, ed., *The Duke Ellington Reader* (New York; Oxford University Press, 1993), 115

23. Richard Mack, *Duke Ellington—In Person* (*Orchestra World*, May 1936; reprinted in Mark Tucker, ed., *The Duke Ellington Reader* (New York; Oxford University Press, 1993), 114–118

24. Duke Ellington, *Music Is My Mistress* (New York; Doubleday, 1973), 104; Robert Wyatt and John Andrew Johnson, eds., *The George Gershwin Reader* (New York; Oxford University Press, 2004), 301

25. Oscar Levant, *Variations on a Gershwin Theme* (*Town and Country*, November, 1936); Robert Wyatt and John Andrew Johnson, eds., *The George Gershwin Reader* (New York; Oxford University Press, 2004), 17

26. Isaac Goldberg, *George Gershwin: A Study in American Music* (New York; Fredrick Ungar Publishing CO., 1938, 1958), 333

27. Quote by Rouben Mamoulian in Merle Armitage, ed., *George Gershwin* (New York; Longsmans, Green & Co., 1938), 51

The Senatorial Roll Call

1. *Gershwin Goes Political After Chats With Rivera* (*New York Post*, December 17, 1935; Howard Pollack, *George Gershwin; His Life and Work* (Berkeley and Los Angeles; University of California Press, 2006), 209; Edward Jablonski and Lawrence D. Stewart, *The Gershwin Years* (Garden City, New York; Doubleday & Company, Inc., 1958, 1973), 242

2. *Gershwin Goes Political After Chats With Rivera* (*New York Post*, December 17, 1935; Howard Pollack, *George Gershwin; His Life and Work* (Berkeley and Los Angeles; University of California Press, 2006), 209; Edward Jablonski and Lawrence D. Stewart, *The Gershwin Years* (Garden City, New York; Doubleday & Company, Inc., 1958, 1973), 242–244

(I've Got) Beginner's Luck

1. William G. Hyland, *George Gershwin: A New Biography* (Westport, Connecticut; Praeger, 2003), 191

2. William G. Hyland, *George Gershwin: A New Biography* (Westport, Connecticut; Praeger, 2003), 191

What Causes That?

1. Isaac Goldberg, *George Gershwin, A Study in American Music* (New York; Frederick Ungar Publishing Co., 1958), 23

2. Isaac Goldberg, *George Gershwin, A Study in American Music* (New York; Frederick Ungar Publishing Co., 1958), 23–24

3. Edward Jablonski and Lawrence D. Stewart, *The Gershwin Years* (Garden City, New York; Doubleday & Company, Inc., 1958, 1973), 273

4. Isaac Goldberg, *George Gershwin, A Study in American Music* (New York; Frederick Ungar Publishing Co., 1958), 347

5. Oscar Levant, *A Smattering of Ignorance* (Garden City, New York; Garden City Publishing CO., INC., 1942), 198–199

6. Robert Kimball & Alfred Simon, *The Gershwins* (New York; Atheneum, 1973), 226–227

7. William Howard Hay, M.D., *Health via Food* (East Aurora, New York; Sun-Diet Health Service, 1929, 1932), 14

8. Larry Adler, *It Ain't Necessarily So* (New York; Grove Press, 1984), 91

9. Fred Astaire, *Steps In Time* (New York; Harper & Brothers, 1959, itbooks, 2008), 229

10. Edward Jablonski and Lawrence D. Stewart, *The Gershwin Years* (Garden City, New York; Doubleday & Company, Inc., 1958, 1973), 292

11. Michael Feinstein, *Nice Work If You Can Get It: My Life in Rhythm and Rhyme* (New York; Hyperion, 1995), 71

12. Robert Kimball & Alfred Simon, *The Gershwins* (New York; Atheneum, 1973), 216

13. Edward Jablonski and Lawrence D. Stewart, *The Gershwin Years* (Garden City, New York; Doubleday & Company, Inc., 1958, 1973), 262–263

14. David Ewen, *A Journey to Greatness: The Life and Music of George Gershwin* (New York; Henry Holt and Company, 1956), 294

15. http://articles.latimes.com/2002/feb/04/news/mn-26284

I'll Build a Stairway to Paradise

1. David Ewen, *A Journey to Greatness: The Life and Music of George Gershwin* (New York; Henry Holt and Company, 1956), 305

2. Larry Adler, *It Ain't Necessarily So* (New York; Grove Press, 1984), 65

3. Quote Eva Gauthier, David Ewen, *Men of Popular Music* (Chicago-New York; Ziff-Davis Publishing Company, 1944), 141

I Found a Four Leaf Clover

1. Deena Rosenberg, *Fascinating Rhythm: The Collaboration of George and Ira Gershwin* (New York; Dutton Books, 1991), 122

2. "*Gershwin Left $341,089 Estate to His Mother; 'Rhapsody In Blue' Appraised at 'Greatest Value' and Opera Rights of 'Nominal Interest' to the Residue* (New York Herald Tribune, September 27, 1938) Files from the Wattenburg firm are in DLC (GC). Robert Wyatt and John Andrew Johnson, eds., *The George Gershwin Reader* (New York; Oxford University Press, 2004), 280

3. "*Gershwin Left $341,089 Estate to His Mother; 'Rhapsody In Blue' Appraised at 'Greatest Value' and Opera Rights of 'Nominal Interest' to the Residue* (New York Herald Tribune, September 27, 1938) Files from the Wattenburg firm are in DLC (GC). Robert Wyatt and John Andrew Johnson, eds., *The George Gershwin Reader* (New York; Oxford University Press, 2004), 281

4. Maureen Paton, *Method in the rhythm madness* (The Telegraph, February 19, 2002); Accessed on the internet http://www.telegraph.co.uk/culture/music/classicalmusic/3573332/Method-in-the-rhythm-madness.html

5. David Ewen, *A Journey to Greatness: The Life and Music of George Gershwin* (New York; Henry Holt and Company, 1956), 18

They Can't Take That Away From Me

1. Eriq Gardner, *Warner Music Sued for Millions by George Gershwin Heirs* (Billboard, January 15, 2013) Accessed on the Internet: http://www.billboard.com/biz/articles/news/legal-and-management/1488288/warner-music-sued-for-millions-by-george-gershwin

Overflow

1. Stephanie Cohen, *A New Push for Old Chestnuts* (The Wall Street Journal, May 31, 2013), D5

Boy Wanted

1. Alan Gershwin, *I Am George Gershwin's Illegitimate Son* (Confidential, February, 1959), 11–13 & 45–46

Do It Again!

1. Tim Page, *Broadway Song Trove Tops Original Hopes* (The New York Times, March 10, 1987) Accessed on the Internet: http://www.nytimes.com/1987/03/10/arts/broadway-song-trove-tops-original-hopes.html

2. Ibid

3. Ibid

Love Is Here to Stay

1. Frances Gershwin Godowsky, *George Gershwin Was My Brother* (Reader's Digest Music Guide, November 1962), 4; Robert Wyatt and John Andrew Johnson, eds., *The George Gershwin Reader* (New York; Oxford University Press, 2004), 4

2. George Gershwin, *Jazz Is the Voice of the American Soul* (Theatre Magazine, June 1926); Robert Wyatt and John Andrew Johnson, eds., *The George Gershwin Reader* (New York; Oxford University Press, 2004), 92–94

3. George Gershwin, *Does Jazz Belong to Art* (Singing, July 1926), 14; Robert Wyatt and John Andrew Johnson, eds., *The George Gershwin Reader* (New York; Oxford University Press, 2004), 98

4. George Gershwin, *Jazz Is the Voice of the American Soul* (Theatre Magazine, June 1926); Robert Wyatt and John Andrew Johnson, eds., *The George Gershwin Reader* (New York; Oxford University Press, 2004), 92–94

5. Oscar Levant, *Variations on a Gershwin Theme* (Town and Country, November 1939), 84; Robert Wyatt and John Andrew Johnson, eds., *The George Gershwin Reader* (New York; Oxford University Press, 2004), 19

6. George Gershwin, *Does Jazz Belong to Art* (Singing, July 1926), 14; Robert Wyatt and John Andrew Johnson, eds., *The George Gershwin Reader* (New York; Oxford University Press, 2004), 97

7. Samuel Chotzinoff, "*New York Symphony at Carnegie Hall* (New York World, December 4, 1925), 16; Robert Wyatt and John Andrew Johnson, eds., *The George Gershwin Reader* (New York; Oxford University Press, 2004), 83

Bibliography

Adler, Larry. *It Ain't Necessarily So*. New York: Grove Press, 1984.

Aebersold, Jamey. *Nothin' But Blues*. New Albany, Indiana: Jamey Aebersold Jazz, INC., 2nd Revised Edition, 1981.

Allen, William Francis, Charles Pickard Ware, Lucy McKim Garrison (compiled by). *Slave Songs of the United States*. Bedford, Massachusetts: Applewood Books, 1867.

Ambinder, Marc, D. B. Grady. *Deep State: Inside the Government Secrecy Industry*. Hoboken: John Wiley & Sons, Inc., 2013.

Armitage, Merle. *George Gershwin: Man and Legend*. New York: Duell, Sloan and Pearce, 1958.

Armitage, Merle. *George Gershwin*. New York: Longmans, Green & CO, 1938.

Armstrong, Louis, Edited by Thomas Brothers. *Louis Armstrong, In His Own Words*. New York: Oxford University Press, 1999.

Astaire, Fred. *Steps in Time*. New York: Harper & Brothers, 1959.

Baldwin, James. *Notes of a Native Son*. New York: Dial Press, 1963.

Bernstein, Leonard. *The Joy of Music*. New York: Simon and Schuster, 1959.

Brackman, Dr. Harold. *Let's Face the Music and Dance: African Americans, Jews, and the Creation of Modern Popular Music*. The Simon Weisenthal Center, October 2010.

Brown, James. *James Brown: The Godfather of Soul*. New York:Thunder Mouth Press, 1986, Reprinted Macmillan Publishing Company 1997.

Callahan, John F., ed. *The Collected Essays of Ralph Ellison*. Modern Library Paperback Edition, 2003.

Carr, Roy. *A Century of Jazz*. London: Hamlyn, 1997.

Carruth, Hayden. *Sitting In*. Iowa City: University of Iowa Press, 1986.

Cassidy, Donna M. *Painting the Musical City: Jazz and Cultural Identity in American Art, 1910–1940*. Washington: Smithsonian Institution Press, 1997.

Cerf, Bennett. *Try and Stop Me: A Collection of Anecdotes and Stories, Mostly Humorous*. New York: Simon and Schuster, 1944.

Clarke, Gerald. *Broadway Legends: George Gershwin: The Celebrated Composer's Manhattan Penthouse*, Architectural Digest, November 1995.

Coker, Jerry. *Improvising Jazz*. Englewood Cliffs, N. J.: Prentice-Hall, Inc., 1964.

Coker, Jerry. *Listening to Jazz*. Englewood Cliffs, N.J.:Prentice-Hall, INC, 1978.

Crow, Bill. *Jazz Anecdotes*. New York—Oxford: Oxford University Press, 1990.

Cugat, Xavier. *Rumba Is My Life*. New York: Didier Publishers, 1948.

Davis, Miles with Quincy Troupe. *Miles: The Autobiography*. New York: Touchstone, Simon & Schuster, Inc., 1989.

Dexter, Dave. *Jazz Cavalcade: The Inside Story of Jazz.* New York: Criterion, 1946.

Dunning, John. *On the Air: The Encyclopedia of Old-Time Radio.* Oxford University Press, 1998.

Ellington, Duke. *Music Is My Mistress.* New York: Da Capo Press, 1976.

Ewen, David. *A Journey to Greatness: The Life and Music of George Gershwin.* New York: Henry Holt and Company, 1956.

Ewen, David. *Men of Popular Music.* Chicago-New York: Ziff-Davis Publishing Company, 1944.

Ewen, David. *Panorama of American Popular Music: The Story of Our National Ballads and Folk Songs, the Songs of Tin Pan Alley, Broadway, and Hollywood, New Orleans Jazz, Swing, and Symphonic Jazz.* Englewood Cliffs, N.J.: Prentice-Hall, 1957.

Ewen, David. *The Story of George Gershwin.* New York: Henry Holt and Company, 1945.

Feather, Leonard. *The Book of Jazz.* New York: Horizon Press, 1957.

Feather, Leonard. *The New Edition of the Encyclopedia of Jazz.* New York: Bonanza Books, 1960.

Feinstein, Michael. *Nice Work if You Can Get It: My Life in Rhythm and Rhyme.* New York: Hyperion, 1995.

Fordham, John. *Jazz.* London-New York: Dorling Kindersley, 1993.

Gershwin, George. *George Gershwin's Songbook.* New York: Simon & Schuster, Inc., 1932.

Gershwin, Ira. *Lyrics on Several Occasions.* New York: The Viking Press, 1959.

Gilbert, Steven E. *The Music of Gershwin.* New Haven: Yale University Press, 1995.

Gillespie, Dizzy with Al Fraser. *To Be, or Not . . . To Bop.* Minneapolis: Doubleday Books, 1979.

Goldberg, Isaac. *George Gershwin: A Study in American Music.* New York: Fredrick Ungar Publishing, 1958.

Goldberg, Isaac. *Tin Pan Alley, A Chronicle of the American Popular Music Racket.* New York: The John Day Company, 1930.

Handy, W. C. ed. *Blues: An Anthology.* New York: Albert & Charles Boni, Inc., 1926, 1949.

Handy, W. C. *Father of the Blues.* New York: Macillian, 1941.

Hentoff, Nat. *Jazz Is.* New York: A Ridge Press Book, Random House, 1976.

Hirsch, Foster. *Kurt Weill on Stage: From Berlin to Broadway.* New York: Alfred A. Knopf, 2002.

Hyland, William G. *George Gershwin: A New Biography.* Westport, Connecticut: Praeger, 2003.

Jablonski, Edward, Lawrence D. Stewart. *The Gershwin Years.* Garden City, New York: Doubleday & Compay, 1958, 1973.

Johnson, Carl, curator. *Paul Whiteman: A Chronology (1890–1967).* Williamstown, MA: The Whiteman Collection, 1977.

Keepnews, Orrin and Bill Grauer, Jr. *A Pictorial History of Jazz, People and Places from New Orleans to Modern Jazz.* New York: Crown Publishers, Inc., 1955.

Kimbal, Robert, Alfred Simon. *The Gershwins.* New York: Atheneum, New York. 1973.

Knox, Donald. *The Magic Factory: How MGM Made An American in Paris.* New York: Praegar Publishers, 1973.

Koenig, Karl, ed. *Jazz in Print (1856–1929): An Anthology of Selected Early Readings in Jazz History.* Hillsdale, New York: Pendragon Press, Hillsdale, 2002.

Lees, Gene. *Cats of Any Color: Jazz Black and White.* New York: Da Capo Press, 1995.

Lees, Gene. *Jazz Lives.* Buffalo, New York: Firefly Books, 1992.

Levant, Oscar. *A Smattering of Ignorance.* Garden City, New York: Garden City Publishing Co., Inc., 1942.

Locke, Alain, ed. *The New Negro.* New York: Albert and Charles Boni, 1925.

Lomax, Alan. *Mister Jelly Roll: The Fortunes of Jelly Roll Morton, New Orleans Creole and "Inventor of Jazz."* New York: Duell, Sloan and Pearce, 1950.

McRae, Barry. *Dizzy Gillespie: His Life & Times.* New York: Universe Books, 1988.

Melnic, Jeffrey. *The Right to Sing the Blues: African Americans, Jews, and American Popular Song*. Cambridge: Harvard University Press, 1999.

Merman, Ethel. *Who Could Ask for Anything More*. New York: Doubleday & Co., 1955.

Osgood, Henry O. *So This Is Jazz*. Boston: Little, Brown, and Company, 1926.

Panassie, Hugues. *Hot Jazz: The Guide to Swing Music*. New York: M. Witmark & Sons, 1936.

Peress, Maurice. *Dvorak to Duke Ellington: A Conductor Explores America's Music and its African American Roots*. New York: Oxford University Press, 2004.

Peyser, Joan. *The Memory of All That: The Life of George Gershwin*. New York: Simon & Schuster, 1993.

Pollack, Howard. *George Gershwin: His Life and Work*. Berekely: University of California Press, 2006.

Pratt, Waldo Seldon and Charles N. Boyd, eds. *Grove's Dictionary of Music and Musicians*. New York: The Macmillan Company, 1920.

Rayno, Don. *Paul Whiteman: Pioneer in American Music*. U.K.: Scarecrow Press, Inc., 2003.

Reisner, Robert George. *Bird: The Legend of Charlie Parker*. New York: Citadel Press, 1962.

Rimler, Walter. *A Gershwin Companion: A Critical Inventory & Discography, 1916–1984*. Ann Arbor, MI: Popular Culture, Inc., 1991.

Rogin, Michael. *Blackface, White Noise: Jewish Immigrants in the Hollywood Melting Pot*. Oakland, CA: Univ. of California Press, 1996.

Rosenberg, Deena. *Fascinating Rhythm: The Collaboration of George and Ira Gershwin*. New York: Dutton Books, 1991.

Sanborn, Larry M. *Musicianship for the Jazz Performer*, a dissertation submitted in partial satisfaction of the requirements for the degree Doctor of Philosophy in Music: Jazz Studies, May 1992.

Sanborn, Larry M. *The Chordal Evolution of the American Jazz Art Form: The Twelve Bar Blues*, 1992.

Schiff, David. *Gershwin: Rhapsody in Blue*. Cambridge: Cambridge University Press, 1997.

Schuller, Gunther. *Early Jazz: Its Roots and Musical Development*. New York: Oxford University Press, 1968.

Seldes, Gilbert. *The 7 Lively Arts*. New York: Harper & Brothers Publishers, 1924.

Shapiro, Nat & Nat Hentoff, eds. *Hear Me Talkin' to Ya: The Story of Jazz as Told by the Men Who Made It*. New York: Dover Publications, Inc., 1966.

Shaw, Arnold. *Honkers and Shouters: The Golden Years of Rhythm and Blues*. New York: Collier Books, 1978.

Sheed, Wilfred. *The House That George Built*. New York: Random House, 2008.

Sidran, Ben. *Talking Jazz: An Illustrated Oral History*. San Francisco: Pomegranate Artbooks, 1992.

Smith, Charles Edward with Fredric Ramsey, Jr., Charles Payne Rogers and William Russell. *The Jazz Record Book*. New York: Smith & Durrell, 1943.

Southern, Eileen. *The Music of Black America*, 1st ed. New York: W. W. Norton, 1971.

Summers, David and Ruth O'Rourke-Jones, eds. *Music: The Definitive Visual History*. London-New York: Dorling Kindersley, 2013.

Suriano, Gregory R. *Gershwin in His Time: A Biographical Scrapbook, 1919–1937*. New York: Gramercy Books, 1998.

Teachout, Terry. *Pops: A Life of Louis Armstrong*. Boston: Houghton Mifflin Harcourt, 2009.

Tucker, Mark, ed. *The Duke Ellington Reader*. New York: Oxford University Press, 1993.

Whiteman, Paul and Mary Margaret McBride. *Jazz*. New York: J. H. Sears & Company, Inc., 1926.

Wilder, Alec, edited by James T. Maher. *American Popular Song: The Great Innovators, 1900–1950*. New York: Oxford University Press, 1972.

Williams, Martin. *Where's the Melody? A Listener's Introduction to Jazz*. New York: Pantheon Books, 1966.

Wyatt, Robert, John Andrew Johnson. *The George Gershwin Reader*. New York: Oxford University Press, 2004.

Index

A

"Aaron Copland and His Jazz" (Goldberg), 88
"Abi Gezunt," 24
Abramson, Max, 110
Academy Awards, 217, 231
Adams, John, 10
"Adams and Liberty," 10
Adderley, Cannonball, 24
Adler, Larry, 156, 237–238, 263
Adventures of Tom Sawyer, The (Twain), 20
Aeolian Company, 112–113, 114, 132
Aeolian Hall, 132, 157
 Éva Gauthier's concert, 126, 132–134
 Whiteman's modern music concert. See *Experiment in Modern Music, An* (concert).
Afro-Americans. See Blacks.
Agar-agar, 180
"Ain't We Got Fun," 49
"Alexander's Ragtime Band," 56, 59, 149–150
Alexandria Hotel, Los Angeles, 94
"All Coons Look Alike to Me," 39
Allen, William Francis, 249
Alvin Theatre, New York, 251
Ambassador Billiards Parlor, New York, 136
Ambassador Hotel, Atlantic City, 94
American Academy in Rome, 157
American Cancer Society, 264
American Federation of Musicians, 26, 40
American in Paris, An, 170, 185, 194, 213–216, 246, 271
 critical reception of, 215–216
American in Paris, An (movie), 126, 216, 217–219
 ballet, 217, 218
American National Association of Dance Masters, 75–76
American Popular Song (Wilder), 41–42, 94
American Rhapsody. See *Rhapsody in Blue*.
American Society of Composers, Authors and Publishers (ASCAP), 56, 137, 257, 272
American Telephone and Telegraph, 245
"America the Beautiful," 66
Ammons, Albert, 62
Amsterdam News, The, 23
"Anacreon in Heaven," 10
Anderson Galleries, 137
Andrew Sisters, 63
Anksy, S., 221
Antheil, George, 85, 87–88
"Anthropology," 238
Anti-Saloon League, 74
Anti-Semitism, 25–26, 53–54, 57, 59, 251–252, 258, 260
Apollo Theater, New York, 49
Arlen, Harold, 238, 245, 246, 263
Armitage, Merle, 5, 77, 106, 173, 194
Armstrong, Louis "Satchmo," 33, 34, 35, 37, 43–46, 47, 81, 94
 racial issues and, 44–45, 75
 relations with Jews, 43–44
 relationship with Karnofsky family, 43–44
Art collections, 193–198
Arthur Gershwin Testamentary Trust, 275
Arthur Pryor Band, 123
Arts Club of Chicago, 193
ASCAP. See American Society of Composers, Authors and Publishers (ASCAP).
Astaire, Adele, 110, 172, 205, 211
Astaire, Fred, 110, 172, 205, 211, 259, 263
Atkinson, Brooks, 251
Auld, George, 27
Avenue de la Grand Armée, Paris, 214
Azpiazu, Don, 226

B

B. F. Keith's Theatre, Washington, D.C., 211
"Baby Seal Blues," 69–70
Bacall, Lauren, 257
Baker, Josephine, 125
Baldwin, James, 25
Ball, Lucille, 257
Ballard, Hank, 56
Balliett, Whitney, 84
Bands
 black, 26–27
 marching, 32
 orchestrated jazz, 93–94
Banjos, 20
Barney Greengrass, New York, 190
Barnum, P. T., 20
"Barnyard Blues," 146, 146
Baron Wilkins Club, New York, 130
Bartók, Béla, 132
Basie, Count, 27
Basin Street, New Orleans, 32–33

310

"Basin Street Blues," 33
Bass lines, 62
Bauzá, Mario, 17
"Be Yourself," 117
Beaven, A. W., 76
Bebop, 17
Bechet, Sidney, 33
Behrman, Martin, 33
Behrman, S. N., 121, 182, 183, 190, 207
Beiderbecke, Bix, 95
Believe It or Not (radio broadcast), 38
Belinni, Vincenzo, 132
Bell, Clive, 84
Bellson, Louis, 27
Benchley, Robert C., 211
Benny, Jack, 245
Benny Goodman Trio, 191
Benton, Thomas, 198
Berkeley Square Orchestra, 205
Berlin, Irving, 55, 56, 57, 59–60, 82, 85, 88, 132, 136, 146, 149–150, 238, 257
  George Gershwin and, 59, 60, 127, 149–150, 169
Berliner, Emile, 78
Bernie, Ben, 70
Bernstein, Leonard, 156, 163
Bertholoff, William Henry Joseph Berthol Bonaparte. *See* Smith, Willie "The Lion."
Bertrand, Jimmy, 68
Bessie Blood's House of Fame, New York, 123
Bigard, Barney, 33–34
Billings, William, 9
Birth of Rhapsody in Blue, The (album), 157
Black Sabbath: the Secret Musical History of Black-Jewish Relations (album), 24
Blackface, 19–20, 22–23, 123, 125–126, 248
Blacks, 16, 19–21
  Christianity and, 16, 29
  relations with Jews, 17, 22–27, 44, 53–54, 62
  stereotypes, 19, 21
"Blah-Blah-Blah," 232
Blake, Eubie, 42, 61, 110, 125
Bland, James A., 21
Bloomer Deussen, Nancy, 200, 279
Blue Monday, 123, 125–126, 136, 246

Blue notes, 66, 67, 70, 73
"Blue Washboard Stomp," 68
Blues, 21, 23, 65–70, 72, 140
  Concerto in F and, 167
  criticisms of, 69
  definition, 148
  origin of the term, 65
Blues: An Anthology (Handy), 69–70
"Bluetooth Blues," 68
Bogart, Humphrey, 31, 257
Bolden, Buddy "King," 33
Boogaloo (dance), 56
Boogie-woogie, 62–63
"Boogie Woogie Bugle Boy from Company B, The," 63
Boomer, Lucius, 226
Boston Symphony Orchestra, 233
Botkin, Henry, 185, 193, 194, 245, 249
Bott, Fenton T., 75
Bowery Theatre, New York, 19
Braggiotti, Mario, 214
"Bring Along Your Dancing Shoes," 114
"Broadway At Home" (article), 184
"Broadway Song Trove Tops Original Hopes" (article), 282
Bronson, Charles, 185
Brooklyn Academy of Music, 241
"Brother, Can You Spare a Dime," 229
Brothers Gershwin, 114, 117, 118–119, 230, 231, 259
Brown, Anne, 255
Brown, Eugene. *See* Hamid, Sufi Abdul.
Brown, James, 24–25
Brown, Jasbo, 85
Brown, John Mason, 251
Brubeck, Dave, 35, 86
Bruce, Lenny, 26
Buchanan, Charles L., 169
Buck, Gene, 257
Buck Privates (movie), 63
Bunny Hug, The (dance), 56
Burleigh, Harry T., 62
Burlesque, 21
Busse, Henry, 95, 145

C

Caesar, Irving, 109, 122–123
Cakewalk (dance), 39, 40
Callender, Red, 33

Calloway, Cab, 24
"Camptown Races," 20
Cantor, Eddie, 21, 211
Carey, Mutt, 43
Carlisle, Kitty, 199–200
Carmichael, Hoagy, 238
Carnegie Hall, 126, 129, 157, 166, 215, 239
  programs, 128–129, 157, 165
"Carnival of Venice," 149
"Carolina Shout," 73
Caron, Leslie, 216, 219
Carroll, John, 194
Carruth, Hayden, 67, 86
"Carry Me Back to Old Virginny," 21
Carter, Benny, 219
Casablanca (movie), 31
Catlett, Walter, 118
Celesta, 214
Cell phones, 264
Cerf, Bennett, 177, 200, 226
Cézanne, Paul, 193
Chagall, Marc, 193, 195, 198
Chaloff, Serge, 27
Champs-Élysées, Paris, 215
"Chansonsette," 150
Chaplin, Charlie, 94, 200, 211
Charles, Ray, 25, 66, 69
"Charleston," 61, 73
Charleston, South Carolina, 248
"Charleston Rag," 42
"Chasin' the Bird," 238
Checker, Chubby, 56
"Chester," 9
Chicago (dance), 76
Chicago, Illinois, 33, 45, 47
Chicago Tribune, 76
Child, Calvin, 94
Chords, 156, 238–239
  blues, 66
Chotzinof, Samuel, 168, 287
Christensen, Axel, 40–41
Christensen School of Popular Music, 41
Christianity, 16, 29
Christy, Edwin Pearce, 19–20
Christy's Minstrels, 20, 122
Civil Rights Act of 1964, 4
Civil Rights Movement, 54, 255
Clarinets, 150, 155, 158–162
Clef Club Orchestra, 129
Club Ebony, New York, 52
Coates, Albert, 169

Cohan, George M., 268
"Cohen Owes Me 97 Dollars," 23
Coker, Jerry, 86
Coleman, Ornette, 69
Colonel Lagg's Great Empire Show, 117
Colored Waifs' Home, New Orleans, 43, 45
Colored Waifs' Home for Boys Band, 45
Coltrane, John, 79, 89
Columbia Records, 22, 25–26, 78
Columbia Street Theatre, Cincinnati, 19
Committee for the First Amendment, 257
Communities
  black, 14–15, 52
  Gullah, 245, 248–249
"Composer In the Machine Age, The" (Gershwin), 203, 204
"Composer's Pictures, A" (article), 193, 195
Compositions, performers relationship to, 86
Concerto in F, 95, 133, 164, 165–170, 182, 217, 218, 246, 271
  critical reception of, 168
Concertos, 166
Confrey, Zez, 42, 146, 149, 153
Congo Square, New Orleans, 32
Connie's Inn, New York, 52
Continental Airlines, 164
Contrafact, 15, 238
Coolidge, Calvin, 211
Coots, J. Fred, 238
Copland, Aaron, 41, 82, 88, 252
Coppicus, F. C., 157
Copyright, 257
Cotton Club, The, New York, 49, 52
Cotton Club Orchestra, 254
"Cotton Tail," 238
Covarrubias, Miguel, 191, 197–198, 274
Coward, Henry, 77
Coward, Noel, 238
Crawford, Richard, 238
"Crazy Blues," 73
"Creole Love Song," 254
Creoles, 37
Crosby, Bing, 21, 96
Crosley, Lewis, 265
Crosley, Powel, 265

Crosley Radio Company, 265
Crosley Xervac, 265–266
Crow Jim policy, 27
Crowninshield, Frank, 144
Crump, Edward "Boss," 72
Cuban Love Song, The (movie), 226
Cuban Overture, 170, 225–228
CuBop, 17
Cueto, Andre Alexis, 264–265
Cugat, Xavier, 226, 227–228
"Cult of Jazz," (Thomson), 154
Cultures
  African, 17
  Afro-Cuban, 17
  black, 14–15, 52
  Gullah, 245, 248–249
"Current Opinions," 160
Curtis, King, 103

D

"Dallas," 70
Daly, William, 167, 183
Damrosch, Walter, 133, 144, 153, 165, 167, 168, 174, 215, 245
Damsel in Distress, A (movie), 263
Dance, 14–15, 17, 32, 49, 52, 56, 62
  Cuban, 226, 227
  public, 75–76
  ring shouts, 249–250
  See also specific styles and names.
Dandy, Walter, 264
Danish Royal Opera, Copenhagen, 255
"Das Pintele Yud," 114
Davening minyan, 250
Davis, Benny, 238
Davis, Miles, 25–26, 89, 206
Davis, Peter, 45
"Daybreak Express," 254
Death Wish (movie), 185
Debussy, Claude, 214
Delicious (movie), 209, 231–232
"Delishious," 232
DeMille, Cecil B., 94, 211
Denver Symphony Orchestra, 91
Derain, André, 193
DeSylva, Buddy, 125, 136
"Detrimental Effects of Jazz on Our Younger Generation" (Guilliams), 76-77
Deussen, Nancy Bloomer. *See* Bloomer Deussen, Nancy.
Dexter's Blues (album), 69

Dickie Wells' Shim Shammers, 253
Dictionary of Modern English, 84
"Dixie Jass Band One-Step," 34, 52
"Dizzy Atmosphere," 238
"Do It Again," 133
Dodds, Johnny, 33, 68
"Does Jazz Put the Sin in Syncopation?" (Faulkner), 74
"Don't Worry, Be Happy," 68
Donaldson, Will, 114
Dorset, Edmund, 145–146
Dorsey, Jimmy, 245
Dorsey, Tommy, 245
Downes, Olin, 146, 153–154, 161, 215, 251
Dresser, Louise, 211
Dreyfus, Louis, 256
Dreyfus, Max, 111, 206
Drummers, 130
Drumming, 16, 17
Du Bois, W. E. B., 23, 25, 52, 54
"Duke Ellington–In Person" (Mack), 253
"Duke Ellington on Gershwin's *Porgy*" (interview), 252–254
Duke Ellington Reader, The (Tucker), 254
Duncan, Todd, 250–251, 254, 255
"Dunkin' Bagel," 24
Durante, Jimmy "The Great Schnozzola," 254
Dutch West India Company, 14
Dybbuk, The, 221–222
Dybbuk, The, or Between Two Worlds (story), 221
Dybbuks, 221

E

East Aurora Sun and Diet Sanatorium, The, 180–181
East New York, Brooklyn, 51, 102
"Easter Parade," 60
Edison, Thomas, 78, 84
Education, 52
Edwards, Gus, 238
18th Amendment. *See* Prohibiton.
Ellington, Duke, 27, 34, 35, 37, 52, 62, 84–85, 89, 94, 156, 163, 238, 239, 254
  interview on *Porgy and Bess,* 252–254
  on Paul Whiteman, 93
Ellis, Mary, 222

Ellison, Ralph, 25
Elman, Mischa, 188
"Embraceable You," 188
Enemas, 181
"Entertainer, The," 39, 42
"Eretz Zavat Chalav," 24
Erlebach, Rudolph O., 113
Ernst, Hugh C., 146
Europe, James Reece, 129, 130
Eveready Hour, The (radio program), 245
Ewen, David, 104, 155, 172, 179, 192, 201, 228, 265–266, 272
Exhibition of Advertising Art, 198
Experiment in Modern Music, An (concert), 34, 42, 114, 134, 144–151
  audience, 144
  critical reception of, 153–157
  introductory lecture, 146
  orchestra, 145, 148
  program, 146–151, 155
  ticket prices, 144–145
Eybeschutz, Jonathan, 221

F

Fain, Sammy, 238
"Farewell to Storyville," 34
Farrell, Charles, 231–232
"Fascinating Rhythm," 172, 242
Fascinating Rhythm (Rosenberg), 191, 206, 211
Fasting, 181
Faulkner, Anne Shaw, 74–75
Feather, Leonard, 83, 155, 239
Feen-A-Mint, 246
Fiber, 180
Fiddler on the Roof, 24
Fiedler, Arthur, 163
Fiedler, Leslie, 25
Fields, W. C., 123
Fillmore, Millard, 181
Fillmore East Auditorium, New York, 103
Film Booking Offices of America (FBO), 259
Finck, Henry T., 154
"Fine and Dandy," 201
"Fine Clothes to the Jew" (poem), 25
Fisher-Price, 181
Fisk Jubilee Singers, 29, 30
Fisk University, 29
Fitzgerald, F. Scott, 49

Flatiron Building, New York, 55
"Flintstones Theme," 238
Folly Island, South Carolina, 249
Fonda, Henry, 257
Ford, Edsel, 187
Ford, Henry, 26, 57
Forsyth, Cecil, 161
Foster, Stephen, 20, 122, 137
Fox City Theatre, New York, 111
Fox Movietone Company, 209, 231
Fox-trot (dance), 56
Frances Gershwin Godowsky Revocable Trust, The, 273–274
Francesconi, Gino, 130, 157, 165
Francis, Arthur. *See* Gershwin, Ira.
Franklin, Aretha, 23–24
Freed, Arthur, 218
Frequency hopping, 88
Frey, Jacques, 214
"Frog-I-More-Rag," 42
Funk, 65
Funny Face, 170

G

Gable, Betty, 202
Gabriel, Gilbert W., 154
Galli-Curci, Amelita, 144
Garland, Judy, 21
Garland, Robert, 251
Garrison, Lucy McKim, 249
Garvey, Marcus, 53–54
Gaskill, Clarence, 24
Gauguin, Paul, 193, 198
Gauthier, Éva, 126, 130, 132–134, 268
Gaynor, Janet, 231, 233
Gee, Mathew, Jr., 239
Geller, Herb, 239
General Federation of Women's Clubs, 77
George Gershwin (Armitage), 5, 77, 106
George Gershwin: A New Biography (Hyland), 160–161, 211, 213, 230
George Gershwin: A Study in American Music (Goldberg), 70, 100, 175, 184, 222, 223–224, 261
George Gershwin: His Life and Work (Pollack), 214 "George Gershwin and Jazz" (Newell), 176
George Gershwin Family Trust, 273
George Gershwin Junior High School, Brooklyn, 225, 268–269

George Gershwin Theatre, Brooklyn College, Brooklyn, 268
George Gershwin Way, New York, 269
George Gershwin's Song Book (Gershwin), 188, 242–243
George White's Scandals, 123
George White's Scandals of 1922, 123, 125, 136
George White's Scandals of 1924, 164, 170
"Georgia on My Mind," 66, 69
Gerber, Isaac, 162
Gerber, Julie, 103, 162, 200, 225, 269, 286
Gerber, Richard, 204
Gerber, Richie, 181, 286
  Bill Graham incident, 103
  Prospect Park tree and, 103
Gerber-Gershwin New York Challenge, 269–270
Gershwin, Adam, 273–274
Gershwin, Alan, 200, 277
Gershwin, Arthur, 100, 116, 120, 271
Gershwin, Frances, 100, 116, 120, 163, 179, 271, 285
Gershwin, George, 88, 247, 284, 285, 287
  accompanist at Éva Gauthier concert, 130, 132–134
  art collection, 185, 193–198
  baldness, 264–266
  birth, 51, 100
  black musicians and, 62, 110, 123, 126–127, 130, 191
  brain tumor, 262–264
  Broadway shows, 110, 115, 114, 119, 137, 138, 151, 164, 170
  cause of death, 263–266, 268
  childhood, 100–104, 171
  children (illegitimate), 200, 277–279
  cigar smoking and, 173, 180, 189
  on composing, 138–139, 171
  conducting, 223–224
  constipation and, 179–180, 181, 261
  Covarrubias caricature of, 191
  Covarrubias *Rhapsody in Blue* painting and, 197–198
  dancing and, 172
  death, 264
  debut on concert stage, 133

diet, 179–181
drive/energy, 166, 172
education, 102, 107
on Ethel Merman's singing, 237
first concert piece, 106
first music memory, 104, 112
first published song, 110, 114
friendship with Astaires, 109–110, 172, 259, 263
funeral, 62, 268
generosity, 210
health, 179–180, 203–204, 261–266
Havana trip, 226
headaches, 262
homes (California), 191–192, 198, 231
homes (New York), 101, 102, 103–104, 182–183, 184–185, 188, 193, 195, 226
honoring memory of, 268–270
improvisation and, 139, 151, 156, 241, 242, 243, 284
Irving Berlin and, 59, 60, 127, 149–150, 169
insecurity, 166, 200
instruments and, 106
James Reece Europe's influence on, 130
jazz, views on, 82, 83, 139, 286
jazz contributions, 239
job cutting piano rolls, 111, 112, 123
job as song plugger, 109–111
job as staff composer at Harms, 111
jobs as pianist, 111, 130, 132–133
on listening, 105–106, 286–287
living/working conditions, 182
"lost" songs, 202, 281
memory lapses, 262
Mexico trip, 257
movie deals, 259–260
music, views on, 100, 203–204, 286
music theory training, 106, 228
music training, 175, 286
as musical bridge, 85, 287
musical output, 170
NBC contract, 157
neck cracking, 174
Newsweek cover, 118
notebooks of, 106–107, 161, 171, 228, 248–249
operas, 123, 125–127, 170, 220–222, 247–256
orchestration and, 166
painting/drawing and, 186, 192, 194–195
Paris trip, 213–14
parties and, 175, 177, 187–189, 190–192
personality, 171–177, 189, 192, 200
piano playing at parties, 187, 188–189, 190, 191, 201, 251
piano roll compositions, 113
piano roll duets, 113
piano rollography, 114–115
piano technique, 109, 134, 151, 241, 242–243, 262
piano training, 104–107
politics, 211–212, 257–258
Portrait of Grandfather (painting) and, 198
on process of songwriting/composing, 117, 119, 175–176, 224, 228
psychoanalytic treatment, 180
pseudonyms, 113
radio program, 207, 241, 245–246
relationship with Ira, 118, 119, 120, 184–186, 241
relationship with parents, 120, 122, 181, 182–183, 188–189, 199
relationships with women, 185, 199–200, 277
rights and management of musical estate, 273, 275
sense of humor, 174
sense of smell, 262, 263
songwriting, 59, 60, 137, 171, 206, 259, 260, 272
spinal tap, refusal of, 262–263
sports and, 172, 179, 184, 261–262
symptoms of illness, 262–264
Tin Pan Alley, views on, 55, 56
tours, 157
wealth, 209–210, 230, 271–272, 273–274
Gershwin, George, musical works
American in Paris, An, 170, 177, 185, 194, 213–216, 246, 271
"Blah-Blah-Blah," 232
Blue Monday, 123, 125–126, 136, 248
Concerto in F, 95, 133, 164, 165–170, 182, 217, 218, 246, 271
Cuban Overture, 170, 225–228
Delicious, 209, 286
"Delishious," 232
"Do It Again," 133
"Embraceable You," 188
"Fascinating Rhythm," 242
Funny Face, 170
Girl Crazy, 170, 237
"I Got Plenty o' Nuttin'," 170, 255
"I Got Rhythm," 156, 191, 217, 237–238, 242, 272
"I'll Build a Stairway to Paradise," 126, 133, 136, 137, 219, 242
"Illegitimate Daughter," 279
"I'm Goin' South in the Mornin'," 126
"Innocent Ingénue Baby," 133, 217
"It Ain't Necessarily So," 170, 255
Lady Be Good!, 110, 114, 164, 170, 205
Let 'Em Eat Cake, 212, 228, 235
"Liza," 177, 191
"Love Is Here to Stay," 284
"Man I Love, The," 205–207, 242, 245
"Mine," 228
"Mischa, Jascha, Toscha, Sascha," 188, 232
"Nice Work if You Can Get It!," 209, 217
Of Thee I Sing, 119, 170, 212, 235, 271, 279
Oh, Kay!, 201
"Oh, Lady Be Good!," 242
135th Street, 126
Pardon My English, 281
Porgy and Bess, 123, 127, 170, 202, 228, 246, 247–256
Preludes for Piano, 170
Primrose, 164, 170, 281
"Real American Folk Song (Is a Rag)," 117
Rhapsody in Blue, 42, 62, 94, 96, 97, 114, 135, 138–142, 150–164, 170, 191, 206–207, 246, 253, 268, 271, 272, 286
"Rialto Ripples," 114
Rosalie, 170, 205
"'S Wonderful," 217, 242
Second Rhapsody, 170, 232, 233–234
Show Girl, 170, 177, 254
"Sing of Spring," 175
"Somebody Loves Me," 242

Someone to Watch Over Me, 170, 201
Strike Up the Band, 170, 177, 205, 206, 212
"Summertime," 170, 175, 249, 255
"Swanee," 22, 23–24, 114, 122–124, 133, 137, 182, 242
"Sweet and Lowdown," 114
Sweet Little Devil, 137, 138, 151, 170
Tell Me More, 170
Tip-Toes, 115, 164, 170, 281
"That Certain Feeling," 115
"Typical Self-Made American, A," 171
"Variations on 'I Got Rhythm'," 228, 241
"Waiting For the Sun to Come Out," 114
Welcome to the Melting Pot, 232, 286
"When You Want 'Em, You Can't Get 'Em, When You Got 'Em, You Don't Want 'Em," 110, 122
"Who Cares," 242
"Will You Remember Me?," 270
"Woman Is a Sometime Thing, A" 202
Gershwin, George, written works
"Composer in the Machine Age, The," 203, 204
George Gershwin's Song Book, 242–243
"Jazz Is the Voice of the American Soul," 139
"Making Music," 117, 141
"Rhapsody in Catfish Row," 252
Singing (magazine), letter in, 140
Gershwin, Ira, 100, 102, 103, 116–119, 136, 137, 141–142, 165, 169, 175, 184, 192, 194, 201, 213, 227, 241, 228, 271, 271
American In Paris, An (movie), 217, 218
bar mitzvah, 116
on glissando, 161
jobs, 116–117
Lyrics on Several Occasions, 118, 206
politics, 257
on process of songwriting/lyric writing, 116, 117, 118, 119
Pulitzer prize, 119, 170, 212, 235

relationship with George, 118, 119, 120, 184–186
pseudonyms, 114, 117
wit, 118–119
Gershwin, Ira, musical works
"Be Yourself," 117
Lady Be Good!, 110, 114
Of Thee I Sing, 119
"Real American Folk Song (Is a Rag)," 117
"'S Wonderful," 118, 119, 217
"Sweet and Lowdown," 114
"Sunny Disposish," 118, 119
Tip-Toes, 115
"That Certain Feeling," 115
"Waiting For the Sun to Come Out," 114
Gershwin, Leonore (Strunsky), 183, 184, 192
Gershwin, Marc George, 274, 275
Gershwin, Morris, 100, 120–121, 142, 153, 188–189, 233, 235
occupations of, 104, 173
Gershwin, Rose (Bruskin), 100, 107, 120–121, 139, 181, 187, 199, 271
Gershwin, Todd, 273–274
Gershwin: Rhapsody in Blue (Schiff), 167, 206
"Gershwin and Musical Snobbery" (Buchanan), 169
Gershwin Estate, 163, 217, 254, 271–272
lawsuits, 273–274
wealth, 271–272, 273–274
Gershwin Family Trust, 274
Gershwin Publishing Corporation, 256
Gershwin Theatre, New York, 270
Gershwin *vs* Gershwin, 273–274
Gershwin *vs* Warner Music, 273
Gershwin Years, The (Jablonski and Stewart), 117, 245, 265
Gershwins, The (Kimball and Simon), 103, 113–115, 140
Gilbert, Steven E., 138
Gillespie, Dizzy, 17–18, 87, 149, 206, 238
Gilman, Lawrence, 153, 154, 168
Gimbel, Adam, 226
Girl Crazy, 170, 237
Gish, Lillian, 265
Glaenzer, Jules, 144, 187, 188

Glaser, Joe, 45
Glissando, 141, 145, 150, 158
Gluck, Alma, 136
"Go Down, Moses," 17, 29
"God Bless America," 60
"God Save the King," 9
Goddard, Paulette, 200
Godowsky, Leopold, 120, 191
Godowsky, Leopold, Jr., 120, 163
Godowsky family, 272
Goldberg, Isaac, 41, 70, 72, 82, 88, 100, 175, 184, 222, 223–224, 252, 261
Goldberg, Rube, 211
Goldmark, Rubin, 106
Goodman, Benny, 26, 237
Gorham, Joseph K., 34
Gorman, Ross, 145, 149, 151, 153
Rhapsody in Blue and, 141, 150, 158–162
"Gott un Sein Mishpet Is Gerecht," 114
Graham, Bill, 103
Grainger, Percy, 205
Gramophone Company, 78
Grand Canyon Suite (Grofé), 96
Grant, Percy Stickney, 76
Grant, Ulysses S., 30
Grauer, Bill, 87
Great Depression, 229, 231
Great Gatsby, The (movie), 49
Green, Johnny, 238
Green Cat, New York, 52
Grizzly Bear (dance), 56
Grofé, Ferde, 94, 96, 149, 174
orchestration of *Rhapsody in Blue,* 139–140
"Groovin' High," 149
Gruenberg, Louis, 82
Guilliams, A. E., 76-77
Gullahs, 245, 248–249

H

"Hallelujah Chorus" (Handel), 148
Ham fat, 19
"Ham-fat Man, The," 19
Hambitzer, Charles, 105–106, 109
Hambone. See Human body, as instrument.
Hamid, Sufi Abdul, 54
Hammond, Johnny, 239
Handel, George Frideric, 148
Handy, Charles, 73

Handy, W. C., 38, 41, 69–70, 72–73, 85, 190, 238, 268
　on the blues, 65, 71
Handy Bros., 73
Hannenfeldt, Zenna, 198
Harburg, Yip, 229, 263
Harlem, New York, 51, 52, 54
Harlem Renaissance, 49, 52
Harmonicas, 156
Harmony, 46, 239
Hart, Charles, 126
Hart, Moss, 184
Hay, William Howard, 180, 263
Hay Diet, 181
Health foods movement, 181
Health via Food (Hay), 180, 263
"Hearts of Oak," 9
Heifetz, Jascha, 136, 144, 188, 200
Heifetz, Pauline, 201
Henderson, Fletcher, 52, 94, 167
Henderson, W. J., 153, 160
Henry, Patrick, 10
Herbert, Victor, 56, 136, 137, 145, 146, 150, 153, 281
Herman, Woody, 33
Hernan, John, 94
Heschel, Abraham Joshua, 54
Hess, Cliff, 113
Heyward, Dorothy, 248, 254
Heyward, DuBose, 173, 246, 248, 254
Heyward, Janie, 248
Higgins, Eddie, 18, 130
High School of Commerce, New York, 107
Hill, Edward Burlingame, 137
"Hindustan," 122
Hines, Earl "Fatha," 190
Hodeir, Andre, 46
Hogan, Ernest, 39
Holiday, Billie, 24, 26, 33, 35, 87, 206
Hollywood Ten, 257
Hollywood Walk of Fame, 163
Holmes, Oliver Wendell, 56
Honkers and Screamers (album), 69
Hootchy-kootchy. *See* Sex.
Hooties' Blues (album), 69
Hoover, Herbert, 211–212
Horns (taxi), 214
Hosier, Harry "Black Harry," 12
Hot Jazz (Panassié), 169
Hotel Almendares, Havana, 227

House That George Built, The (Sheed), 88
Hudson River, 215
Hughes, Langston, 25, 52
Hughes, Spike, 156
Human body, as instrument, 68
Hunter, Alberta, 24, 70
Hunter, Laura, 37
Hurst, Fannie, 144
Hutcheson, Ernest, 106
Hyland, William, 160–161, 211, 213, 230
Hyman, Dick, 160, 239

I

"I Am George Gershwin's Illegitimate Son" (A. Gershwin), 277
"I Got Plenty o' Nuttin'," 170, 255
"I Got Rhythm," 156, 191, 217, 237–238, 242, 272
　chords, 238–239
"I Love You," 149
"I'll Build a Stairway to Paradise," 126, 133, 136, 137, 217, 218, 242
"I'm Goin' South in the Mornin'," 126
"I'm Just Wild About Harry," 125
"Ich Hob Dich Tzufil Lieba," 24
"Illegitimate Daughter," 279
Imagen Music Group, 275
Improvisation, 3, 45, 62, 78–79, 81, 86–87, 92, 139, 151, 156, 239, 241, 242, 243, 286
"In God we trust," (motto) 9
Individualism, 3, 286
"Innocent Ingénue Baby," 133
Instruments, 68, 106
　See also specific types.
International Jew (Ford), 57
"Invitation to the Blues," 120
Ireland, John, 205
Irving, Washington, 65–66
"It Ain't Necessarily So," 170, 255
It Ain't Necessarily So (Adler), 237–238, 263
"It Don't Mean a Thing (If It Ain't Got That Swing)," 89
Ives, Charles, 239

J

Jablonski, Edward, 117, 245, 265
Jackson, Jesse, 53

Jacob, 11–12
Jacob, Max, 198
Jacobs, Everett, 226
Jacobsen, Sascha, 188
Jasmine, 85
Jay McShann Orchestra, 69
Jazz, 3, 15, 26, 34, 71, 81–89, 140, 144, 156, 168, 285–287
　birth of, 32–35, 82
　chords, 66, 156, 238–239
　campaigns against, 74–77
　Chicago and, 33, 45, 47
　conducting and, 224
　definitions, 81–89
　first stage concert, 132–134
　first concerto, 167
　first published song, 37–38
　first piano solo record, 73
　first recording, 34, 52
　Gershwin and, 239
　history, 17, 32–35, 37–38, 74–77, 155–156
　Jews and, 23, 88
　New Orleans and, 32–35, 83
　New York City and, 47, 49–50
　operas, 125–127, 170, 220–222, 247–256
　orchestrations of, 93, 139–140, 167
　origin of term/use of the term, 5, 74, 81–82, 85
　performance, 86–87
　symphonic, 93, 140–141, 155–156, 163, 169, 213, 241
　See also specific styles.
Jazz: Its Evolution and Essence (Hodeir), 46
Jazz Age, The, 49, 77
"Jazz Fiddler, The," (article), 161
Jazz Is the Voice of the American Soul" (Gershwin), 139
"Jazz Singer, The," 23
Jazz Singer, The (movie), 22, 23, 154, 231, 281
Jefferson, Thomas, 10, 12
"Jelly Roll Blues," 37
Jerome H. Remick & Company, 109–110, 114, 282
Jethro Tull (musical group), 15
Jewface, 22–23
"Jewish Jazz–Moron Music–Becomes Our National Anthem" (Ford), 26, 57
Jews, 102

relations with blacks, 17, 22–27, 44, 53–54, 62, 255
stereotypes, 23
Johnson, Eldridge R., 78
Johnson, J. Rosamond, 251
Johnson, James P., 61, 73, 110, 167, 191
Johnson, James Weldon, 249–250
Johnson, Pete, 62
Johnson, Rahassan, 164
Johnson brothers, 190
Jolson, Al, 21, 22, 23, 114, 123, 248
Jones, Spike, 68
Joplin, Scott, 39
Journey to Greatness (Ewen), 104, 155, 172, 179, 192, 201, 228, 265–266, 272
Jubilee, 29–30
"Jump Jim Crow," 19
Jungle, The, New York, 52
"Junk Man Rag," 42

K

Kahn, Gus, 114
Kahn, Otto H., 144, 187, 248
Kandinsky, Wassily, 193
"Kangaroo Hop," 114
Karnofsky, Alex, 43
Karnofsky, Morris, 43
Karnofsky family, 43–44
Kaufman, George S., 235
Kaufman, S. Jay, 144
Keeler, Ruby, 254
Keepnews, Orrin, 87
Keith-Albee-Orpheum (KAO), 259
Kelly, Gene, 216, 217, 218
Kennedy, Joseph F., 259–260
Kennedy, Joseph F., Jr., 260
Keppard, Freddie "King," 33, 34
Kern, Jerome, 82, 127, 132, 175, 238, 281
Key, Francis Scott, 10
Kid Ory's Jazz Band, 45
Kilenyi, Edward, 106, 161, 223
Kimball, Robert, 103, 113–115, 140, 282
King of Jazz (movie), 96–97, 209
Kirk, Rahsaan Roland, 15
Kitt, Eartha, 24
"Kitten on the Keys," 42, 149
Klee, Paul, 193
Knopf, Alfred, 187
Knox, Donald, 217–218

"Kol Nidre," 24
Koussevitsky, Serge, 223, 234, 251
Krehbiel, Henry E., 5
Krupa, Gene, 237

L

La Guardia, Fiorello, 268
Laban, 11
Lady Be Good!, 110, 164, 170, 205
Lady Day. *See* Holliday, Billie.
Lafayette Baths, New York, 104, 116
"Lafcadio Hearn and Congo Music" (Krehbiel), 5
Lamarr, Hedy, 87–88
LaMothe, Ferdinand Joseph. *See* Morton, Jelly Roll.
Land of the Blacks. *See* Washington Square Park, New York.
Land, ownership of, 14
Lane, Burton, 238
Lantz, Walter, 97
LaRocca, Nick, 51, 146
Laws, Jim Crow, 19, 26, 51, 75
Léger, Fernand, 193
Lenox Hill, New York, 185–186
Leo Reisman Orchestra, 157
Let 'Em Eat Cake, 212, 228, 235
Levant, Oscar, 118, 163, 174–175, 176, 179–180, 186, 190, 191, 200, 209, 217, 218, 219, 254, 262
Lewis, Meade "Lux," 34, 62
Lewisohn Stadium, New York, 223, 227
"Liberty Song, The," 9
Liebling, Leonard, 136, 144, 215–216
"Lilliputian Musicians, The" (article), 16
"Limehouse Blues," 149
Lining out, 12
Liszt, Franz, 210
"Livery Stable Blues," 34, 51, 52, 141, 146, 147, 157
"Liza," 177, 191
Lloyd, Harold, 94
Loft, George W., Mrs., 76
Lopez, Vincent, 134, 136
Los Angeles Symphony Orchestra, 96
"Love Is Here to Stay," 285
Lower East Side, New York, 51, 59, 102
Ludwig, John M., 282
"Lullaby for String Quartet," 106
Lulu White's, New Orleans, 37

Lyons, Arthur, 259
Lyrics, 9, 10, 72, 116, 118
Lyrics on Several Occasions (I. Gershwin), 118, 206

M

M. Witmark & Sons, 282
Macedonia Church, South Carolina, 249
Mack, Richard, 253
Madame White's Mahogany Hall, New Orleans, 33
Magic Factory, The (Knox), 217–218
Mahara's Colored Minstrels, 72
Mahesh Yogi, Maharishi, 204
"Mahogany Hall Stomp," 33
Majestic Hotel, Paris, 213
Majestic Theatre, New York, 255
"Making Music" (article), 141
"Mama Loves Papa," 148
Mamoulian, Rouben, 174, 188, 251, 253, 256
"Man I Love, The," 205–207, 242, 245
Manhattan, purchase of, 14
Manners, Margaret, 277
"Maple Leaf Rag," 39, 42
Mardi Gras, 32
Margin call, 229
"Marie from Sunny Italy," 59
Marijuana, 46
Marsalis, Wynton, 26
Mary, Queen, 76
Marx, Chico, 111
Marx, Groucho, 257
Mashed Potato Time (dance), 56
Mason, J. W. T., 148
Mathis, Johnny, 24
May, Earl Chapin, 161
McFerrin, Bobby, 68
McGlinn, John, 282
McHugh, Jimmy, 238
McMahon, John R., 75
Medicine
alternative, 180–181, 203–204
quack, 264–266
Melnick, Jeffrey, 26
Melody, 3, 10, 46, 60, 78–79, 86, 92, 238
Melody (magazine), 88
"Melody in F," 104, 112
Memory of All That, The (Peyser), 277–278, 279

"Memphis Blues," 70, 72, 85
Mencken, H. L., 211
Menéndez, Nilo, 226
Meredith, Burgess, 200
Merman, Ethel, 237
Messiah (Handel), 148
"Method in the Rhythm Madness" (Paton), 272
Metropolitan Music Bureau, 157
Metropolitan Opera Company, 220, 221, 222, 248
Metropolitan Opera House, 137, 227
Meyer, Sam, 87
Midnighters, The, 56
Milhaud, Darius, 132
Millay, Edna St. Vincent, 211
Miller, Betty Kern, 282
Miller, Glenn, 163, 237
Miller, Marilyn, 205
Mills, Irving, 24, 89
Mills Artists, 253
"Mine," 228
Minelli, Vincente, 217
Minstrel shows, 19–21
Minton's Playhouse, New York, 49
Minuit, Peter, 14
"Mischa, Jascha, Toscha, Sascha," 188, 189, 232
"Misunderstanding Gershwin" (Schiff), 213, 239
Moderwell, Kelly, 132
"Modest Proposal, A" (Moderwell), 132
Modigliani, Amedeo, 193, 198
Monk, Thelonious, 88
Monkey (dance), 56
Montgomery, Michael, 114–115
"Moose the Mooche," 238
Morrow, Edward, 252–254
Morton, Jelly Roll, 21, 33, 37, 42
Mosbacher, Emil, 226, 241
Moscow Art Theatre, 185
Moskowitz, Henry, 54
Mottos, 9
Mountbatten, Lady, 206
"Mr. Crump," 72–73
Mr. Jelly Lord. *See* Morton, Jelly Roll.
Mr. Whiteman and the Fox Trot (Dorset), 145–146
Mueller, Paul, 265
Murphy, Jeannette Robinson, 42
Music, 40, 66, 87, 92
  ability to read, 60, 93, 109, 129
  African, 12, 16–17, 21, 40, 67, 83
  African-American/black, 26, 40, 42, 67–68, 82, 128–130, 252
  Afro-Cuban, 17, 226–227
  American, 9–10, 12, 14–15, 20–21, 22, 60, 70, 77, 82, 85, 132, 136, 150, 169, 227, 252, 286
  cantorial, 23, 24, 59
  classical, 85, 86, 166, 239
  dance, 39–42
  European, 67
  folk, 83
  Klezmer, 159, 160
  Latin, 17
  New Orleans and, 32–35
  New York City and, 49–50
  popular, 26, 40–42, 55–56, 82
  rights to, 56, 70, 72–73
  Yiddish, 102–103, 114, 159, 160
Music By Gershwin (radio program), 207, 241, 245–246
Music Is My Mistress (Ellington), 254
Music of Gershwin, The (Gilbert), 138
Music School Settlement for Colored People, 129
Musical Courier (magazine), 40
Musical quotation, 133
Musicals, Yiddish, 102
Musicians Symphony Orchestra, 227
"My Yiddishe Momme," 24

N

NAACP (National Association for the Advancement of Colored People), 54
Naguchi, Isamu, 185, 195
Nast, Condé, 187
National Theatre, Washington, D.C., 254–255
Native Americans, 14
NBC, 157
Negro Drawings (Covarrubias), 197
Nest, The, New York, 52
New Christy Minstrels, 20
New Edition of the Encyclopedia of Jazz (Feather), 155, 239
New England Psalm Singer, The (Billings), 9
New Negro, The, 52, 85
New Negro Movement. *See* Harlem Renaissance.
New Orleans, Louisiana, 32–35
New Orleans—The All-Musical Tribute to the Birth of Jazz 1947 (movie), 33
New World Music Corporation, 164
New World Publishing Company, 256
New York City, 51, 49–50
New York City Ballet, 216
New York Herald Tribune, 136, 271
New York Symphony Orchestra, 164, 165–166, 215
New York Times, 41, 75, 76, 126, 242, 268, 282
New Yorker, The, 106–107, 121, 182, 183, 188, 189, 206, 222
Newell, George, 111, 176
Newman, Ernest, 140
Newport Jazz Festival, Rhode Island, 15
Newsweek, 118
"Nice Work if You Can Get It!," 209, 217
"Nickel in the Slot," 149
Nigger Mike's, New York, 59
Nightclubs, 52
Niles, Abbe, 69
Noone, Jimmy, 33
Notes, flattened, 66
Notes on the State of Virginia (Jefferson), 12
"Now's the Time," 60
Nudity, 181

O

O'Hara, John, 268
O'Hare International Airport, 164
Of Thee I Sing, 119, 212, 235, 271, 279
Offbeats, 39
"Oh! Susanna," 20
"Oh, Dem Golden Slippers," 21
Oh, Kay!, 201
"Oh, Lady Be Good!," 242
Okeh Records, 73
"Old Black Joe," 20
"Oleo," 238
Oliver, Joseph "King," 33, 45
Olympics (1964), 163
Omnibook (Parker), 238
135th Street, 126
"Orange Blossoms In California," 149, 150

Original Dixieland Jass Band, The, 34, 51–52, 146
Ory, Kid, 33, 45
"Oscar for Treadwell, An," 238
Osgood, Henry O., 84, 101, 154, 160

P

Pace, Harry, 73
Pace & Handy, 73
Paine, Robert Treat, 10
Palais Royal, New York, 94, 142
"Pale Moon," 150
Paley, Emily, 261
Panassié, Hugo, 169
Pardon My English, 281
Parker, Charlie "Bird," 17, 35, 69, 87, 238
Parker, Henry Taylor, 133, 134
Parties
   Gershwin and, 175, 177, 187–189, 190–192, 201, 251
   integrated, 190
   rent, 50
Pascin, 194, 198
Paton, Maureen, 272
Paul Whiteman and His Ambassador Orchestra, 96, 149
Paul Whiteman and His Palais Royal Orchestra, 94, 145, 148
Paul Whiteman Archives, 162
Paul Whiteman Orchestra, 94, 96, 97, 126, 136, 140
"Peanut Vendor, The," 226
Pelham, George F., 185
Pennsylvania Orchestra, 137
Percussion instruments, 226, 227
Peress, Maurice, 66, 146, 149, 150, 155, 157, 250
   re-creation of *Experiment in Modern Music* concert, 157
Perfection Studios, East Orange, New Jersey, 112
Peyser, Herbert, 216
Peyser, Joan, 277–278, 279
Piano playing, 61–63, 242–243
   boogie-woogie, 62–63
   ragtime, 39–42, 59, 60
   stride, 61–62
"Piano-Rag-Music," 42
Piano rolls, 111, 112, 113
Pianos, 39, 55, 56, 113
   player. *See* Player pianos.
Picasso, Pablo, 193, 198

"Pine Top's Boogie Woogie," 62
Pingatore, Mike, 145
Pitch, 66, 85
Plato, 40
Player pianos, 104, 111, 112–113
Pogroms, 59
Pollack, Howard, 214
Pollock, Muriel, 113
"Pomp and Circumstance," 151, 157
Porgy (Heyward), 248
Porgy and Bess, 123, 127, 170, 202, 228, 245, 247–256
   critical reception of, 251–254, 255
   Nazis and, 255
Portamento. *See* Glissando.
Porter, Cole, 211, 281
"Portrait of the Lion," 62
Pozo, Chano, 17
Prayers, 250
Prelude in C-sharp Minor (Rachmaninoff), 149
Preludes for Piano, 170
Presley, Elvis, 275
Presley, Gladys Love, 275
"Pretty Girl Is Like a Melody, A," 149, 150
"Primitive Savage Animalism, Preacher's Analysis of Jazz" (Beaven), 76
Primrose, 164, 170, 281
Prince of Wales and Other Famous Americans (Covarrubias), 191
"Profiles: Troubador" (article), 188
Prohibition, 47, 52, 74
Prospect Park, Brooklyn, 103
Prostitution and prostitutes, 32–33, 84
Publishing, music, 55–57, 69–70, 109, 110
Pulitzer Prize, 119, 163, 170, 235

R

Rachael, 11
Rachmaninoff, Sergei, 136, 144, 149, 185
Racial barriers, 26, 51
Racial issues, 4, 22–27, 44–45, 53–54, 57
Racism, 4–5, 19, 22–27, 37, 39, 57, 84
Radiation, electromagnetic, 264
Radio Corporation of America (RCA), 259

Radio shows, 207, 241, 245–246
Radiofrequency energy, 264
"Raggedy Ann," 149
Ragtime, 39–42, 59, 60, 66, 96, 132, 150
   protests against, 40–41
"Ragtime," (article), 41
Rainey, Ma, 21
Raphaelson, Samson, 23
Ravel, Maurice, 132, 213, 239
Ray, Man, 181
"Real American Folk Song (Is a Rag)," 117
Record industry, 78–79
Records, 78–79
   first blues by a black singer, 73
   jazz, 81, 146
   race, 68
   Rhapsody in Blue, 157, 164
   sales, 52, 122, 206
"Red Cross," 238
Red light districts, 32–33
Redman, Don, 26
Reisenweber's, New York, 51
Reisman Symphonic Orchestra, 241
Religion
   Afro-Brazilian, 17
   African, 17
   African-American, 26
   Christianity, 16, 29
Remick, Jerome, 109
Renoir, Jean, 193
Republic, The (Plato), 40
Revel, Harry, 238
Rhapsodies, 138
Rhapsody in Black and Blue, A (movie short), 34
Rhapsody in Blue, 114–115, 138–142, 150–164, 170, 191, 206–207, 246, 253, 268, 271, 272, 286
   clarinet glissando, 158–162
   creation of, 135, 138–142
   critical reception of, 153–157
   improvisation and, 139, 151, 156
   orchestration of, 139
   piano rolls of, 157, 163
   première, 42, 62, 150–151
   recording of, 157
   rehearsals for, 94, 142
   right to use in *King of Jazz,* 96, 209
   sheet music sales and licensing rights, 157, 163–164
   titling, 140

United Airlines' use of, 163–164
Rhapsody in Blue (painting)
 (Covarrubias), 197–198
"Rhapsody in Catfish Row"
 (Gershwin), 252
Rhythm, 16, 17, 37, 39–40, 46, 60,
 83, 93, 141, 168, 250, 287
 Caribbean, 37
 Charleston, 167
 Cuban, 226
 Habanera, 37, 73
 ragged, 39
"Rialto Ripples," 114
Rice, Thomas D., 19
"Richmond, Blues, The," 69
Riddell, John, 211
Right to Sing the Blues, A (Melnick),
 26
Rimsky-Korsakov, Nikolai, 133
Ring shouts, 249–250
Rivera, Diego, 257
Riverboats, 33
RKO Pictures, 259
Roach, Max, 238
Roaring Twenties, 49–50, 155, 159
Roberts, Luckey, 42, 61, 110
Robeson, Paul, 25, 125, 190
Rocca, Lodovico, 222
Rodgers, Richard, 184, 189, 238
Rogers, Ginger, 237, 259
Romberg, Sigmund, 238
Roosevelt, Theodore, 51
Rosalie, 170, 205
Roseland Ballroom, New York, 94
Rosen, Jody, 23
Rosenberg, Deena, 191, 206, 211
Rosenfeld, Monroe H., 55
Rosenfeld, Paul, 155
Roth, Murray, 110
Rouault, Georges, 193, 194
Rough Riders, 51
Rousseau, Henri, 193, 198
Roxy Orchestra and Chorus, 96
Roxy Theatre, New York, 96
Rubinstein, Anton, 104, 112
Rubinstein, Beryl, 127
Ruby, Harry, 192
Rue George Gershwin, Paris, 269
Rumba, 226–227
Rumba Is My Life (Cugat), 226,
 227–228
Rumshinsky, Joseph, 102
Runnin' Wild, 61

"Russian Rose," 149
Ryskind, Morrie, 235

S

"'S Wonderful," 118, 199, 217, 242
"Sabbath Prayer," 24
Salmagundi (magazine), 65–66
"Salt Peanuts," 238
San Francisco Symphony Orchestra,
 91, 92, 239
Sanborn, Larry, 68, 81
Sanborn, Pitts, 155, 227
Santeria, 17
Saulter, Mike, 59
Savoy Ballroom, The, New York, 52
Saxophones, 69
Scales
 African (microtonal), 67
 European (diatonic), 67
 solfège, 66
Schacht, Al, 192
Scheherazade (Rimsky-Korsakov), 133
Schiff, David, 167, 206, 213, 239
Schillinger, Joseph, 228
Schirmer, Mabel, 214, 265
Schneider, Albert. *See* Gershwin,
 Alan.
Schneider, Ben, 277
Schneider, Fanny, 277
Schönberg, Arnold, 132, 287
Schrader, Paul, 141
Schuller, Gunther, 38, 41, 46, 86
Schwartz, Arthur, 238
Schwartz, Charles, 213
"Score by George Gershwin," 252
Scott, Bud, 33
Second Rhapsody, 170, 232, 233–234
Segonzac, André de Dunoyer, 198
Segregation, laws of. *See* Laws, Jim
 Crow.
Seidel, Toscha, 188
Seldes, Gilbert, 41, 87, 123–124,
 144, 176–177
"Sequestration Blues," 68
"Serenade to a Cuckoo," 15
Sert, Jose Maria, 226
Sert Room, Waldorf-Astoria, New
 York, 226, 227
Servants, indentured, 11–12
7 Lively Arts, The (Seldes), 41, 87,
 123–124
7th Heaven (movie), 231
Sex, 19

Shabbetai Zvi, 221
Shango cult, 17
Shanley's Restaurant, New York, 56
Shaw, Artie, 26
Sheed, Wilfred, 88
Sheet music, 55–56, 59, 112, 122,
 123, 157, 206, 242–243
Shim Sham, New York, 52
Shim Sham Shimmy (dance), 56
Shocking Miss Pilgrim, The (movie),
 202
Shofar, 29–30
"Sholem," 24
Shouts, 249
Show Girl, 170, 254
Shuffle Along (Blake and Sissle), 125
Silverberg, Danny, 226
Simon, Alfred, 103, 113–115, 140
Simon & Schuster, 242
Simone, Nina, 24
Sims, John Haley "Zoots," 206
Sinatra, Frank, 257
Sinbad, 22, 114, 123
"Sing of Spring," 175
Singing, 67, 87
Singing (magazine), 140
Singleton, Zutty, 33
Siqueiros, David Alfaro, 193, 198
Sissle, Noble, 125
Skyscrapers, 55
Slave Songs of the United States
 (Allen, Ware, and Garrison),
 249
Slave trade, 17, 32
Slavery, 11, 12, 20, 29, 42, 285
 Christianity and, 29
 economics and, 16
Slaves, 16, 20, 29, 32, 67
 emancipated, 21, 29
 half-freedom of, 14
 music and, 12, 67
 treatment of, 12, 16, 32
Slides. *See* Glissando.
Slim Gaillard Quartet, 24
Sloper, L. A., 251
Smalls, Samuel, 248
Small's Paradise, New York, 49
Smith, Al, 211
Smith, Bessie, 167, 190
Smith, John, 62
Smith, Kate, 60
Smith, Mamie, 73
Smith, Pine Top, 62

Smith, Willie "The Lion," 61, 62, 73, 144, 191
Smoot-Hawley Tariff Act, 231
So This Is Jazz (Osgood), 84, 101
"So This Is Venice," 148–149, 151
Solos, 3, 86
    clarinet, 150, 158–160
"Some Wonderful Sort of Something," 111
"Somebody Loves Me," 242
Someone to Watch Over Me, 170
Song pluggers, 109
Songs, 15
    American, 9–10, 20, 21, 22, 133
    call and response, 12, 67
    comedic, 148
    publishing of, 55–57, 73
    recovered, 281–283
    See also specific types.
"Sophisticated Lady," 254
Sousa, John Philip, 77
Spaeth, Sigmund, 169
Spanish-American War, 51
Speakeasies, 33, 52
Spirituals, 29, 41, 82, 132, 249
Spontaneity, 81, 86
Spread spectrum, 88
SS *George Gershwin*, 269
"St. Louis Blues," 72, 73
St. Nicholas Baths, New York, 104, 116
Stale Bread (person), 34
"Stale Bread's Sadness Gave 'Jazz' to the World" (article), 34
Stale Bread's Spasm Band, 34
Standard Music Company, 112
"Star-Spangled Banner, The" 9, 231
Steely, Blossom, 126
"Steeplechase," 238
Steinert, Alexander, 119, 173–174
Steinway & Sons, 198
Steps in Time (Astaire), 110, 263
Stewart, Lawrence D., 117, 245, 265
Sting, The (movie), 39
Stock market, 229
Stokowski, Leopold, 144
Story of Jazz, The (Welles), 34
Storyville, New Orleans, 32–34, 45
Storyville (club), Boston, 35
Straus, S. W., 94
Stravinsky, Igor, 42, 239
Street Angel (movie), 231
Street naming, 269

Street performances, 68
"Strength of the Nation, Dedicated to the Proposed Colored Regiment," 130
Stride piano, 61–62
Strike Up the Band, 170, 177, 205, 206, 212
Stroll, The (dance), 56
Suite of Serenades, A (Herbert), 150
"Summertime," 170, 175, 249, 255
"Sunny Disposish," 118, 119
Sunrise (movie), 231
"Suppression of Ragtime" (article), 66
"Swanee," 22, 23–24, 114, 122–124, 133, 137, 182, 242
"Swanee Rhapsody," 254
"Swanee River." *See* "Old Folks at Home."
"Sweet and Lowdown," 114
"Sweet Georgia Brown," 70
Sweet Little Devil, 137, 138, 151, 170
Swift, Kay, 60, 184–185, 200–202, 241, 243, 261
Swing, 46, 169
Symphony in Black: A Rhapsody of Negro Life (movie short), 34
Syncopation, 39, 41, 59, 130

T

T. B. Harms Publishing, 111, 256, 282
Tait's, San Francisco, 92
Talented Tenth, 49, 52
Tatum, Art, 61, 191
Tavern, The, New York, 144
Taylor, Deems, 133, 144, 153, 215
Telephone Hour, The (radio program), 245
Tell Me More, 164, 170
Temple Emanu-El, New York, 62, 268
Temptations, The, 24
Tenney, Jack B., 258
Tenney Committee, 258
Texas Tommy (dance), 56
Texidor, Joe, 15
"That Certain Feeling," 115
Theaters, 230
Theatre Guild, 248
"There She Is, Miss America," 150
33 Riverside Drive, New York, 185, 188, 190, 193, 194, 195, 226
Thomas, Michael Tilson, 239

Thompson, Oscar, 127, 154, 168
Thomson, Virgil, 84, 154, 251–252, 255
Three Stooges, The, 123, 126
"Tiger Rag," 51
Tilzer, Harry Von, 110
Tin Pan Alley, 52, 55–57, 59, 82, 109
"Tip-Toe Through the Tulips," 228
Tip-Toes, 115, 164, 170, 281
"To a Wild Rose," 150
To Be, or Not . . . to Bop (Gillespie), 17
Tootsie (movie), 120
Trains, 138
Treaty of Paris (1898), 51
Tribes, African, 17, 32
"True Negro Music and Its Decline, The" (Murphy), 42
Trumpets and trumpet playing, 33, 34, 43
Tubmen, 68
Tucker, Mark, 254
Tucker, Sophie, 73
"Turkey in the Straw," 19
Turkey Trot, The (dance), 56
"Turn Back the Pharoah's Army," 29
Twain, Mark, 20
Twelve-bar blues, 66, 72, 167
Twist, The (dance), 56
"Typical Self-Made American, A" 171

U

U.S. Department of State, 255
U.S. House. Committee on Patents, 257
U.S. House. Un-American Activities Committee, 257
U.S. Navy, 33
Underground resistance, Danish, 255
Union Square, New York, 55
United Airlines, 163
United States, rise as global power, 51, 55
"Unspeakable Jazz Must Go!" (McMahon), 75
Utrillo, Maurice, 194, 198
"Utt Da Zay," 24

V

Vallee, Rudy, 245, 257
Van Dyke, Henry, 84
Van Norman, Julia Thomas, 279

Van Vechten, Carl, 59, 132, 133, 144, 154, 187, 190, 191
Vanity Fair (magazine), 211
Vardi, David, 222
"Variations on 'I Got Rhythm'," 228, 241
Variety (magazine), 47
Vaudeville, 21
Venuti, Joe, 95
Vibrational Medicine (Gerber), 204
Vibrations, 204
Victor Records, 34, 52, 157, 164
Victor Talking Machines Company, 78
Victoria, Queen, 30
Victrola, 78
Vodery, Will, 110, 111
"Volga Boat Song, The" 149
Voliva, Wilbur Glen, 74
Volstead Act, 74
Voodoo, 17, 75
Vote, right to, 20
Voudun. *See* Voodoo.

W

"Waiting For the Sun to Come Out," 114
Waldorf Astoria, New York, 226
Waldorf-Astoria Orchestra, 105, 226
Wall Street crash (1929), 229
Waller, Fats, 61, 190, 191, 238
Walling, Rosamond, 173
Warburg, James P. "Jimmy," 201
Ware, Charles Pickard, 249
Warehouses, Secaucus, New Jersey, 281–283
Warner Bros. Records, 281–282
Warner Bros. Studios, 281
Warner Brothers, 256, 281, 283
Warner/Chappell, 275
Warner Music Group, 271–272, 273
"Warner Music Sued for Millions by George Gershwin Heirs" (article), 273

Washboard Band, 68
Washboards, 68
Washington Rhythm Kings, The, 68
"Washington Square," 15
Washington Square Park, New York, 13–15
Waters, Muddy, 19
Weary Blues, The (Hughes), 52
Weber, Max, 193, 195
Weems, Ted, 245
Weill, Kurt, 252
Wein, George, 35
Welcome to the Melting Pot, 232, 286
Welles, Orson, 34, 84
Wells, Dickie, 253
"West End Blues," 46
Wetmore Lecture series, 25
"When Mose With His Nose Leads the Band," 23
"When You Want 'Em, You Can't Get 'Em, When You Got 'Em, You Don't Want 'Em," 110, 114, 122
"Where Jazz Comes From," (May), 161
"Whispering," 94, 96
White, George, 29, 123–124
White, "Slaps," 148
"White Christmas," 60, 69
Whitehall Hotel, New York, 183
Whiteman, Paul, 26, 81, 91–97, 126, 127, 149
  commissioning *Rhapsody in Blue*, 97, 126, 137–38
  Covarrubias *Rhapsody in Blue* painting and, 197–198
  concerts and tours, 156–156, 191
  Experiment in Modern Music concert and, 134, 136–137, 144–146, 153, 154, 155–156
  on glissando, 160
  on jazz, 4, 84, 91, 144
  King of Jazz (movie), 96–97

"Whiteman at Carnegie Hall" (poster) (Covarrubias), 274
"Who Cares," 242
Who Could Ask for Anything More (Merman), 237
"Why Can't We Be Friends," 201
Wilder, Alec, 41–42, 94
"Will You Remember Me?," 270
Williams, Bert, 110
Williams, Martin, 45
Williams, Spencer, 33
Williams College, 162
Willis, Helen, 211
Wilson, Don, 245
Wilson, Edwin E., 113
Wilson, Teddy, 26
Wilson, Woodrow, 211
Wireless communication, 88
Wise, Stephen S., 268
WJZ (radio station), 207, 245
Wolpin, Harry, 104
"Woman Is a Sometime Thing," 202
Wood shedding, 92
Woollcott, Alexander, 179
WOR (radio station), 246
World Health Organization (WHO), 264
Wynn, Ed, 113

Y

"Yes! We Have No Bananas," 148
Yiddish, 24
Yiddish Theatre District, New York, 103
Youmans, Vincent, 281
Young, Lester, 206

Z

Zeitlan's Restaurant, New York, 116
Zelayo, Alfonso, 84
Ziegfeld, Florenz, 177, 254
Ziegfeld Follies, 123
Zilboorg, Gregory, 180, 261
Zimbalist, Efrem, 136
"Zip Coon," 19

About the Author & Illustrator

Author **RICHIE GERBER** is a musician, performer, comedian, and impresario. Over the years, he has produced hundreds of jazz concerts that featured his band The Free Radicals, playing straight-ahead jazz, bebop, and swing with jazz greats like Eddie Higgins, former Count Basie alumnus Pete Minger, five-time Grammy nominee Ira Sullivan, and Buddy DeFranco.

During Gerber's Brooklyn years, he created a solo street act called *Alone on the Saxophone*, which combined solo sax and stand-up comedy. In 1974, he moved to Maine with his Cuban-American wife, Julie. They moved and renovated a barn into a house and started an organic farm. All the while, Gerber continued to perform *Alone on the Saxophone* and began leading his newly formed band of *Maine-iacs* called The Compost Blues Boys. As Gerber's popularity in Maine grew, he caught the eye and ear of Maine humorist/artist/musician Tim Sample, leader of Tim Sample and the Dubious Brothers. Sample asked Gerber to join the band, and the rest, as they say, is Maine history. Also a talented artist, Sample designed the logo for Gerber's *Alone on the Saxophone* act, which is now Gerber's book-publishing logo.

Gerber and his wife moved to Florida after realizing that Maine had only two seasons: winter and July. They quickly realized that Florida had only two seasons as well: summer and winter (which is exactly the same as summer, except it included lots of folks from Maine, trying to thaw out).

Upon arriving in sunny Florida, Gerber quickly got a gig in the Chip Hoehler Big Band, playing sax on the world's largest cruise ship at the time, the *SS Norway*, with some music legends like

Frankie Laine ("Rawhide" and "Mule Train" Gold Record hits). After leaving the cruise scene, Gerber started to perform *Alone on the Saxophone* at various South Florida venues. He also started playing in various bands such as the R&B Soul group The Blue Notes ("If You Don't Know Me By Now" and "Bad Luck" chart hits) and R&B Rock and Roll Hall of Famer Hank Ballard and the Midnighters (Ballard wrote the smash hit "The Twist," made enormously famous by Chubby Checker).

In addition to playing sax with various bands, Gerber signed on to create, develop, write, and produce a children's television show for the Broward County Schools in the early 1980s. The deal included Gerber writing the music as well as the script for a TV show to teach English to the Spanish-speaking children who fled from Communist Castro's Cuba (known as "Marielitos") and were attending public school.

The Gerbers bought a small health food store with a juice bar, the Bread of Life Natural Foods Market, in the early 1980s. Gerber's father had owned grocery stores since the early 1900s, so Richie literally grew up in the grocery business. The Bread of Life grew quickly, compelling the Gerbers to move the business into a much larger storefront and include one of Richie's dreams: a full-service natural foods restaurant. This afforded him the venue for weekly jazz performances, which he called Jazz Goes Natural. Upon partnering with Jim Oppenheimer and moving the store and restaurant to an even larger location, Gerber changed the name of his jazz group from The Nutrients playing "music you can assimilate" to The Free Radicals, saying, "It don't mean a thing if the registers don't ring." The Free Radicals performed Friday and Saturday nights as well as during Sunday brunch and featured many world-renowned jazz cats as well as the best jazz musicians South Florida had to offer.

The business continued to boom, convincing the Gerber/Oppenheimer team to open up a second, much larger location. They built a 33,000-square-foot natural foods supermarket, and once again Gerber and The Free Radicals performed on weekends with some of the greatest jazz musicians. As the store's popularity grew, the natural foods behemoth Whole Foods Markets made the Gerber/Oppenheimer team a deal they could not refuse. In 1997, Whole Foods Markets merged with Bread of Life and formed the Whole Foods Florida Region. Gerber stayed on as the regional vice president and continued the weekend music concerts. After a few years, he retired from the natural foods business.

Being so avant-garde, Gerber had attended Woodstock in 1969. In the 1960s, he was a New York City cab driver and a public school teacher for ten years, first in Brooklyn, then in Maine, and finally in South Florida. While converting the barn into a home and operating his organic farm, la Finca Loca, Gerber also taught T'ai Chi Ch'uan, which he learned from master Herman Kauz in New York City's Chinatown.

Leveraging his knowledge as an organic farmer and natural foods store owner/operator, Gerber became a licensed nutrition counselor and went on to produce and host *The Natural Grocer Radio Show* for ten years, the longest-running health talk radio show in South Florida at the time. In 2014, the Gerbers were included in *Natural Prophets*, a book about the pioneers of the health food industry. **Visit www.jazzamericasgift.com.**

Illustrator **MIGUEL COVARRUBIAS** (November 22, 1904–February 4, 1957) can arguably be called the chronicler of "The Jazz Age." Moving from his birthplace of Mexico to New York City as a nineteen-year-old in 1923, carrying his pen and sketchpad, he instantaneously took the Big Apple by storm. He shared a studio on 42nd Street with Al Hirschfeld, a caricaturist greatly influenced by "El Chamaco" ("The Kid"—Covarrubias's nickname). Covarrubias's original, unique, and innovative style of drawing celebrity caricatures catapulted him into a teenage/twenty-something storied celebrity artist, landing him gigs at top-tier magazines such as *The New Yorker* and *Vanity Fair*. Ultimately, Covarrubias became one of *Vanity Fair's* preeminent caricaturists. "El Chamaco" had a special talent of penetrating and capturing the essence of a celebrity (his "victim") in caricature, which earned him another nickname "The Murderer." If one wanted to be an A-list celeb, then Covarrubias had to "murder" you! His "victims" were both terrified as well as delighted to be "murdered" by the satirical pointed pen of Miguel Covarrubias. It has been said that his fresh modern, economical use of line made him the quintessential artist of the Jazz Age, the Roaring Twenties, and the Harlem Renaissance.

One can easily see that Covarrubias was a modern-day renaissance man. Besides writing and illustrating books and creating knockout caricatures, he was also a painter and lithographer. In addition, he developed theater costumes and set designs, including the famous *La Revue Negre*, which starred Josephine Baker. He was a muralist, cartographer, and a self-taught expert and author of books on ethnology and anthropology. In 1933, Covarrubias was awarded a Guggenheim Fellowship, which he used to study the Island of Bali and write and illustrate a highly celebrated book by the same name. In 1940, he was awarded a second Guggenheim Fellowship. He won numerous awards for his advertising artwork as well.

Jazz: America's Gift is the perfect marriage between Miguel Covarrubias's artwork and the colorful history of the Jazz Age. The interplay of Gerber's words and Covarrubias's images gives each page a rhythm all its own. Who could ask for anything more?

www.ingramcontent.com/pod-product-compliance
Lightning Source LLC
Chambersburg PA
CBHW082107230426
43671CB00015B/2630